Indigeneity in Latin American Cinema

Indigeneity in Latin American Cinema

Milton Fernando Gonzalez Rodriguez

BLOOMSBURY ACADEMIC
NEW YORK • LONDON • OXFORD • NEW DELHI • SYDNEY

BLOOMSBURY ACADEMIC
Bloomsbury Publishing Inc
1385 Broadway, New York, NY 10018, USA
50 Bedford Square, London, WC1B 3DP, UK
29 Earlsfort Terrace, Dublin 2, Ireland

BLOOMSBURY, BLOOMSBURY ACADEMIC and the Diana logo are trademarks of Bloomsbury Publishing Plc

First published in the United States of America 2022
Paperback edition published in 2024

Copyright © Milton Fernando Gonzalez Rodriguez, 2022, 2024

For legal purposes the Acknowledgements on pp. viii–ix constitute an extension of this copyright page.

Companion website: https://uni.hi.is/mfg1/

Cover design: Eleanor Rose

Cover image © Milton Fernando Gonzalez Rodriguez

All rights reserved. No part of this publication may be reproduced or transmitted in any form or by any means, electronic or mechanical, including photocopying, recording, or any information storage or retrieval system, without prior permission in writing from the publishers.

Bloomsbury Publishing Inc does not have any control over, or responsibility for, any third-party websites referred to or in this book. All internet addresses given in this book were correct at the time of going to press. The author and publisher regret any inconvenience caused if addresses have changed or sites have ceased to exist, but can accept no responsibility for any such changes.

Library of Congress Cataloging-in-Publication Data
Names: Gonzalez Rodriguez, Milton Fernando, author.
Title: Indigeneity in Latin American cinema / Milton Fernando Gonzalez Rodriguez.
Description: New York : Bloomsbury Academic, 2022. | Includes bibliographical references and index. |
Summary: "The book critically reviews the portrayal of indigenous characters in Latin American films produced after the turn of the century (2000-2018)"–Provided by publisher.
Identifiers: LCCN 2022005389 (print) | LCCN 2022005390 (ebook) | ISBN 9781501384707 (hardback) | ISBN 9781501384677 (paperback) | ISBN 9781501384691 (epub) | ISBN 9781501384684 (pdf) | ISBN 9781501384660
Subjects: LCSH: Motion pictures–Latin America–History and criticism. | Indigenous peoples in motion pictures.
Classification: LCC PN1995.9.I49 G66 2022 (print) | LCC PN1995.9.I49 (ebook) | DDC 791.43/652998–dc23/eng/20220429
LC record available at https://lccn.loc.gov/2022005389
LC ebook record available at https://lccn.loc.gov/2022005390

ISBN: HB: 978-1-5013-8470-7
    PB: 978-1-5013-8467-7
    ePDF: 978-1-5013-8468-4
    eBook: 978-1-5013-8469-1

Typeset by Newgen KnowledgeWorks Pvt. Ltd., Chennai, India

To find out more about our authors and books visit www.bloomsbury.com and sign up for our newsletters.

Contents

List of Illustrations	vii
Acknowledgements	viii

	Basis: Introduction	1
	Indigeneity: Conceptualization, perception and representation	16
	Syntonic versus histrionic indigeneity	35
1	Mimesis: Circulation of ideas and images	47
	Figment, art and fabrication	47
	Cinema and indigeneity	61
2	Metropolis: Production of audiovisual cultural artefacts	89
	Mexico and Central America	89
	South America	99
3	Lexis: Portrayals of linguistic topologies	123
	Accented inclusion and vocative framing	124
	(In)discernible sounds and authenticity	143
4	Emphasis: Embodiment of indigeneity	153
	Nature–technology nexus as an ontological genre	154
	Ethnicity, senses and knowledge	164
5	Axis: Identities and global imaginaries	175
	Intersectional paradigms	175
	Arrayed figures	188
6	Catalysis: Paradigms and disruption	201
	(In)visibility and representation	201
	(Re)drawn blueprint	210
7	Wääjx äp: Epistemic and ontological repositioning	227
	The cybernetics of self-representation	228
	Screen(ed)/(ing) intimacy and clusivity	239

Synopsis: Conclusion	253
Notes	269
Bibliography	281
Filmography	303
Index	313

Illustrations

Diagrams

1	Mental schema of the term *indigenous*	27
2	Position of *Roma* (Mexico, 2018) within a (re)drawn blueprint for indigenous ethnotypes	218

Figures

1	*America with those known parts in that unknowne worlde both people and manner of buildings* (c. 1662), Abraham Goos	51
2	Screenshot of the film *El Violín* (Mexico, 2005)	96
3	Screenshot of the film *La carga* (Mexico, 2016)	171
4	Film location of *Roma* (Mexico, 2018) in Mexico City	220
5	Homemade copy of *El Pecado* sold in a market in Cuzco	244

Tables

1	The Main Corpus of Representational Films (68)	11
2	The Main Corpus of Self-representational Films (53)	12
3	Taxonomy of Traits Identified in Representational Films Depicting Historical Communities	30
4	Films Depicting Modern Indigenous Communities (N = 62)	31
5	Modern Times Films	33

Acknowledgements

This page is dedicated to thanking and acknowledging all those people who contributed to the completion of this book. Most of them are still here and I hope that by mentioning them, I can express my sense of gratitude. Along this long journey, the most important person to me passed away and in this way, this page is also meant to serve as a brief posthumous homage to her. More than anyone, I would like to thank and dedicate this book to my dear mother, María Melba Rodriguez de Gonzalez.

In like manner, I would like to express my deepest thanks to Bibi, Gísli, Leo, Nando and Paul for their encouragement, patience, time and support: gracias, takk fyrir! One person was there with me through every step along the way: Martin. I am indebted to him for his infinite patience, unconditional encouragement, hours of conversation, uncountable (un)requested pieces of advice and for being there during the most difficult moments: mange tak! A special thanks to Eric, whose beliefs in this book and in me were such motivators: dank je! Also 'dank je' to Irene, a true listener, great encourager and loyal friend.

It goes without saying that a book project requires more than family and friends.

Above all, I want to thank the participants, respondents, interviewees and informants from all corners of Latin America and the world for their kind cooperation. Important parts of this book had not been possible without their participation. Their insights truly enriched the depth and quality of the data.

From the academic world, I would like to express my sincere gratitude to Professors Arij Ouweneel, Michiel Baud, Hólmfríður (Hóffý) Garðarsdóttir, Pamela Innes and Björn Ægir Norðfjörð. I owe very special thanks to Arij for his unflagging encouragement, support, honesty, motivation and insightful feedback: dank je! In many ways, the idea of this book first emerged in Iceland, and from day one Hóffý was part of it. I am greatly appreciative of her involvement and commitment: takk fyrir! From my time at the University of Iceland, I also want to thank the School of Humanities, the Faculty of Languages and Cultures and the Vigdís Finnbogadóttir Institute of Foreign Languages for a couple of travel grants and a one-year teaching assistantship. From my time at the University of Amsterdam, I want to thank Centro de Estudios y Documentación Latinoamericanos/Centre for Latin American Research and Documentation (CEDLA), Amsterdam School for Regional, Transnational and European Studies (ARTES) and Michiel Baud, for allowing me to complete important stages of this book project. I will forever be indebted to Michiel.

Crucial parts of the research behind this volume were carried out while I was a student at Malmö University and Associate PhD Student in Cambridge. My special gratitude goes to the academic staff and researchers of the Communication for Development program, Faculty of Culture and Society, Malmö University and Centre of Latin American Studies (CLAS) at the University of Cambridge. A special word of appreciation is due to Professors Oscar Hemer, Rosalva Aída Hernández Castillo, Charles Jones and Joanna Page. I will never forget Aída's generosity in inviting me to attend her seminars and the kindness shown by Professors Jones and Page in hosting me at CLAS. From my time in Cambridge, UK, I cannot thank Julie Coimbra enough for her warmth, support and hospitality. I will always be indebted to the University of Cambridge for providing me access to its library and digital resources during two important stages of this book.

Throughout the preparation process of this monograph, a recognition from the Erasmus Prize (Praemium Erasmianum) Foundation offered great encouragement. I am grateful for their kindness.

At Bloomsbury, I am indebted to Katie Gallof, Stephanie Grace-Petinos, Jonathan Nash, Eleanor Rose, Saranya Manohar and all the members of the global team involved at every stage of the production of this book for their commitment, efficiency and professionalism.

Finally, I would like to sincerely thank this book's reviewers for their engagement, guidance, feedback, immense wisdom and intellectual generosity. This monograph benefitted enormously from their comments, suggestions, advice and recommendations, and I cannot thank them enough for being so helpful and encouraging.

The research behind *Indigeneity in Latin American Cinema* received no specific grant from any funding agency in the public, commercial or not-for-profit sectors at any stage. The author of the book is the author of the image (*Histrionic Indigeneity*) on the cover and owns its copyright.

Basis: Introduction

At the intersection of art and technology, films have become global conveyors of visuals that navigate between places, pollinizing ideas about the peoples, cultures and languages of those being cinematically represented. During a set of interviews about portrayals of Andean communities in media spaces, one Aymara respondent expressed his firm belief that a film about an Aymara- or a Quechua-speaking superhero would end a long-established tradition of stereotypical misrepresentations. According to him, an 'indigenous Batman would force others to see Andean people and life in a different way'. Representations are entangled processes and complex cultural artefacts. This explains why Kaqchikel scholar Sandra Xinico Batz, reacting on the film *Ixcanul* (Guatemala, 2015), wonders, '¿Para quién o quienes está hecha la película? [For whom (singular/plural) is this film made?]'.[1] Quoting Ayuujk linguist, writer and activist Yasnaya Elena Aguilar Gil (2020), 'es una lástima que la mayoría de las personas que se interesan por los pueblos indígenas lo hagan mediante el folclor, la idealización o la caricaturización de nuestras culturas, que además son tan distintas entre sí [it is sad that most people interested in indigenous peoples become so through folklore, idealizations and caricatures of our cultures that, besides, are so different from each other] (99). Art as the ultimate outlet for human expression has the capacity to feed imaginaries. This volume explores how contemporary filmmakers (2000–20) are participants in the evolution and circulation of images and sounds that in many ways define how Latin American indigenous communities are imagined, at a local, regional and global scale.

Depictions do not exist in nature; they are human creations that can be explained as repositories of reactions, emotions and attitudes. Rightfully, Hacking (1983) observes, 'Human beings are representers. Not *homo faber*, I say, but *homo depictor*. People make representations' (132). Since visual culture production is intrinsically not objective, no visual representation can take place without a reconfiguration and categorization of some sort. After all, the first step to represent is to extract and distil details and aspects of an object/subject that are eventually used to embody and ideally retain part of its essence. This process of collecting and selecting invariably implies reducing and discarding. In this sense, representations become materializations of the imaginary tightly linked to social reality and power structures, and since both are embedded in political and economic processes, hierarchies emerge. A case in point is the main concern expressed by indigenous female directors, Magda Cacari (Purepecha), Ángeles Cruz (Mixtec), Dinazar Urbina Mata (Mixtec), Dolores Sántiz Gómez (Tzotzil), María Candelaria Palma Marcelino (San Antonio Afro-Indigenous community in Guerrero) and curator Amalia Córdova, during a panel about stereotypes and diversity, organized in the context of the seventeenth edition of the Morelia International Film Festival (2019): media content produced and mobilized by non-indigenous producers and directors often deploys stereotypes that have a negative impact on how Latin American indigenous peoples are perceived. By screening their films and voicing their apprehension about ethnotypes (ethnicity-based stereotypes), self-identified indigenous filmmakers and collectives, sometimes in collaboration with filmmakers from outside of their communities, prompt a reflection about the agency, rhetoric and power dynamics at play behind contemporary cinematic portrayals of the native peoples of the region. At many points, indigeneity as a theme, and as I argue in this book, a (sub) genre, in films has been commercialized or, at least, transformed into a driving element to appeal to (paying) audiences, draw attention from prize-awarding committees and position future generations of filmmakers. The response of transnational spectators (feedback) to the exoticization of indigenous peoples defines the continuation (feedforward) of a theme/genre that secures access to funding, success or, at least, international visibility. Trapped in a loop, *histrionic indigeneity* emerges as the audiovisual artistic representation of an imagined version of Latin America's first peoples in films, managed by funding, exhibition and distribution networks, and susceptible to the feedback/feedforward of global viewers. Ultimately, in a market of visual experiences, enticing and awe-inspiring subjective aesthetic externalizations have a symbolic and cultural value that eventually secures funders and exhibitors (e.g. film festivals) a sense of branding, cosmopolitanism and nostalgia.[2] Above all, overtly histrionic portrayals of an indigenous figure emerge as products of a system that emulates and preserves the longue durée visual culture tradition of deriving entertainment from difference.

Enhanced core–periphery structures are not new, and neither is the fact that one-sided depictions exclude the possibility for under-/misrepresented communities to negotiate, rebrand, reposition or contest how they are depicted. The legacy of colonizing hierarchies still rules the channelization of media content, especially in cultural industries highly dependent on substantial amounts of financial support. Commercial cinema today is regulated by international distribution networks, similar to those trade networks of objects mobilized by conquering endeavours, religious enterprises and commodities exchanges between core (Global North) and periphery (Global South). Historical processes have materialized in iconic characterizations through which a dominant group articulates its hegemonic ideas and assumptions about an imagined Other. Since indigenous societies are mostly represented by non-indigenous cinematographers, it is a matter of hope 'that the success of fictionalized lives of Indigenous peoples may help increase access for Indigenous directors that aspire to one day complete a feature film in their own communities and on their own terms' (Córdova 2017a: 115). Non-indigenous Latin American filmmakers also face difficult challenges as competition is intense and national funding schemes are ubiquitously scarce. Often, they are forced to compromise their artistic creativity, approach and style, in order to obtain funding and support to complete their projects. Financial support comes with demands in terms of content. Global funding and distribution networks have a direct impact on how fictionalized indigenous-themed narratives emerge to satisfy an all-encompassing, cultural, capital-driven, entertainment-oriented, exploitation-dependent market of images, overlooking the implications thereof for fragile, mis- and under-represented societies.

Ever since the colonization of Latin America, indigenous peoples have been portrayed as inferior or uncivilized subjects, both in narratives and iconography. The need of Europe to present and position itself in relation to its imagined distant Others from all the corners of the globe still informs the creation of distorted, simplistic, reductive and exotifying depictions of native societies. While visual articulations of idyllic, alluring and evocative indigenes bolster a sense of romanticized imperialism, adventure and mysticism, these images also risk trivializing the materiality of racism, social inequality, abuse, invisibility, oblivion and violence experienced by cotemporary communities tracing their origins to pre-Columbian societies. Across the region, few social groups are subject to such levels of discrimination as the ones faced by indigenous communities. External articulations, engendered in various modes, formats and outlets, cinema being one of them, contribute to retain hierarchical structures in which Amerindian cultures and languages are not acknowledged. Films operate as cultural artefacts that evolve and strengthen canons of representations. In the process, visuals circulate ideas that inform imaginaries and partly shape how indigenous societies and cultures are culturally, epistemically and ontologically present in media outlets. The international character of contemporary film production and the nature of cultural artefacts as objects that travel explain why these narratives are conceived to align with non-indigenous, mostly Western, viewers. Although pre-Columbian legacy, linguistic heritage, epistemologies, values and lifestyles serve as inspiration and raw material for artistic expression, commercial indigeneity-oriented films in the twenty-first century, just as engravings and drawings in the sixteenth century or photographs in the early twentieth century, mirror the optics of their funders and creators, not necessarily the peoples they allegedly portray.

This explains why representation and self-representation differ considerably. Contemporary Latin American large-scale, commercial fictional films, produced to be exported and screened outside the region, echo editorial strategies used by early modern European artists to render their depictions of the New World's natives acceptable and attractive for continental audiences (van Groesen 2008). The scripted optics of films that have a global and general outlook, and yet retain a specific and local character, is symbiotically entwined with characterizations that target audiences understand. Alternatively, Indigenous Cinema expresses the ways in which self-identified indigenous communities adopt the medium, their relation to it, their sensitivities about it, the praxis in which it is inscribed and their need to present themselves on their own terms. Above all, and despite lack of resources, limited access to distribution, production and exhibition networks, and relatively little interest from mainstream media outlets and academic circles, Indigenous Cinema thrives, evolves and grows. Images and sounds emerged from within indigenous communities reveal attempts to reconfigure, efface or dislocate silencing structures. Simultaneously, they reveal the contradictions, paradoxes and perpetuation of hegemonic, well-gatekept systems that regulate who speaks on behalf of whom, often supported by ideological screeds that do not necessarily hold. Spotlights still cast on films where faces, voices and themes are indigenous, but not their authors. While urban, often foreign-educated/trained Latin American directors present their works in Berlin or Sydney, Indigenous Cinema finds its outlet in itinerant screenings in informal venues across the Andes or in unperceived corners of easy-access platforms, such as YouTube or Facebook. Not surprisingly, self-identified indigenous filmmakers or communities involved in collective productions and non-indigenous directors, either from Latin America or from other parts of the world, working on the subject (e.g. Dana Ziyasheva from Kazakhstan filming in Costa Rica), share few commonalities in terms of approaches, sense of aesthetics, contexts, topics and, of course, the set of ideas and references that their contributions mobilize.

But there is hope. Globalization, political change, economic growth, access to technology and democratization have had an impact on the Latin American film industry in recent decades. The first films depicting indigenous communities needed to make the choice of either advocating for or condemning their existence, emulating a hierarchy that relegated them to a peripheral position. Alternatively, some contemporary depictions of modern indigenous nations allow for wider understandings of sameness and difference, deviating at times substantially from colonial rhetoric perspectives. In recent visual representations, the spectator is introduced to strong young indigenous women amidst male-dominated communities, for example, *El corazón del tiempo/Heart of Time* (Mexico, 2008); an indigenous scholar aware of the importance of knowledge dissemination, for example, *Dauna: Lo que lleva el río/Dauna: Gone with the River* (Venezuela, 2015); a generation of independent, affluent indigenous women, for example, *Zona Sur/Southern District* (Bolivia, 2009); an indigenous violinist and political activist, for example, *El Violín/The Violin* (Mexico, 2005); and an Aymara-speaking president, for example, *Evo Pueblo/Evo People* (Bolivia, 2007).

Yet, the decisive role of funding and the criteria imposed on filmmakers to become eligible for financial, post-production and distribution support weigh heavily on aspiring directors. The imagined Other aligns with canons upheld in arthouse cinema and prestigious festivals, in stark contrast with the canons observed in commercial films, destined mainly for local Latin American audiences (e.g. comedy), screened in urban multiplexes, online media platforms and public spaces (e.g. airline entertainment systems), and rarely entering global circuits of exhibition or receiving attention from international critics, academics or journalists. In commercial cinema targeted at local spectators, the inclusion of indigenous themes is quite limited, as it is in nationwide mass media outlets across the region. In the case of cinema, until now, indigenous elements have been assumed to produce a sense of foreignness among Latin American spectators. Reinforced and widespread ethnotypes have maintained a symbolic order in which Amerindian societies play a subaltern role. Their assumed otherness has set them apart, leading them to be considered by many as primitives or rendering them invisible (Franco 1993, 2013; Nahmad Rodríguez 2007; Tompkins 2018). Consequently, in modern times, indigenous heritage is absent in most mass media productions catering to mainstream audiences. When it is present, indigeneity is mainly staged according to hegemonic parameters in which being of European ancestry is favoured and promoted.

Since circulation of preconceptions and assumptions, wrapped in entertaining productions, contributes and informs public discourse, counterhegemonic projects at a mass communicational level are crucial. While #BlackLivesMatter, for example, rise as a movement and a symbolic hashtag, it also emerges as a tool to render visible the embodiment of ethnotypes as a symptom of inequality, privilege and racism. In similar ways, as I intend to show, acknowledgement of films made by indigenous communities is key to reconfigure the mobilization of mono-dimensional, simplified, reductive portrayals, many of which uphold racist caricatures and exoticist depictions. Media outlets operate as central nods of interaction to exchange and recalibrate, sometimes regrettably, the ways in which identity, nationhood, ethnicity and community as concepts are understood and acknowledged, and hence, the power of audiovisual input, today more than ever, cannot be underestimated. At the core, stereotypes, at times, considered passé lines of inquiry or theoretically overestimated notions, unproductively chained to constructivist ideologies, reappear at the surface as derivatives of a human tendency to simplify the Other, according to a repertoire of ready-made assumptions. Understanding that a study of how a social group is represented is not a study of that social group in the 'real world' is of paramount importance. The founding principle of this work, and a constant throughout its various writing and revision stages, has been to distinguish between indigeneity in cinematic spaces, and indigeneity in 'real life'. This is not a project inscribed in the anthropological tradition of reporting or assessing the nuances and contrivances of a society in a given place. The object of study here is cultural artefacts, not people, and the main geographical dimensions considered are the cinematic (media production) and virtual (social media engagement) spaces in which these narratives operate. Central to this work is a review of the processes by which imagination, imitation and mimesis materialize in audiovisual narratives that circulate across global screens.

The present monograph aspires, in as suggestive and varied manner as possible, to shed light on the fact that cinematic portrayals rely upon ethnotypes to present those considered to be different. Imagology, the central theoretical and methodological framework of this book, is concerned with the convention and strategies by which a group ascribes a set of characteristics to other specific groups, making in the process claims of referentiality not necessarily supported by empirical reality (Leerssen 2007, 2016; Ouweneel 2018). The first takes distance from the second, for instance, by producing visual artefacts in which they deploy aesthetic, artistic and narrative strategies to depict cinematically the divergent elements that set them apart. This study focuses upon cultural productions in which a group exposes its impressions of another group, without seeking to test, verify or falsify those claims. It plays nonetheless close attention to the manipulation of identity and its objectification as an intangible commodity. This does not necessarily mean that there is a rigid Us (non-indigenous)–Them (indigenous) dichotomy. Identity is a continuum, and cinema production reflects this, particularly, because different from many other art formats, films are large projects involving large numbers of people at various stages. Yet, a difference is made between those who speak in first person (self-representational cinema/auto-images) and those who speak on their behalf (representational cinema/hetero-images). An important observation is that Latin American non-indigenous directors find themselves in a tripartite position, as they are perceived as outsiders not only by Western funding and distribution bodies but also by the communities they intend to depict in their fictionalized features. This is an aspect addressed in various parts of the book.

A radical ontological discrepancy with respect to a general tendency in the analysis of representation in films is that the vantage point does not lie on the specific milieu only. Films belong to the realm of the visual. As such, this study starts by interrogating in which ways present-day cinema is part of a five-century convention of characterizing indigenous peoples visually. This implies recognizing the impact of formats that chronologically preceded and informed the emergence of cinematographic representations (e.g. paintings). The goal is to place contemporary portrayals into a broader historical and iconographic perspective. The volume does not take stock of films, but of indigeneity *in* films. Beyond examining the onset of current paradigms, offering a full picture entails reflecting on the convergence of renderings authored by filmmakers from within indigenous communities, often overlooked as producing agents of their own representation. In line with the premise that images reflect the global circulation of ideas, special attention is paid to specific films according to their content, international and local reception, particular characteristics and inclusion of linguistic elements, at all times, from a long history of pattern-oriented viewpoint. In this sense, the overarching goal is to explore canons of representation in as many films as possible, how they are traversed by the mobilization of ideas and how stereotypes emerge as generalizations. Bearing in mind the repetitive referential character of the paradigms found in indigeneity-focused cinematic productions, I suggest, these films constitute a (sub)genre in their own right.

The methodological framework I propose to explore these audiovisual cultural artefacts is based on qualitative and theoretical instruments. Content and close (textual) analysis, interviews, surveys and social media posts' analysis were the main instruments chosen to make inferences about paradigm continuity in feature films and audiences' attitudes towards these productions and their meanings. By means of content and close analysis, the corpus of films was studied to elicit patterns of representation of indigenous communities. A focus point in this review concerns the inclusion, to varying degrees, of Amerindian languages, and the ways in which filmmakers present the linguistic legacy of the indigenous characters depicted. Emphasis is placed upon assessing how Latin American indigenous groups are represented in cinema from a mainstream cultural and sociolinguistic standpoint. Within this framework, an important aspect to consider is that films operate at a local and international level, and that many of the reviewed narratives have prompted discussions of the plight of undermined segments of the population and their cultures.

Yet, in spite of an increased number of self-representational and representational films that touch upon indigenous themes, limited academic attention has been devoted to recent portrayals of indigeneity in cinema from a longue durée transnational visual culture context. The dynamic of visibility, and lack thereof, of minorities in public discourse spaces does not necessarily overlap with parallel ongoing scholarly debates. Nothing prevents continuously evolving lines of enquiry and discussion within academic circles from operating asynchronously with respect to transformations at a social level. Whereas stereotypes in cinema are overlooked, they are nevertheless commonly mentioned by the indigenous communities as a challenging obstacle in their path to more acceptance, inclusion and recognition. So far, studies have been attuned to representations in early stages of cinema, focused upon one specific country, concentrated on analysing specific filmmakers, engaged with a particular film or examined new trends of self-representation.[3] Until now, limited research has been conducted on cinematic depictions of indigenous peoples and languages across Latin America as a region, taking into account the different nature of visual representation and self-representation. While previous research findings are useful when approaching specific countries, filmmakers or films depicting these communities, few studies have explored recent representations of indigeneity as a sign of cross-border processes in themes and foci, specifically in a Global North–Global South context. Can we afford to write about films (as by-products of culture, media, communication, technology and epistemic systems), without realizing that aesthetic qualities, magistral composition, innovative cinematographic techniques, genre specificities, symbolism and compelling narratives can also be repositories of long-standing caricatures, folklorizing simplifications and recycled depictions?

Reviewing previous studies on the topic, it becomes evident that there are gaps in the ways cinematic portrayals of indigenous groups have been outlined. Beyond this point, this book also seeks to provide deeper understandings of how cinema becomes a public platform for the dissemination of iconographic and ideological shifts, while proposing to contribute to the growing number of recent studies focusing upon the inclusion of indigenous linguistic heritage in films.[4] Bearing in mind those aspects of this vast topic that have not been subjects of study until now, the main concern throughout this project is how contemporary depictions portray indigenous ethnotypes in contemporary cinema. By addressing this question, this volume aims to analyse multiple depictions of indigenous peoples in contemporary Latin American films (2000–20), focusing especially upon how social changes have been reflected, interpreted and echoed by audiovisual production. Central to this inquiry is a critical review of whether indigeneity, as it is presented in recent films, is a cinematic construction, or a reflection of contemporary states of affairs in these communities. The overall goal is to participate in an ongoing discussion of cinematic depictions of indigeneity by shedding light on the ways in which representations operate as input/inspiration across an ever-evolving worldwide circulation of ideas.

This project has endeavoured to include as many indigeneity-oriented films as possible, originated from Spanish- and Portuguese-speaking countries of Latin America, and released between 2000 and 2020. Specifically, the corpus of this study consists of sixty-eight fictional features directed by non-indigenous filmmakers (hetero-images) and exhibited outside Latin America, thirty-one works of various formats, mostly short films and documentaries, produced by indigenous filmmakers and indigenous communities collectively, and twenty-two sample works of Peruvian *Cine regional* (Regional Cinema), an unsupported, overlooked and peripheral but thriving Andean cinematic tradition, unique in several respects. Thus, in total, the corpus includes fifty-three auto-images. In addition, a significant number of engravings, drawings, paintings, photographs and films produced between 1493 and 2000 have served as primary sources and the backbone for the historical review of the evolution and circulation of visual representations of indigeneity (Chapter 1). In this sense, the sample of sources is considered fairly representative.

An ontological distinction is made between the two main parts of the corpus and pertains to their nature, on the one hand, as representational and, on the other, as self-representational visual cultural artefacts. In the case of representational films (hetero-images), the films are selected based on the summaries, plot descriptions, premiere presentations and festival press conferences provided by directors, producers, distribution companies, fund and grant organizations, festival organizers, editorial publicists and cinema houses. During interviews, extended presentations, festival entry descriptions, publicity editorials, academic conferences and promotional events, the selected productions have been, at some point, presented as indigeneity-oriented films or as narratives that include indigenous characters and/or themes. The selected films are productions conceived by filmmakers who publicly identify themselves as non-indigenous (e.g. in interviews). Since the focus of this book is on productions that depict a world imagined by a filmmaker, except in the case of self-representational productions, documentaries have not been considered. The main reason for this conscious omission is that documentary filmmaking distinguishes itself with elements of veracity, actuality and precision that make it difficult to determine which elements of the narrative are products of the imagination and creativity of the directors, and which elements are real facts. Consequently, this study focuses upon fiction as it is apparent from the beginning that the story is fine-tuned according to the inventiveness and creativity of filmmakers, and that the characters are unique to the screen as they are also a figment of their creation. In terms of genre, with a couple of exceptions, the majority would fall in the category of drama, although as I suggest in Chapter 4, indigeneity-themed films can be considered as a genre, or at least a subgenre, in its own right, based on their intrinsic characteristics.

The corpus of selected films, listed in Tables 1 and 2, purposely includes films that have circulated outside their registered producing countries and, as such, have participated in the mobilization of images and ideas about Latin American indigenous societies, heritages and cultures. Although some of the hetero-images have not been widely distributed, they have all been shown at international

Table 1 The Main Corpus of Representational Films (68)

A terra dos homens vermelhos (Birdwatchers); Brazil, 2008
Alamar (To the Sea); Mexico, 2009
Alicia en el país (Alicia in the Land); Chile, 2008
Antes o Tempo Não Acabava (Time Was Endless); Brazil, 2016
Bien esquivo (The Elusive Good); Peru, 2001
Brava gente brasileira (Brave New Land); Brazil, 2001
Burwa dii ebo (The Wind and the Water); Panama, 2008
Caramuru; Brazil, 2001
Cenizas eternas (Eternal Ashes); Venezuela, 2011
Climas (Climates); Peru, 2014
Cochochi; Mexico, 2007
Corazón del Tiempo (Heart of Time); Mexico, 2008
Dauna: Lo que lleva el río (Dauna: Gone with the River); Venezuela, 2015
Defensores de la vida (Defenders of Life); Costa Rica, 2015
Diarios de Motocicleta (Motorcycle Diaries); Several countries, 2004
Dioses (Gods); Peru, 2008
Distancia (Distance); Guatemala, 2011
El abrazo de la serpiente (Embrace of the Serpent); Colombia, 2015
El destino (The Man Who Came to the Village); Argentina–Spain, 2006
El facilitador (The Facilitator); Ecuador, 2013
El niño pez (The Fish Child); Argentina, 2009
El ombligo de Guie'dani/Xquipi' Guie'dani (Guie'dani's Navel); Mexico, 2019
El regreso (The Return); Venezuela, 2013
El regreso de Lencho (The Return of Lencho); Guatemala, 2010
El sueño del Mara'akame (Mara'akame's Dream); Mexico, 2016
El traspatio (The Backyard); Mexico, 2009
El verano de los peces voladores (The Summer of Flying Fish); Chile, 2013
El Violín (The Violin); Mexico, 2005
Erase una vez en Bolivia (Once upon a Time in Bolivia); Bolivia, 2011
Erendira Ikikunari; Mexico, 2006
Espiral (Spiral); Mexico, 2008
Evo Pueblo; Bolivia, 2007
Feriado (Holiday); Ecuador, 2014
Guaraní; Paraguay, 2015
Hamaca Paraguaya (Paraguayan Hammock); Paraguay, 2000
Ixcanul; Guatemala–France, 2015
Könun Wenu; Chile, 2010
La carga (The Load); Mexico, 2016
La Ciénaga (The Swamp); Argentina, 2001

La Jaula de Oro (The Golden Cage); Mexico, 2013
La mujer sin cabeza (The Headless Woman); Argentina, 2008
La niña santa (The Holy Girl); Argentina, 2004
La Sirga (The Towrope); Colombia, 2012
La teta asustada (Milk of Sorrow); Peru, 2009
La Tirisia (Perpetual Sadness); Mexico, 2014
Las niñas Quispe (The Quispe Girls); Chile, 2013
Los ojos azules (The Blue Eyes); Mexico, 2012
Los viajes del viento (The Wind Journeys); Colombia, 2009
Madeinusa; Peru, 2005
Magallanes; Peru, 2015
Nosilatiaj. La belleza (Nosilatiaj. Beauty); Argentina, 2012
Pájaros de Verano (Birds of Passage); Colombia, 2018
Play; Chile, 2005
¿Quién mató la llamita blanca? (Who Killed the White llama?); Bolivia, 2007
Retablo; Peru, 2017
Rito Terminal (Terminal Rite); Mexico, 2000
Roma; Mexico, 2018
Siguiendo las estrellas (Following the Stars); Panama, 2010
Sueño en otro idioma (I Dream in Another Language); Mexico, 2017
Tainá; Brazil, 2000
Taínos: La última tribu (Taínos: The Last Tribe); Puerto Rico, 2005
Tiempos menos modernos (Not so Modern Times); Argentina, 2012
Vaho (Becloud); Mexico, 2009
Xingu; Brazil, 2012
Yvy Maraêy: Tierra sin mal (Yvy Maraêy: Land without Evil); Bolivia, 2013
Zama; Argentina, 2017
Zona Sur (Southern District); Bolivia, 2009

Table 2 The Main Corpus of Self-representational Films (53) Clustered into Two Categories: Indigenous Cinema (31) and Cine regional/Regional Cinema Films (22)

Indigenous Cinema Films

Apaylla; Ecuador, 2011
Atempa, sueños a orillas del río (Atempa: Dreams by the River); Mexico, 2013
Cholitas con fútbol de altura (Cholitas and Football at High Levels); Bolivia, 2014
¿Cuando te vuelva a ver? (When I See You Again?); Ecuador, 2008
Cuidado/Paktara (Attention); Ecuador, 2008
Dulce convivencia? (Sweet Coexistence); Mexico, 2004
El conflicto en el sueño mapuche/Pewma jadkulu (Conflict in the Mapuche Dream); Chile, 2000

Indigenous Cinema Films

El día de las comadres (The Godmothers' Day); Argentina, 2013
Ella (She); Ecuador, 2011
Equilíbrio (Equilibrium); Brazil, 2020
Hidrofractura: El agua, el aire, la tierra … la muerte (Hydrofracture: Water, Air, Land … Death); Argentina, 2012
Inacayal; Argentina, 2011
Jiisa weçe – Raíz del conocimiento (Roots of Knowledge); Colombia, 2010
Justicia sin palabras (Mute Justice); Mexico, 2011
Kotkuphi; Brazil, 2012
La flor que vive (The Living Flower); Peru, 2013
La limpia/Chiqui Pichay – Wayrachirina (The Purging); Ecuador, 2012
Los descendientes del jaguar/Puma chirikuna (The Jaguar's Descendants); Ecuador, 2012
Mala Junta (Bad Influence); Chile, 2016
Mari Mari; Chile, 2011
Minkakuy; Peru, 2014
Palabras de agua/Ga tëya sziaya co'c (Words of Water); Colombia, 2012
Por la tierra vivimos (We Live for the Land); Mexico, 2012
Q'uma chuyma (Clean Heart); Bolivia, 2013
Razón de estado (The State's Reasons); Chile, 2009
Txejkho Kham Mby (Warsome Women); Brazil, 2011
Varayuqkuna (Ancestral Authority); Peru, 2015
Vestimenta Sapara: Una tradición en peligro (Sapara Clothing: A Tradition in Danger); Ecuador, 2019
Wachikua: Nuestra Historia (Wachikua: Our History); Colombia, 2014
¡Y siguen llegando por el oro! (And They Keep Coming for More Gold!); Colombia, 2012
Zhamayama: Nuestra música (Zhamayama: Our Music); Colombia, 2012

Cine regional/Regional Cinema Films (Peru)

El destino de los pobres (The Fate of the Poor); 2011
El destino de los pobres II (The Fate of the Poor II); 2017
El hijo del viento (The Son of the Wind); 2008
El misterio del Kharisiri (Kharisiri's Mystery); 2004
El Pecado (The Sin); 2007
Frágil (Fragile); 2007
Jarjacha vs. Pishtaco: La batalla final (Jarjacha vs. Pishtaco: The Final Stand-Off); 2011
La leyenda del Ekeko (Ekeko's Legend); 2010
Madre, una ilusión convertida en pesadilla (Mother, an Illusion Turned into a Nightmare); 2009

Cine regional/Regional Cinema Films (Peru)
Marcados por el destino (Cursed by Fate); 2009
Nakaq; 2003
Niños pobres (Poor Children); 2009
Pishtaco; 2003
Qarquacha, el demonio del incesto (Qarquacha, the Devil of Incest); 2002
Sangre inocente (Innocent Blood); 2000
Sangre y traición (Blood and Treason); 2005
Secuelas del terror (Terror After-Effects); 2010
Sin sentimiento (Without Feelings); 2007
Trampas de tu lado oscuro (Traps of Your Dark Side); 2013
Triste realidad (Sad Reality); 2004
Vicio maldito (Wicked Vice); 2000
Wiñaypacha (Eternity); 2017

festivals, representing the country that coincides with the filmmakers' nationality or the film's main location. These productions can be considered as outlets in which authors attempt to depict what nations hold to be the 'essence' of other nations, or communities in relation to themselves. On this account, they are samples of national cinema. They are believed to forge a representation that encapsulates the contrivances of Latin American nation states, even if their borders are problematized by the presence of ethnicities and cultures perceived to be dissimilar or unrelated. In the case of self-representational films (auto-images), it is not feasible to put together a sizeable corpus of feature films, simply because, except for a few cases, the lack of (inter)national support has not made it possible for most indigenous filmmakers/collectives to complete large-scale projects. The set of thirty Indigenous Cinema works revised in this study is composed of short films, documentaries and fiction. By virtue of its entangled relationships with art, entertainment, technology, ethics and politics, cinema has different meanings and serves different purposes for the various producing communities. Through new cinematic vocabularies, Indigenous Cinema productions address the deep-seated conflict of self-representation. In many ways, these recent new formats are agential attempts to reclaim media spaces. Indigenous media operate as a tool for these communities to express their own visions and to mediate content on their own terms (Schiwy 2009). The auto-images included in this analysis are not necessarily produced with the ultimate goal of contesting misconceptions and stereotypes or appeal exclusively to indigenous viewers.

Alternatively, the corpus of self-representational films by exponents of *Cine regional* is composed mostly of fictional features, predominantly informed by local realities, oral tradition and Andean epistemologies. These productions, completed under strenuous circumstances, embody the effort of neglected filmmakers attempting to tell their stories, even if they remain unconnected to Lima-based and international networks of production and circulation. *Cine regional* productions not only contest hegemonic industrial cinema but also operate as canvases where boxed conceptualizations about ethnic identities, sociolinguistic practices and Amerindian heritage become diffuse and somehow unproductive. By creating spaces to tell their own narratives in their own terms, self-representational Indigenous Cinema and *Cine regional* complicate the triangular relation between cinema, identity and ethnicity.

Another aspect taken into account is that while representational fictional works are regarded as reflections of the producer's imaginary, moulded by the aesthetic and industrial constraints of commercial cinema, self-representational productions are approached as relatively recently founded outlets where under-represented communities find a media safe haven. This book does not intend to scrutinize productions conceived by communities systematically being ostracized, misrepresented and forgotten.

In terms of gender, this study seeks to answer how it is depicted, staged, construed and defined in the selected corpus. Due to the nature of the topic, particular emphasis is placed upon the intersection of predetermined social roles and ethnicity. The main concern is to present a critical review of processes of intersectionality in contemporary cinema. Furthermore, this study attempts to address how indigenous elements are present and presented vis-à-vis collective identities, and how they are inscribed and translated into imagery to which audiences can relate. There is no chapter specifically dedicated to gender as it is a subject discussed throughout the entire volume and in relation to the topic, when pertinent, of each section. As I intend to show, renderings of indigenous women from a nation state, linguistic, ontological, visibility and self-identification perspective are critical to understand how cinema operates as a conveyor and circulator of representations. The historical (Chapter 1), intersectional (Chapter 5) and paradigm-related (Chapter 6) accounts, in particular, delve into the evolution of tropes surrounding gender. As I show, gender characterizations are extremely varied, ranging from background nameless figures to iconic dramatis personae (e.g. María Candelaria in the eponymous *María Candelaria* and Cleo in *Roma*).

Finally, given a long-established tradition of exoticizing indigenous elements, it seems logical to review the connection between contemporary portrayals and various present-day processes, for instance, cross-border interconnectivity, standardization of media platforms, globalized economies of cinema and multidimensional funding systems. Hence the rationale behind this approach is to explore how films produced across the continent operate as encapsulations of hetero-images. An important clarification is that while an in-depth analysis is offered for key films, not all the productions are discussed to the same degree of detail: an impossible task given the size of this monograph.

Due to spatial constraints, the corpus omits important, groundbreaking and innovative cinematic productions that deserve to be mentioned, but also addressed and discussed in detail. To do justice to their qualities, chapter-length discussion would be needed, and unfortunately, the size of this volume does not make it possible. Some of them are *Canción sin Nombre/Song without a Name* (Peru, 2021), directed by Melina León, and César Diaz's *Nuestras Madres/Our Mothers* (Guatemala, 2019), which offer insightful and monumental interpretations of indigenous realities in modern Latin America. While films such as *Tiempo de Lluvia/Times of Rain* (Mexico, 2018), directed by Itandehui Jansen and written by Armando Bautista García, creatively exemplify the refreshing hybrid nature of representation, self-representation and epistemic reflections, Jayro Bustamante's *Llorona* (Guatemala, 2019) reinscribes the global and the particular in a myth-laden illustration of the effects of civil war. Vis-à-vis self-representation, the panorama is being reshaped by contributions such as Ángeles Cruz's *Nudo Mixteco/Mixtecan Knot* (Mexico, 2021), Mauricio Franco Tosso's *Samichay/In Search of Happiness* (Peru, 2020) and Diego Mondaca's *Chaco* (Bolivia, 2020). These are films that confirm the broadness of the subject this volume humbly intends to cover at a regional level, even if the subject, indigeneity, is in itself a concept difficult to define.

Indigeneity: Conceptualization, perception and representation

Etymologically, the term *indigenous* denotes those native to a territory, 'sprung from the land' (Late Latin: *indigena*), or who are born in a given place. In his prominent dictionary, specifically in the edition published in 1492, Elio Antonio de Nebrija included the Latin locution with the meaning 'native from there'. In

Spanish, there are examples of the word used as an adjective to refer to plants from the Americas in the eighteenth century, but only in the early nineteenth century, dictionaries register it as a term to refer to human beings. The first appearance of *indigène* as a word to designate the inhabitants of the so-called New World was its inclusion in the 1798 edition of the *Dictionnaire de l'Académie Française*, an addition also included in Spanish dictionaries published in the subsequent years.[5] *Indigena*, from Old Latin *indu* (in, within) and *gignere* (produce, beget), have been used in combination or as synonyms of other terms, such as *native* and *aboriginal*. The former draws upon those who are natural to a place, who belong to it or who are 'produced by birth' in a specific region. Conversely, *aboriginal* which became a popular term among Australians of European descent in the eighteenth century, came to invoke those earliest settlers, without referring to their birthplace. *Indigenous* came to replace the controversial *Indian*, which had been used since America was first settled by European explorers in 1492. The term derived from 'Las Indias' (the Indies), as the Spanish possessions in the New World were known until 1824. As a perpetuating reminder, this misnomer, derived from Columbus's unfounded belief he had reached India, has lived in the interstices of the Latin American psyche for centuries. Product of a wrong assumption, this mistaken designation has given rise to objections not only due to its origins but also in light of the negative connotations it invokes, although this has not always been the case. In point of fact, the category *Indio* entitled individuals to specific rights within the legal framework by which the *República de Indios* (Indigenous Republics) were established in the sixteenth century, reinforced by the Laws of Burgos (1512) and the New Laws (1542) (Schwaller 2016). The independent, autonomous *pueblo de indios* operated as the basic unit of these republics and entitled their citizens to be assigned a *fundo real* [landed property] (Ouweneel 1996). Once the republics were dismantled and most of the land became property of non-indigenous elites, the term *Indio* ceased to grant indigenous citizens political autonomy. Gradually, the connotation of this former legal category changed.

Due to its homogenizing, standardizing and reductive character, the word *indígena* (indigenous) renders invisible the fact that major differences exist between each ethnic group (Aguilar Gil 2017). The term reminds many of the oppression, internalized colonialism, marginalization and stigma that have led mainstream societies to assume that indigenous communities are primitive, inferior and ignorant. The notion that an educated 'Indian' ceases to be considered an 'Indian' denotes the association that the term has with inferiority, exclusion and discrimination. As a concept, it has long implied that all indigenous peoples can be categorized as one ethnicity regardless of each of their individualities, or as simplification of an instant Other who is not European by origin. But like other parts of the world, the Americas were set to gain their independence in the aftermath of the French Revolution. Ideologies of equality swept across most of the European colonies, and Latin America was no exception. Historical evidence shows that there were attempts to abolish the use of the term *Indio* and other racial categories for being considered incompatible with notions of equality. Effectively, the main goal was to dismantle the system linked to the *Indio* categorization that had previously secured autonomy and access to land.

A new wind of change dictated that Latin Americans were not to be regarded based on the taxonomy imposed by European rulers. Although noble in nature, this shift never materialized completely and the widespread notion of *mestizaje* (race mixing), encouraged by the church, among others, only enforced already established hierarchies. Paradoxically, the figure of the mestizo strengthened existing differences between ethnicities across the continent. Mestizo has been used as a category that conveniently conveys a sense of fixity and permanence, even if originally, it revolved around the negotiation of identity according to various contexts (Rappaport 2014). Scientifically disputed, the socially constructed notion of *mestizaje* has evolved to operate as a strategy to define the mixed population of modern Latin American nations (Ouweneel 2018). As a result, *mestizaje* is still problematic for those who identify themselves as indigenous. In several passages of Latin American history, the position of self-identified indigenous communities has been imperilled by the idea that differences between indigenous and non-indigenous segments of society should be erased, but without reconfiguring the hegemonic power structures which ensure that the indigenous figure is in a subaltern position (Hernández Castillo 2010; Chirix 2015; Xinico Batz 2016).

An important aspect to consider here is that indigenous and indigeneity are 'scholastic concepts' (Ouweneel 2018), used to define, as Mary Louise Pratt (2007) observes, the identity of a group that inhabits a territory prior to the invasion or unwelcome arrival of another group. These are global terms that render invisible the real names of the nations they encompass, but that have gained certain degree of political and legal recognition. Across continents formerly colonized by European empires, at present, this categorization and what it entails is often one of the few tools these societies have to face the effect of neoliberal policies, abusive governments and discrimination.

In Latin America, indigenous/indigeneity suggests that party A (pre-Columbian societies) is defined by the actions of party B (Europeans). Party A is to be understood according to party B's actions, and the all-encompassing party A (all indigenous groups), composed of many other groups (A1, A2, A3, etc.), emerges in opposition to, as a response to and as a result of historical events brought about by a dominant group (Europeans).[6] Indigeneity has a generalist connotation in the sense that all the pre-Columbian groups (A1, A2, A3, etc.) that it circumscribes are in fact an amalgam of those groups that faced invasion by Europeans (party B), even if many of these distinct nations have expressed their desire to be referred to according to the name of each of them. Those who self-identify as members of a surviving party A are perceived as *indígenas*, and 'constitute a transnational mnemonic community in their own right as country dwellers, protectors of forests and nature, or as victims of military powers' (Ouweneel 2018: 6). A1 is by no means a subaltern of A2, but they are clustered and labelled as elements of A (the indigenous) in virtue of the existence of B, also composed of B1, B2, B3 and so on. As De la Cadena and Starn assert, 'indigenous cultural practices, institutions, and politics become such in articulation with what is not considered indigenous within the particular social formation where they exist' (De la Cadena and Starn 2007: 7). Similar to discourses of race, their significance 'only becomes apparent in the interaction of the two' (Malik 1996: 268).

Time is a key aspect as, 'it is only with reference to B's that A was *already there*' and 'until B arrived bearing a different temporal frame, A was most likely not the first subject on the scene, but the *last*, that is, the most recently arrived' (Pratt 2007: 398). The human landscape also includes other groups (party C) forced by party B to resettle in the invaded territories (large groups of enslaved Africans), and through violence reduced to subaltern positions, as is party A (the indigenous). Throughout the centuries, other groups (party D) have also settled in the region (e.g. large groups of immigrants from Asia, Europe and the Middle East), in many cases intermingling with party A, B and C, and gradually adding to the diversity introduced by first Europeans.

In order to understand the contrivances and complexities around the concept of indigeneity, one should consider that a combination of party A (pre-Columbian societies), B (Europeans), C (communities of African descent) and D (immigrants of various ethnicities) has emerged as the main constituent of the Latin American population. A logical consequence of centuries of intermingling is that the precise contours, if any, that demarcate membership of today's A,

B, C or D parties extend beyond a specific clear-cut division. This does not mean that identities and cultures have been eroded and weakened completely by the formation of modern nations. On the contrary, the survival of many elements of pre-Columbian and African cultural identities is evidence that the extermination, colonization and standardization projects put in place by Europeans and incipient states were not entirely successful. Yet, it is undeniable that all parties have extensively blended through intermarriage and cohabitation at a multigenerational level, resulting in the process in national, conflated identities and mixed cultures, cemented by memory and history.

In contemporary times, Latin Americans of European descent are hardly the same group that came to the Americas in the fifteenth century. Party B recognizes that it has mixed with indigenous communities, Afro-descendants and other ethnic groups to such an extent that it is difficult to refer to non-indigenous Latin Americans as Europeans. Indigenous biological, cultural, historical and social legacies (party A) are a fundamental aspect of most of the inhabitants of the region, to varying degrees. The same applies to areas of the continent with a noticeable African, Asian or Middle Eastern presence. *Indígena* is in many ways the concept used by Latin Americans (party ABCD) to refer to the social groups that trace their roots back to pre-Columbian societies (party A), and those who actively defend, promote, uphold, represent and embody the cultural identity that distinguishes them from other ethnic groups. Individuals actively articulate their adherence to a party they believe embodies their sense of identity, cultural background, ancestral roots, set of beliefs, worldviews, epistemologies and, most importantly, social and political standing. Contexts vary greatly, but many *indígenas* feel the enforced process of amalgamation never eroded, interrupted or broke their genealogical lineage. Historically oppressed identities logically inspire and embolden social and political movements to demand acknowledgement, equality and recognition.

Modern Latin American societies (ABCD) are a continuum in which subjective experiences, sensitivities and worldviews play a vital role in defining to what extent individuals claim affiliation to indigenous groups (A1, A2, etc.). Graham and Penny (2014) note that 'indigeneity as a global identity emerged during the Cold War era [and] the performance of Indigenous identity as a means of establishing membership in this community' has since become 'increasingly important' (4). Pratt observes that 'A was living a temporal narrative whose projection into the future did not include B', and hence, 'A's relational status as "indigenous" depends on the perdurance of that prior, nonrelational self-identity'

(Pratt 2007: 398). Preservation of cultural identity, combined with political acknowledgement and social inclusion, is vital for self-identified indigenous members to safeguard their constituency as a cultural and political entity and, in certain ways, to dissipate some of the consequences of the European invasion. A well-justified, identity-oriented, political and tactical endeavour, however, does not undo the multilayered ramifications that distinguish a social fabric that reflects an interweave of all ethnic groups (ABCD). There is a reason to celebrate the fact that this diversity is not lost, but one also has to admit that the clash, encounter, in/voluntary coexistence and in/accidental fusion has produced levels of diversity that do not necessarily reflect idealized distinctions accurately.

In present-day Latin America (ABCD Continuum), individuals are known not only for embracing their indigenous ancestry but also for denying it or taking distance from it, according to various contexts, temporalities, political climates, discriminatory settings or simply their own convenience. In this convoluted continuum, social status and class are linked to ancestral origin, as Wade (2005) explains, 'blackness and indigenousness can still be subjected to hierarchical orderings in which they are made to occupy inferior locations and are discriminated against and/or rendered exotic' (255). This is evidence that the project of homogenizing all parties – in particular indigenous and African ones – in order to erase animosities based on ethnic background, *mestizaje*, has actually redrawn social hierarchies. In general terms, 'the relationships between whites, indians, and mestizos have been long, violent, and frequently intimate [and therefore] distinctions between these groups are more likely to be characterized by ambiguity than clarity' (Canessa 2005: 24). Latin Americans' sense of individuality and belonging, cultural affiliation and, most importantly, self-identification are nuanced, complex and fluctuate along a wide spectrum.

Cinema replicates the tension between identity and perceived ethnicity, because the homogenization and amalgamation processes were profoundly rooted in stratified cultural expressions. As a 'supposed reconciliation between the Spanish and Indian worlds' (De la Cadena and Starn 2007: 5), the mestizo has been central to artistic productions aimed to represent the spirit of the modern Latin American nations. This book does not have as a purpose to dispute, make a case or present new ways of understanding indigeneity as a concept within social sciences (e.g. Anthropology) or humanities (e.g. Cultural Studies). Notwithstanding, it cannot ignore that there is a continuum in the way indigeneity is presented in recent Latin America cinematic productions, just as there seems to be a continuum in the way individuals regard themselves and others as indigenous. Whereas films produced by self-identified indigenous filmmakers stand out for their didactic, militant, communicational and contestatory approach, the spectrum of productions by non-indigenous filmmakers includes sophisticated, transfixing, awe-inspiring narratives, ethnographic films and productions that seek to denounce, articulate or enhance the subalternity of those considered to be the Other. The notion of alterity is crucial in many films that are allegedly conceived to condemn social inequalities and ethnicized hierarchies, while resorting to a frequent use of ethnic labels, preconceived typologies, caricatured renderings and, above all, stereotypes.

Perception

Even if the study of stereotypes has been considered as a passé, outdated remnant of structuralist approaches, it matters, as still today, in the second decade of the twenty-first century, stagnant, simplistic and stereotypical representations are often cited as obstacles for peripheral groups in their fight for inclusion, acknowledgement and equality. In the lived daily experience of millions of Latin Americans, stereotypes are not conceptual, abstract derivatives of system-oriented perspectives refusing to embrace new understandings of identity, diversity and ethnicity, as malleable notions fluctuating along a continuum. They have real implications in everyday lives. Stereotypes in mass media outlets, including cinema, help keep a narrative in place that legitimizes hierarchies and practices that benefit or harm under- and misrepresented segments of the population. Media outlets of all sorts reflect stifling and reductive stereotypes, often disguised as strategic dismissal of social groups that are not considered aspirational. In Argentina, Brazil and Mexico, for instance, indigenous and Afro-descendant traits are systematically avoided in advertisements. An analysis of 274 cases reveals that commercials conceived and produced in the three countries creatively avoid including references to the least favoured social groups and ethnicities in each country (Izquierdo Iranzo, Martínez Pastor and Galmes Cerezo 2017). Invisibility and under-representation operate in similar ways as stereotypes, as they denote which physical and cultural traits are considered to be positive, desirable, dominant and preferred. In Peru, four out of ten people do not feel in any way represented in mass media outlets, either in television programmes or in advertisement (Ipsos 2018). Cinema, likewise, draws organically on discourses of power and representation that replicate views of societies at large.

In an extensive study of the traits that mainstream Mexicans assign indigenous groups in the country, *Perception of the Image of the Indigenous Peoples of Mexico* (CDI 2006), the research team established that pre-Columbian societies and modern indigenous communities are perceived differently.[7] Pre-Hispanic civilizations are entwined with notions such as authenticity, intellectual superiority and ferocity, whereas contemporary urban and rural indigenous communities are perceived as poor, opposed to modernity, enclosed, traditionalist, efficient cheap labour and monolingual. Stereotypes are particularly negative about indigenous peoples residing in enclosed villages, agrarian zones and geographically isolated areas. Studies have shown that indigenous characters in mainstream media are mostly secondary characters typified according to their appearance and occupation. Identifiable by their accent and dark skin, often depicted as farmers, fishermen, domestic workers and healers/midwives, indigenous characters in Mexican telenovelas, for instance, are portrayed as not only loyal, friendly, hard-working but also angry, annoyed and not intelligent (Muñiz, Marañón and Saldierna 2014).

In contrast, idealizations about glorious pre-Hispanic civilizations seem to translate into positive conceptualizations of *historical* indigenous societies. In a large-scale study conducted by ninety-three researchers among 1,200 Mexican informants, Gutiérrez Chong and Valdés González (2015) observe the *dead Indian*, pre-Hispanic, civilized and archaeologically relevant is preferred over the marginalized, poor and discriminated *alive Indian*. A logical conundrum of this finding is that these are groups that none of the respondents has ever encountered. Perceptions about indigenous groups residing in urban areas show, above all, a direct link to socio-economic status, rather than specific traits such as epistemologies. In general, Mexicans seem to embrace indigeneity as a historical notion, or as a marker of ancestral legacy, but they are less positive about the economic and social disparities than the term seems to imply in modern contexts. In the most extensive poll commissioned by the Mexican government about discrimination, 75 per cent of the 102,245 informants agreed that indigenous communities were one of the least acknowledged segments of the population. Among the findings, the poll indicated that 36 per cent of the 39,101 interviewed households believed that poverty among indigenous communities was directly linked to their cultural background (INEGI-CONAPRED 2018). Surveys from other Latin American countries have reached similar conclusions. A study among six hundred Costa Ricans revealed that the term 'indigenous' is perceived to be intrinsically linked to other terms such as 'forefathers', 'discrimination', 'ethnic traits', 'archaeological traits', 'specific clothes' and 'humble people' (Solano Acuña 2008). Findings of surveys support the taxonomy of ideas that circulate about the indigenous Other across the region. The results serve as an entry point to understand the repertoire of assumptions about indigenous peoples, sometimes in paradoxical ways. In a Chilean study involving 7,333 informants, for instance, according to 81.1 per cent of the interviewed, indigenous peoples are hard-working, but in order to find employment, 61.7 per cent agree that a foreign last name facilitates matters as opposed to having an indigenous surname (INDH 2018).

Similarly, results of a study among 569 Peruvians clearly show that most informants link someone's indigenous background to preconceptions about specific sociolects and dress style (Chirapaq 2015). There are certain ideas about the physicality of those perceived to be indigenous in one way or another, and in urban contexts particularly, less visible aspects, such as customs and place of origin, become important identity markers. Those interviewed recognize that an individual's self-perception is fluid and that self-identification varies according to ancestry, linguistic affiliation, a family's political engagement and personal choice. In another study among 3,700 Peruvians from the twenty-five regions of the country, one of the main findings was that skin colour, phenological traits in general, place of birth, style of speech/accent and customs increased the possibility of discrimination (Ipsos 2018). Informants agreed on the fact that not all terms used to denote ethnic self-identification across the country (e.g. *originario*, *provinciano*, *nativo*, *campesino*, *indígena* and *mestizo*) elicited the same sensitivities. In general terms, Genna and Espinosa (2012) identify that Peruvians are stereotyped on the basis of their birthplace and distinctions are made between *amazónicos* (Amazonians) and *andinos* (Andeans). There is a widespread idea that levels of indigeneity are higher among Peruvians from either of these groups. Amazonians are generally coupled to notions such as backwardness, conformism, failure, incompetence and 'underdevelopment', whereas Andeans are typified as sad, industrious, backward, caring and conformist (in that order). An important difference in the stereotypes affixed to the two groups is that the former is regarded as unreliable, and the latter is perceived to be quite reliable and trustworthy. In the mental schema of many Peruvians, a connection is made between a set of categorizations and the notion of indigeneity.

Findings from *Stereotypes about Mapuches: A Recent Evolution* indicate many Chileans perceive Mapuche communities through a spectrum of categorization similar to those identified in Mexico, Peru and Costa Rica (Saiz, Rapimán and Mladinic 2008). With the participation of 407 informants, this study sought to determine and outline the longitudinal perpetuation of stereotypes and attributes mainstream Chileans ascribed to the Mapuche community.[8] As in similar studies, informants describe historical pre-Hispanic societies in positive terms, and except for their hostile and stubborn character, they are imagined to have been noble, brave, honest, intelligent and strong free spirits. Modern-day Mapuches are described not only as good citizens, loyal, industrious, responsible and willing to be useful to society but also as unfairly privileged, uneducated opportunistic, troublesome, wary and heavy drinkers, perceived by some as destructive, troublesome and incendiary. In Chile, as in Mexico and Peru, the spectrum of stereotypes affixed to ethnic groups is rather unbalanced. Indigenous societies settled across the continent before the European colonization are regarded with high esteem, whereas those identified as their descendants are regarded less positively. The various surveys and polls conducted throughout the region provide key insights into the set of preconceived ideas that Latin Americans share about those considered to be indigenous. These findings are stark reminders of how pervasive categorizations are. Humans use traits of perceived difference as a method to organize their understanding of others.

With important exceptions discussed in the subsequent chapters, the cinematic landscape is dominated by images of indigeneity that reflect and recycle many of the generalizations and clichés reported by the informants of the surveys. Ethnotypes lie at the core of Latin American indigeneity-oriented films, as much as repetitive, long-lasting formulas and mental schemas are central to frame or unfavourably contextualize, for instance, African Americans in Hollywood, Muslims or Roma communities in Western European news programmes, religious minorities across South Asian television networks and LGBTQ+ (as problematic as this acronym is) individuals in Eastern African media, to name a few. Images embody ideas and consequently imaginaries that scaffold the materiality and physicality of the consequences that stereotypes have in the lived experience of the people being framed. As is the case in the region, for many, media outlets, including cinema, are some, or the only, outlets or points of contact between spectators and segments of society unknown to them otherwise. At present, inclusion, tolerance, acceptance and equity can hardly become tangible insofar as mediascapes impossibly sketch scenarios in which this can happen. In fact, as it has been asserted by indigenous filmmakers, stereotypical misrepresentations in media are quite damaging for the communities involved.

An important part of the audiovisual vocabulary used to epitomize indigenous figures in fiction are preconceived schemas, many of which surround a distant Indian dwelling in a petrified state that retains an alluring sense of colonial nostalgia, comfortably couched in close contact with the natural world from which self-referential civilized societies assume they have distanced themselves.

Schemas are not only webs of categorizations and of interconnected sets of references, abstractions and concepts but also blueprints that denote the perceived relations between people and things, based on their similarities or contrasts[9] (Merskin 2011; Davis 2013). Diagram 1 is an attempt to sketch a mental schema of the term 'indigenous' possibly shared by many Latin Americans, based on the findings from previously mentioned studies and surveys, even if a visualization could not possibly account for the diversity found across a region as ethnically rich as Latin America. Schemas, or schemata, as they are also known, constantly change in sync with incoming data, which explains why concepts are reassessed when new information is received (Davis 2013). *Indígena* or mestizo ethnotypes, for instance, as they are understood in Argentina, Colombia or Mexico, are not necessarily perceived in identical ways in Bolivia, Ecuador, Guatemala or Peru (Ouweneel 2018). Diagram 1 does not suggest that the connections and clusters of ideas are not subject to constant revision and change, or apply in all cases and contexts. Yet, many of the concepts and terms found in the above-mentioned studies and depicted in the diagram overlap with ethno-typifications that reshape the lived experiences of millions across the region. A social manifestation of mental schemas is that they materialize in discriminatory practices against those who bear certain characteristics.

Perceptual identities have real implications for those considered to have purportedly different ethnic and cultural backgrounds, and for those who self-identify as members of communities widely regarded as peripheral. Discrimination does not seem to go out of style, and remains a pressing challenge in ethnically diverse regions, such as Latin America. For the affected communities, it matters how their representations mobilize images and ideas about their cultures, customs, worldviews and role within larger societies.

Representation

Cinema is a moving reflection not only of a society but also of its evolving process of self-definition, identification and nation-building campaigns that, in the case of the Americas, emerged as a response to the Eurocentric impressions

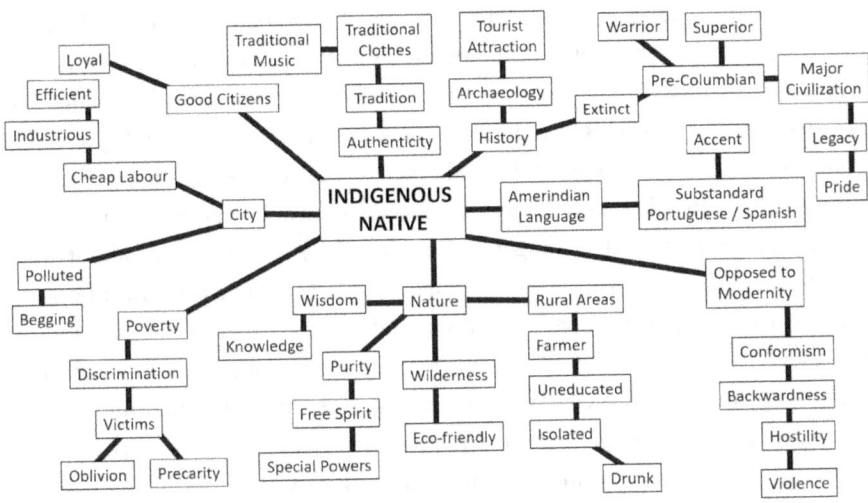

Diagram 1 Mental schema of the term *indigenous*.

of what was, and still is, considered a *different* world (Bataille 2001; Wernitznig 2007; de la Garza 2010; Flores 2014; Tompkins 2018). In this distinctive reality, unexplored geographies and, more importantly, unfamiliar peoples became central to narratives and artistic expressions that intended to represent the sensitivities that these new Others provoked among European and eventually mestizo mindsets. In fact, in several pages of the history of cinema, filmmakers were hesitant about their role and positionality, either as critical observants or as empathetic bystanders towards unfranchised groups, with many fluctuating across the two ends of the spectrum. The indigenous has traditionally complicated the production of visually consumed cultural artefacts that could emblematize the emergence of new republics. Ultimately, early visual representations were reproductions of discourses that made a clear difference between the European legacy and any other ancestry and set of conventions that lay at the periphery. To this day, as a general norm, representations of what is perceived to be different readily translates into exotifying practices that are supported by perpetuated, but not always substantiated, ideas, preconceptions, analogies, comparisons, exaggerations and fears.

Throughout most of the history of the medium, the inclusion, reference and portrayal of an imagined indigenous figure (party A) on the screen has been in the hands of mestizo and European cinematographers (ABCD Continuum). Whether for scientific or archival purposes, most images of pre-Columbian societies in the history of the so-called Seventh Art are hetero-images.[10] It seems logical that films made by self-identified indigenous directors (party A) are preoccupied with a different array of topics and themes than are films conceived by directors who seemingly represent a mainstream mestizo identity (ABCD Continuum). Due to historic and social processes, ABCD filmmakers are mainly informed by cultural tenets heavily influenced by European artistic conventions. A sense of distance and estrangement among the mestizo classes about what they perceive to be indigenous has aligned with Eurocentric preconceptions. In other words, these films have been attempts to create visual representations of how they imagine party A ought to be. The frequent use of ethnotypes to portray indigenous and Afro-descendants reflexively and iconically document social spaces where *blanqueamiento* (whitening) is the rule.[11] An indigeneity-oriented film is not necessarily a cinematic narrative conceived to denounce negative preconceptions about those perceived to be indigenous. Filmmakers create, actively and referentially, narratives that reflect their own worldviews and those of their funders, remaining attentive to the themes that draw the most attention.

The fact that cinema is a European invention introduced to Latin America through Western filmmakers cannot be disregarded (Carreño 2006). Considering that the first motion pictures focusing on the native peoples of the Americas were made in Europe explains some of the most pervasive archetypes (e.g. indigenous people are sage creatures, spiritual beings, guardians of nature, wild hunters and exotic women).[12] The impact of iconographic models kept and reinforced for centuries remained latent within the ideological fabric of cinematography about and from Latin America, especially present in films directed by filmmakers educated abroad. European conceptualizations served as the backbone for the implementation of this new form of art in the region, and in the context of the economies of the film industry, they have remained dominant and prevalent. Historical processes materialize in visual narratives, leaving in them inherent traces of the intersections between power and ethnic/racial ideologies, translated into discourses of dominance. The subalternity of indigenous societies in the realm of mainstream cinema exemplifies the subordinate role assigned to communities when they do not narrate in first person. For instance, while many self-representational films have indigenous epistemologies, ontologies and cosmologies as main subject, attention to traditional knowledge systems is less common in representational cinema.

Consonant with an imagology-oriented approach, this study seeks to delve into traditions of representation rather than societies at large. An assessment of indigenous ethno-typifications in cinema requires establishing the spectrum of attributes, generalizations and characterizations affixed to the social group being depicted. Ethnotypes are at their core stereotypes, and as such, they convey prejudices towards other social groups by implying and suggesting their identity and behaviour are static. Scripted representations of under-represented segments of society echo assumptions and preconceived ideas desultorily and arbitrarily used as points of reference about them.[13] Mental representations and their perceptual processes dwell in a parallel world vis-à-vis social reality. Their relation is asymptotic, hence actual manifestations of indigeneity are not necessarily reflected in cinematic spaces and vice versa. Images from films are not accurate depictions of the real world. I focus upon indigeneity as an abstract conceptualization that encompasses or makes direct or indirect reference to a broad spectrum of concepts (e.g. *andino, cholo,* Mapuche, *indio, indígena, serrano, campesino,* etc.) that have different meanings in different contexts and settings. They are imaginatively materialized in artistic artefacts conceived according to the discretion of an artist (e.g. a filmmaker).

Evidence gathered by the above-mentioned empirical studies confirms the centrality of stereotypes in the evolution and circulation of ideas about indigenous peoples. Yet, the set of traits revealed from those surveys and studies does not entirely coincide with the nomenclature of traits identified in the corpus of representational films (hetero-images), listed in Tables 3–5. Although many of the stereotypes mentioned by the informants overlap with a wide range of typifications found in the selected films, as subsequent chapters will show, diversity in cinematic portrayals at an individual level surpasses group-oriented generalizations observed in the surveys. More than an inventory of traits, Tables 3–5 list identified stereotypes as means to recognize their role in weaving stories that visually register and shape the history of representation of indigenous peoples in cinema.

As for films made by indigenous filmmakers and *Cine regional* directors, no nomenclature of ethnotypes, or rather self-ethnotypes, has been drawn for the corpus of self-representational cinema for two reasons. Firstly, it is beyond the scope of this book and beyond my positionality as non-indigenous researcher to review a fledgling, unsupported and contestational cinematic tradition that bespeaks the needs for self-expression of unfranchised communities.[14] Secondly, there is a limited number of surveys that could provide empirical background or an indication of how indigenous communities regard themselves in terms of characteristics or traits.

Table 3 Taxonomy of Traits Identified in Representational Films Depicting Historical Communities

	Traits	Main character (Individual)		Secondary characters (Community) Mixed genders	Historical films
		Female	Male		
Films depicting historical indigenous communities (N=6)	Original and credible			3	*Bien esquivo*; Peru, 2001
	Fierce warriors			4	*Brava gente*; Brazil, 2001
	Interesting for tourists			1	*Caramuru*; Brazil, 2001
	Brave warriors, strong leaders, free spirits	1		5	*Erendira Ikikunari*; Mexico, 2006
	Hostile, stubborn, violent, wary	1		4	*La carga*; Mexico, 2016
	Makers of colourful art, archaeologically relevant		1	3	*Zama*; Argentina, 2017
	Noble, loyal, honest	1	1	3	
	Survivors in extreme conditions		1	3	
	Intellectually superior			1	
	Industrious, responsible			4	
	Interesting lifestyle			2	

In light of the importance of gender as a social categorization, separate columns provide data on the gender of the main characters. As the tables show, the range of traits identified in the films is quite broad, particularly if the variable 'main character' (individual) is compared to 'secondary characters' (community), and a contrast is drawn between female and male main characters. In general terms, there is a tendency in films to portray indigenous women as foreign and poverty-stricken in rural settings, and as cheap labour in urban contexts. Overall, filmmakers seem to suggest that more women than men move from the countryside to the cities, and that they are more likely to become part of urban

Table 4 Films Depicting Modern Indigenous Communities (N = 62)

Traits	Rural Communities			Urban communities		
	Main character (Individual)		Secondary characters (Community)	Main character (Individual)		Secondary characters (Community)
	Female	Male	Mixed genders	Female	Male	Mixed genders
Credible, pure	2		17			5
Impoverished, abject, forgotten	4	3	23	1	2	7
Intelligent		1	7		1	1
Free spirits		1	19			5
Different, foreign	5		20	1		4
Knowledgeable about nature	1	1	21			4
Willing to adhere to their traditions	1	2	19	2	1	6
Willing to preserve their linguistic heritage			14			5
Lacking education	2		22			5
Wary, stubborn, heavy drinkers		2	23			6
Troublesome, extremists	1		19			4
Efficient workers, industrious	4		7	1	1	4
Cheap work labour, willing to engage in informal sources of income		2	18	6		5
Unpolluted unless they come in contact with urban traditions	1		13	1	1	2
Opposed to modernity.			8	1		2

Traits	Rural Communities			Urban communities		
	Main character (Individual)		Secondary characters (Community)	Main character (Individual)		Secondary characters (Community)
	Female	Male	Mixed genders	Female	Male	Mixed genders
Own worldviews about wealth	1		5			2
Arrogant			8	1		1
Self-enclosed, showing a tendency to reject civilization		2	13			1
Quiet		3	5			3
Good citizens, responsible, loyal	2	2	5			2
Able to progress, ambitious about education	2		1	2		3
Destructive, aggressive		1	21	1		3
Willing to become part of the nation	1		2	2	2	1
Engaged in begging	1		1			1
Unfairly privileged		1				1

society. Directors seem to affix traits such as aggressiveness, self-enclosure and wariness more readily to indigenous male characters. The taxonomy also indicates that most films depict indigenous characters as not only convincing, pure, intelligent and relatively free but also impoverished, forgotten, abject and, at first blush, different.

The results shown in Tables 3–5 suggest that recent films stand out not only for their recognition of the ethnic legacy of the continent but also for their

Table 5 Modern Times Films

A terra dos homens vermelhos; Brazil, 2008
Alamar; Mexico, 2009
Alicia en el país; Chile, 2008
Antes o Tempo Não Acabava; Brazil, 2016
Burwa dii ebo; Panama, 2008
Cassandra; Argentina, 2012
Cenizas eternas; Venezuela, 2011
Climas; Peru, 2014
Cochochi; Mexico, 2007
Corazón del Tiempo; Mexico, 2008
Dauna: Lo que lleva el río; Venezuela, 2015
Defensores de la vida; Costa Rica, 2015
Diarios de Motocicleta; Several countries, 2004
Dioses; Peru, 2008
Distancia; Guatemala, 2011
El abrazo de la serpiente; Colombia, 2015
El destino; Argentina–Spain, 2006
El facilitador; Ecuador, 2013
El niño pez; Argentina-Paraguay, 2009
El ombligo de Guie'dani/Xquipi' Guie'dani/Guie'dani's Navel; Mexico, 2019
El regreso; Venezuela, 2013
El regreso de Lencho; Guatemala, 2010
El sueño del Mara'akame; Mexico, 2016
El traspatio; Mexico, 2009
El verano de los peces voladores; Chile, 2013
El Violín; Mexico, 2005
Erase una vez en Bolivia; Bolivia, 2011
Espiral; Mexico, 2008
Evo Pueblo; Bolivia, 2007
Feriado; Ecuador, 2014
Guaraní; Paraguay, 2015
Hamaca Paraguaya; Argentina–Paraguay, 2000
Ixcanul; Guatemala–France, 2015
Könun Wenu; Chile, 2010
La Ciénaga; Argentina, 2001
La Jaula de Oro; Mexico, 2013
La mujer sin cabeza; Argentina, 2008
La niña santa; Argentina, 2004
La Sirga; Colombia, 2012

La teta asustada; Peru, 2009
La Tirisia; Mexico, 2014
Las niñas Quispe; Chile, 2013
Los ojos azules; Mexico, 2012
Los viajes del viento; Colombia, 2009
Madeinusa; Peru, 2005
Magallanes; Peru, 2015
Nosilatiaj. La belleza; Argentina, 2012
Pájaros de verano; Colombia–Denmark–Mexico, 2018
Play; Chile, 2005
¿Quién mató la llamita blanca?; Bolivia, 2007)
Retablo; Peru, 2017
Rito Terminal; Mexico, 2000
Roma; Mexico–United States, 2018
Siguiendo las estrellas; Panama, 2010
Sueño en otro idioma; Mexico, 2017
Tainá; Brazil, 2001
Taínos: La última tribu; Puerto Rico, 2005
Tiempos menos modernos; Argentina–Chile, 2011
Vaho; Mexico, 2009
Xingu; Brazil, 2012
Yvy Maraêy: Tierra sin mal; Bolivia, 2013
Zona Sur; Bolivia, 2009

---

acknowledgement of the diversity that exists within, until now, only superficially explored communities. In fact, newer portrayals problematize older paradigms of representation because they debunk the incomplete characterizations upon which these narratives were constructed. Using the scenarios set in rural areas as a reference point – as they are the majority – it is possible to deduce that the renderings of indigenous communities and individual characters differ considerably. This concerns in particular the rendering of negative traits. While only a few films focus on troublesome, destructive and wary protagonists, these negative connotations are easily found in the portrayals of the communities to which they belong. There is a clear tendency to separate the individual from a sense of collective identity, or to refuse to generalize about a standard imagined indigenous prototype, as films from previous decades commonly do.

As previously discussed, identity and representations cannot be reduced to a binary of stereotypical and counter-stereotypical representations. The set of traits does provide nevertheless an overview of how non-indigenous filmmakers depict indigenous characters in contemporary cinema. Deducing from many of the representational films of the corpus, urban Latin American film directors entwine the concept of indigeneity with the cognitive noble savage schema (CNSS), the embodiment of the uncorrupted innate good indigene sentimentally positioned to dwell perennially in nature (Ouweneel 2018). Filmmakers can only present the figure of the indigenous from their own mindset, but more importantly, according to their own position with regard to this figure. From a social, political, ethnic and cultural standpoint, it is not certain where the boundaries of indigeneity lie, either in imaginary or 'real-life' contexts, and this project does not aim to answer this question. It does intend to delve into the set of filmic characterizations of indigenous identities in hetero- and auto-images. The porousness of 'borderlands' (Anzaldúa 1987), where mestizo and indigenous individuality overlap and collide, results in areas of contention and tension. As a public medium, cinema relies on its capacity to engage viewers by complying with predetermined criteria, traditions and approaches. If indigeneity has a performative dimension along the identity politics landscape (Graham and Penny 2014), contemporary films seem to suggest that it also has a theatrical applicability and potentiality across international screening venues.

Syntonic versus histrionic indigeneity

Indigeneity emerges as a theme with leverage and currency across a competitive market of images that thrive on entertaining content that spices up global mediascapes hungry for iterative formulas. During the process of transposing indigenous ethno-typifications into screened productions, representations acquire not only an artistic but also a social and political value for the societies being represented. Caricatures, clichés and recycled formulas are perhaps more easily digestible narrative strategies for viewers in Sundance or Venice, but less savoury for the ostracized communities that serve as inspiration or point of reference in exotifying films. A distinction can be made between a zoomed-in perspective with built-in social commentary on the individuality of indigenous characters (syntonic), and a zoomed-out angle on the exoticism of members of a community, recognizable for elements that mark their difference and that strengthen upheld preconceptions and long-established canons (histrionic).

Understanding 'histrionic' as a term that connotes excessively theatrical, deceitful and stagy representations, *histrionic indigeneity* refers to the hyperbolized, manipulated and caricatural portrait of indigenous identities. In these representations, pre-Columbian cultures, traditions and languages are adjusted, distorted, enhanced and reconfigured in an attempt to produce attractive, awe-inspiring visual narratives. Replicating the trope of a set of distant, imagined Others, essentially different from a central continuum of Selves is instrumental in harnessing shock value, increasing the capacity to provoke reactions and securing visibility. Ethnotypes widen the distance between professedly peripheral characters and mainstream spectators, recirculating Western (post)-colonial precepts that tap into the enormous nostalgia of (inter) national audiences for the figure of the noble savage. An overtly histrionic version of indigeneity comfortably allows for exaggerations, reductions, inaccuracies, misimpressions, condensations and omissions at will, fulfilling criteria of funders, exhibitors and distributors.

Falicov (2017, 2019) convincingly makes a case for the level of influence festivals have on the content, approach and aesthetics of the films they circulate and co-create directly (i.e. funding, post-production assistance) or indirectly (i.e. training workshops). An especially problematic aspect of institutions involved in instructing new generation of filmmakers is the intangible effects of their pedagogical endeavours. From a tripartite position of co-producers (i.e. through funding schemes), assessors (i.e. through shortlisting and awards) and gatekeepers, one might wonder to which extent creativity, agency and artistic independence are fostered or brought into conformity with a predetermined standard. Festivals are important showcases that offer not only financial support, access to distribution networks and notoriety but also seals of excellence that secure visibility. It remains unclear how diversity is adjusted or attenuated to secure consistency in the body of visual narratives being promoted. Simplistically, festivals can be compared to a large factory producing chocolate of the best quality. While the cacao beans are the ingredients, a number of stages ensure that the final product meets certain standards, before it is wrapped in a modish package that oozes sophistication, duly labelled with the name of a glamourized country and shipped to all the corners of the world, concretely to those with adventurous and refined palates. How far the cacao beans are from the industrially produced bonbons remains a second-order matter. The final product moves around precisely *because* it has gone through a number of filters. In a similar manner, Latin American films that circulate at a global level are thrust by the invisible support and influence of the festivals that at different stages have been involved in various ways in their production and exhibition.

Disparagingly, this modus operandi hardly includes self-identified indigenous filmmakers/collectives. Beyond the easily observable asymmetry in terms of inclusion and participation, festivals reinforce the horizontal and vertical hierarchies that define the production and distribution of cinema. In stark contrast, indigenous film festivals have emerged as spaces that 'reconfigure Indigenous film praxis from a marginal practice to a vibrant transnational and transcultural cinema', prompting a 'productive reckoning, updating and reimagining of what counts as Indigenous Cinema, contributing sophisticated renderings to questions that haunt indigeneity across diverse public spheres worldwide' (Córdova 2017b: 164). Commercial cinema networks thrive on novelty, as long as it adheres to a specific optic, register and aesthetic. Although films that could be inscribed as Indigenous Cinema are occasionally screened in a specific theme-oriented section of the programme in large-scale prestigious festivals, they are contextualized on the basis of their provenance. Regrettably, in this sense, festivals fail to work as spaces that propel interaction, collaborations and strategies to further the production of self-representational films.

Across exhibition outlets, a Latin American indigeneity-oriented film is an addition because it is, at least, in principle, made in the continent and touches upon a so-perceived interesting topic. As Falicov (2010) observes, 'while it may be true that the South needs opportunities and support from the North to survive, it is equally true, in Saidian terms, that the North needs the South to be *avant la lettre*' (18). It is impossible to ignore the array of opportunities and possibilities yielded by global financing and distribution networks, particularly in a continent with reduced economic support for cinematic efforts from the state. A valid observation is that economic manipulation of national cinema can result in films inscribed within hegemonic Western frameworks aligned with neo-colonial paradigms. In fact, comparing films focusing upon indigeneity made by foreign and local filmmakers reveals undeniable commonalities and confirms that the viewpoint in many of the 'national' films mimics Eurocentric ideologies (Shaw 2014). Yet, it is not clear how exotic landscapes, colonialist nostalgia, fabulism and mysticism work as indictments of social inequality, discrimination and oppression. These films prompt us to wonder whether viewers have a fascination with the sense of mystique, remoteness and authenticity of the imagined Other, or whether seductive, idealized, provocative and fabricated Otherness holds an innate fascination for the audiences. Aesthetic strategies can be effective methods to create reduced but seductive versions of reality. Central to these films, consumed paradoxically by global rather than national audiences, are the dimensions and determinants behind the disenfranchisement of indigenous communities. Ironically, as the following example confirms, (allegedly) altruistic goals of the filmmakers are used as a key piece in the promotional machinery around many indigeneity-themed films.

Addressing the popularity of *Ixcanul* (2016) in her native Guatemala, Sandra Xinico Batz (2016) asserts that its director, Jayro Bustamante, is not a 'héroe por desnudar la desgracia de la vida indígena en contraste con la majestuosidad de los paisajes naturales y de un imponente volcán cuya traducción (de volcán) en kaqchikel fue escrita como ixcanul en lugar de xkanul, resultado del gran desconocimiento que impera alrededor de los idiomas mayas' [a hero for unveiling the misfortune of indigenous life in contrast with the majesty of the natural landscapes and of an imposing volcano of which the translation (of the word volcano) in Kaqchikel was written as *ixcanul* instead of *xkanul*, resulting from the great ignorance that prevails about Mayan languages] (Part III). Thematically, poverty, rituals, monolingualism, trafficking of newborns and exuberant nature, indeed, are the main topics in Bustamante's debut film. *Ixcanul* follows María (María Mercedes Coroy), a seventeen-year-old girl who is to marry Ignacio (Justo Lorenzo), the landowner of the coffee farm where she lives with her parents. Speaking only Kaqchikel, the family has limited possibilities and hence, in spite of her love for impoverished America-bound Pepe (Marvin Coroy), the wedding seems unavoidable. The film revolves around the drama that ensues after Ignacio finds out about María's infidelity and pregnancy, and the local hospital tricks the disenfranchised family into believing the newborn has died, only for them to discover that the staff has clandestinely given the baby up for adoption. According to some critics, *Ixcanul* manages to epitomize women 'continually disparaged by their cultures' (Merry 2016: para. 5), and certainly, the film does address the resilience of María and her mother, Juana (María Telón). During a screening in Amsterdam, Bustamante vaguely specified that he had heard the story from his nanny, and explained that, unlike 'average' Guatemalans, 'only audiences like us' (the ones sitting in the Dutch auditorium) were able to appreciate María's story and 'Guatemalan indigenous stories and traditional clothes' (Rialto Theatre, August 16, 2015). A reverse gender-oriented analysis of the story would have it that the Guatemalan director appropriated the story he heard from his Kaqchikel employee and decided to transform it into a strong candidate entry for a film festival.

In her reflection about the film, Xinico Batz prompts us to entertain the possibility that *Ixcanul* is a French-Guatemalan, not a Guatemalan-French film, proudly endorsed by the French Ministry of Europe and Foreign Affairs and Guatemalan Institute of Tourism. Quoting a guide who organizes one of the many tours around the Pacaya volcano national park (Parque Nacional Volcán de Pacaya y Laguna de Calderas) departing from Antigua, 'the life as is shown in Ixcanul does not exist but the movie is good to attract tourists'. Certain aspects of the *life* shown in the film are not inventions though. Bustamante does draw attention to the apathy and abuse committed by local authorities towards non-Spanish-speaking, low-income and impoverished citizens. Yet, as Castillo (2019) observes, this is a film where the figure of the indigenous is entirely decoupled from any conceptualization of modernity, for instance, by editorially removing an international fast food sign so that it does not spoil the impeccable photography that taps into viewers' romantic yearning. Hence, it is normal that 'perceptive Indigenous commentators have taken issue precisely with this variant on colonialist nostalgia and liberal guilt' (120), contained in a story that apparently grants access to an enticing and authentic reality. Scholars Judith Maxwell and Brett Nelson, specialized in Kaqchikel language and culture, regret that the film disparages the community's belief system and frames its members through the optic of superstition, drunkenness and bestiality. Their conclusion is that 'the movie is beautifully filmed and acted. María Mercedes Coroy is lovely as the eponymous heroine. But Ixcanul [sic] is racism made beautiful' (2018: para. 16).

María's heroic characterization bears resemblance to the portrayal of Madeinusa in Claudia Llosa's eponymous *Madeinusa* (Peru, 2005). A connection between the two films is apparent as they revolve around young women reclaiming their agency and challenging social norms. Both girls are central feminine figures amidst the constraints of realities staged by the assembly of exotifying elements and ethnotypes. The two productions are made by directors educated in Europe, Bustamante (France) and Llosa (Spain), supported by European institutions and, as expected, widely screened at film festivals where Western paradigms of exoticism are the benchmark. Controversial *Madeinusa* focuses upon a fourteen-year-old young girl about to be deflowered by her father and town mayor, Don Cayo, during the Holy Week festivities (see Chapter 4). Anticipating a keen appreciation of international audiences for ethnographic yet fabulist narratives, the story is set in the village of Manayaycuna, a lost town in terms of space and time. As noted by Cisneros (2013), there are certain commonalities and registers at play in productions engineered by directors educated abroad and whose works have been endorsed, distributed and awarded internationally. Language is one of them. Cisneros's reflection invites us to think in which ways, for instance, Quechua (*Madeinusa*) and Kaqchikel (*Ixcanul*) are elements that successfully convey a sense of credibility and genuineness: perhaps at the level of scripted stimuli enhancers. Their inclusion reminds spectators of the achievements of Amerindian societies in terms of language preservation. Alternatively, they presumably operate as tokens of authenticity that increase the marketability of films, the core topic of discussion in Chapter 3.

In terms of realistic representation, cinema is one of those domains that facilitate the global adaptability of imagined local and national expressions. *Madeinusa* and *Ixcanul* are representative of cultural artefacts that perpetuate stereotypical colonialist notions of indigeneity by recycling long-established paradigms (i.e. drunkenness, amorality, savageness, monolingualism, ingenuity, isolation). Other examples of this optic and approach, of what I understand as histrionic indigeneity, include *Xingu* (Brazil, 2012), *El facilitador/The Facilitator* (Ecuador, 2013) and *El abrazo de la serpiente/Embrace of the Serpent* (Colombia, 2015). More films along this line are detailed in the subsequent chapters, but also contributions that attest to the multiplicity of approaches in indigeneity-themed cinema. Across a spectrum between what I identify as histrionic and syntonic representations, there is an ecosystem of nuanced diversity and variance in constant evolution.

Understanding syntonic as 'responsive to and in harmony with the environment so that affect is appropriate to the given situation' (Oxford Dictionary 2016), at the other end of histrionic portrayals, I suggest that Indigenous Cinema and *Cine regional* are examples of syntonic representations. At their core, these are artistic self-expressions of identities, until now, mostly spoken for, above all, committed to use cinema as a medium to promote social advancements for the communities involved. In their process of creation and exhibition, auto-images increase our understanding of those considered as distant Others, and are likely to receive increased attention, support and recognition in the coming decades. Self-representational films of the stature of Claudia Huaiquimilla's *Mala Junta/Bad Influence* (2016) and Óscar Catacora's *Wiñaypacha/Eternity* (Peru, 2017) are already reshaping the expansion of the cinematic vocabularies used to represent indigenous cultures in cinematic spaces (see Chapter 7). Along a similar line in terms of its ramifications socially, culturally and even politically, *Roma* (Mexico, 2019), discussed in detail in Chapter 6, can be considered a syntonic cultural artefact.

Cuarón's film syntonically transcends and outflanks reiterative interpretations and aesthetic codes that have served as the backbone of long-established stereotypes. The sense of (e)motion(s) that Cuarón elicits in *Roma* bears the hallmarks of a new approach to the (re)presentation of under/mis/(re)presented groups. In certain respects, *Roma* seems to suggest that a changing attitude to the topic of indigeneity is not linked to the social life of the images presented, but the focus, depth and magnitude of the story, on- and off-screen. There is more beyond the veil of visually arresting images disguising (recycled) representations informed by assumptions spectators recognize and embrace. Cinema also has the power to create new cultural memories. These emerge from the experience spectators have of images that reduce a figure's apparent distance from those observing them.

Indigeneity in contemporary cinema does not always denote a reinforcement of fossilized paradigms of representation. Challenging some of the preconceptions audiences might have about Bolivian society, Juan Carlos Valdivia's *Zona Sur/Southern District* (2009), for instance, depicts a country in the process of embracing its ethnic legacy. Actors Ninón del Castillo (Carola) and Pascual Loayza (Wilson) perform impeccably as embodiments of a nation where the distribution of wealth is slowly changing social dynamics. In charge of three children and responsible for all expenses a large house implies, Carola embodies the ruling classes of a country in times of upheaval and restructuring. Scanning the carefully decorated, white-walled house, the mobile framing of the camera gives the idea that time does not linger, nor does it make concessions to any of the family members. This approach resembles Valdivia's non-concessional stance when it comes to foreign funding, refusing external endorsement if it comes with demands in terms of content.

In *Zona Sur*, the private realm of the servants, on the other hand, remains enclosed and difficult to approach, to the extent that their exchanges in Aymara are not subtitled.[15] This might suggest that the indigenous elements in the film need to be observed, rather than explained (Molina Ergueta 2010). Ties of affection between all members of the household are clear, and moments of tension, such as the death of Wilson's son, serve to remind audiences that class, ethnicity and gender are not foregone determinants. There is no space for artificial histrionic codes in the representations of the Aymara servants (Erika, Marcelina and Wilson), and therein lies a crucial point of reflection. A tentative observation is that external funding is more likely than not to translate into uncoerced, less prescriptive and honest cinematic portrayals of indigeneity, if no restrictions on content accompany the support.¹⁶ Also widely acclaimed, but for different reasons, *Zona Sur* embodies a tangible commitment to create deep, panoramic visual statements about Bolivia's social evolution. *Ixcanul, Madeinusa, Roma* and *Zona Sur* showcase that canons of representation in indigeneity-oriented films can vary considerably. The goal of the present volume is to explore this diversity from a chronological, geopolitical, linguistic, epistemic-ontological, transnational, paradigm/point-of-view changing and self-representational perspective, in this order. Based on an analysis of histrionic and syntonic elements, the films appear in a sequence that reserve the last sections of the book for the groundbreaking approaches and contributions that are envisioned to shape the cinematic representation of indigeneity in the coming decades.

Thus, the volume has been structured into seven chapters, each subdivided into two sections and followed by a brief conclusion. Except for Chapter 7, *Wääjx äp* (WhatsApp), a Mixe phonetic transcription coined by linguist Aguilar Gil, the names of the chapters bear Greek and Latin words that summarize the topic of each. A European approach to name-giving symbolically alludes to the fact that many of the films analysed in the first six chapters are informed by traditional approaches to (re)presenting an imagined Other. The influence of canons originally featured in European works of art and cinema is central in Chapter 1, 'Mimesis'. This chapter explores the historical processes behind the canons of representation of the pre-Columbian societies of the continent. In terms of approach, it contends that although films are believed to serve as representations of social reality, a close analysis reveals that indigeneity in visual culture has, from the beginning, been partly fabricated. This part of the book charts how the image of the American natives has historically been registered as the embodiment of a noble savage in works of literature, paintings, photography and cinematic spaces. Chapter 1 is further subdivided into 'Figment, Art and Fabrication' and 'Cinema and Indigeneity'. While the first section situates fine arts as the origin of ethnotypes, the second charts the inclusion of hetero-images in cinema from a historical perspective. This section is concerned with the stages these portrayals have undergone from the time filmmaking was introduced at the beginning of the twentieth century. In a broader context, this relatively extensive chapter provides background information about the visual representations that precede, and introspectively explain, approaches commonly identified in Latin American contemporary cinema.

Subdivided into 'Mexico and Central America' and 'South America', Chapter 2, 'Metropolis', presents an analysis of the films produced in various countries across the region. In numerous ways, the reviewed films can be considered as (metro/cosmo)politan cultural artefacts that reflect how societies choose to understand themselves. Each section focuses upon the links between national identities, social realities and the representation of indigeneity, which is mainly conceived by filmmakers based in the capital cities. The discussion in this chapter summarizes how the codes, conventions and symbols found in the objects of analysis can be linked to processes and reconfigurations of group affiliations and identities. A focal point in this analysis is to assess how geopolitical divisions and long-established canons of representation are maintained, strengthened or contested at a national level. Furthermore, this chapter explores not only the commonalities but also the striking differences in the way Latin American filmmakers approach indigeneity in recent films. Whereas Andean directors are notorious for resorting to indigenist practices reminiscent of previous decades, Mexican visuals highlight the importance of identity. In the case of Brazil, natives are still regarded through a tropicalist optic, and historical chronicles are preferred over confrontational, present-day stories. Meanwhile, the Southern Cone region presents two clear approaches. Argentine cinema seems to address indigeneity as a *part* of newly rediscovered rural geographies, while Chilean films are critical about what indigeneity actually entails. Due to a lack of resources, and widespread indifference to the plight of self-identified indigenous communities, the number of Central American and Paraguayan films on the topic is limited.

Language is the central theme in Chapter 3. 'Lexis' documents the ways in which Amerindian languages are included in filmic narratives, and outlines formularizations on hegemony, audiences and globalization from a sociolinguistic standpoint. Divided into 'Accented Inclusion' and '(In)discernible Sounds and Authenticity', this chapter focuses on the role played by Amerindian languages in the selected films as tokens of realism, exoticism and authenticity. As a marker, language is an integral part of heterogeneous cultural production. This is particularly the case in contexts in which it is required to convey a sense of authoritativeness and realness. As this chapter suggests, it is not accidental that forty-four of the sixty-eight selected representational films include conversations of various kinds and lengths in Amerindian languages.

Chapter 4, 'Emphasis', subdivided into 'Nature–Technology Dichotomy as an Ontological Genre' and 'Knowledge, Senses and Ethnicity', argues that epistemic and ontological considerations are key to review the iconic representations of Latin America's pre-Columbian societies in cinema. In this chapter, I argue that a revision of indigeneity-themed films from a longue durée perspective suggests these productions constitute a genre or, at least, a subgenre in their own right. Focusing on the centrality of nature and technology as concepts explicitly or implicitly addressed in the narratives, the discussion revolves around the frame of reference in which indigeneity and modernity are antonyms. Subsequently, the second section revises the incursion of knowledge as an aspect of indigenous cultures that has gained recognition in the last two decades.

Based on the findings of a close reading analysis, Chapter 5, 'Axis', offers an assessment of the artistic fabrication of otherness, contemporary archetypes, regnant ideologies of representation and intersectionality of social categories in the selected corpus. As I show in the first section, 'Intersectional Paradigms', ethnicity and gender remain within an outwardly positioned realm. A prevalent pattern seen in most of the reviewed films is that cinematic imagery of female characters is influenced by their ancestry and, in particular, by a well-defined 'pigmentocracy' (Lipstchutz 1944: 70-1). As Chirix (2015) asserts, the universality of hegemonic gender and ethnic discourses do not explain, they just operate. The fascination for the unknown remains a symptom of a Self–Other binary within Latin American and global cinematic tradition. The second section, 'Arrayed Figures', revises how indigeneity implies conspicuousness and continues to lie outside the range of normality. In this part of the chapter, I discuss the tendency to script, exotify and above all histrionize what constitutes indigeneity according to canons and paradigms that secure recognition, popularity and attention internationally.

In stark contrast, Chapter 6, 'Catalysis', argues that the release of *Roma* (Mexico–United States) in December 2018 marks a paradigm shift in the portrayal of indigenous characters in Latin American cinema. In this chapter, I suggest that Alfonso Cuarón's film redraws a blueprint for the representation of indigeneity by presenting a syntonic, rather than a histrionic, approach. While the second section, '(Re)drawn blueprint', focuses on *Roma*, the first one, '(In)visibility and Representation', theorizes and retrospectively reflects on the actual practice and canons of representation that have been deployed to create cinematic ethno-typifications.

The last chapter, 'Wääjx äp', summarizes the spectrum of themes and approaches found in self-representational films (auto-images), some of which are collaborations between indigenous communities and non-indigenous directors, but nevertheless steered by those being represented. The first section, entitled 'The Cybernetics of Self-Representation', looks at films made by self-identified indigenous collectives/filmmakers and the systems where they operate. The second section, 'Screen(ed)(ing) Intimacy and Clusivity', touches on the proclivities identified in works commonly known as *Cine regional*. This chapter suggests that Indigenous Cinema and new forms of cinema produced in so-perceived peripheral regions of Peru challenge notions of (self)-identity, ethnicity and representation.

At last, the subsequent conclusion seeks to present a general synthesis of the results of this research and summarize the findings of this study. In order to make the chapters independent of each other, some of the most prominent films, for example, *Zona Sur/Southern District*, are introduced and analysed according to the context of discussions in each section, allowing for occasional reiterations. Repetition makes it possible to read each analysis without reviewing previous sections, while offering different reflections on key films from various standpoints and critical angles.

Conclusion

This book explores the evolutionary path of audiovisual representations of indigenous cultures and languages in Latin American cinema. The focus lies on how films have played a role in mobilizing stereotypical notions about Latin American pre-Columbian communities (ethnotypes) and their cultural and linguistic heritage. The underlying premise is that images have served as repositories and conveyors of ideas that have fed national, regional and global imaginaries, while framing, favouring and diffusing perspectives, attitudes and narratives that have not necessarily taken into account the standpoint of the indigenous peoples. The overarching term *indigenous* refers to the inhabitants – and their descendants – of territories preceding the subsequent arrival of settlers, eventually rendered into colonized communities, often through strenuous methods. Ancestry and culture are used as markers among/about those commonly (self)-identified as indigenous. Indigeneity alludes to the aspects of identity shared by societies whose individualities are defined in relation to the creation of hegemonic societies in occupied territories. As a concept, indigeneity implies an autochthonous, uninterrupted nature articulated in an identity expressed through ethnic affiliation. The main objects of study in this volume are sixty-eight representational films, thirty-one self-representational productions and twenty-two *Cine regional* cinematic works. The main argument is that recent Latin American narratives elucidate commonalities in the processes of creation, technique and ideology, because they lie at the heart of a cinematic scene reshaped by a common trend to incorporate a new compendium of cultures, ostensibly brought about by globalization processes. Understanding 'histrionic' as a term that connotes excessively theatrical, deceitful and stagy representations suggests that the term *histrionic indigeneity* seems appropriate to describe productions in which filmmakers design and decorate indigenous identity, rather than reflect on the subjectivities of the social groups depicted.

1

Mimesis: Circulation of ideas and images

Images evolve and circulate, not only disseminating attitudes but also documenting and establishing ways of interpreting and imaging ourselves and others. Aesthetic attempts to mimic reality have constituently manifested in visual artefacts that unequivocally provide more information about the creators and their worldviews than about the societies being depicted. As this chapter aims to show, in terms of themes and formats, current portrayals of indigenous societies are intrinsically linked to paradigms originally featured in European artworks; canons of difference and judgement eventually transferred into the world of cinema. The first section, 'Figment, art and fabrication', addresses the impact of the Western tradition of fine arts in the creation of paradigmatic portrayals of the natives of the so-called New World. The second section, 'Cinema and indigeneity', presents a historical overview of the various stages, approaches and themes that have distinguished the depiction of indigenous characters and elements since cinema was introduced in the region. It analyses how cultural trends and shifts in the sociopolitical climate of the continent have had an impact on the inclusion of indigenous characters and elements in each of the producing countries. In relation to advances in technology, the introduction of sound is understood to be a chronological division line as it reshaped the way audiences related to cinema. Since contemporary portrayals are linked to visual practices established during the silent and sound periods of cinema, a historical overview of canons of representations foreshadows eventual cultural developments.

Figment, art and fabrication

The practice of expressing thoughts and sensitivities in works of art appears to be inherently human. Throughout the centuries, the archival nature of visual arts has granted the possibility of knowing how tribal affiliation has materialized in aesthetic codes. First encounters between the natives living in the Americas and Europeans encouraged the creation of visual (re)presentations that sought to register this major *discovery*. Engravings, drawings and paintings constituted the first repositories of comprehensive iconographic representations of distant human and geographical landscapes for early modern Europeans. Visually arresting works of art were intended to mediate and register the exploration of new territories and their peoples. In the process, the figure of the indigenous started to emerge as part of the European cultural repertoire. When trying to create visual artefacts accompanying his descriptions of Brazilian natives in the sixteenth century, Jean de Léry asserted that there was a gap between mental and artistic images (Rubiés 2009). The first refers to the iconic image, while the second one alludes to how the image is perceived and understood. The focus of this section lies on the initial iconic images of American indigenous societies and the paradigms behind their composition.

An important observation is that self-representation was not entirely absent. Through collaborative works between indigenous and European artists and writers, such as sixteenth-century *La Historia General de las Cosas de Nueva España* (*The Universal History of the Things of New Spain*), compiled by friar Bernardino de Sahagún, indigenous knowledge production, lifestyles, history, social codes and epistemic praxis found their way into Europe.

English, French, Flemish and Dutch artists stand out for the promptness, preponderance and popularity of their paintings featuring the first expeditions to the *New World*. The first representation, presumably the engraving ornamenting *La lettera dell'isole che ha trovato nuovamente il Re di Spagna* (1493), depicting Columbus's arrival to *Insula Hyspana*, set the tone. It depicts a king sitting in a throne while he contemplates from a distance the encounter between the semi-nude natives of the island and Columbus's fleet. Less than a decade later, an important work would visually mark the onset of a strategic tacit alliance between art, religion and indigeneity. *The Adoration of the Magi* (1501–6), an altarpiece panel commissioned for the chancel in Viseu Cathedral (Portugal), and depicting the visit of the Three Wise Men to Jesus, replaces the magus Baltazar for the image of a Brazilian native. It is a symbolic gesture, nonetheless because the Tupinambá appears in full regalia (not naked), as expected in such a formal setting. The tradition of dressing and undressing American natives editorially became more prominent with the emergence and circulation of so-called costume books. Cristoph Weiditz's *Trachtenbuch* (*c.* 1530) is notorious for including Aztec ethnotypes, mostly representations of indigenous men brought by Hernán Cortés to Europe. America as a territory also became an object of interest and by *c.* 1535, Jan Jansz Mostaert encapsulates in *Landschap met een episode uit de verovering van Amerika* (*Landscape with an Episode from the Conquest of America*) one of the first images of an imagined part of the New World, but also of Spanish soldiers subduing the local populations.

In many cases, illustrators sketched drawings based on descriptions provided by the explorers after their return to Europe or based on their extensive chronicles and letters. A widespread practice was to include a member of the crew assigned to piece together maps of the uncharted territories, and of reproducing illustrations that could complement their cartographic work. European audiences were fascinated by the sense of novelty of the Americas. Paintings, engravings and derivative works of art conceived (in)directly by artists such as John White, Theodore De Bry and Jacques Le Moyne gained widespread popularity, and their sense of accuracy or veracity was hardly scrutinized. Often, illustrations were conceived based on previous visualizations but ornamented with additional elements. Drawings such as *Mother and the Child* (1585) and *Man of the Secotan* (1585) by English artist and colonist John White (*c.* 1540–*c.* 1593) are believed to have served as sources of inspiration to mass-produced collections.

The initiatory and precursory nature of White's images explains their importance as points of reference and benchmarks for much of the 'Indian' iconography to follow (Pratt 2009). Any allusion to the New World evoked feelings of unfamiliarity.

The Age of Discovery (as it is known by many authors) bestowed on the artists a degree of freedom that resembled the creative immunity experienced during earlier encounters of Europeans with civilizations they considered to be exotic, mysterious and alluring. The trend was to fuse older paradigms applied to other parts of the world with an underlying plethora of inaccurate images of the Americas and their peoples. Admittedly, even the encounter with the new involves a retrieval of previously accumulated cultural references, images and notions (Beller 2007). Some of the aspects of the indigenous ethnotype seem to have existed even before the arrival of Columbus in Hispaniola. White's paintings are often described as objective illustrations, probably because they were less prone to astonishing distortions and exaggerations, if compared to visualizations conceived by his contemporaries. His drawings also enjoyed a high degree of verisimilitude because of their quality and his reputation as former explorer of the West Indies. White's creations served as points of reference for royals, writers, scholars and artists in England and continental Europe. His detailed watercolours were used, among other sources, by Theodore De Bry. Collections about the Great Voyages sought to transmit the impressions documented by explorers, complemented and enhanced with awe-inspiring details. Art documents intention. There are clear differences in approach in paintings such as *The Flyer* (c. 1585) by White, and *The Indian Conjuror* (1590) by De Bry.

Some of the most widely circulated images and depictions of American natives and landscapes across Europe are collections edited either by De Bry or his sons, Johann Theodor and Johannes Israel. To a large extent, one of the birthplaces of exoticism and indigenous ethno-typification was the Frankfurt-based publishing house run by this German-Dutch family. Throughout the seventeenth century, their volumes focusing on the Americas became points of reference for subsequent illustrations depicting the New World, framing the Black Legend or portraying cannibalism as a practice. In many cases, artists engaging in the elaboration of adaptations or imitations were hesitant to deviate from the canons established by the prominent De Bry volumes. De Bry's works sought to present to sixteenth-century audiences images of American natives that aligned with the unmitigated sensationalism incited by the era of European explorations. Connection to nature, exuberant but simplistic weaponry, nudity and decorated bodies were prominent allusive features of these pieces. These are key observations in the context of contemporary films because some of these aspects still play a significant role in the construction of the indigenous ethnotypes in cinema. One canon, in particular, especially noticeable in present-day cinema, is linking the notions of birthplace and occupation to a specific iconography that overlooks specificity at an individual level. An example thereof is *America with those known parts in that unknowne worlde both people and manner of buildings* (c. 1662) (Figure 1).[1]

Another canon that has survived through various formats and into the cinematic realm is the custom of entwining the figure of the native with inhospitable landscapes and dangerous topographies. European artists in the sixteenth and seventeenth centuries went as far as their nostalgic, phantasmagorical and unlimited imagination allowed them. The quests to the newly found continents evoked not only biblical and mythological idealizations but also apocalyptical fears. At the other side of the Atlantic, giants, Amazons, headless men, mermaids and unicorns allegedly roamed around in lush but threatening landscapes. Enticing sceneries dominated by fantastic creatures could only be inhabited by humans with characteristics that would suit such a

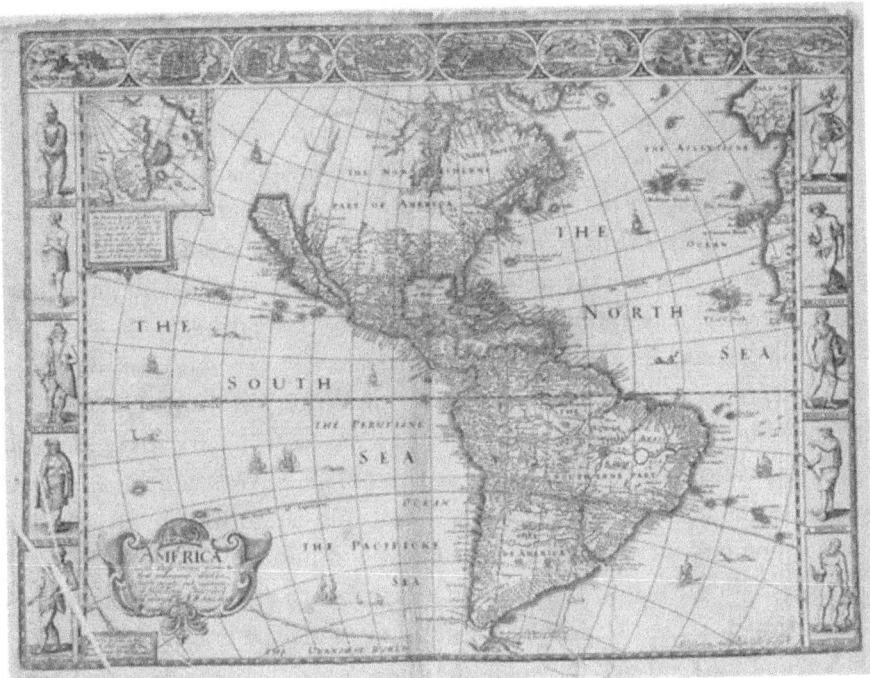

Figure 1 *America with those known parts in that unknowne worlde both people and manner of buildings* (c. 1662), Abraham Goos. Courtesy of the National Gallery, Washington, USA.

diverse environment. In short, the fourth terrestrial continent was home to the most fantastic beings ever imagined by anyone (Pizarro Gómez 1997).

Visualizations where Blemmyes or *akephaloi* (Greek ἀκέφαλοι) [headless men] are part of the American human landscape denote two aspects of the European imaginary. On the one hand, chronicles and visual representations were in line with the well-established convention of affixing exuberant, unrealistic, animalistic and surreal characteristics to non-European societies. On the other hand, there was a tendency to look for explanations in previously (un)documented encounters, common beliefs or myths. Chimerical beings (headless people with a tail) mentioned by renowned authors such as Herodotus, Mela and Pliny the Elder figuratively matched with preconceptions about any distant corner of the world. Mythological creatures or outlandish races, such as the Blemmyes, commonly assumed to *live* in Ethiopia, India or Guinea, could all be part of the narrative about the New World. The depiction of headless men in pieces of art produced during the Age of Discovery can be traced to Walter Raleigh's book *Discovery of Guiana* (1595). An aspect to consider about the English conquest, probably applicable to other European colonizing campaigns, is that images were used to infer where to place newly encountered civilizations historically (Pratt 2009). The European self-referential standpoint was limited, except to underscore the striking cultural differences between explorers and natives. Unfamiliar rituals or unusual daily practices among the newly *discovered* peoples were a common theme in iconographic representations and subsequent imitations (e.g. *Solemn Ritual in Consecrating a Deerskin to the Sun*).

Chronicles such as *L'Histoire d'un voyage faict en la terre du Brésil, autrement dite Amérique* (1578) by French colonist Jean de Léry (1536–1613) served as backbone to many subsequent written and visual works. Léry wrote passages where he reflected about the paradoxical nature of stereotypes, and the elaborated notion of the good savage. He asserted that this categorization envisioned a natural, tranquil, faithful and hospitable type of human, capable of living in harmony with the nature they idolized, worshipped and followed in a religious and pragmatic sense (Rubiés 2009). The figure of the good savage has survived throughout the centuries, but not in the same format that Léry described in his passage. Writers and artists have consistently recurred to sheer sensationalism as a means to create crowd-pleasing, provocative and enthralling versions of it. De Bry's collections addressed the conceptualization of the good savage in the engravings and commentary, but carefully alluding to the most upsetting aspects of what savagery entailed. Natives were entwined with habits such as drunkenness, consumption of abject types of food, and special attention was devoted to topics such as mutilation and self-mutilation (van Groesen 2008). Disgraceful portrayals of little-known societies became the most accessible one-dimensional narrative presented to audiences and readers across Europe. An exception to this convention was the documented passages in diaries and letters attesting, for instance, that the natives were considered quite attractive, healthy, strong and of high stature, even intimidating to European explorers (Sánchez 2011). Nevertheless, these observations rarely materialized in widely circulated works of art.

Each colonizing nation developed its own tradition of creating a national approach and visual strategy to portray the natives from their newly reprehensibly acquired territories (Rubiés 2009). By the end of the sixteenth century, chronicles and letters with passages about sacrifices, cannibalism and paganism became points of reference for the fabrication of decorative items and works of visual art. Johann Theodor and Johannes Israel De Bry oversaw the publication and reproduction of collections that highlighted the 'afición desmedida a la carne humana' [immeasurable fascination for human flesh] (Gutiérrez Usillos 2017: 193) of the natives.

Lack of Christian values was often associated with abhorrent practices, and cannibalism was one of them. American natives' alleged anthropophagy quenched European thirst, obsession and interest in cannibalistic practices. In fact, the word 'cannibal' emerged and evolved from the first attempts to conceptualize linguistically man-eating societies (i.e. recalling canine voracity), self-identified as *Cariba* but redefined by Columbus's conviction to have reached territories ruled by the Great Khan (i.e. *Caniba*) (Davies 2016). This allegedly customary practice among Brazilian aboriginals drew so much attention during the Renaissance that it became a prominent element in works of art portraying the New World. Cannibalism and other characteristics that could sound frightening confirmed the superiority of the Europeans and their bravery; after all, conquering fierce, violent peoples signalled mental and physical strength (Sánchez 2011). The natives were apparently not reserved about their appetite for human flesh or about their presumably sinful nakedness – tropes that have been retained and reproduced, for instance, in the Brazilian film *Caramuru* (2001).

Attitudes and assumptions about the natives were paradoxical and contradictory. On the one hand, their nudity was equated with ideas about an elusive Eden where vivacious figures hovered in a Genesis-inspired garden. On the other hand, the lack of clothes was explained as a marker of their lack of civilization and their status as emergent human groups. In their position of prominent referential works, the centrality of nudity in De Bry's illustrations strengthened associations with promiscuity, unruliness and wildness. Absence of clothes operated as visual evidence of a lack of other attributes, such as godliness and morality. For centuries, naked bodies in artistic portrayals of exotic peoples were used as tropes and references for animalistic and barbaric behaviours. Ornaments, body paintings and feathers became canonical elements in the depiction of the peoples of the New World.

For evangelical purposes, solemn attires, capes and fans exhibiting feathers soon became part of the artefacts used by missionaries to promulgate Christianity among the natives. The distinctive character of the feathers among indigenous societies became almost instantly an iconic identity marker for the American native peoples. Staged animalistic regalia added a sense of solemnity, stupefaction and allure to the ordinary, unostentatious garments typically worn by some of the newly encountered nations. Fascination with the idea of an imagined feathered Other progressively encouraged the production, circulation and appreciation of feather work artefacts as highly prized rarities among European elite circles (Farago 2010). Along with feathers, cannibalism and nudity, practices such as maiming, feasting in peculiar ways and holding strange rites and ceremonies systematically merged into the figure of the instant Indian, a figure that has survived and has indiscriminately relied on cultural and myth-making narratives (Wernitznig 2007).

In contrast, explorers who travelled to the West Indies more than once came to notice that the stereotypical images were often based on falsehood or manipulated descriptions (Sánchez 2011). Their journeys across the Atlantic made them realize to which extent editorial malapropism or tactical changes were used to create an alluring visual version of the Americas. Yet, images of an iconic native spread extensively both in geographic and contextual terms. Besides paintings and books, home decorative artefacts, engravings, utensils and maps became spaces inhabited by the identifiable portrayal of *Indians*, all attentively and imaginatively enhanced, according to national and personal tastes. The conquest and colonization campaigns forced stereotypes to become more specific and make distinctions between the various ethnic groups. For Spaniards, the Caribs came to represent a barbaric, evil, cannibalistic and primitive race, in complete opposition to the noble, innocent and good-hearted Tainos (Chicangana-Bayona 2008). Art became a reflection and a tool of the colonizing projects of the Spanish Crown in the West Indies. Distortional iconography seemed to result, on the one hand, from an interest in using colonial ideologies to denigrate the Other, justifying in the process the colonial enterprise and validating the presence of Europeans as civilizing agents (Rubiés 2009). On the other hand, depicting American natives as civilized victims of European rapaciousness apparently emerged as a visual strategy in the fabrication of the debatable Spanish Black Legend. In this sense, the Carib/Taino, good/bad Indian dichotomy had not only artistic and cultural but also political connotations.

The establishment of colonies and hierarchized societies in the Americas in the seventeenth and eighteenth centuries was registered by artists, writers and scholars. Racial category labels prompted the creation of iconographic taxonomies of the various social types, according to ethnicity-based criteria, commonly known as 'pintura de castas'. This tradition of depicting racialized understandings of the social diversity in colonial Latin America became an important theme in nineteenth-century *costumbrista* circles.² *Casta* paintings intended to depict the various racial mixtures found in the social fabric of the colonies but were in fact visual idealizations targeted at European viewers and aligned with eighteenth-century ideologies (Rappaport 2014). The racial taxonomy retained stereotypical elements, but their pedagogical and illustrative scope prevented artists from venturing into exaggerations, or from creating overtly sensationalist images. Those considered to have indigenous and African blood were categorized as inferior, compared to the intermixtures between Spaniards and creoles, or Europeans stationed in the Americas. Those natives who had resisted the European colonization were ranked at the bottom of the hierarchy. In the canvases conceived by Miguel Cabrera (1763), *Indios gentiles* (Heathen Indians) are considered as a separate group. As a matter of fact, they are the only couple where woman and man belong to the same *casta*.

Andrés de Islas (1774) proposes a similar taxonomy where the most inferior position is given to *Indios Mecos bárbaros* (Barbarian Meco Indians). The portrayals of the natives imbued prevailing conventions. Scanty clothes, feathers, partial nudity and a wild setting were characteristics commonly associated with the figure of the good savage. The innovative dimension of the *casta* paintings was to attempt to make a division between a wild and an educated 'Indian'. The underlying notion throughout the sixteen categories identified in the *casta* system is that skin colour and clothing style are markers of identity.³ These widely circulated canvases suggest that the indigenous identity is complex and convoluted. The civilized version of a native is one who grooms his/her hair, wears clothes and shoes, marries outside her/his ethnic group and has an occupation other than gatherer or hunter. *Casta* paintings normalize the figure of the *Indian*. The savage version of the native is the one who has remained isolated, uncivilized and somehow quarantined.

Europeans believed their accomplishments and presence in the Americas confirmed the superior character of those elements derived from their culture and lifestyle (Rabasa 1993). An attire and grooming standards that according to Spanish conventions implied pre-Columbian habits had been abandoned. The introduction of more versions of an indigenous figure was followed by the production of works of art where even the wild Indian was depicted as less frightening. In subsequent paintings, an indigenous woman is seen carrying a basket with children, instead of pieces of human corpses, as in previous versions (Gutiérrez Usillos 2017). Europeans were still fixated with cannibalistic practices, but the focal point had become the newly found anthropophagous *tribes* living on islands scattered across the Pacific Ocean (Chicangana-Bayona 2008). More importantly, from the seventeenth century onwards, there had been an important number of mestizo and creole artists, trained according to European conventions but born in Latin America. Apprentices from the School of Lake Titica and Cuzco became prominent for including indigenous elements in their works, often in discrete but symbolic ways. Pieces of art modelled according to purposely syncretic canons were the rule for the centuries to come. The visibility of indigenous ethno-typifications, followed by the depiction of a native constructed according to Eurocentric ideologies, was the norm once the pre-Hispanic themes became objects of stigma, or were altogether banned, as it was the case in eighteenth-century Peru (Pizarro Gómez 1997).

Portrayals of indigenous characters and elements in the eighteenth and nineteenth centuries had an overall *Costumbrismo*-oriented mood. The main inspiration of this pictorial and literary style was the habits and customs of imagined characters', often laborers and peasants, idealized attires and behaviours. Mestizo emblematic figures and indigenous typifications disguised in reviewed versions of the paradigmatic noble savage (Olson 2014). Ideologically, *Costumbrismo* responded to creative vocabularies heavily influenced by the social climate of young Latin American nations in the making. Towards the end of the nineteenth century, new attitudes started to inform canons of representations of native societies. Propelled by travel narratives and the images that accompanied them, a new approach emerged also among European and North American academic, art and cultural scenes. Interest across international circuits eventually influenced Latin American artists to identify and rediscover new sources of inspiration in their immediate surroundings. Indigenous ethnotypes did not disappear with the waning interest in exotifying canvases and watercolours. In fact, a clear connection can be traced between *Costumbrismo* approaches in hand-made works and its inception in the other mediums, particularly in photography (Moriuchi 2018).

Paintings dominated the representational landscape and, despite their inaccuracy, prevailed as solid and primary sources of visual information, until the arrival, development and commercialization of photography in the nineteenth century. Its introduction changed dramatically the position of the fine arts. This new format and its mechanical nature certainly allowed for new possibilities, but in terms of content, photos quickly confirmed that they were not immune to the cultural biases of their makers. On the contrary, photographs containing Edenic scenes of real natives in their traditional attires gained major interest as early as 1865–70 (Carreño 2002). At first, photography was primarily a technique used to document the physical and human landscape of the Americas with the goal of circulating these images in more accessible formats than collotypes, woodcuts or works developed using other printing techniques. The first stages of photography in Latin America were mainly defined by its use as a medium to register aspects of the region that could interest European receptors in the context of projects commissioned and funded by foreign publishing houses and academic institutions.

Mexico, Brazil and Argentina pioneered the adoption of photography as a medium. Leverger Brothers and Jean François Prelier are credited for their contribution to the introduction of photography as a format in Latin America with photos made in Mexico, and Louis Compte with those taken in Brazil and Uruguay in 1839. The first photographs made in the region had as central theme the cathedrals of Mexico City and Montevideo, the Palace in Rio de Janeiro and the Portuguese Royal family. In progressive order, daguerreotypes, ambrotypes, tintypes (also known as ferrotype or melainotypes) and eventually albumen prints were all adapted by local photographers, soon after their development as innovative photo development processes. Bellido Gant (2002) notes that assuming photography as an entirely European and North American invention nevertheless silences contributions made by Esteban Martínez in the form of experiments, although Frenchman Hércules Florence is credited for the technique of combining the use of camera obscura with the effect of the sun. Florence, based in Brazil, named this technique 'photographie' (Bellido Gant 2002: 114) before renowned figures such as Niépce, Daguerre, Talbot and Herschel did so.

During the nineteenth century, portraits of social events, nudes, personalities and deceased relatives; photography for academic purposes heavily influenced by pictorialism; along with documentary-oriented images, mostly vistas, landscapes and *Costumbrista*-style compositions became popular genres of photographs in Mexico (Salas-Zamudio and Atilano-Villegas 2020). By the beginning of the twentieth century, deltiologists had identified ethnography as one of the most popular categories of postcards circulating across the Atlantic, many of which included imagery of so-considered interesting peoples, customs and dressing traditions. Unsuspectingly, postcards played a crucial role not only in the rediscovery and revived interest of foreigners in Latin

America and its people but also in feeding their imaginaries and diffusing an anthropological optic.

Indigenous societies became a popular theme across networks of Austrian, American, French, German and Swiss publishing houses involved in the commercialization of postcards. Foreign photographers saw a great potential in recording the natural and social landscapes of the recently formed Latin American nations. Political instability and other travel-related hindrances did not discourage European photographers from venturing into short visits and expeditions for the purpose of taking photographs. Although panoramic vistas of isolated corners of the region were at first the main subject for the production of photographical work, the local communities in remote rural areas gained progressively more attention and interest. The fascination of collectors of postcards, readers of tourist books and academic circles had an impact not only on the editorial choices of prestigious publishers and magazines but also on the circulation of images of indigenous peoples of Latin America among the local elites.

Foreign-born photographers, in particular, Ernst Hugo Brehme, Albert Frisch, Franz Keller-Leuzinger, Christiano Junior, Tina Modotti, along with prominent ethnologists, such as Guido Boggiani and Carl Sofus Lumholtz, had a profound influence on subsequent generations of visual artists and scholars in the way indigenous peoples were photographically recorded, either from a humanist or academic viewpoint. Brehme and Boggiani were among the first to use cameras as tools to document until-then considered trivial aspects of indigenous lifestyles in Brazil, Mexico and Paraguay.[4] Applying meticulous ethnographic methodologies resulted in delicately curated photographs that in themselves conveyed detailed accounts of the lives of their subjects. Yet, at all times, indigenous peoples remained excluded as participants in their own representation, privileging the gaze of the eventual editors, receptors and buyers of the images, and reigniting the indigenous-as-object frame of reference observed in previous formats of visual representation. Photography allowed those interested in anthropological reflections not only to register undisputable evidence of their experiential immersion among unknown societies but also to circulate images that encouraged examination, comparison and essentialist attitudes.[5] At a local level, in the case of Mexico, the cultural landscape of the Porfiriato period had an impact on the reception of photography and its use among local elites, longing to welcome practices, customs and innovations embraced by European, particularly French, bourgeoisie.

The impact of European and North American photographers on the emergent scene of local visual artists was profound and left long-standing traces, especially in the blooming Mexican intellectual circles that were finding a language to express the spirit of the revolution. Brehme's approaches eventually influenced important figures such as Manuel Álvarez Bravo, Lola Álvarez Bravo, Mariana Yampolsky Urbach and local filmmakers Emilio Fernández and Gabriel Figueroa Mateos. German-born Brehme was interested in creating impressions that conveyed the human essence of forgotten indigenous communities at an individual level and through magnified representations of otherwise imperceptible, perhaps mundane instants and small daily rituals. His camera allowed him to create idyllic pieces that forced viewers to notice the diversity of a nation by privileging illustratively the everyday lives of often forgotten indigenous communities.

Traces of the approach to rituality in Brehme's work might presumably be found in Sergei Eisenstein's avant-garde conceptualization of how Mexico should be presented cinematographically, although this will never be known with certainty as his film was never completed. Yet, even if inconclusive, *Да здравствует Мексика!* (*¡Que Viva México!*/*Long live Mexico!*), Eisenstein's halted film project, left traces in the history of Mexican renderings of the indigenous soul of the nation. Disseminated through various attempts to convey what he would have conceivably done himself, the aesthetic approach of the footage had a profound effect on contemporary filmmakers. The Russian director had a vision of Mexico before travelling to the country in December 1930, possibly further reshaped and informed by his interaction with important figures of the national intellectual and artistic scene, such as Diego Rivera, Frida Kahlo, Adolfo Best Maugard, Luis Márquez and Roberto Montenegro. Eisenstein intended to crystallize in images the allure that the Mexican nation evoked in him, and he was not alone, as Mexico was a source of inspiration for many artists of the time. He was not alone either in the sense that the government did not allow him to travel unaccompanied, minimizing the risk that he could register in film, discrediting images of the nation's state of affairs. Eisenstein's footage frames indigenous cultures as testaments to the monumentality of their ancestors. Aesthetically, they imply Mexico is the amalgamation of syncretic sacredness and carnivalesqueness dotted with ancient ruins and tinted with arid open spaces. In these compositions, the pre-Hispanic component of the nation dwells in Eden-inspired landscapes, reminiscent of Paul Gauguin's renderings of Tahiti.

Pre-Hispanic cultural legacy was invoked as an integral part of emblematic representations of a region rediscovering itself. Photographs and artworks emerging from the Mexican muralists during the first half of the twentieth century resembled each other in terms of fixity and motionlessness, but also in creating imaginatively canvases that inspired and informed trends in other visual arts. Innovations in image-printing technologies propelled the circulation of images and ideas, and, in the process, amplified the impact of the Mexican cultural revolution on the rest of the region. Introduction and widespread diffusion of photography coincided with the mobilization of indigenist and Americanist ideologies across countries trying to reconcile the notions of modernity, national identity and indigenous legacy. Aesthetically, stylistically and thematically, the indigenous was depicted, portrayed and presented according to canons stablished by non-indigenous onlookers. Pre-Columbian roots, best epitomized by the centrality of architectural vestiges of powerful civilizations, became sources of inspiration for visual artists at the time. Photography was instrumental for local urban classes in their discovery of rural topologies and peoples. Internationally, a collection of photographs was also fundamental in the diffusion of the first-ever images of Machu Picchu, published in a special edition of *National Geographic* in April 1913 and accompanied by an account of how Hiram Bingham had *discovered* the impressive Incan ruins.

Diffusion of images that fed imaginaries about the material heritage, ancestry and lives of peoples that had survived for centuries awoke the curiosity of tourists who responded to the attention drawn by the awe-inspiring images of Peru. In terms of self-representation, Martin Chambi (1891–1973) stands out for his contributions as a photographer engaged with the documentation and registrations of the habitus and modus vivendi of the Andean communities not only in his native Peru but also in Chile. Chambi's works found a podium in prestigious outlets such as *National Geographic*, February edition 1938, and several expositions across the continent. Memorable works include *El gigante indio Paruro* (1929), *La familia en el cementerio* (1928), *En la hacienda La Angostura* (1931), *La línea de ferrocarril de Cuzco a Santa Ana* (1930) and *La mujer india con el niño* (1934).

Progressively, photography as a medium became more accessible, retaining nevertheless its function as a documentation tool of the unknown. Portraits of Tehuelche chief Casimiro Biguá during his visit to Buenos Aires between 1864 and 1866 by Benito Panunzi (1819–1894) were, for example, among the first registered photos of members of an indigenous community while still retaining their political status as sovereigns of their territories. The introduction and expansion of photography as a format to capture reality overlapped with the inquisitive enthusiasm of scholars and experienced travellers. A desire to articulate reality through mechanically produced images encouraged the revision of themes endemic to the fine arts. Photographers sought to synthesize and create renewed versions of sceneries, situations and 'subjects' commonly depicted in paintings, and the figure of the native was one of them. Visual framing of feathers, scanty clothes, mystic rituals and arrows were transposed from paintings onto photos and eventually onto films. The invention of motion picture cameras paved the way not only for the art/industry of cinematography but also for an even wider circulation of indigenous ethnotypes.

Cinema and indigeneity

As in the fine arts, during the first stages of cinematic production, European ethnotypes served as cultural referents in films produced throughout the region, among other reasons, because cinema was introduced by European directors and Latin American filmmakers educated in Europe. Apart from Eurocentric evocations, local realities inspired local directors to create visual representations of the young nations of the continent. Examples included cinematic productions that sought to advance an indigenist ideology in line with perspectives in public discourse of the time. On the one hand, there was a relentless search for the core of the national identity, and on the other hand, there was a need to question or appear to be willing to question the moral implications of a system that marginalized its indigenous citizens (Baud 2003, 2010). These visual narratives endowed with a sense of paternalism were followed by a wave of cinematic portrayals in which the indigenous subject was depicted as the revolutionary driving force. Latin American films have consistently reflected the creation of national identities, as well as the global impact of Western cultural production. Classical Hollywood style, in particular, has served as a cultural referent in the conception of indigeneity-oriented films, in terms of generic form and conventions. As subsequent paragraphs discuss, film production in the region has passed through various stages and has addressed indigenous topics from various standpoints.

Silent cinema

A focal point of many of the first films shot in the continent was to transmit the sense of otherness that indigenous peoples would elicit among viewers in Europe. Although many productions had as their main focus to educate viewers, others chose to participate in a ubiquitous racialization of these communities on screen (Rony 1996). Since the first producers of films in the continent were mainly Europeans, in great measure, inclusion of indigenous cultures in cinema stemmed from the sense of exoticism and inquisitiveness.

During the silent period of Latin American films, between 1895 and 1936, indigeneity was central to over twenty films produced mainly in Mexico and Brazil, although there were also examples of Bolivian, Chilean, Colombian and Peruvian productions during this period. In total, around thirty-eight films produced during the silent period of cinema focused on indigenous characters and elements.[6] The first film focusing on Latin America's indigenous communities is believed to have been *Desayuno de indios/Indians' Breakfast* (1896) by Gabriel Veyre. This short film originally born out of the curiosity of a young European on his first trip around the Mexican countryside is credited for having introduced the art of cinematography in Mexico (Mora 1989). In *Desayuno de indios*, the French filmmaker obviously adopts the same set of ideas about indigeneity commonly portrayed in literature, painting and sculpture customary in Europe at his time.[7]

In September 1898, Veyre, this time a representative of the Lumiére company, shot *Danse indienne/Indian Dance* in the Kahnawake Mohawk reservation, carefully staged to fit into the European stereotype of a wild Canada. Indigenous communities of North, Central and South America were all regarded as a novelty and similar patterns of representation could be perceived in the way directors presented what they identified as exotic. Cinematic indigeneity emerges then as an instant formula containing all the elements audiences might want to see in films about native peoples. Paradoxically, inclusion of indigeneity in cinema, although problematic, is in its origins strongly related to ethnographic documentation. Scientific and intellectual interest has thus played a central role in the attention cinema paid to the indigenous legacy of the continent, casting a light on the fact that many of the directors were scholars.[8]

Members of European academic circles started a tradition of recording the reality of Latin American indigenous communities moved by the novelty and an eagerness to share their experiences with audiences thirsty for discovery.

A political viewpoint runs through many of these films. As happens with other types of cultural outputs, inclusion of certain lived experiences and perspectives can be in themselves omissions and erasures of other lives and vantage points (Eide 2011). In most cases, films produced with a scientific scope had as a main goal to offer insights into an unknown world, especially popular among European and North American audiences. Yet, domestic productions were no less driven to transmit a sense of allurement in order to astonish local viewers about the reality outside their immediate environment. Ultimately, the omitted groups were the urban indigenous communities. Their reduced sense of foreignness and enlarged sense of geographical proximity to the audiences presumably made their stories less gripping to audiences eager to be amazed. Arguably, spectators were mainly interested in confirming preconceived ideas and images drawn from colonial times, rather than being confronted with the social reality of oppressed segments of the population (Contreras 2008).

Since cinema remained an innovation mostly available to urban audiences and aimed at the bourgeoisie, it is obvious why rural indigenous areas offered many possibilities as a topic, especially if spiced with fantasized and overtly exaggerated features of 'Indian' life (Getino 2007). At the end of the nineteenth and twentieth centuries, spectators came to the movie theatres mainly interested in cinema as a technological innovation, and a social event. With an increasing number of audiences and screenings, producing companies started to categorize films according to genres, but only after researching taste and preferences of each type of audience.

From early on, Hollywood adopted the arbitrary Euro-American dichotomization that made a distinction between noble natives and godless warriors (Adare 2005). Primitive westerns quintessentially entwined with the figure of the 'Indian' are recognized as one of the first categorizations created by major studios. Edison Manufacturing Company, American Mutoscope and Biograph Company, Vitagraph Company of America, la Société Lumière, Star Films-Geo Mélès, Pathé Frères de Paris and León Gaumont et Compagnie endorsed the establishment of genres and their definition as strategies to create thematic conventionalities at a global scale. Ultimately, the western genre became a point of reference for the creation of indigeneity-oriented visual narratives, nonetheless, across Latin American fledgling cinematic landscapes (Carreño 2006). In this sense, North American westerns played a key role in determining how the figure of the 'Indian' was to be portrayed in cinematic spaces (see Chapter 4). There exist some broad commonalities and recognizable conventions in the portrayal of Amerindian societies in films produced across the Americas. From early on, the impact of North America and Europe on Latin American cinema has been related to economic and cultural proclivities. Direct and indirect training of local filmmakers overseas has had an impact on local production from the inception of cinema in the region. As discussed in Chapter 5, some of the most exotifying indigeneity-inspired films are conceived by directors educated in the United States or Europe.

National directors, in the initial stages of local filmmaking, were interested in showing the novelties of the countryside, in many cases moved by their experiences as members of a secluded elite or students abroad. For instance, Mexican director Carlos Martínez de Arredondo is often considered as the first Latin American director who ventured into making films about the indigenous legacy of the continent, after dwelling away from home for an extended period of time.[9] Most of his films can be interpreted as samples of melodramas of great ambition told from a historical and nationalistic perspective (García 1999). Evidently, the Mexican Revolution (1910–20) was having a profound influence on the cinematic production and the other way around. Martínez de Arredondo was inspired by a nation in the process of making itself, a sense of hope for a future similar to an almost forgotten glorious past and interest in the roots of his birth country. His most renowned production, *Tiempos Mayas/Mayan Times* (1914), takes the audience on a journey through pre-Columbian Mexico and the splendour this civilization had reached before the arrival of the Europeans. It is a historical tale about a legendary quest taking place in the Mayan city of Uxmal and the bravery of its citizens. A common paradigm in cinema, frequently encountered in countries going through massive transformations, was the glorification of pre-Columbian elements through stories where indigenous courage was being exalted, as in the case of Mexico after the revolution (1910–20). Along with *Tiempos Mayas*, the films *El suplicio de Cuahtémoc/Cuauhtemoc's Torture* (1910) and *La voz de su raza/The Voice of Their Race* (1914) stand out for denouncing the loss of major sovereign states and for reminding audiences of what Latin America used to be prior to its colonization. Like in other similar films, reinstating the sense of belonging and self-identification deeply distorted by the Europeanization of the Americas is a central theme.

Indigeneity drew interest among directors as a tool to elevate and provoke feelings of nationalism and pride, mainly by idealizing pre-Columbian ancestors and distant empires lost in time. In early Latin American films, contemporary indigeneity was not present but masked in the form of tales about fierce and legendary empires. Most directors focusing on the continent were interested in shedding light on the indigenous legacy as an exotic part of the social fabric but remained overly attentive to the rural aspect of it (Ramírez Berg 2002). This is mainly explained by the anthropological approach that many of the filmmakers applied to the subject and the format they used, which resembled more documentary filmmaking than fiction. Central to the genre of ethnological film was venturing into little-known and isolated corners of the world where endemic communities shared their daily lives with a distant audience, mainly in Europe and North America. These films were and are still conceived of as a means to obtain access to remote places and forms of living while educating, amazing and drawing viewers by offering encounters with the unknown (Mateus Mora 2012). Aside from European directors, local production started emerging soon after the arrival of cinema in most Latin American countries.

In Mexico, figures such as Carlos González, José Manuel Ramos, Aurelio de los Reyes, Enrique Rosas and Fernando Sáyago became noticeable for drawing attention to the indigenous legacy of the nation and their contributions to domestic cinema. *El milagro de Tepeyac/The Miracle of Tepeyac* (1917) by Carlos González is particularly prominent for touching upon the conflict that European beliefs pose to indigenous communities from a religious perspective (Wilt 2004). It is considered the longest sample of silent Mexican cinema. The importance of *El milagro de Tepeyac* lies in the fact that it presents syncretism as a logical result from meshing traditional indigenous folklore and beliefs with religious rites introduced by Europeans during the Conquest (Ojeda Llanes 2007). The film revolves around Juan Diego, a naïve, infant-like and easily manipulated figure of humble indigenous roots, who is believed to have had a spiritual encounter with the Virgin Mary. González introduces the idea that clerks, priests and monks had the task to guide, instruct and introduce indigenous communities to more elaborated forms of worshiping than sacrifices, chanting or dancing. For many, the film mobilizes a patronizing and condescending way to approach the syncretic nature of Catholicism in Latin America (Dávalos 1989).

El milagro de Tepeyac raises questions about the paradigms of representation of ethnic groups in films by presenting indigenous reality as an isolated, distant and almost imaginary condition far from the rest of Mexico, where a revolution was being fought. One possible interpretation of the film is that even during an upheaval, indigenous communities were to retain their rural, far-flung and relegated status. Sketching a scenario in which social unrest hardly affects them can be seen as a critique to the idea that indigenous communities live in a parallel and secluded dimension (de España 2006). Another interpretation of *El milagro de Tepeyac* is that it denounces the fragile social condition of native societies at times of uncertainty and serves as a reminder of the values the nation might learn from its indigenous legacy. On his own terms, González invites the audience to dream of a Mexico where other revolutions are also being fought, although in a less mediatized way (i.e. unacknowledged communities against oppressing authorities).

Cinematic indigeneity becomes central to many films produced in the 1920s in Mexico. Hershfield and Maciel (1999) relate this to the fact that the Mexican Revolution promoted a strong sense of nationalism and pride intrinsically entwined with the revivification of indigenous elements. Four films produced in this period introduced the notion of native communities as dauntless, brave and highly elaborated societies not easily subjugated: *El último malón/The Last Indian* (1918), *Tabaré* (1918), *Cuauhtémoc* (1919) and *De raza Azteca/Of Aztec Blood* (1921). Directed by Lezama and Holms, *Tabaré* is conceived as an epic to the resistance of indigenous societies against the conquest in what today constitutes Uruguay.[10] The story presents the tale of Tabaré, a Charrúa who falls madly in love with Blanca, daughter of a European conqueror trying to seize his people's land. Interracial relationships between indigenous and non-indigenous characters were a common theme in indigeneity-oriented cultural outputs (Young and Cisneros 2011). A revolt of the Charrúa against Blanca's father, Gonzalo de Orgaz, serves as the background for this love story. Tabaré's bravery is central to the film as it is evident from the beginning that his love for Blanca and his attempt to overrule her father's dominance will result in conflict. This is one of the first films from the region displaying an indigenous hero, already a common feature in European and North American films delving into similar topics.

Along the same line, the underlying ideology in *Cuauhtémoc* (1919) and *De raza Azteca* (1921) is that indigeneity is by default interwoven with bravery and pride, while pro-European precepts, to a certain extent, are interwoven with abuse and dominance. In *Cuauhtémoc*, Manuel de la Bandera explores Cuauhtémoc's murder under Hernán Cortés' orders and the consequences this act of cowardliness brought about for the Aztecs. *De raza Azteca* invites the audience to rediscover their indigenous legacy and bravery for which past civilizations of the continent were known.[11] The figure of the so-called 'good Indian' thus becomes a recognizable topic in Latin American cinema from its early stage.

Outside Mexico, a comparable trend of inclusion and glorification of indigeneity in cinema became noticeable in films produced across the continent. Brazil, Chile and Argentina stood out for the production of films where enhanced indigeneity played a significant role. In the case of Brazil, unlike Mexico, inclusion of indigenous elements in cinema was institutionalized and funded by the state through the so-called Rondon Commission, which was charged with promoting the inclusion of indigenous peoples in all sectors of social life and furtherance of their legacy. De Tacca (1999) observes that among the most prominent members of this commission, Luíz Thómas Reis stands out for encouraging the production of films where indigenous issues are presented with the intention of sensitizing audiences.[12]

Historically, Reis is considered as the first Brazilian director who aimed for inclusion of indigeneity as a means to achieve social justice. His most renowned film resulting from this initiative is probably *Os Sertões do Mato Grosso/The Backlands of Mato Grosso* (1912), where he explores the determination of the workers installing the Mato Grosso-Amazonas telegraph lines. Furthermore, Reis is praised for his second and third films, *Expedição Roosevelt/Roosevelt Expedition* (1913) and *Rituais e festas/Rituals and Feasts of Boror* (1916), as genuine attempts to document Bororo culture free of indigenist propaganda. Despite their irruptive political agenda, the three films resemble one another in retaining a subtle paternalistic undertone. By shedding light on the indigenous component of the Brazilian nation, in a way, they signalled the onset of a tradition. Visually, these cinematographic works suggest that a predefined agenda (acknowledgement) and a specific set of goals (bridging native communities and mainstream audiences) can operate as tools to redeem a (peripheral) segment of the population. As suggested by Guzmán (2013), media can purposely agree on which ideology to impart among audiences in order to instigate a response among viewers. The outcome has been that the Brazilian perception of indigeneity in modern times is still interwoven with the institutionalization of preconceived idealized identities. Morphologically and structurally, the state is conceived as a static entity to which subjects ought to adapt, even if that implies sacrificing their cultural identities or social affiliation.

In the case of Argentina, *El último malón* (1918), directed and entirely funded by Alcides Greca, is the first film to focus on indigenous characters as individuals with their own desires, agendas and agency. Greca recreates the revolt of the Mocovís (1904) against the citizens of San Javier (Santa Fe Province), a historical event that drew national attention, mostly because it required the involvement of the army. As in real life, the community in the film protests against their seclusion in shantytowns surrounding the European neighbourhoods they had helped to build at the turn of the century. Indigenous characters are presented as resilient, brave and part of the social fabric of the town until they decide to demand more rights, specifically, land rights. The film problematizes the idea that an encounter between two civilizations is feasible if indigenous communities do not surpass the boundaries established by European settlers. Partially a documentary, partially fiction, *El ultimo malón* is intended to denounce abuses committed against the Mocovís, and yet it remains at the level of a 'romántica huida bucólica' [romantic bucolic flight] (Alba 2015: 415) that sentimentalizes the function of a paternalistic state. The revolt is crushed by force and those involved received reprisals under orders of the provincial government. The climate of violence in which the Mocovís live serves as background to a love story between the main cacique's brother and his wife.[13] Rosa is a matter of conflict between brothers Jesús Salvador and Bernardo, but their primary disagreement is their approach to the hierarchy imposed by the settlers.

El Último Malón follows a twofold ideology in its framing and narration. On the one hand, it champions the view that indigenous communities and European descendants had their own space and status within the relatively new Argentinean nation. On the other hand, Greca starts a practice still put into practice by contemporary Argentinean directors and which entails approaching indigenous cultures as objects of ethnographic gaze. The illustrative value of displaying differences between European and non-European lifestyles seems to be the need to explain divergence. It involves focusing on those aspects that are missing, or need to be completed or disciplined in order to reach modernity, and finally become part of the Argentinean nation.

Since the release of these productions, within Argentinean cinema, indigeneity as a trope has become a way to confirm the assumption that the country is non-indigenous by nature. Argentinean self-image builds on a tendency to portray themselves as South America–based Europeans, a particularly common perception in urban centres in coastal provinces (Schneider 2007). As subsequent chapters explore in more detail, Argentinean audiences are used to the perpetuation of predetermined roles. With some exceptions, another characteristic of Argentinean cinema is a strong tendency to cast primarily and preferably *real* members of native communities in order to play indigenous roles. In this respect, Argentinean visual art canon has differentiated from other Latin American national cinemas.

Besides censorship, 'orientalizing depictions' (Lucero 2009: 261) played out by non-indigenous actors was the most striking characteristic of Bolivian early films. Even though indigeneity was central to the first feature film ever made in the country, only professional actors of the Círculo Lírico Dramático group were cast to play in it. Released in 1925, *Corazón Aymara/Aymara Heart*, directed by Pedro Sambarino, presents the tale of Lurpila, a woman struggling against accusations of infidelity and who, according to some reviews, exemplifies the core of the Bolivian nation (Dagrón 1982). In general, it is considered as a first attempt in the short-lived cinematic tradition of this Andean nation to reclaim the indigenous past of the country as it explores the Aymara way of life. But its importance lies also in foreshadowing Jorge Ruiz's and Jorge Sanjinés's groundbreaking productions in terms of themes and artistic approach.[14] Although the film can be read as the product of an 'archaeological excavation of a national identity and heritage' (Himpele 2008: 106), it can also be interpreted as an endeavour to log the birth of Bolivia as a cinematic entity. Two other films would follow, the never released *La Profecía del Lago/The Prophecy of the Lake* (1925) and widely promoted *Wara Wara* (1930). Directed by José María Velasco Maidana, *La Profecía del Lago* narrates the struggle of an interracial couple in a country where ethnicity has always been synonymous with status.[15] The government eventually forbade screenings of the film because it implied that indigenous communities were exploited, under-represented and excluded.[16] Velasco Maidanas's second attempt to showcase the complexity of interracial love within Bolivian social conventions was *Wara Wara*.[17]

Released in 1930, the film explores the romantic story between an Inca princess and a Spanish conquistador during the decline of the Inca Empire. Following a rigorous line of succession, Princess Wara Wara ostensibly embodies the resistance against the invaders and gives a sense of hope to her people. In terms of impact on audiences, although *Wara Wara* received considerable attention, it remained lost for almost sixty years, until it was rediscovered and restored.[18] It remains the only surviving example of Bolivian silent cinema (Villazón 2010). *Wara Wara* is understood to exhibit the avant-garde movement of Bolivian intellectuals and artists concerned with the recognition and inclusion of indigenous communities and their heritage. Approval of the authorities to the release of images with indigenist themes was allegedly a response to a collective desire to acknowledge, at least partly, the foundations of the country.[19] These early representations of Bolivian society are essential to disseminate the synthetic notion of visual indigeneity, promoted by the state, as a trope linked to a glorious past and free of any sense of contemporaneity. Along the same lines, these first films disclose and elaborate on the weak position women were to play within the building of this new mestizo nation. Gender inversion of the characters in *Wara Wara*, as well as in *La Profecía del Lago*, to avoid prohibition mirrors the complexity of intersectionality of indigeneity and femininity within the Bolivian societal hierarchy.

Another film addressing indigeneity and released during the silent period was *La Gloria de la Raza/The Glory of Race* (1926) by Arturo Posnansky. Set along the Titicaca Lake, it is the story of a native Uru who shares with an archaeologist the chronicle of his people. Recalling the history of this lost civilization, the story spans from prehistoric times until Uru civilization started to decline before disappearing completely. In line with comparable stories from the 1930s and 1940s, the narrative sought to elevate and evoke the glorious past of indigenous peoples across the region, an approach commonly seen in the Peruvian cinema of the time.

From its onset, national cinema as a format was enthusiastically embraced by Peruvian audiences. Viewers were fascinated by the transposition of known faces and places into motion pictures, even if there was not always a defined storyline. In general, 'actuality films – short views of current events – were plentiful during the silent era in Peru' (León Frías 1996: 275). In this sense, films such as *El Oriente peruano/Peruvian East* (1921), *Tras los Andes/Beyond the Andes* (1925) and *La conquista de la selva/The Conquer of the Jungle* (1929) can be considered as reflections of reality, rather than political statements. With a strong pre-Columbian legacy, cinema in Peru is noticeable for paying tribute to the roots of the nation from its early days. Inclusion of Amerindian elements was not strategical but rather a logical method to present the state of affairs.

In Chile, indigeneity was first introduced as a cinematic topic in *La Agonía del Arauco/The Agony of the Indian* (1917), a film by Gabriela Bussenius. Also known as *The Oblivion of the Death*, the story touches upon the confrontation between Mapuche and Spaniards over Wallmapu, their homeland, seen through the eyes of a Mapuche mother who has just lost her husband and son. Seven years later, another film addressing the theme of conflict is released, *Nobleza Araucana/Araucanian Nobility* (1924) by Iquiquez de la Fuente. Again, central to the narrative are the clashes between European colonizers and native communities. In spite of a boom in Chilean cinema during the silent area, indigenous topics were not a central focus for any other films until sound was introduced decades later.

The encounter between ethnic communities and Eurocentric ideologies also plays a significant role in the first indigeneity-oriented film produced in Ecuador. In spite of being seventeen minutes long, Carlos Crespi's *Los Invencibles Shuaras del Alto Amazonas/The Unbeatable Shuars from High Amazonas* (1926) retains its importance as the first attempt to document the daily life of isolated native communities. The film was also the first cinematographic approach to register the process of evangelization in the tropical part of the country (Noboa 1995). In his position as a Salesian priest and evangelizer, Crispe saw in cinema a venue to record indoctrination practices in remote regions.

Meanwhile, in neighbouring Colombia, there is no evidence of any silent feature films addressing indigenous topics. The first images of Colombian native communities are believed to be part of a series of videos shot by brothers Álvaro and Gonzalo Acevedo in 1929 along the Chocó region (Mateus Mora 2012).

All things considered, across the continent, the number of cinematic productions increased thanks to technological advancements. Sound in particular is believed to have exerted influence on the diversity of themes and approaches that emerged at the beginning of the 1930s. More variety in topics translated into more productions focusing not only on indigeneity but also on the construction and emergence of ethnicity, national identity and the role of native communities and their linguistic diversity. Increased attention to indigeneity stemmed from scientific and anthropological interest, but eventually shifted into historical and legacy-oriented themes. Due to the economic implications of cinema at the time, Argentina, Bolivia, Brazil, Mexico and Peru became the most influential countries in terms of cinematic production in South and Central America.

Sound cinema and indigeneity

Introduction of sound in 1926 made films more realistic as it meant inclusion of linguistic features, accompanying soundtracks and surrounding noises. This technological advancement in the industry redrew cinema as it opened the door for new possibilities in terms of topicality, style of narrative and therefore new ways of interpreting images. Compared to the silent period, sound cinema brought about an unprecedented thematic diversification, related to both diegetic and non-diegetic applications. New patterns of representation emerge as cinematic indigeneity becomes less tightly entwined with visual features such as typical dresses, exaggerated physical characteristics or nudity. Furthermore, although conflicts between native communities and authorities remained a common topic, with the incorporation of sound, directors began to look at indigenous peoples as part of the social fabric of the relatively young Latin American nations (King 2000).

A monolinguistic paradigm emerged as by-product of technological advances in acoustics. Cinema became a stage for audiovisual encounters between nations and their own voices, which led to the emergence of markets defined by the language spoken by their spectators. The introduction of sound marked the onset of not only a series of changes at all stages of production and exhibition but also the circulation of spoken dialogues needed to align with the linguistic reality of audiences. Performers whose mother tongues did not overlap with the needs of specific characters would be replaced by native speakers of the language. A cinematic linguistic identity expressed in the relation audiences had with the movie stars changed the landscape. The singularity of sound cinema replaced the plurality and versatility of silent productions that could be screened in several countries unaffected by linguistic constraints (except for intertitles).

Inclusion of spoken language gave voice to the 'Indian' characters and underpinned diversification in the range of native characterizations with whom audiences became acquainted. Political changes, above all, the new social climate in post-revolutionary Mexico, made directors aware of shifts in power and the ways in which cinema could mirror this reality. The notion of mestizo as a synonym of unity and nation soon made its way into fictional narratives that touched upon exclusion, isolation and assimilation of indigenous communities for the first time in the history of cinema in the continent. In some countries like Bolivia and Mexico, an increased number of films with an activist edge were produced during the first decades after sound was introduced (Hedrick 2003). In a relatively brief time, some motion films advocating for acknowledgement of native societies became part of the cultural repertoire of audiences intrigued by social change. Ethnographic and anthropological films, along with historical accounts, regained their status as a common genre across the continent. Introduction of sound rendered cinema more attractive, translating quickly to larger audiences and a major proliferation of ideologies and images depicted in films. In combination with changes in the political climate of the region, the end of silence reconfigured the representation of indigenous characters in Latin American cinema. In total, around 149 films focusing on indigenous communities were produced between 1926 and 1980 throughout the region.[20]

Mexico stands out for playing a significant role in this new stage of cinema in the continent. As in the silent period, political shifts in the country became a central theme in the production of films not only at the national level but also across the continent. After the civil war (1910–20), the post-revolutionary spirit translated into a fruitful decade in terms of the number of films made in the country. Pro-indigenous themes remained high on the agenda and some of the titles released during the 1930s are still highly regarded as milestones in Mexican cinema.[21] During the 1940s, several directors felt compelled to explore religion and its relation to indigeneity, probably as a response to the assumption that the whole nation, regardless of ethnicity, shared common beliefs.[22] This underlying trend remains well into the 1970s, propping up the inclusion and empowerment of mestizo culture as a unifying element.[23]

Several directors saw in religion another common ground for the various segments of the Mexican population, including native peoples, and explored it from different standpoints (Rist 2014). Adherence to Catholic values is presented side by side with recognition of native heritage and culture as important pillars of Latin American identity. Central to most films mentioned above was the notion that indigenous communities should be given the place they deserved within the established structures. Since pro-indigenous narratives had become, during and after the Mexican Revolution, a self-standing literary genre, they were embraced by cinema soon after that. Some characteristics of this genre, known as *indigenismo* (indigenism), were elevation of indigeneity, promulgation of a pro-indigenous agenda or affiliation to the idea that native communities were entitled to regain possession of their lost status. Across the history of Latin American cinema, cultural changes and trends instigated by social and political shifts have translated at specific moments into the production of films with an indigenist agenda on its own and with different understandings of *indigenismo*. Central to many of the titles released in Mexico between the 1930s and 1960s was to reclaim a space to revive the glorious past of extinct pre-Columbian civilizations and the process of folklorization and amalgamation of indigenous elements into mestizo mainstream culture. Directors felt compelled to demystify indigeneity while catering to urban audiences highly accustomed to Eurocentric films and exotified images of native peoples.

In the specific case of the films made in the 1930s, the indigenist agenda tended to accentuate the notion that a synthesis of a merged identity was preferred to an exaltation of either indigenous or European heritage. Re-released in 1939, *La Noche de las Mayas/The Night of the Mayas*, by Chano Urueta, is considered 'paradigmatic' (Lienhard 2002: 86) in terms of indigenist elements. Here, director Urueta, like other directors of the time, attempts to portray realistic representations of Maya cultural heritage in Yucatán, social conventions, iconography, customs and beliefs.[24] Venturing into exalting an imagined lost civilization that is being revived confirms the strong influence indigenism had on literature and cinema at the time.[25] Moreover, attempting to reproduce Maya reality can be understood as an effort to apply an anthropological or ethnographical approach to cinema.[26]

Part of this journey for the viewers included becoming accustomed to non-professional actors who were members of the communities being depicted; an example thereof is the film *Janitzio* (1934). This production stands out not only for being the first Mexican sound movie focusing on indigeneity and the social implications of belonging to a disfranchised social group but also for integrating part of a Purepecha community in its making.[27] Zirahuén, the main character, contributed to establishing Emilio Fernández as one of the leading figures in the history of Mexican filmmaking, and the actor ever after became known as 'El Indio Fernández' among national audiences.[28] In the movie, he plays an indigenous hero defending a community of anglers working along the Patzcuaro Lake (Michoacán) from Don Manuel, an abusive trader. Since fish is the only steady source of income, Don Manuel feels free to oppress the community at his will, often by means of violence. Not being able to withstand the situation, Zirahuén attacks Don Manuel and is imprisoned, leaving his wife Eréndira unprotected. Don Manuel seizes the opportunity and as a means of revenge offers Eréndira the option of liberating her husband in exchange for sexual favours. She accepts and in spite of the circumstances, both Zirahuén and her Purepecha people resent her for it. *Janitzio* concludes with the death of Eréndira stoned by her community for adultery, even if her husband had already forgiven her in light of the course of events.

Janitzio explores the duality in which native communities live in terms of the legal system, enforcement of law and subsequent punishment. On the one hand, they are ruled by Mexican legal and judicial structures (i.e. imprisonment), but on the other hand, they are simultaneously bound by rules embedded in social codes dating from pre-Columbian times. Through the figure of Eréndira, Navarro invites viewers to experience the constraints of being female and indigenous in a paternalistic, male-dominated and unequal society riddled by violence (Lienhard 2002). *Janitzio* draws attention to the position of women within the Mexican hierarchical order. More importantly, the film touches upon indigeneity from a personal and not a collective perspective, which can be considered a trend introduced during the sound era. Both Eréndira and

Zirahuén calculate risks, make decisions and abide the consequences regardless of tradition, depicting in the process individuals subscribing to a culture but not entirely defined by it.

A decade after *Janitizio* was released, *María Candelaria* (1943) would confirm that cinematic indigeneity was not to be understood only as a theme to broadcast the struggle between ethnic groups and a ruling mainstream society. Iconic traits and physical features were now less instrumental in conveying the idea of ethnic and cultural affiliation. Indigenous knowledge engendered in the figure of an indigenous healer is included, but subtly mocked, and presented as peripheral to modern medicine. Directed and written by Emilio Fernández, the film also revolves around a couple who struggle against an oppressing social system and social values embodied in members of their community. But María Candelaria (Dolores del Río) and Lorenzo (Pedro Armendáriz) are determined to stay together and marry in spite of social exclusion and hostility stemming from the fact that the girl's mother is a prostitute. Matters complicate when María Candelaria contracts malaria and becomes fatally ill.

Since the film tacitly serves as a vehicle to disseminate information about the mosquito-borne infectious disease, quinine receives special attention. María Candelaria needs it if she is to survive, but the only provider in town is Don Damián (Miguel Inclán), an abusive influential figure in love with María. Enraged by unrequited feelings, he refuses to provide the young couple with the pharmaceuticals, abusing his position, as the medicine is part of an antimalarial governmental programme. Although María and Lorenzo receive help from a painter (Alberto Galán) obsessed with the idea of capturing the beauty of the young girl on a canvas, the gesture of kindness comes with a price. She is expected to pose for him. While Lorenzo is in prison for stealing quinine and a wedding dress, María Candelaria dies at the hands of the community. It is a retaliation for a work of art in which she appears to be naked, even if she is not aware the painter uses her face, but somebody else's body to accidentally and figuratively sketch her death sentence. The story makes clear that a system embodied in figures such as Don Damián is to blame for the hardship indigenous peoples endure across Mexico and which eventually leads Lorenzo to break the law.

As in Navarro's film, colonialism and male dominance are depicted as endemic and widespread problems hindering progress and limiting the possibilities of individuals within their community. Abuse of power, like microorganisms causing malaria, cause symptoms of major ailments that need to be treated. In cultural terms, indigenous heritage is presented through a syncretic optic and the film aligns linguistically with monolinguistic discourses. The fact that reality is more described than staged might explain why Nahuatl is included in the narrative, although only briefly in moments of animosity or attack. Notwithstanding, with *María Candelaria*, Mexico started a convention of recognizing Amerindian linguistic heritage in fiction. Being two of the most iconic films ever made in Mexico, both *Janitzio* (1934) and *María Candelaria* (1943) are understood to have had significant impact on directors across Latin America in terms of topics, approach and technique.

Similarly, *Río Escondido/Hidden River* (1947) and *Maclovia* (1948), both directed by Emilio Fernández, and *Rebelión de los Colgados/The Rebellion of the Hanged* (1954) were soon to become classics of Mexican cinema, widely applauded both by domestic and international audiences. In hindsight, Mexican filmmakers set the bar in terms of depiction for canons of indigeneity across the continent. This was especially the case in countries where the sound era and indigeneity only crossed paths towards the end of the 1940s, like Brazil (1940), Colombia (1942) or, even later, Bolivia (1948).

The most productive filmmaking venue during this second period was Argentina. The list of important films focusing on indigeneity includes productions such as *Enigma de las llanuras/Turay: Enigma of the Plains* (1950), *Muerte y pueblo/Death and People* (1967), *Señalada en Juella/Incaic Earmarking Ceremony* (1969) and *Carnaval en el Norte/Carnival in the North* (1969). Amerindian voices and sounds were first brought to Buenos Aires' screens in 1948 through a short documentary (twenty-three minutes) by Leo Fleider based on the rites of the Coya people and titled *Pueblos dormidos/Sleeping Towns*. In terms of approach, this production resembles other ethnologic documentaries directed by European filmmakers inquisitive about Latin America's native peoples, a trend which remained popular within Argentinean cinematic circles well into the 1970s. Examples include detailed images by Nemesio Suárez of communities celebrating death (*Muerte y pueblo*), Carlos Nelson's depictions of carnivals as points of intersection between well-preserved traditions, meshed heritage and modernity (*Carnaval en el Norte*) and Preloran's work on festivities in honour of Mother Earth (*Señalada Juella*). Since sound productions in Argentina had until this point approached indigeneity from a collective and not an individual standpoint, these directors are understood to have introduced an already well-known trend in Mexico. In this regard, Irish-Argentinian Jorge Ricardo Prelorán (1933–2009) remains the most prominent and influential Argentinean filmmaker in the field of documentaries focusing on indigeneity.

Prelorán became also mostly recognized for his innovative ethno-documentaries and ethno-biographical films (Sherman 1998). Most of his productions were the result of years of in situ research, fieldwork, consultation with the communities being filmed and their participation in all stages of production.[29]

Another aspect to consider is Prelorán's prominent role in acknowledging Amerindian languages as valid tools of communication within cinematic circles. Much of his work includes full interviews and major part of the narratives in indigenous languages, including various dialects of Quechua, Warao and Mapuche. *Los Warao/The Waraos* (1974) and *Zulay frente al Siglo XXI/Zulay Facing the XXI Century* (1989) are examples of Prelorán's films where indigenous communities share their stories in their native languages. Although Spanish remained dominant, in many documentaries and short films produced between the 1940s and 1970s, the linguistic diversity of Argentinean native communities is also celebrated. Central to Prelorán's filmography was to establish a close bond with a community and become acquainted with their practices before capturing their daily lives on film. For the Argentinean director, a meaningful relation between filmmaker and subjects was an essential component of a movie, in particular because most of his films focused on subjective experiences. His titles became known for depicting members of ethnic groups while they revealed their communities, social life, customs, cultural heritage, festivities and religion.

Syncretism and ethnic diversity were presented in Prelorán's works as unavoidable nods of connection between European mainstream Argentina and its native communities. *Fiesta en el Volcán Higueras/Celebrations in the Higueras Volcano* (1969), for instance, depicted how the whole Uriyá community paid homage to two Catholic saints iconically presented in a mestizo way. Although Prelorán's focus was anthropological and ethnological in nature – probably reactionary to the foreignism associated with indigenous topics among urban Argentineans – he avoided exotifying the subjects of the film (Rossi 1987). *Hermógenes Cayo* (1969) is probably the film that afforded him the most noteworthy acknowledgement as a filmmaker at national and international levels, placing him next to Fernando Birri, Octavio Getino or Fernando Solanas in terms of influence within Latin American cinema.[30] *Hermógenes Cayo* contests the notion that proximity, race, ethnicity and social constraints define individuals and that, on the contrary, shared humanity goes beyond external features.[31]

Simultaneously, indigeneity was central to many of the films produced in Bolivia between the 1940s and 1970s, several of which are still highly regarded for their content and iconic value. Jorge Sanjinés and other members of the Group Ukamau were soon to become renowned figures both at the national and international level for their innovative forms of filmmaking.[32] They were also the first directors in the continent who were concerned with attracting indigenous communities to cinema, making them participants in the audience as well as characters in the films being produced. The ultimate goal was to create a channel of interaction with segments of Bolivian society that had been relegated and oppressed. For Sanjinés and his collaborators, this was a matter of concern in light of the fact that the country remained majorly indigenous in terms of ethnicity. In this sense, they were pioneers since until then, *Vuelve Sebastiana/Come Back, Sebastiana* (1953) had been the only Bolivian sound film touching upon indigeneity. Produced in 1953 by Jorge Ruiz, this short motion picture can be classified as a semi-documentary, being partly a fictional story (Córdova 2007). It represents the tale of a young Chipaya girl who decides to migrate to an Aymara town because she is disappointed in belonging to an isolated, impoverished and disfranchised community.[33] *Vuelve Sebastiana/Come Back, Sebastiana* was the first Bolivian film awarded an international prize in the category of ethnography and many consider it as one of the most representative titles of the indigenist stage of Latin American cinema (Richards 2011).

A year after Sanjinés became director of the ICB (Instituto Cinematográfico Boliviano/Cinematographic Institute of Bolivia), he managed to release *Ukumau/And So It Is* (1966). However, since Bolivian authorities feared that the movie could potentially encourage revolts among oppressed groups, the film was banned.[34] *Ukumau* represents the tragedy of Andrés, an Aymara man seeking revenge on Rosendo, a mestizo man who raped and murdered his wife, Sabina. Besides this horrific crime, the perpetrator is also a dishonest buyer who short-changes and swindles the peasants of the region, including Andrés, in order to make higher profits for himself. Easily understood by audiences across the country and beyond, Andrés and Sabina represent the indigenous peoples of Bolivia being abused. The Aymara couple is split up by the greediness and abuse of a mestizo ruling class. Afflicted by an unbalanced social order, indigenous communities are depicted as an injured party, but simultaneously are being spoken to in their own language. Sanjinés's approach is understood to have induced the onset of a Revolutionary Stage of cinema in the country (Third Cinema), which logically coincides with the years in which militant governments ruled most of the continent.[35]

An important aspect of this stage is the recognizable independence and emancipation of directors as economically self-sufficient artists involved in and aware of the need of promoting social change. In order to do so, and because of the sanctions imposed by the authorities on Sanjinés, the Ukumau group opted for self-funding as the only way to ensure artistic and aesthetic quality, but above all, that their political ideals would not be compromised, constrained or manipulated. Subaltern groups that paradoxically accounted for the majority of the Bolivian population were to be central to the narratives, not for the purpose of display but to be presented as possibilities of change (Gamboa 1999).

The role of cinema for Sanjinés was to include the community in the creation process in order to produce a message shared by a group. According to him, this was especially important in the case of Andean societies, which he found to be community-oriented. More than narratives, his films can still be understood as analogies of the state of affairs in his native country and stories crafted to denounce injustice and raise awareness. The highlight of his career is by many considered to be *Yawar Mallku* (1969), meaning *Blood of the Condor* in Quechua. Sanjinés denounces in this film the horrors of unconsented sterilization programmes carried out by American aid organizations stationed in isolated rural areas.[36] Based on actual facts, the narrative intended to mirror the imperialist approach of the United States in regard to Bolivian domestic affairs. Sanjinés's film is considered as a sample of militant cinema as it contests, scrutinizes and encourages viewers to fight back and take a stand against oppression.[37] It managed to mobilize segments of the population to protest publicly once the authorities banned the movie due to its subversive contents. Censorship, however, was only enforced for twenty-four hours, but it was enough to backfire and ensure that Bolivians were eager to attend the screenings. For Sanjinés, these challenges were not a novelty since the beginning stages of production had been quite conflictive too.

The convincing dimension of Sanjinés's film among Bolivian audiences is believed to have influenced the expulsion of the American Peace Corps from the country in 1971, confirming the militant character of Group Ukumau's productions (Hart 2004). During this same year, General Hugo Banzer Suárez managed to plot a military uprising, allegedly backed up by the United States, and became head of state for seven years. In the aftermath of the coup, Sanjinés and his close collaborator Ricardo Rada were forced into exile and remained abroad until democracy was reinstalled in 1979. *El enemigo principal/The Principal Enemy* (1973), titled in Quechua *Jatun Auka*, set in Peru, and *Fuera de aquí/Out of Here* (1976) set in Ecuador became Sanjinés's representational ways to express his concerns about the state of affairs in Bolivia while he was away. An anti-imperialist agenda is easily recognizable as these films touch upon ownership of land, distribution of wealth, foreign manipulation and multinational powers, exploitation of resources and workforce, and unfranchised indigenous communities (Giukin 2015). Moreover, in later releases, instead of focusing on individuals, he seemed to focus on communities in order to appeal to the collective identity of the indigenous audiences he intended to address.

Similar to the silent period, during this militant stage, cinematic indigeneity appears to be depicted as a collective rather than an individual notion where characters seem to strategize for a communal cause. Group Ukumau's main contribution can be described as an attempt to instil an ideology of social equity and recognition of oppressed communities through films where the addressees play a vital role in the process of production. These new depictions stand out for extricating 'the indigenous' from being a static, passive and one-dimensional trope and transmuting it into a more fluid notion where objectified characters are also subjects. By offering new alternatives of representation, imagining social change and attracting more ethnically diverse audiences, including impoverished native groups, cinematic indigeneity in Bolivia entered a period of perceived de-colonization during the 1960s and 1970s. This process was not restricted to the Andean country as cinema in Latin America was shifting to become a tool of social awareness detached from individual or commercial interests.

As mentioned before, films produced by Sanjinés and Group Ukumau are commonly considered as examples of Third Cinema, understood as the production of films outside the system it seeks to criticize, without depending on it. As observed by Solanas and Getino, Third Cinema films ought to promote revolutionary ideals among oppressed masses and attract filmmakers aiming to raise awareness, militate and oppose against imperialism, censorship and constraints imposed by neoliberal governments through films denouncing injustice.[38] As an innovative approach to visual arts, the term Third Cinema was coined explicitly with reference to the so-called Third World, and hence to Third Estate (*Tiers État*), the lowest social order, as understood in the context of the French Revolution. On that account, these films differ from productions Solanas and Getino considered to belong under the category of First and Second Cinema. While First Cinema articulates and promotes bourgeois, imperialist and above all capitalist ideologies (Hollywood), Second Cinema refers to 'auteur films'/'auterism' and 'national cinemas'.[39] Paradoxically, although Second Cinema rejects the conventions established by a standardized, profit-driven system, it relies on it in terms of funding and distribution. Aesthetically and ideologically, they resembled the preliminary stages of Brazilian *Cinema Nôvo* (*New Cinema*), Cuban Pre- and Post-Revolution Cinema, and Argentinean *Cine de la Base* (Macdonald 1994). They all shared the same pan-continental position on the role of cinema as a tool to denounce social inequality, abuse and repression. Both *Cinema Nôvo* and *Cine de la Base* were committed to encouraging critical debate, registering the political events affecting underprivileged social groups and activating oppressed audiences.[40]

In the specific case of Bolivia, Sanjinés and his collaborators felt committed to broadcast the doubly systematic disparities experienced by communities in rural areas for being indigenous and under-represented peasants. Jorge Sanjinés and the Group Ukamau became also notable for their contributions to the cinematic landscape of the country by using indigenous languages. Their aim was to deploy cinema as a tool to inform, reach and communicate with rural communities and to instigate a sense of social change, pride and inclusion. In this respect, *Ukumau* (1966) by Jorge Sanjinés and produced with funds from the ICB, excels for its recognition of ethnic heritage. It is the first film entirely spoken in a South American indigenous language, Aymara. Through the film, linguistic inclusion operates as a strategy of open contestation and a critique of the language approach endorsed by the 'modern' nation.

Also from this perspective, *Yawar Mallku* (1969) stands out for including Quechua throughout, an aspect that renders it a major work within Latin American filmic tradition. In general terms, linguistic awareness and appreciation of the Amerindian legacy might explain how Sanjinés and his collaborators managed to introduce the seventh art into the cultural repertoire of Quechua and Aymara societies.[41] Before this initiative, cinema in Bolivia was a privilege of the ruling urban classes and an unknown notion for Andean rural segments of the population.

Meanwhile in Brazil, the last stage of the above-mentioned *Cinema Nôvo* (1968–72) soon became prominent for focusing on indigeneity and rejecting a system where disparity was entwined with race. Until then, Brazilian cinema had not approached the native population as tropes to engage audiences in a reflection on destruction and abuse. By depicting images of hostile groups, inhospitable jungles and even cannibalism, directors sought to draw attention to violence as a tool against oppression. In *Como era gostoso e meu frances*/*How Tasty Was My Frenchman* (1971), Nelson Pereira dos Santos is thought to imply that colonizers would only become aware of the brutality of their acts once they would experience annihilation first-hand (Johnson and Stam 1995). The story revolves around a Frenchman captured by an indigenous group in 1557 as a reprimand for not bringing any presents to honour them. Befriended by the French and enemies of the Portuguese, the Tupinambás take him prisoner and decide to feed him intensely in order to feast on his fattened body months later. The film is considered to be a satire against pro-European and North American imperialist structures ruling the country and which should be *swallowed* and overtaken by common Brazilians (Nagib 2006). Pereira dos Santos's film was nominated for the Berlin Golden Bear and was widely praised for its original storyline.

Other Brazilian films from the 1970s focusing on indigeneity were primarily documentaries or short films, some of which include *Iracema, uma tramsa amazônica/Iracema, an Amazon Affair* (1974), *Uira, um indio em busca de Deus/Uira, an Indian in Search of God* (1974) and *A lenda de Ubirajara/The Legend of Ubirajara* (1975). Most of them were an initiative of the Serviço de Proteção ao Índio (Service of Indian Protection), an organization founded in 1910 to handle all issues concerning Brazilian native peoples.[42] Furthermore, renowned anthropologist Darcy Ribeiro was involved in the making of a couple of documentaries. Although Ribeiro became popular in Brazil because of his role as an educator and politician later on, he got international attention for unlocking the cultural riches of Brazil's indigenous communities for the rest of the country. Notably, a number of short films by Darcy Ribeiro released under state support acknowledged native languages as samples of indigenous legacy, for example, Tupi and several dialects of Karaja. *A lenda de Ubirajara* has a bearing for being entirely spoken in Macro-Gê. In terms of linguistic inclusion and acknowledgement, although several films allow viewers to experience and hear some fragments in various Amerindian languages, both on- and off-screen, or within the non-diegetic frame, Spanish and Portuguese remained the dominant languages used to communicate with audiences. Elsewhere in the region, the trend of recognizing the linguistic heritage of indigenous communities in films only began in the 1990s.

After a period of stagnation in Peruvian cinema, *Kukuli* (1961) was released. The film enacts an ancient legend, set in the mountains of Paucartambo. It is the story of fifteen-year-old Kukuli who falls in love with Alaku on her way to a local festivity. Their affair is short-lived as a frightening creature, half-man/half-bear (Ukuku) takes Kukuli prisoner and murders him. Both lovers only meet again after death when they transform into llamas and in their new shape become inseparable once again. Although the film was appreciated and welcomed by audiences, it was criticized for its amateurish cinematography (Middents 2009). If analysed in light of the national literary scene, *Kukuli* can be situated at the border between *indigenismo* and *indianismo*. As mentioned earlier, *indianismo* regards indigenous figures as exotic, melancholic and imaginary beings difficult to relate to in terms of contemporaneity, whereas indigenism (*indigenismo*) considers indigeneity from a realistic standpoint, particularly based on the social disfranchisement faced by native communities within the context of modernity (Escajadillo 1990). It is considered to touch upon indigeneity from an artistic and imaginary approach, but it is also realistic in its portrayal of religion versus syncretism, forbidden love, social control, inadequate conditions in rural Andean communities and the historic implications of colonization. *Kukuli* was also the result of years of collaboration between the filmmakers in a studio known as Foto Cine Club del Cusco, later known as School of Cusco. Founded in 1955, this institution played a key role in the production of short motion pictures and documentaries.[43]

In neighbouring Venezuela, *El bohío rebelde/The Rebel's Hut* (1961) stands out for being the first sound film produced in the country that includes indigenous elements. Focusing on the arrival of Christianity to the country, the motion picture includes scenes about the use of tools, basket weaving, decoration of musical instruments and weaponry. As mentioned earlier, Argentinean Jorge Prelorán contributed to Venezuelan cinema with his film on the Warao people, *Los Warao* (1974). Furthermore, indigenous Venezuelan communities were mostly depicted in documentaries with anthropological, ethnological and preservationist interest.[44]

As for Colombia, the first sound film focusing on indigeneity is understood to have been *Amanecer en la selva/Sunrise in the Forest* although it is not clear in which year it was produced. Similar to other Latin American productions from the silent era, the story revolves around the evangelization of indigenous communities from isolated Chocó region, paying particular attention to the Katio people. The underlying message is that once the natives Westernize, they are spiritually, morally and socially saved (Mateus Mora 2012). Framing an encounter with a Claritin brotherhood, the narrative invites viewers to witness how an isolated indigenous group becomes assimilated into a dominant culture. Other Colombian films and documentaries addressing indigenous themes include *San Agustín* (1942), *La leyenda de El Dorado/Legend of Dorado* (1968), *La fiesta del indio en Quibdó/An Indian's Feast in Quibdó* (1970), *Dabucuri: ceremonia de intercambio/Dabucuri: Scenes from an Exchange Ceremony* (1975), *El pecado de ser indio/The Sin of Being an Indian* (1975) and *El rugido de los dioses/The Roar of the Gods* (1976). In early Colombian cinema, the figure of the indigenous was mainly characterized to reflect on projects of Europeanization or as metaphors about the essence of the nation.

The situation was different in Chile where even though cinema throve during the 1950s and 1960s, indigeneity was not entwined with ideals of national identity, and so remained largely ignored. Although over twenty films were produced in the country after the introduction of sound and before the onset of the socially conscious *Nuevo Cine Chileno* (New Chilean Cinema) in 1960, indigenous elements did not play a meaningful role in any of them. It was only in 1962 that Sergio Bravo y Enrique Zorilla embarked on a 100,000 km journey in order to complete *Amerindia*, a documentary about Latin American native communities. The filmmakers were awarded the FIPRECI prize at the Oberhausen Film Festival in 1964 for their original work. A decade later, a critique on the destruction and expropriation of land belonging to Mapuche peoples was released. Directed by Carlos Flores, Guillermo Cahn, Samuel Carvajal, Luis Araneda and Antonio Campi, *Nutuayin mapu/Let's Get Back Our Land* sought to draw attention to the historical and social implications of dispossessing and evicting native nations from their centuries-old dwelling places. Thematically, both films differed from most mainstream productions released at the time. Although there was a trend to produce socially committed cinema in the country, in line with the rest of the continent, Chilean filmmakers did not readily aim attention at indigeneity until the 1990s.

Similarly, indigenous topics were not central in early Ecuadorean cinema. The first director keen to display the ethnic diversity of the country was Demetrio Aguilera Malta with *Los salasacas/The Salasaca Peoples* and *Los colorados/The Red Ones* in 1955. Twenty years later, Ronny Velásquez and Cuesta Ordóñez made the documentary *Los Shuar: Hijos de las cascadas/The Shuar: Sons of the Waterfalls* on the Shuar customs and way of living. Finally, *Entre el sol y la serpiente/Between the Sun and the Snake*, produced by José Corral in 1976, stood out for exploring how history was embedded in ancient traditions, focusing on the Cañari peoples.[45] Meanwhile in Brazil, the ideological approach in *Iracema, uma tramsa amazônica* (1974) was about to create controversy. This realistic documentary with a fictional approach, directed by Brazilian directors Jorge Bodanzky and Orlando Senna, offers an implicit critique of the changes brought by modernity. *Iracema* revolves around the journey and interactions of a prostitute while hitchhiking her way back home. Due to government-induced media censorship, the film was only publicly screened in 1981. Critique of the Brazilian answer to 'development' and how this affected native communities is also the underlying topic in *India, a filha do sol/India, the Daughter of the Sun* (1982) and *Kuarup* (1989).

The collapse of dictatorships would define the cultural landscape in the years to come. Particularly during the 1980s, newly re-established democracies were soon to be echoed in films with a higher sense of equity and ethnic inclusion. Anthropological interest and militant attitudes became less prominent than the need to come to terms with national identities. This range of ideological precepts constituted a postcolonial approach that drew attention to the long-established core–periphery/Self–Other dichotomies. Progressively, the first attempts emerged to focus on indigenous societies as a political entity from a more nuanced and accurate perspective (Rist 2014). Nevertheless, a problematic aspect of this stage was the insistence of Latin American cinematic production in positioning itself within a 'ghetto of Third World cinema' (Hart 2004: 10). This deep-rooted tendency reiteratively integrated fabulist and realist elements that ultimately tapped into a sense of allure and nostalgia among international viewers. A democratic approach to cinema started to emerge out of resistance to the unequal practices of dictatorships. After all, censorship, political repression and persecution had had profound influence on the cinematic landscape under dictatorial regimes.

These new attempts of creating films that would endorse horizontal social relations paved the way for indigenous filmmakers to create their own productions. For the first time, certain segments of the population had access to technology that gave them the possibilities to produce and edit films. This influenced the growth of new formats of cinema and increased the diversity of topics and standpoints. Indigenous communities saw the opportunity to become agents in the recording of their own history. Prior to the 1980s, self-representation had not been an option for native segments of the population, least of all those dwelling in isolated regions or unfamiliar with cinema as a concept (Hearne 2012). The new wave of indigenous works meant a shift in the way indigeneity was depicted, as it was no longer the exclusive domain of mestizo or European directors. Native filmmakers were now able to create their own narratives and broadcast them to the world. Either as tools of cultural transmission, educational material, statement, protest, denouncement or artistic expression, many indigenous groups grasped the opportunity to produce their own version of self. Indeed, by the end of the 1980s, the advent of video cameras and access to new methods of filmmaking prompted the emergence of Indigenous Cinema. A major characteristic of self-representational filmmaking was its group-authored approach. It strikingly differed from the auteurist praxis behind the production of indigeneity-themed films released during the first eight decades of cinema in Latin America.

After the collapse of New Latin American Cinema, due to lack of funding, new methods, approaches, topics and orientations emerged. Rediscovery of roots became prominent in the production of motion pictures evoking the glorious past of ancient civilizations. The five hundredth anniversary of the 'New World' in the early 1990s influenced the imaginary of filmmakers willing to embody the character and identity of a continent still in the making. Some of the new formats that emerged in the continent included productions in which blended techniques were put into practice.

In Mexico, a trend of making films focusing on the clash between the Native American and European worlds developed in different directions. Generally speaking, a connection can be traced between the commemoration of five centuries of colonization of the Americas and pre-Columbian heritage characterizations in cinema. Some filmmakers opted for offering colourful images of an imagined, idyllic past where allegoric legends would explain the differences between ancient and new civilizations, as in *Retorno a Aztlán* (1991). There were also examples of films based on historical events, mainly based on archaeological evidence, such as *La otra conquista/The Other Conquest* (1998). A third option was to present audiences with a narrative where both natives and colonizers were victims of historic circumstances, as was the case in *Cabeza de Vaca* (1991). Directed by Nicolás Echevarría, the story of how Álvar Núñez Cabeza de Vaca shipwrecked, survived and later on encountered the Karankawa people remains a highlight in Mexican cinema. Similar to other countries across the continent, conjectural accuracy informed the making of most motion pictures released during the 1980s and 1990s. This included linguistic diversity, which resulted in the use of Nahuatl in many of the films touching upon indigeneity, even if it was not accurate to assume that all ancient civilizations spoke that particular language.

In spite of failed attempts, like the fake indigenous languages spoken in *Cabeza de Vaca*, filmmakers sought in native voices a vehicle to make a difference between the Old ('Us') and the New World ('Them'). Social awareness remained high on the agenda, especially in the Andean region. Segregation, forced migrations, environmental violations, aggressions and inequalities among ethnic and non-ethnic sectors of the population are widely explored in the Colombian *La Voz de los Sobrevivientes/The Voice of the Survivors* (1980); and Venezuelan *Caño Manamo/Manamo Cain* (1983), *Amazonas: El Negocio de este Mundo/Amazon: The Business of This World* (1986) and *Piaroa* (1993). Economic interest and infringement of landownership are the main focus in Guatemalan *Ecos de Feria/Echoes of Fair* (1998), which to a large extent resemble Bolivian *Las Banderas del Amanecer/The Flags of the Dawn* (1983) and *Nación Clandestina/Clandestine Nation* (1989) by Jorge Sanjinés. Still militant in nature, these cinematographic works have in common the desire to expose the unbalanced interaction between defenceless peasants and an oligarchic state. *Nación Clandestina* moreover denounces the obstacles faced by those moving from rural areas into urban centres where indigenous elements are rampantly unacknowledged (Quispe Escobar 2007). As in Mexico, an organization known as CEFREC was founded in 1989 in Bolivia to train potential indigenous filmmakers, encouraging them to create their own cinematic expressions. As a result, there was an increase in the number of films and documentaries voiced entirely in a native language, as opposed to Spanish or Portuguese. Besides a broader sense of equity and inclusion, modernity brought about changes and innovations in the imaginary of filmmakers and their depictions of Latin American reality.

Conclusion

Cinematic spaces retain their value as carefully crafted art works that adumbrate social attitudes and sensitivities, still today, intrinsically linked to canons originally featured in European works of art. Visual cultural artefacts provide more information about the worldviews of the producing society than about the communities being depicted. The figure of the indigenous emerged from a need of registering the 'discovery' of a New World and its peoples. Unmitigated sensationalism, incited by the era of European explorations, encouraged the imaginary of painters, writers and sculptors. Chronicles and works of fine arts enhanced the tendency of affixing surreal, exuberant and unrealistic characteristics to non-European societies. Their presumed inferior lifestyles, attires, practices and physiognomy confirmed not only the superiority of the colonizing powers but also the proliferation of attitudes up until today. For centuries, the image of the American natives was registered as the embodiment of a noble savage only external forces could save. The introduction of photography and easier ways of travelling opened up new possibilities for those wanting to study these communities. Later on, common themes and approaches identified in the fine arts were transposed onto the cinematic world. Hollywood characterizations of Native Americans had an impact on Latin American representations. By the same token, the ethnographic and auto-ethnographic stance taken by the first local filmmakers has also reshaped the renderings of indigeneity. Social upheaval, expansion of *mestizaje* as an ideology, new waves of immigrants from Europe, academic interest and commercialization of movie theatres had an impact on the creation of a cinematic version of the indigenous.

This chronological overview of the inclusion of native communities in cinema leads one to conclude that ethnicity has held a key role since the inception of the medium. Mostly framed as exotified characters or as foci of anthropological and ethnological approaches, indigenous figures soon became a part of the cultural repertoire of those who had access to film screenings. The underlying assumption was that cinema afforded mainly mestizo or Westernized directors the freedom to choose how to depict these communities for over half a century, or until self-representation emerged. Latin American filmic industries struggled to gain a sense of identity built on mestizo elements but embedded in majorly Western canons. Shifts in the political climate of most countries, specifically in light of dictatorships and hardship, influenced the ideological and pedagogical value of films. This explains how images of native communities became crucial to deploy a message of nationalism, not least when it was entwined with allegorizations of ancient empires or extinct magical worlds. By the end of the century, cinematic indigeneity becomes synonymic with times of change in which ethnic communities allegedly ceased to be forgotten social groups, with filmmakers seeking to draw this awakening on the screen. Ultimately, self-representation emerges as a sustainable approach to contest hegemonic approaches.

2

Metropolis: Production of audiovisual cultural artefacts

This chapter focuses on narratives enmeshed in recomposed frames of references and formulations that mirror local, national and regional concerns, in most cases conceived as articulations of metropolitan centres of production. Cities such as Buenos Aires, Lima and Mexico City operate as core venues where artistic expressions materialize, while an imagined periphery is perceived as a source of inspiration. In the Peruvian case, for instance, *Cine regional* (Chapter 7) renders the urban–rural dichotomy most apparent. Common alignments identified in these productions include the centrality of rural areas; fixation on agency, identity and ethnicity; and, most importantly, a revived interest in the indigeneity/collectivity dichotomy. The synthesis of this chapter is thus to consider these orientations from the various positions presented by filmmakers across the continent. Central to this reflection is to recognize indigenist practices abundant in the Andean cinematic tradition, examine exoticizing ideologies in Brazilian films, review discourses of empathy and indifference in Central American productions, explore romanticized mixed elements in Mexican narratives and scrutinize the democratic, but paternalistic, approach to minorities in motion pictures from the Southern Cone region.

Mexico and Central America

In Central America, the modest number of film productions limits the diversity of themes, and partly explains the dwindling visibility of indigeneity in cinematic spaces. Due to several factors, mainly lack of technical development, state support and funding, except for Cuba, cinematic production across Central America remained limited throughout most of the twentieth century. Since 2001, improved conditions have contributed to an increase in the number of films produced in the region (Durón 2014). Although artisanal modes of production are still the norm, a 'huracán cinematográfico' [cinematic hurricane] (Cortés 2010: 85) has started. Artistically, it is not surprising to find external influences in Central American films, mainly from Cuba, Europe and the United States, places where most of the aspiring film directors received academic training. Furthermore, the creation of platforms where filmmakers in the region can interact seems to have not only stimulated and encouraged production and distribution but also expanded the diversity of themes and formats with which Central American directors choose to work.

Thematically, civil war, gangs and migration flows are the three main recurring themes in the cinema of the region (Durón 2014). These three topics are indeed easily recognizable in films where indigeneity is a focal point. Similarly, contemporary portrayals seek to give women prime consideration. Young females are protagonists in many of the films produced across Central America. A shift in paradigm is noticeable in narratives that discursively participate in the demystification, deconstruction and redefinition of structures that rigidly prevent the emergence of alternative social identities (Garðarsdóttir 2014). Even though the limited number of Central American films focusing on indigenous communities denotes indifference towards their cause, the centrality of womanhood in these narratives reflects a high sense of empathy for the most vulnerable social group across the region, that is, young indigenous women.

Turning to Puerto Rico, *Taínos* (2005) appears to be the only example of Puerto Rican national cinema illustrating the presumably lost indigenous legacy of the island country. Directed by Benjamin Lopez, this 116-minute production is set in modern times and revolves around the academic devotion of an archaeology student, Sara (Christie Miró), for the glorious, highly celebrated but vanished Taino Empire. As part of her research, the young student organizes an excursion along with four friends and a guide, Yabey (Josué Reyes), into the Mora Cave. The climax of the story is reached when Sara discovers that Yabey is actually an emissary of an undiscovered last remaining Taino clan, and that this empire is not entirely extinct. In spite of excessive sentimentality and a number of overtly melodramatic episodes, Lopez's film stands out for contesting a tendency in contemporary Puerto Rican cinema. Distancing from contemporary local cinema, it does not recur to sensationalism, sex or violence as commodifiable narrative strategies (Rodríguez 2015).

In stark contrast with Caribbean postcolonial premises, attempts to conflate pre-Columbian heritage with national identity convey the idea of ancestral continuity and racial purity (Martínez-San Miguel 2011). In this sense, *Taínos*, rather than presenting an iconoclastic celebration of an ancient civilization, intends to appeal to the sense of nationalism and belonging. The love story that emerges between Sara and Yabey captures the sensitivities and nostalgia that the concept of indigeneity prompts in the Puerto Rican psyche. Their fable exemplifies the tendency in Latin American cinema to favour private individual experiences as a means to sketch collective-level identities (Podalsky 2011). As Martínez-San Miguel (2011) asserts, the production of *Taínos* is symptomatic of a society that fantasizes about an extinct autochthonous indigenous identity. Paradoxically, the production of a film featuring the reminiscence of a society about its pre-Columbian past unveils the indifference of other countries in the region where these communities make up part of their social fabric but are deliberately omitted from mediatized spaces.

Directing the attention to Costa Rica, the core emphasis of its filmic discourse is consistently put on the importance of 'unicidad' [oneness] (Sandoval García 2002: 7); this is a notion frequently cited in national narratives and promotes the idea of unity and homogeneity. Inclusion of elements lying outside a uniform nucleus seems only possible as long as a considerable distance is established between mainstream and subaltern. In spite of an increasing number of films made in Costa Rica in the last decade, only one film touches upon indigeneity. Bearing in mind that under 2 per cent of Costa Rican population is considered to be indigenous, this might explain the absence of this theme from the mainstream cinematic scene. However, the fact that the filmmaker of *Defensores de la vida/Defenders of Life* (2015), Dana Ziyasheva, comes originally from Kazakhstan raises questions on the indifference these communities (a population of approximately 64,000) face in the cultural landscape of the country. Ziyasheva's agency to tell the story and her interest in it, compared with the disinterest shown by local filmmakers, constitute a reminder of the impact of transnationalism, globally consumed visual artefacts and postcolonial exoticism in the production of stories where indigeneity plays a central role.

After transferring to Costa Rica as a UNESCO civil servant, Ziyasheva had the opportunity to work closely with the Ngöbe community and gradually befriended Carmen Romero, president of the women's association. The film revolves around Carmen's life at the centre of a matriarchy and the internal conflict experienced by Pamela (Beatriz Brenes), an anthropologist who struggles to understand the Ngöbe culture. Social codes dictate that Carmen's granddaughter, Esmeralda, is to get married once she has completed the rite of passage that marks the beginning of her life as a woman. The so-called *Mongo* ritual is charged with biological connotations, as it is to take place after Esmeralda's first menstruation. Since Claudio, the seventy-year-old shaman, decides to propose to the young girl, Carmen faces a difficult choice, of either preserving the Ngöbe customs or adapting them to *modern* times. Besides exploring the complexities of intergenerational marriages, the narrative delves into adolescent pregnancy and the advancement of indigenous women's rights. Esmeralda is not only young but also enchanted by Feb (Aman Darbo), Pamela's teenage son who follows her to do fieldwork during his school holidays.

Politically, the story questions indigenous morality vis-à-vis Western values, and the clashes between different readings of what constitutes identity and culture. Femininity is a crucial aspect as it serves to reflect on a myriad of standpoints where audiences might disagree with Ngöbe epistemologies. Separated by time, grandmother and granddaughter do not seem to share the same cultural lens. Ziyasheva (2015) explains that 'for Carmen, culture is a set of forms, skills and rituals that must be passed to the next generation in its most purist, unaltered form', while her granddaughter Esmeralda perceives it as 'a creative and emotional outlet, a living substance that evolves, absorbs and feeds on new concepts' (para. 5). The film stands out for shedding light on the inextricable relations between indigeneity and gender, modernity and tradition. Reflecting on Ziyasheva's preoccupation with the recognition of indigenous linguistic heritage, Ngöbe is a fundamental aspect of the film. All chants and songs that accompany the rituals and ceremonies are sung in the original language. English is mainly used to denote the outsider's point of view, while Spanish operates as a bridge language between the Ngöbe and the non-indigenous. As the filmmaker has openly discussed, one of the conditions set by the community before joining the project was that the film had to include Ngöbe, an understandable request from an under-represented community.

Invisibility and omission of indigenous groups across media landscapes is perhaps most alarming in Guatemala. These diverse communities remain grossly under-represented on national screens, even if almost half of the country's population (40 per cent) is assumed to belong to an ethnic group. Partly, this is due to the fact that the Guatemalan film industry is considerably restrained and underfunded. As in other Central American countries, government support to cultural enterprises is limited, and conditions for filmmaking projects are strenuous (Durón 2014). The artisanal and inventive methods (in some aspects) behind the production of the three films concerning indigeneity released after

2000, *El regreso de Lencho/The Return of Lencho* (2010), *Distancia/Distance* (2011) and *Ixcanul* (2015), attest to the challenges that local filmmakers confront. In general terms, comicality, awareness-raising and social critique are the main argumentative lines identified in the few Guatemalan films released nationwide each year (Cajas 2013). Across various outlets for public discourse, indigenous cultures are evocatively portrayed as folklore, rather than a vital component of the country's social fabric (Rasch 2008).

A case in point is the insistence of Jayro Bustamante in creating a nostalgic and romantic setting as background for María's hardships in *Ixcanul*, discussed in the introduction. Situating the story in an idyllically remote context taps into the fascination for the unknown that aligns with imaginaries about those living with 'nature'. A visually coherent topography, according to Bustamante's criteria, involves creating a 'wholly imaginary distance from specific markers of Western modernity in the actual locality – the nearby McDonald's, for instance, that had to be carefully *not* included in the shots' (Castillo 2019: 120). The film successfully denounces Guatemalan linguistic attitudes and tendency of entwining levels of proficiency in Spanish and ethnic identity (Rasch 2008). It follows the formula in local cinema of employing documentary-inspired techniques to add a realistic undertone to the narratives, and having untrained actors in key roles.[1] María's dismaying story is realistic in all its aspects, but so is the power dynamic behind the conception of the film.

While Bustamante prevents McDonald's to pollute the perceived wilderness of *Ixcanul*'s backdrop, Sergio Ramírez uses a location dominated by a Pepsi sign to open up one of the scenes in *Distancia* (2011). Indeed, aesthetic choices play a crucial role in contextualizing the cultural distance between characters and audiences. A camera bestows power to infer associations that articulate identification and proximity, or stagnation and fossilization. As its title suggests, *Distancia* explores not only the metaphoric and symbolic but also the intimate and tangible aspects and implications of distance. Ramírez narrates the journey of Tomás (Carlos Escalante) to encounter his daughter Lucia (Saknicté Racancoj), who was kidnapped from her parents as a small child and given up for adoption. After sacredly attending the exhumation of bodies buried in common graves every day with the hope of finding her, Tomás receives with joy the news that the girl is alive. She is now twenty-three years old, but having been allocated to a Kek'chí-speaking (also spelled Q'eqchi') family, she is unable to communicate with her father who is fluent in Ki'ché and Spanish. Kek'chí is the only language she speaks. After a two-day journey and a two-decade interval, Tomás will not let linguistic barriers tarnish his reunion with Lucia. An interpreter serves as a bridge to connect father and daughter in the challenging attempt to get to know each other.

His 150-kilometre journey to Nebaj, the town where Lucia resides, is presented as a symbolic pilgrimage throughout rural Guatemala, although the lack of resources of these communities mirrors their subalternity. Ramírez insists in using symbols, for instance mobile phones, as elements that denote the coexistence of resources and poverty as parts of the same reality (Liano 2015). In this sense, *Distancia* illustrates that indigeneity does not convey the notion of backwardness and reclusiveness. Now that Lucia's mother is dead, Tomás feels compelled to register in a notebook the family chronicles so that Lucia gains some knowledge about her ancestry and heritage. Puzzlingly, the ultimate metaphor which bespeaks the concept of distance is the separation of father and daughter after their memorial encounter. Lucia is not only married, and belongs to another ethnic group, but she is also part of a family who aligned with the army during the war, a fact that separates them at an emotional and political level. Realism eclipses a more optimistic closure; Tomás returns to the farm where he works, and to the memories of his dead wife.

Although a certain sense of folklorization is to be found in Guatemalan fictional representations of indigenous groups, a common characteristic is to present impressions of the subalternity these communities face. Awareness about economic disparities, long-term effects of civil war and social unrest are also recurrent subthemes in these productions, as is the case with most Central American cinematic portrayals. Ensuing chapters will furnish examples of films from the region where the main topics also include dispossession, abuse of power and failed state policies.

Mexico: Hybridity and romanticization

Considering films in Mexico, it is worth noting that the country has the most productive cinematic industry in Latin America, a fact that partly explains the long list of indigeneity-oriented films it has produced since the turn of the century. The list of works addressing indigenous elements include *Rito Terminal/Terminal Rite* (2000), *El Violín/The Violin* (2005), *Erendira Ikikunari* (2006), *Cochochi* (2007), *Corazón del Tiempo* (2008), *Espiral/Spiral* (2008), *Alamar/To the Sea* (2009), *El traspatio/The Backyard* (2009), *Vaho/Becloud* (2009), *Los ojos azules/The Blue Eyes* (2012), *La Jaula de Oro/The Golden Cage* (2013), *La Tirisia/Perpetual Sadness*

(2014), *El sueño del Maraákame/Maraákame's Dream* (2016), *La carga/The Load* (2016), *Sueño en otro idioma/I Dream in Another Language* (2017), *Roma* (2018) and *El ombligo de Guie'dani/Xquipi' Guie'dani/Guie'dani's Navel* (Mexico, 2019).

The rich diversity of Mexican native groups has for a long time served as a breeding ground for the production of imagery that epitomizes the country in the imaginary of local and international audiences. Portrayals of indigeneity have evolved, as has been the case with other elements considered central to the creation of national narratives. Progressively, new forms of understanding ethnicity have emerged. The relative freedom to present innovative approaches and impressions about under-represented social groups probably stems from the ideological autonomy that new structures of production and distribution offer (Miquel 2006). Diversity and high quality are traits that have helped Mexican cinema to reconquer its national audience. Yet, as in the past, the discourse about indigenous communities is still slightly illuminated by indigenist attitudes. It must be noted that many of the reflections featured in the selected films echo solidified ideas about mystical societies with arcane connections to their territories and which are unequivocally rural. These newer forms of indigenism resemble preceding strategies that sought 'to liberate the country from the deadweight of its native past' (Brading 2008: 88) by highlighting the nostalgia of mestizo populations, rather than the agency of subaltern ethnicities. The need to externalize a romanticized journey of self-discovery is prominent in the Mexican films touching upon indigenous themes. Even if outdated stereotypes are preserved, contemporary cinematic portrayals give centrality to until now overlooked identities.

Attention to the pre-Columbian themes has been considered as a means to challenge and contest American hegemony, and as a strategy to differentiate Mexican cinema from more dominant discourses (González Manrique 2009). After all, the impact of globalization on the production of films in Mexico has been considerable and its repercussions, especially in the context of funding, raise questions about the liberty local cinema really enjoys. A drawback to this scheme is the tendency to underestimate the individual characters of the various indigenous groups and consolidate their epistemologies under a common hybrid label.[2] In this sense the mestizo/Indian dichotomy miscalculates the importance of acknowledging difference, and the realization that reductions and simplifications can be as damaging as omissions.[3]

In the case of *El Violín* (2005), the film constitutes the first depiction of a key figure from an indigenous movement actively involved in deciding how he is being portrayed (Martínez Sotelo 2012). Directed by Francisco Vargas, the film narrates the story of an eighty-eight-year-old violinist, Plutarco Hidalgo (Ángel Tavira), who witnesses the military occupation of his hometown. Due to the army set-up, limited access to the village blocks the possibilities of the community to rebel against the oppressing armed forces, particularly because the armament is hidden underneath the houses occupied now by soldiers. Don Plutarco captivates the captain of the troops with his music and gradually manages to smuggle the munitions his son and grandson so desperately need to combat the abusive army (Figure 2).

The theme resonated with audiences all over the world, as indigenous movements have gained empathy in the last decades, in particular as a response to the attention received by the Zapatista movement in Southern Mexico. *El Violín* has been acclaimed not only for giving voice to the silent but also to scrupulously shedding light on the sense of vulnerability in which self-identified indigenous peoples live. Vargas has stated that the underlying approach behind the cinematography of the story was to capture and transport reality onto the screen and, in the process, to convey the idea that Mexican neorealism is possible.[4]

Figure 2 Screenshot of the film *El Violín* (Mexico, 2005).

In fact, as Vargas explains, the choice of shooting in black and white is linked to the degree of severity of the topic (Rueda, Vargas and Saint-Dizier 2006).

Due to the political connotations of the story, *El Violín* is perceived as an attempt to portray the evolution of how Mexico can understand the various components of its social fabric, and what makes up its identity. Since violins are considered quintessentially European, the symbolism of the story relies on the appropriation by a subaltern body of an element that belongs to the hegemonic institutions. Don Plutarco is not represented as a weak figure in any moment of the film; on the contrary, he emerges as a hybrid hero (civilized but warlike), trying to defend his community by resorting to noble strategies (music) in order to engage in a dialogue that a sightless, detached and violent army fails to appreciate. The end of the film invites viewers to reflect on the allocation of power and recognition of sovereignty. Since the film does not denounce any specific real-life event, the language chosen for the dialogues is Spanish, as opposed to an Amerindian language spoken in a particular region of the country.

Along the line of *El Violín*, the film *Corazón del Tiempo* (2008) provides a nuanced insight into the intimate side of Zapatista resistance. Set in La Esperanza de San Pedro (Chiapas), this is the story of Sonia (Rocío Barrios), a young girl destined to marry Miguel (Leonardo Rodríguez), despite being romantically involved with insurgent Francisco Jiménez (Julio). Marriage is not considered a private commitment between a couple but rather a traditional community custom with a long history. The situation is particularly problematic because Miguel has already provided Sonia's family with a dowry (a cow), and also because insurgents are only to marry other fellow insurgents. If Sonia is serious about being with Julio, she would be requested to leave the village and join him in his dangerous life as a militant. The film opens up a space to dissect the situation and power of decision of women within Chiapanec societies who find themselves trapped between two worlds. An important aspect of the *Corazón del Tiempo* is the figure of Sonia's father, who shows admirable, rather romantically idealized, support for his daughter's decisions, regardless of the consequences. Paradoxically, the story revolves around the uprising against an order within a mandate that is rebellious in its own right. Women and the community at large dwell in a climate of intrinsic and extrinsic duality at a political and social level with cultural reverberations that scape the realm of the private. This duplicity encompasses, for instance, in which terms and what Chiapanec societies choose to share with those outside their immediate environment. The film is fictional, but largely informed by the collective experience of those involved in its production.

In line with long-established communicational practices, it is worth noting that the community, for instance, decided that Spanish would increase the visibility and accessibility of the story to (inter)national audiences. Delivering a message was more relevant than any attempt to seek acknowledgement of their linguistic heritage. Admittedly, the linguistic diversity of the inhabitants of many Zapatista towns explains why Spanish operates as lingua franca. Behind *Corazón del Tiempo*, dissemination was the main concern.

In several respects, privileging stories, such as *Corazón del Tiempo* and *El Violín*, where indigenous resistance is celebrated, raise questions about Indianist trends, as opposed to indigenist approaches. A distinction needs to be made, nevertheless, between these two forms to articulate support and perceive Mexican indigenous communities (Leyva Solano 2005). Indeed, whereas indigenism advances attitudes informed by paternalism, indianism supporters campaign for the independence of indigenous peoples.[5] Although, or perhaps *because*, these concepts are originally political and ideological discourses rather than cultural strands, they are continuously present in Mexican motion pictures.

In the case of *La Jaula de Oro* (2013), director Diego Quemada-Díez explores the journey of three teenagers who attempt to emigrate illegally to the United States in spite of the external and internal obstacles. The film delves into the positionality of ethnicity vis-à-vis social class. It focuses on the obstacles faced by a Tzotzil teenager, Chauk (Rodolfo Domínguez), who is unable to speak Spanish but who nevertheless shares the same dream as his mestizo companions, Sara (Karen Martinez) and Juan (Brandon Lopez). Within a social grid, envisioning America as their exit out of poverty situates the three of them under a horizontal, rather than a vertical line. Exploring more than a violent clash between mestizo and indigenous values, the film positions itself from a questioning perspective. The Guatemalan–Mexican trio is making their journey northwards, through Mexico, and the distance from their homeland works as an element that equalizes their disparities; after all, they all want the same thing. The centrality of language within discourses of difference at a microscopic level makes the film an excellent venue to reflect on the incursion of indigenous languages in recent cinematic portrayals of indigeneity, discussed amply in Chapter 3.

Conclusively, the Mexican approach to indigeneity in cinema centres on romanticized but often painstakingly respectful images of communities where the sense of individuality prevails over the collective legacy. If thinking of a nation in Mexico requires relying on shared elements, such as territory, population, language and customs, contemporary films question to what extent this applies in the case of indigenous societies. Thematically, the diversity in focal points and viewpoints has resulted in a national cinema engaged with the peoples it represents. From this perspective, there is less space – compared to other national cinemas in the region – for outdated versions of indigeneity, or single, reduced and reductionist attitudes. Although the number of films is limited when compared to the size of the national film industry, contemporary motion pictures have introduced and enriched established canons. Recent depictions of indigenous groups in Mexico thus revive, at their outermost points, a dialogue about the individual/group dichotomy, and contribute to a repertoire of imagery where diversity, hybridity and plasticity replace homogeneity, consistency and firmness. This is particularly the case of *Roma* (2018), examined in detail in Chapter 6.

South America

South American cinema is rich in indigenous ethnotypes. They operate as cultural constants and serve as a reflection of visual conventions anchored in ideologies and hierarchized social orders. In the case of the Andean region, films produced after the turn of the century confirm political shifts have resulted in major visibility of indigenous heritage. In many ways, recent titles suggest indigenist approaches might have been reconfigured or reformulated. Originally, local forms of indigenism denoted the use of a benevolent mestizo and criollo voice to denounce the exploitation and marginalization of indigenous communities on their behalf. A tendency of speaking on behalf of those who imaginatively lack agency explains one-dimensional, city-oriented and paternalistic portrayals not only across the Andean region but also in films from the Southern Cone countries. As for Brazilian cinema, with few exceptions, tropicalist ethnotypes are dutifully displayed, although sometimes in a caricatured way.

Andean region: Reconfiguring indigenism

Due to the ethnic diversity of Bolivia, Colombia, Ecuador, Peru and Venezuela, it is not surprising to find a wide spectrum of recent films focusing on indigenous ethnotypes. In the light of a long history of inclusion of indigeneity in cinema, both through political and militant approaches, vestiges of older models of portraying indigenous characters and elements are easily found in films produced across the region, particularly in Bolivia and Peru. The most salient characteristic is the prominence of indigenist features that distinguish some of the stories produced after the turn of the century.

The key aspect of twentieth-century indigenism is the tradition of non-indigenous figures of using public discourse to reflect on the lived experience of oppressed indigenous communities, without necessarily considering their opinions, positions or sensitivities (Bigenho 2015; Barrow 2018, D'Argenio 2020). From an early twenty-first-century standpoint, this is seen as problematic in a region with large numbers of indigenous populations, particularly in the case of Bolivia, Guatemala and Peru, because it suggests the right of a group to speak up on behalf of other groups, silencing them in the process. Films become platforms to attest disparities in agency and advocacy of discourses of identity, specifically for under-represented communities across countries where cinematic productions cater mainly to non-indigenous audiences (both at a national and global level). In this sense, they act as instruments to interpret and translate between two coextending groups, but not necessarily in an equitable, unbiased format. This is the case even if those following indigenist agendas are aware of their interpellant role, and seek to favour indigenous elements.[6] Considering long-established structures of discrimination, they act as heterogeneous cultural outputs as their recipients, referents and interlocutors do not share the same cultural background. An overview of films produced across the Andean region attests to a well-established, decades-old practice of denunciation and social critique that seeks to increase awareness among audiences. Despite this, many of the reviewed narratives insist on presenting indigeneity as a non-standard, irregular, somehow unrepresentative and, at times, even aberrant notion.

In the case of Bolivian cinema, a clear resurgence in the production of films touching upon indigeneity followed the election of Evo Morales as president of the country in December 2005. At least six films focusing on the Quechua and Aymara populations have been produced in the last decade, out of which most have received wide attention from national and international audiences. Spearheading this trend, *¿Quién mató a la llamita blanca?*, directed by Rodrigo Bellot, broke national office records in 2007. Bolivian audiences were quick to respond to this satirical road comedy and its take on attitudes about ethnic diversity and failed governmental structures. Almost instantly, Bellot's film entered the ubiquitous circle of pirate DVDs and became a favourite in public spaces (e.g. buses) where American movies used to be the norm (Steagall 2009). The main characters are Domitila (Erika Andía) and Jacinto (Miguel Valverde), a couple of criminals, also known as *Los Tortolitos* (Lovebirds), whose mission is to deliver fifty kilograms of cocaine to the Brazilian border at any cost. The couple ignores how dangerous the task can become. Two unscrupulous counter-narcotic police officers assigned to apprehend them complicate matters further.

Descriptively, *¿Quién Mató a la Llamita Blanca?* is a documentary-style portrait of modern Bolivian society which uses ridicule to offer a sketch of a society struggling with its self-identity. Like Domitila and Jacinto, most characters serve to make a parody of topics such as so-perceived backwardness, criminality, corruption and discrimination. This film is considered as a space where Bolivian audiences have an opportunity to witness the unmeasurable diversity of the country. Bellot describes his movie as 'un retorno a Sanjinés con una visión contemporánea' [a return to Sanjinés with a contemporary vision] (Mastodonte 2006: para. 6). His own statement corroborates the indigenist approach of the iconography that characterizes *La Llamita* (*Little Llama*), as the film has been popularly renamed.[7]

By using Sanjinés's works as point of reference, Bellot attests his interest in producing films that engage audiences. Alluding to one of the most celebrated symbols of Andean culture – llamas – in the title of the film, he presumably implies that Bolivia is the ultimate victim of the acts of injustice and abuse committed by its ruling classes (Ríos Gastelú 2006). His skilful use of cinema to raise awareness about the state of affairs of his native country materializes in images of precarity and discrimination. *La Llamita* also echoes a desire of embodying the ills of a nation in the portrayal of an indigenous couple in need because, after all, they are not criminals but survivors of a system that marginalizes them.

The film makes use of an omniscient commentator who appears in between crucial scenes and explains the context of the images in relation to the social and political climate of the country. A non-indigenous narrator who takes all possible formats, including indigenous ones, and recites condescendingly how *Los Tortolitos* face several mishaps resembles a parent commenting on the pranks of her or his child. Thus, the undertone becomes paternalistic, and in this sense, *¿Quién mató a la llamita blanca?* unquestionably extolls indigenist attitudes. By presenting Domitila and Jacinto as victims, Bellot ratifies the notion that their agency is subaltern to the agency of non-indigenous structures. Defending oppressed ethnic groups on account of their perceived vulnerability strengthens the tendency of altruistic paternalism (Tarica 2008). Even if *La llamita* is a satirical comedy, the limited fictive scenarios do not entertain any reconfiguration in the power structures, attitudes towards ethnicity or gender, or the dichotomy between urban and rural spaces. It does, though, blatantly critique the canons of beauty that are widespread in Bolivia and that favour European physical traits over indigenous features. In the film, mestizo characters, and in particular those from the eastern part of Bolivia, demand recognition of their white legacy while they reject everything that is indigenous (Banegas Flores 2008).

La Llamita demonstrates Bolivian national cinema is becoming attentive to self-introspection and acknowledgement of the cultural, social and political interests of its local audiences. The film offers not only ample displays of indigenous folklore but also of Domitila and Jacinto's mindset, dreams and agony. However, even if *La llamita* works as a platform to express the fury and suffering of the subaltern, it offers *Los Tortolitos* a false sense of hope that does not seem to lead anywhere, in terms of social hierarchies. In spite of committing several crimes, Bellot conveys the idea that the couple is to be acquitted once they decide to return to a law-abiding life, a decision prompted by Domitila's pregnancy. Once the police officers capture the head of the drug-trafficking operation, *Los Tortolitos* are redeemed, and the 'happy ending' offers a glimpse of the possibility that they can start a new life. Thus, nothing has really changed. In line with Bellot's film, other Bolivian filmmakers have also explored the clash between past and modernity and the intersection of urban and indigenous cosmologies.

Evo Pueblo (2007), *Zona Sur* (2009), *Erase una vez en Bolivia/Once upon a Time in Bolivia* (2011) and *Yvy Maraêy: Tierra sin mal/Yvy Maraêy: Land without Evil* (2013), which will be discussed in subsequent chapters, are all examples of this trend. Other films produced in Bolivia and which portray indigenous elements, although to a much lesser extent, include: *Los Andes no creen en Dios/Andes Do Not Believe in God* (2007), *Bicicletas de los Huanca/The Huancas Bicycle* (2007), *Escríbeme postales a Copacabana/Write Me: Postcards to Copacabana* (2009) and *Manuelas, heroínas de la Coronilla/Manuelas, Heroines of Coronilla*, (2012). All these films have in common a desire from mediatized circles to corroborate the significant political value of indigeneity at a national and international level. Up to a point, this return to the country's roots has nevertheless implied reverting to outdated paradigms of representation.

In the case of Colombia, recent films have adopted New Latin American Cinema approaches. These include the use of untrained actors, documentary-inspired techniques and realistic scenarios set in unstaged locations. The importance given to the urban areas might explain why indigenous elements have not been given prime consideration, if compared to narratives taking place in cities like Bogotá or Medellín. A commonality among the selected films is to suggest that indigenous communities inhabit mainly distant areas of Colombia, and that they remain relatively isolated.[8] According to these stories, their seclusion stems not only from the remoteness of the areas where their communities have dwelled for centuries but also to cultural traits, such as language. Although Spanish remains the dominant language, filmmakers have made efforts to recognize the linguistic heritage of the indigenous communities represented in their narratives. Since the urban/indigenous dichotomy seems to determine the linguistic choice, Spanish is the chosen language in most scenes shot in urban settings. Among the filmmakers that have ventured beyond the Colombian metropolises, Ciro Guerra stands out for *Los viajes del viento* (Colombia–Germany–The Netherlands, 2009), Oscar-nominated *El abrazo de la serpiente* (Argentina–Colombia–France–Spain–The Netherlands–Venezuela, 2015) and *Pájaros de verano/Birds of Passage* (2018) (Colombia–Denmark–Mexico), while William Vega is known for *La Sirga* (2012). Vega's work is worth further analysis because it illustrates the ahistorical link filmmakers seem to make between current topographies, extinct documented ethnicities and imagined ancestries. In the case of Colombia, probably related to the system of *resguardos indígenas* (indigenous reserves), there is a notion that specific peripheral regions of the country still operate as embodiments of their indigenous past. Along these lines, Vega's film suggests that the essence of his chosen location extends to modern-day communities living in the area, a connection he epitomizes and traces through the figure of a young girl (see Chapter 4). The aesthetic appraisal of the rural in Colombian cinema seems to be infused with tropes that seek to create an antithesis of what metropolitanism entails.

Unlike Colombia, since the turn of the century, Ecuador has produced visual narratives where indigeneity is posited as an integral, nonetheless subaltern, part of the modern national fabric. Topics such as rural flight, migration to Western countries, homosexuality and corruption are central to films such as *Sara, La Espantapájaros/Sara, The Scarecrow* (2008), *En el nombre de la hija/In the name of the Girl* (2011), *El facilitador* (2013) and *Feriado* (2014). In comparison to the total number of motion pictures produced in the country, indigeneity remains a minor focal point. At present, Ecuadorean film tradition remains heavily influenced and informed by Western canons. Its aspirations to adopt European and North American cinematic repertoires and style explain its reluctance to include indigenous or African cultural elements (Luzuriaga 2014). Sanjinés's efforts to use cinema as a tool to demand justice in the 1970s have shifted paradigms. Ecuadorean cinema today is highly racialized and especially skilful in stressing markers of allegiance and difference. For instance, central to both *El facilitador* and *Feriado* is the internal conflict that upper-class, white adolescents from Quito experience once they come in contact with the Andean world. Although the storylines could not differ more, they do have in common the marked gap that appears to separate non-indigenous from indigenous characters.

In *Feriado*, we follow introverted, well-to-do Juan Pablo (Juan Manuel Arregui), as he spends some days at his uncle Jorge's (Peky Andino) second home in the countryside. It is 1999 and Ecuador is faced with a major banking crisis that might result in the imprisonment and ruin of his uncle, who happens to be implicated in the disappearance of copious quantities of money. The movie explores the conflicting realizations Juan Pablo experiences after meeting Juano (Diego Andrés Paredes), a Kichwa-speaking car mechanic based in a nearby village. Juan Pablo's immediate fascination for Juano is the core of the storyline. But their acquaintanceship and subsequent closeness unmask how different their worlds are. After all, they met when Juano attempted to escape after being caught stealing the hubcaps of one of Don Jorge's cars. Even if we learn that Jorge is responsible for the loss of millions of pesos saved by families like Juano's, the structure of power in place counterbalances their deeds according to different scales.

Director Diego Araujo regards his film as the chronicle of an awakening and the onset of a self-discovery process. By portraying a friendship between Juan Pablo and Juano, Araujo seems to suggest that social inequality does not necessarily pose an obstacle to establishing a bond. A closer look, though, does reveal that throughout this coming-of-age story, several elements are used to remind audiences of the disparities between these two young men. Juan Pablo's inner quietness, epitomized in his passion for poetry, is contrasted with Juano's nonchalant, carefree attitude, even in crucial moments. It is not clear whether their affection is mutual, but the end affirms what audiences foreshadow from the beginning. Their friendship reaches a peak after which there is no point of return. The film leaves many unanswered questions, most importantly, whether Juano is at all gay, or whether he has been all along the *object* of affection of an allegedly superior figure. Ultimately, the narrative is told from Juan Pablo's point of view, and it is through his eyes that viewers contemplate Juano. A notable example is the telephoto shot used to explore the hut where Juano's aunt lives, starting and ending with Juan Pablo. In line with indigenist discourse, Juano is portrayed as subaltern to Juan Pablo. Through imagery of difference and paternalism, *Feriado* presents an asymmetrical visual framing of ethnic and non-indigenous characters. It does so by advancing a position where indigeneity is staged as an amalgam of childlike traits, which include carelessness, innocence and naiveté. The linguistic choice strengthens this parallelism, as the few exchanges in Quechua, accompanied by subtitles, are about clandestine activities, subversion or revenge. Alternatively, in one scene, Juano's older relative uses Quechua to express fascination for Pablo's blue/green eyes, denoting admiration for his ancestry.

The storyline in *El facilitador* is similar, as it tells the story of Elena (María Gracia Omegna), the spoiled daughter of a high-ranking businessman, Miguel (Juan Carlos Terán), who is sent to the countryside to reflect on her abusive use of alcohol and drugs. As this is her grandparents' land, she is not new to the area and soon she reunites with Galo (Marco Bustos), the son of the maid with whom she used to play as a child. Except for being in the same age group, there could not be more differences between them. The tripartite binaries urban/rural, white/indigenous, haves/have-nots become evident in every new discovery cosmopolitan Elena makes about her own life and the challenges Galo's community faces, as in their struggle for access to water. These realizations prompt a change in the young girl, who believes it is her duty to get involved in their cause. Audiences witness how Elena turns into the figure of a superior outsider who feels compelled to stand for those in need. Inevitably, as other core–periphery relations, the missionary attitude is articulated through apparent altruistic actions to save those who are perceived to be incapable of helping themselves. Her position is reminiscent of a Western saviour trying to shield those who, otherwise, could not avoid being exploited and abused.

Galo helps Elena rediscover a hidden Ecuador, ancestral medicines, a cause to fight for and, in many ways, the essence of her roots. Oddly enough, Galo's inconsistent use of Quechua puts forth questions about his cultural background, the dividing lines between linguistic and ethnic realms, and the ambiguities of indigenous youth in rural Ecuador. In doing so, director Victor Aregui revisits the seemingly unresolved question about national identity.[9] *Feriado* and *El Facilitador* critique the fact that the country is harmed by imperialist ideologies and by abusing its indigenous communities, while championing the portrayal of urban, empowered, privileged saviours as a means to resolve the dilemma. These films do not offer new insights to this question or entertain the idea that bottom-up contestation is also an option, reducing the indigenous figures to mere bystanders or onlookers.

In the case of Peru, a long cinematic tradition with a militant undertone seems to have made way for newer formats and approaches. As has been pointed out, international awards and box office records allow one to foresee a productive future for the country's cinematic spaces (Barrow 2018). Since the turn of the century, Peruvian filmmakers have released several feature films, short films and documentaries focusing on indigeneity, many of which have been widely acclaimed, particularly in Western film festivals. The most renowned ones include *Bien esquivo* (2001), *Madeinusa* (2005), *Dioses* (2008), *La teta asustada* (2009), *Climas* (2014) and *Retablo* (Peru, 2017). Yet, while foreign attention might work in favour of a more productive cinematic scene, its impact on the themes, stylistics and filmmakers' approach cannot be ignored.

Director Claudia Llosa stands out not only for her widely acclaimed *Madeinusa* and *La teta asustada* but also for paving the road for other women filmmakers and female-centred narratives in the region, particularly if one bears in mind that Latin America is a continent where distinctive femininities are to be found. Local women live in a continent born out of a mixture of ethnicities (African, European and indigenous). They are conditioned by Catholic values, shadowed by the economic, political and cultural strength of the United States, constrained by patriarchal institutions, and overexposed to Western conventionalities and precepts. They live in male-oriented societies, where gender equality and social inclusion are as recent as the re-establishment of democracies after decades of oppressive regime (Garðarsdóttir 2005). Compared to previous decades, Peruvian narratives produced in the last decade invite viewers to reflect on the role of women on the screen, and certainly behind it.

Llosa's films are somehow reminiscent of *Paloma de Papel/Paper Dove* in the centrality that childhood plays in the narratives. In this film by Fabrizio Aguilar, Juan's childhood (Antonio Callirgos) is interrupted by the social unrest caused by Sendero Luminoso during the 1980s. After discovering that his stepfather, Fermín (Aristóteles Picho), is involved in his father's murder, Juan is forced to join the guerrilla movement in order to secure his silence. Sitting in a bus headed to his hometown, grown-up Juan recounts the horrors he experienced as an eleven-year-old boy recruited into a criminal organization and later incarcerated for his participation. Embodied in an urban Spanish-speaking protagonist, *Paloma de Papel* brings to the screen the dramatic experience of Andean Quechua-speaking communities (Barrow 2014). The devastating consequences of Sendero Luminoso's policy – mainly recruiting indigenous children – are narrated by using flashbacks of special moments Juan spent with his friends Rosita (Anaís Padilla) and Pacho (Angel Josue Rojas Huaranga). The film resonated with national and international audiences as it touched upon one of the most challenging times in recent Peruvian history. Its popularity has been linked to its temporality, approach and articulation of a child's perspective about a complicated and traumatic episode, refusing to let this passage of Peruvian history to fade away into oblivion (Mandler 2012; Barrow 2014).

In terms of representation, however, there are principally two aspects that need to be addressed. On the one hand, the unquestionability of the figure of a child, especially because there is evidence that the forcibly recruited children came mostly from vulnerable Andean villages. On the other hand, since Juan is presented as a child, his condition as an infant seemingly prevails over his intersectional position as an indigenous minor within an isolated war-ridden community. The film succeeds in avoiding a recriminating tone but does not retain the same perspective when approaching Juan as an adult. As a grown-up, he is presented in terms of his ethnic background and he is notably portrayed as a distant '"otro" (guerillero forastero)' ['other' (outsider militant)] (Ferreira 2015: 159). Thus, indigeneity is rendered as a symbolic notion that alternates and can be manoeuvred accordingly. As such, the film mirrors the convention of voicing the plight of Andean communities and epitomizes their past and present on their behalf, but mostly excluding their points of view. This can be a particularly debatable position in the case of narratives that involve extreme cases of violence and brutality.

Two other recurrent tropes are noticeable in the portrayal of the nation's ethnic composition. Firstly, the exaltation of elements that are considered autochthonous and where the main premise is that the mestizo essence is the desirable one, but that idealized indigenous elements lie at the core.[10] Secondly, indigenist trends in Peruvian cinema have stood out for underlining the telluric condition of the Andean communities; indigenous and land are regarded as synonyms. *Bien esquivo* (2001), *Dioses* (2008), *La teta asustada* (2009), *Climas* (2014) and *Altiplano* (2009), for example, tend to suggest that indigeneity is intrinsically linked to a specific topography. Conversely, as mentioned earlier, Llosa's *Madeinusa* (2005) stands out for inviting audiences to consider the life of an Andean girl anxious to experience a life away from her birthplace.

In the case of Venezuela, a fixation on equating indigenous peoples with their land is also present in the three films considered in this study: *Cenizas eternas* (2011), *El regreso/The Return* (2013) and *Dauna: Lo que lleva el río* (2015). Even if most of Venezuela's productions focusing on native populations are made by indigenist directors, most of these filmmakers do not belong to the communities they seek to portray. This translates into narratives where the main argument is that these are isolated communities, in need of protection, ruled by traditions deeply rooted in their social fabric, and vulnerable to an insuppressibly malignant modernity that threatens their existence. A recurrent theme, as in other films from the Andean region, is that indigenous populations are mainly secluded in inaccessible geographies far away from urban areas, even if there is plenty of evidence of a large immigration influx to the cities. Many of these productions contest the stereotypical *good savage*, a recurring ethnotype in renderings of indigeneity, but tend to highlight a link between supernatural forces and ancient wisdom. Ideologically, Venezuelan films are indicative of political positions that hold the state responsible for grievous breaches against ethnic communities, but portray the indigenous figure as static.

For instance, *Cenizas eternas* (2011), directed by Margarita Cadenas, depicts the Yanomami people in a predominantly positive light, but focuses on the centrality of the non-indigenous figure accidentally discovering the existence of a parallel reality within her country. The story revolves around a daughter, Elena (Danay García), who decides to travel to the Orinoco River region to search for her mother, Ana (Patricia Velásquez). Elena is convinced that her mother survived the accident where she allegedly died more than four decades ago according to the local authorities. With the support of her aunt, she ventures into the jungle to find the truth. Ana is alive and ever since her disappearance, she has dwelled among the natives of the jungle, under the name *Napoyomi*. The film highlights how the Yanomami have 'saved and nurtured' (Rist 2014: 239) Ana and how they have lessons to teach non-indigenous people about hospitality, tolerance and respect for nature. While the first half of the film draws attention to the epistemologies of the natives, the second half considers the experience of foreigners in unknown territories dominated by autochthonous populations. *Cenizas eternas* conceptualizes the position that indigeneity and modernity do not need to be incompatible and irreconcilable terms. A problematic aspect in the narrative is, nevertheless, the portrayal of the Yanomami as an undifferentiated collectivity while Ana's experience is presented from different angles. The interweaving and juxtaposition of gender and ethnicity, explored mainly from a metropolitan perspective, is another questionable aspect.

Director Cadenas does not explore Yanomami womanhood to any great extent as the film only delves into the position of an urban Venezuelan female vis-à-vis an unknown civilization in a secluded geography. Since most Venezuelan filmmakers are men, *Cenizas eternas* is a noteworthy contribution to national cinema, particularly because it offers a feminine perspective. Artistically, like many other films produced in Venezuela, it features a cast that includes untrained actors and uses real locations as scenic backdrops. The originality of the narrative lies in the involvement of the Yanomami community, both from a histrionic and linguistic standpoint, and the inclusion of several elements of their culture as part of the story. In its idealization of the natives, the film has commonalities with other motion pictures from the Andean region that are reminiscent of indigenist cinema from earlier decades. Although it is important to distinguish between cultural and political indigenism, the former focuses on questions of origin and heritage while the latter addresses questions of land. Both stances make demands on behalf of oppressed groups. A debatable aspect of an indigenist agenda is that its cultural formats do not necessarily contribute to close the perceived gap between indigenous and non-indigenous societies (Coronado 2009; D'Argenio 2020). In the case of the selected films, the narratives have in common an outspoken desire to denounce the social exclusion endured by natives but without presenting contemporary indigenous peoples as the desirable subjectivity. The elements that indigenist paradigms do seek to elevate are the emblematic, ancient and idealized identities of long-gone ancient civilizations. In essence, in indigenist and mestizaje discourses, 'the *mestizo* is the iconic citizen' (Canessa 2012: 244), not the indigenous one.

Throughout the Andean region, recent cinematic productions are therefore evidence that indigenist cultural products, instead of drawing closer past with present or idealization with reality, and closing the breach between them in the process, mark the distinctions between them. Through various formats, the cinematic approach to indigeneity across the Andean region is inflected with indigenist imagery. Visually, stories are conceived from a sympathetic viewpoint that nevertheless tend to result in films that make a clear distinction between the desirable mestizo and the ethnotype of the idealized earth-bound, rural and unequivocally 'wise Indian'.

Brazil: Visual exoticism

Researching Brazilian film production demands considering the importance that the creation of the *mestiço* figure, as a state ideology, has had in the national psyche. The notion that Brazilians are the products of combining African, European and Native American physical and cultural traits has been central to the genesis of nationhood. Indigenous ethnotypes have been focal points in the literary scene and also in films, as a parallel figure to the emblematic, modern and progressive Brazilian nation (Pacheco de Oliveira 2005; Flores, 2013). In general terms, indigeneity has mainly been approached through tropicalist ideologies that uphold the notion that *Índio* (indigenous) and *selva* (jungle) are synonymous terms. Following Eurocentric paradigms, in modern times, Brazil has become a key figure of the decontextualized vilification of the tropics in Western(ized) imaginaries (Shohat and Stam 2012). At its core, its main point of reference is the differentiation between those emerging from the tropics and those who trace their ancestry to more 'quotidian' places (i.e. Europe). Still today, native peoples are freely associated with stereotypical visual representations of nude bodies displaying connections to archaic lifestyles and wild landscapes.

In a country with a relatively productive cinematic scene, the number of fictional narratives where indigenous themes play a central role is quite low. There is also evidence of a reluctance to touch upon the topic of the *Índios*. A long history of oppression and extermination explains why the matter remains quite sensitive. After the turn of the century, six films stand out for drawing attention to indigenous themes, mainly though from a historical perspective: *Brava gente brasileira* (2001), *Caramuru* (2001), *Tainá - Uma Aventura na Amazônia / Tainá: An Adventure in the Amazon* (2000), *A terra dos homens vermelhos* (Italy–Brazil, 2008), *Xingu* (2012) and *Antes o Tempo Não Acabava* (2016). With the exception of *A terra dos homens vermelhos* and *Antes o Tempo Não Acabava*, the films resort to a temporal distance in order to explore indigeneity without problematizing the current situation of the native communities and their struggles for recognition and land rights. The sense of historicity chosen by filmmakers has allowed them to construct stories that resonate with modern audiences, both at a national and international level. Yet, they tend to imply that social critique is directed at past events, events it is now impossible to correct.

This is best exemplified by the Brazilian-Portuguese co-production *Hans Staden* (1999), directed by Luiz Alberto Pereira and released right before the turn of the century. Central to the story are the chronicles of the German soldier

Hans Staden during his forced stay in Brazil in the sixteenth century. Even though the viewpoint seems to advocate for the position of the natives being colonized, it truly champions a Eurocentric approach to history (Da Fonseca 2010). The vulnerability of either extinct or static native communities evokes the aspiration that audiences are to understand the film in a way similar to how they approach relics in a museum. Along this line, *Xingu* (2012) revolves around the creation of the Parque Nacional do Xingu (Xingu National Park) by virtue of the Villas-Boas' brothers, and how their efforts contributed to the preservation of a considerable number of Amazonian indigenous groups. The film manages to transmit a message of awareness about the perils faced by natives in isolated areas. By conveying the idea that only urban, white, European-looking men could have been up to the task, it nevertheless questions the agency of those being saved. *Xingu* chronicles how these three brothers became key figures in the establishment of protected zones. It is a historical account of the processes by which the first priority conservation areas emerged across the Amazon basin. Besides the white explorers, *Xingu* is not particularly accurate in representing ethnicities. As a matter of fact, it exemplifies a long-established Brazilian practice of presenting a 'mestiço actor representing the Indian' (Stam 1997: 9). Various dichotomies are central to the story (e.g. mainstream/exotic, European power/indigenous vulnerability, saviours/victims and metropolitan/tropical). Accidental or not, the film resorts to exotifications, particularly tangible in each scene where an individual (white) Self stands out among a collective tribal (indigenous) Other. For instance, the first attempts by the Villas-Boas brothers to make contact with the local natives are arguably tainted by their mistrustful spears and apprehensive attitude. It is evident that the story is told from the perspective of an explorer who fails to understand why he is regarded as an intruder.

In this sense, bewitching 'Indians', as they are referred to in the dialogues, are not necessarily portrayed negatively, *only* as a tropical Other that needs to be understood and, as the film unfolds, saved. In order to bolster an issue difficult to address, director Cao Hamburger presents a story from a temporal and geographical distance. *Xingu* transports us to the early 1940s when Cláudio (João Miguel), Leonardo (Caio Blat) and Orlando (Felipe Camargeo) ventured into the Roncador-Xingu expedition. This military quest, commissioned by the government in order to map out the strategic possibilities of the region, is documented by the Villas-Boas brothers in a log-book known as *A marcha para o oeste* (*The East-Bound Trail*). Furthermore, historic events, such as the construction of the first airstrip in the Amazon basin and the secret plans of the government to build a military base, serve as backdrop to the story that spans over three decades. The historical drama makes it clear from the beginning that the focal point is not the natives, but how three benevolent outsiders can change the course of their lives, arguably for the better. As might be expected, the recognition of the linguistic heritage of the portrayed communities is confined to few exchanges in Tupi. It is not evident whether Hamburger intends for the utterances to be unintelligible, or to replicate a long-standing tradition of using Amerindian languages as background sound, especially because translations are not always offered.

Each of the main characters epitomizes distinctive attitudes and sensitivities that indigenous communities prompt among Brazilians. For instance, Cláudio believes that entering the territory occupied by the natives, even with the goal of 'helping' them, exposes these fragile communities to unnecessary dangers. In effect, in the film, a type of flu brought by the Villas-Boas brothers almost caused the decimation of one of the communities that hosted them. At a certain point, the conflict between the indigenous societies and the white man becomes a central part of the narrative. Orlando is then portrayed as the mediator between authorities and the affected ethnic groups, always bearing in mind that the power structures are not balanced. The film does not elaborate on why and how the Villas-Boas brothers managed to become so prominent and influential in the Brazilian political scene, but it highlights how their perseverance led to the creation of a protected area in 1961. Except for Chief Izaquiri (Tapaié Waurá), the involvement of the natives in the creation of the protected area is not given prime consideration. Beyond the lack of agency that the film endows its indigenous characters, Hamburger is uncritical about the losses that impel Brazil to establish an area where indigenous communities are concentrated, regardless of their mutual affiliation. In general terms, *Xingu* has certain pedagogic value, and due to the credibility of the scenery and the inclusion of known figures from Brazilian history, it resembles an ethnographic film at times, rather than a biographical film.

Comparatively, directors Fabio Baldo and Sergio Andrade also recur to documentary techniques, blended with an anthropological and intersectional optics in *Antes o Tempo Não Acabava*. Released in 2016, in the film, Baldo and Andrade explore the challenges faced by Anderson (Anderson Tikuna), a young Saterê trapped between his difficult family situation, the beliefs stablished by his Amazonia-based community and his sexuality.

Paradoxically, either home-brewed ethnographies (foreign-funded or not) or external impressions conceived for Western audiences seem to show recurrent themes when approaching Brazilian native communities. Symptoms of an underlying tendency to tropicalize the notion of indigeneity in Brazilian cinema have not necessarily been influenced by newly emerging trends. National identity resides on selective inclusiveness of certain non-European elements as engrained constituents (Signorelli Heise 2012). The metropolitan optic weighs heavily on local directors, connoted by older models and canons. The individual-based approach seen in recent Brazilian films, for instance, has not successfully replaced the custom of linking indigeneity and collectivity. Except for *Brava Gente Brasileira*, the general approach is that indigeneity is subaltern, and easily reduced to another peculiarity endemic of territories with unconquerable nature. The secrets behind their grandiosity seem to lie behind a cultural and epistemic threshold that filmmakers do not seem to be interested to cross. Language is presented as a marker of interaction, but not necessarily of cultural intelligibility. Rather, Amerindian linguistic traits operate as folkloric additions aimed to further the sense of otherness. Among the exceptions, *A terra dos homens vermelhos* stands out for naturalizing and equating Guaraní with Portuguese. Two ambivalent systems allow their users to understand one another. Even if a predominantly Western optics dominates the narrative, the inclusion of the indigenous language conveys a sense of realism, rather than staged exoticism.

Conclusively, imagery devoted to presenting Brazil's native legacy gives the impression of being inflected by a tendency to do so in past tense. The rationale is likely an attempt to avoid shedding light on developments, such as the ones in 2020, even if this would contribute to advance a deeper understanding of what it entails to be *Índio* in Brazil today. In the present moment of Brazilian history, being native means facing confiscation of their land, experiencing reduction of their dwelling areas and having limited access to resources.

Southern Cone: Democracy and paternalism

In the case of Argentina, the absence of portrayals where aboriginal cultures are included has been linked to the reduced survival of indigenous groups. With regard to Chile, there is reluctance to approach narratives that raise questions about historical processes, or that contain social critique that aligns with Mapuche standpoints. With a limited film scene, Paraguay is slowly freeing itself from a motionless state, while no films concerning indigeneity have been produced in Uruguay after the turn of the century. Almost certainly, this has to do with the extinction of the local indigenous population. At large, measurable and memorable shifts in the political and social climate of the Southern Cone have unfolded in a considerable number of stories featuring, either partially or centrally, the various indigenous peoples of Argentina, Chile and Paraguay.

Symptomatic of a long-established cinematic tradition, Argentine cinema is prominent not only for its resilience, diversity and responsiveness to new trends and themes but also for its devotion to the notion of contemporaneity. In the last decades, local filmmakers have reaffirmed their commitment to innovative, artistically compelling and commercially competitive formats (Piedras 2012; Tompkins 2018). At the crossroads of a burgeoning need to create newer understandings of national identity with an optics heavily influenced by global tendencies, Argentine filmmakers have gradually directed their attention to indigenous themes. Newer visual reflections with traces of indeterminacy carry with them emotional connotations that question older prevailing approaches. On the surface, younger generations of Argentine directors avoid mimicking explicit denunciations of the social disparities of indigenous communities or calling for assertive action. Indeed, many of them claim not to be interested in politics (Podalsky 2011). Yet, there is a tendency to reconsider the centrality of rural societies and regional realities, as opposed to cosmopolitan, European identities. An increased preoccupation with the peripheral areas of the country denotes a revived interest in those most affected by social inequality and unfavourable state policies.

Representation is in itself an externalization of assumed hierarchical orders, often with cultural, economic and political undertones. Indigeneity-themed films remain few compared to the number of Argentine cinematic productions released each year. It is not axiomatic to find films set in regions such as Salta or Patagonia. At times, recent portrayals of indigenous characters tend to give the impression that it is almost by accident that filmmakers notice that the Argentine social fabric includes non-European ancestry. In varying ways, indigenous elements are included as part of the non-urban *landscape*. To a certain extent, the roles assigned to ethnically defined characters reflect the asymmetric representations of European, mestizo and indigenous social groups. Abusive white employers, mestizo bystanders and indigenous ethnotypical figures as mistreated serving staff epitomize society's attitudes, disparities, tension and the sense of displacement of disfranchised communities. Set in isolated locations, the aporetic dialogues illustrate the filmmaker's need to make discrete statements about the discrimination and abuse native communities face in Argentina, particularly in small villages. Opposing the urban, where limits are defined by restrictive codes of what and who belongs or what and who does not, the rural is presented as an open space where abusive behaviour appears to be less monitored, policed and denounced. In contemporary films, the spotlight is thus not only on the reconfiguration of spaces and borders but also on the use of the camera as an instrument to pose questions regarding authority, agency, otherness and violence in its various forms (Pinazza 2011). Ideologically, these are films that champion democratic views (all subjects are equally part of Argentina) but paternalistic attitudes (one subject speaks on behalf of another subject).

From the turn of the century, indigenous characters are the central figures in films such as *El niño pez* (Argentina–Paraguay, 2009), *Tiempos menos modernos* (Argentina–Chile, 2011), *Cassandra* (Argentina, 2012) and *Nosilatiaj. La belleza* (2012), while other narratives approach ethnicity as a subtheme, as in *La Ciénaga/The Swamp* (2001), *La niña santa/The Holy Girl* (2004) and *Zama* (Argentina, 2017), or as important as Eurocentric elements in films like *El destino* (2006). Through a myriad of configurations, these motion pictures address a question put forth since the foundation of Argentina: 'How is it possible for indigenous people to be considered "first Argentineans" (or Argentineans at all) by those who believe, simultaneously, that Argentina was born in the 19th century, precisely through the foundation of a national state project that did not include them and deemed their destruction necessary?' (Carretero and Kriger 2011: 183). Expanding upon this question, it is worth pondering how contemporary films demonstrate that imagery of 'Indians' reflects the creators behind them more than those perceived to be represented.

In the case of *La Ciénaga* (2001), by director Lucrecia Martel, the indigenous is epitomized in the figure of Isabel (Andrea Lopez), a domestic servant who is humiliated and constantly mistreated by her white employer, Mecha (Graciela Borges). In her powerful position, Mecha is unapologetic in her attitudes and sensitivities about Isabel's ethnic background, and in doing so, she fails to realize the reproachful and unacceptable nature of her behaviour. Beyond its artistic qualities, *La Ciénaga* has the merit of exposing a problem the director has openly discussed. Martel sheds light on the various mechanisms through which upper classes in the northern region of Salta regard indigenous workforce as commodities. She has stated a desire to expose the state of confinement of indigenous citizens and the ways in which criollo society violates their rights, either by pretending they are invisible or by assuming they are born to fill in specific low-paying occupations. The narrative does not stand out for exposing an unknown side of contemporary Argentina but for highlighting how problematic it is to assume that the current state of affairs is natural, logical and moral. Martel's work confirms the contingency and self-scepticism of New Argentine Cinema (Page 2009).

Strategically, *La Ciénaga* renders visible what daily routine rituals in their monotony actually conceal. The quietness of the story offers a glimpse into a scarred past that is intertwined with the debatable present: attested, for instance, by the way Joaquín (Diego Baenas) insults the indigenous for sleeping with dogs, implying they constitute a sexually deviant Other (Martin 2016). The story shows signs of intersectionality of *yesterday* and *today*, but also of attitudes of fatigue and desertion (Amado 2004). Martel might imply that Argentina struggles with a past that it has confronted (the dictatorship), while it is still reluctant to recognize a present that needs to be addressed (ethnic discrimination). *La Ciénaga* offers an illusionary reticent world, while it resorts to subtle outcries of consternation that seek to expose hypocrisy and racism. The centrality of silence is also perceivable in the limited dialogues allocated to the indigenous characters. These are mainly short exchanges in Spanish with their abusive employers, and slightly more extended conversations with well-intentioned characters. It is mainly through the use of language that spectators learn about the employer's dismissive attitudes towards native communities.

A sense of superiority is also present in the characterization of Don Diego de Zama (Daniel Giménez Cacho), the main character in Martel's successful attempt to transpose Antonio di Benedetto's novel (*Zama*, 1956) on to the screen (*Zama*, 2017). A profoundly frustrated server of the Spanish Crown posted and forgotten in an outer rim of the empire offers plenty of opportunities to reflect on Latin America's hybrid roots. It is 1790 and in line with ideologies of his time, Don Diego publicly spurns native women in an attempt to affirm his social position as honorific European, even though he has a child with one of them. In her own words, Martel uses his personal crisis to echo the notion that 'identity is a trap' (Lerer 2017: para. 9), a consistent trope in her films.

Effectively, as *La Ciénaga* and *Zama*, *Nosilatiaj. La belleza* (2012) by Daniela Seggiaro advances the notion that indigeneity in Argentine rural areas is disturbingly, but easily linked to servility. This is the story of young Yolanda (Rosmeri Segundo) who is employed in a home where she is treated with disdain due to her ethnicity. The climax point is reached when she is tricked to sacrifice her precious hair (an important symbol within the Wichí culture) so that Antonela (Camila Rogmanolo), her employer's daughter, can benefit from a set of hair extensions for her fifteen-year birthday celebration. The film suggests that there are two versions of womanhood, presenting evidence that indigenous women are subaltern to mestizo/European females. After all, the paternalistic treatment is expressed through an attitude of condescension and loftiness. Another key element is the fabled conflict of two allegedly different worlds that Seggiaro disputes by showing that both young girls share more commonalities than divergences. Even though the film offers an anthropological reflection of the power structures that society has established, it does so by favouring the view that indigenous communities are violated and abused. *Nosilataj. La belleza* is based on real-life events that took place within a Wichí community visited by the filmmaker's mother (Seggiaro 2012).

At the same time, Seggiaro invites the viewer to reflect upon the challenges faced by this oppressed community from a cultural, ecological, economic and social perspective. Probably inspired by ethnographic concerns, one of the goals of the film was to include the language Wichí Lhamtes to denounce the lack of awareness about the linguistic diversity of the country but also the beauty of variety. Seggiaro exemplifies the receptive approach of a younger generation of Argentine directors turning their attention to indigenous themes. As indicated by the title of the film, beauty plays a significant role, specifically how it is understood by Eurocentric and Wichí societies. For the Wichí, it is represented through beliefs, convictions and nature, while the criollo family gives importance to external acknowledgement and superficiality. This is best exemplified by Yolanda's grief after her tresses were cut, contrasted by Antonela's sense of accomplishment – void of cultural meaning – after learning the superposed hair would add to her sense of security during the celebration. It is in the *quinceañera* party where Yolanda also learns that she has been deceived. In line with paternalistic views (adults trick minors), deceit is a key element in the representations of indigeneity. It is a recurrent theme and strategy to criticize or allude to the trope that natives can easily be deluded, or that they have simplistic goals.

Hence, the complexity of the representational axis in which indigeneity is positioned within Argentine cinema is similar to the confrontation modern Argentines have understanding their own identity. On the one hand, democratic principles demand acknowledgement of cultural diversity, and on the other hand, nationalistic discursive ideals ooze admiration for the builders of the nation. As subsequent chapters will explore in more detail, Argentine cinema stands out for its heterogeneity (Varas and Dash 2000). Its impressions of mainstream society, but also its approach to indigenous groups, are informed by a problematic, self-doubting optic on what and how the nation is to be understood. Spanish operates as a common element that unifies this nation, and except for unclear background voices or very brief dialogues, the above-mentioned films do not include extended dialogues in Amerindian languages. In most cases, subtitles are not offered.

In neighbouring Chile, national cinema is generally observed to put emphasis on films that highlight or characterize processes of democratization, or stories that offer spaces to explore processes in general. Aware of its insularity when compared to hegemonic centres of production, local imagery seeks mainly to offer alternatives that show self-respectfully their urban spaces, desires, resources and fantasies. The principal question is how this approach accommodates the notion of indigeneity. For instance, as a reaction to the conflictive relation Mapuche groups have with the Chilean state, they have become targets of sustained vilification across media spaces. An important aspect to consider is that the local cinematic tradition stands out for being conservative, both thematically and artistically. In the last years, recent identity-related explosions have subtly introduced new topics. Gradually, scant attention to peripheral realities and monochromatic depictions has been replaced by diversity-oriented narratives. Specifically, indigenous themes are central in *Play* (2005), *Alicia en el país* (2008), *Könun Wenu: La entrada al cielo* (2010), *El verano de los peces voladores* (2013) and *Las niñas Quispe* (2013). This approach might signal a novel short-lived trend, or an attempt to provide a nuanced and multilayered insight into the lives of indigenous segments of society.

Directed by Alicia Scherson, *Play* explores the life of Cristina (Viviana Herrera), the caregiver of a terminally sick Hungarian émigré who develops a curious relation with the contents of a briefcase she finds by accident. Tracing the origin of the alluring item, she gradually becomes obsessed with Tristan (Andrés Ulloa), the affluent former owner. The recently divorced architect ignores that he has become the object of Cristina's delusion and compulsion. In line with these observations, according to Scherson, *Play* is about reclaiming spaces. Cristina has emigrated from southern Chile and does not intend to go back to her hometown, a key aspect that denotes her power of self-determination. Interestingly, her attitudes echo the behaviour of Irene (Aline

Küppenheim), who refuses, also in accordance with her own conviction, to stay married to Tristán. *Play* weaves a narrative around agentic permutations, triviality and otherwise insignificant people and ordinary places. Scherson has noted that the film explores the need and desire of *Santiaguinos* (inhabitant of Santiago) to emigrate somewhere else, mainly because the metropolis already belongs to them, while Cristina is a newcomer (Greene and Scherson 2005). The protagonist is depicted as a lonely but never self-doubting woman who blocks her outer world and its noises through the use of her prominent headphones, while she explores and makes Santiago hers. Even her romantic relationship with Manuel (Juan Pablo Quezada), a gardener in service of the municipality, is to be determined according to her own pace. Artistically, the notion of identity is transmitted by the portrayals of a bustling but apathetic metropolis, and the efforts of its citizens to reclaim the uniqueness of their identities, for instance, through tattoos and other signs of self-chosen identity.

Scherson (2005) asserts that 'los gringos le fuerzan mucho a que ella es mapuche, y de ahí le dan lectura política, de la invisibilidad de los indígenas en la ciudad' [Americans/Europeans insist in highlighting the fact that she is Mapuche and hence they read the film from a political perspective, about the invisibility of the indigenous in the city]. She emphatically explains this is not the case. Yet, Cristina's Mapuche background problematizes the sense of alterity and power structures the story seems to invert. As findings from *Stereotypes about Mapuches: A Recent Evolution* indicate, many Chileans perceive Mapuche communities as societies prone to hostility and conflict. *Play* recurs to the Mapuche ethnotype of a warrior, fond of martial arts, stalking Tristan and Irene, in similar ways, as the figure of the indigenous hovers around Chilean self-identity. Music and Japanese videogames are Cristina's tools to playfully detach from her daily life. The question that emerges in light of these comments is to what extent she needs to refract her own experience as Mapuche to accommodate the Santiago dream into her life. Even if, according to Scherson, inattention to indigenous groups in the city is not a key theme in *Play*, it is worth observing how well the film registers the urban Mapuche practice of concealing their identity. This is, of course, a mechanism to cope with discrimination, ultimately an ethnicity-related dilemma.

In spite of valid attempts to *normalize* the notion of indigeneity in Chilean cinema, most notably through the vindication of agency, there are plenty of examples of marginalization and subalternity in contemporary portrayals. Since precariousness is entwined with signs of economic dispossession and symbolic profligacy, indigenous themes are approached with caution, but they are acknowledged. As ensuing chapters will explore, recent Chilean films have faithfully translated into spaces that offer reflections of the country's diversity and insist on the importance of including indigenous themes in national cinema.

Approaching Paraguayan films, there is a sense that a challenging climate for cultural endeavours has resulted in limited presence of cinema produced in the country, or directed by local filmmakers. As Leen (2013) observes, Paraguay was 'culturally and economically marginalised for much of the twentieth century, with the result that it has virtually no presence at all in the realm of cinema' (156). The recurrent appearance of the country as point of reference, for example, *El niño pez*, discussed in Chapter 5, as intersectional fringe space in *Guaraní* (Paraguay–Argentina 2015), or as main location in *Hamaca Paraguaya* (2006), provides reason to be hopeful. The three films have in common to pay special attention to the linguistic dynamics of the country, or how they perceive it to be. The unique case of Guaraní, an Amerindian language spoken by around 80 per cent of a nation with less than 2 per cent of indigenous population, is indeed akin to a paradox.[11] Cinema registers the complexities of linguistic praxis in line with the imaginaries at play. As it appears, Paraguayan filmmakers include Guaraní as part of the linguistic realm of their films, seeking to capture its idiosyncratic character, as opposed to non-Paraguayan directors.

In the microscopic reading of a thriving market in Asunción, Juan Carlos Maneglia in *7 Cajas/7 Boxes* (Paraguay, 2012), for instance, includes Guaraí, along with Spanish and Korean, as part of everyday life. In Maneglia's 'high-paced mix of thriller and noir that incorporates local accents and locales' (Falicov 2019: 75), languages are hands-on tools for interaction. Films *about* Paraguay but conceived *outside* Paraguay approach Guaraní differently, mainly because they show a tendency to imply that the terms Paraguay, Guaraní and indigenous are synonyms. One could argue that filmmakers are remarkably prescient or overtly reductionist for exotifying the linguistic heritage of the country. In the context of linguistic hegemonies and the imagined values attached to languages, it is not surprising that Paraguay is regarded as a synthesis of an imagined geography dominated by pre-Columbian traditions that are promoted through the use of a non-European language. In many ways, previously distorted or perhaps doubly voided idealizations about ethnic groups might account for the role of Guaraní in the creation of Paraguayan indigenous ethnotypes. In transnational productions, the Amerindian linguistic heritage of the country renders it ethnically more *indigenous*. There are thus discernible similarities in the portrayals of indigenous societies retaining their native languages and a non-indigenous nation preserving a non-European language. The relation between linguistic considerations and the construction of the notion of indigeneity in Paraguayan films and the rest of the region is the subject of study in the next chapter.

Conclusion

Five geopolitical subdivisions have been observed based on cultural affinities, historical processes and production practices: Andean region (Bolivia, Colombia, Ecuador, Peru and Venezuela), Brazil, Central America (Costa Rica, Guatemala and Puerto Rico), Southern Cone region (Argentina, Chile and Paraguay) and Mexico. Most of the films selected for analysis from each country share the common denominator of having indigenous characters playing a leading role. These are titles primarily conceived by urban filmmakers and prominent for having had an impact beyond their countries of production. In Central America, a common feature of Guatemalan films is to depict the disparities faced by indigenous communities at a social, economic and political level. As in the past, the approach of Mexican films focusing on native groups is illuminated by indigenist ideologies. The ethnic diversity and prolific cinematic industry of the country has positioned it as a point of reference for local and global audiences. Two films in particular, *El Violín* and *Corazón del Tiempo*, raise questions about the celebration of indigenous resistance and Indianist attitudes. In general terms, Mexican directors tend to romanticize, but respectfully pay homage to communities rarely represented in other local media outlets.

In South America, across the Andean region, contemporary films mirror not only a long-established convention of social critique but also a tendency to present indigenous legacy as non-standard, foreign or even aberrant (e.g. *Madeinusa*). In Bolivia, local directors focus on the discordance between urban and rural contexts, and tradition vis-à-vis modernity. As in the past, national cinema mirrors the political value of ethnic identity, group affiliation and linguistic heritage, in all aspects of daily life. Similarly, in Ecuadorean films, much greater emphasis is now placed on the interrelation between indigenous and non-indigenous modus vivendi. In contrast, Colombian and Venezuelan filmmakers depict indigenous elements and characters as part of a parallel and distant reality. Isolated locations serve often as context for narratives where modernity is presented as a threat to cultural legacy and identity. This overarching theme is also found in some Peruvian films. Yet, most Lima-based directors opt for either narratives that underline the perceived telluric nature of Andean societies, or storylines that insist on an ethnicity-based hierarchy (i.e. mestizo characters are the preferred centre, but indigenous characters are the idealized periphery). In contemporary Brazilian cinema, recurrent tropicalist ideologies inform and define the portrayal of native societies in fiction. Exoticism, fabulism and primitivism are common tropes in recent films – not surprisingly – unanimously set in secluded parts of the unhospitable Amazon basin. Geographical considerations are also important referents in Argentine, Chilean and Paraguayan films. Whereas Argentine indigeneity-oriented films bear the stylist earmarks of ethnographical, perspectivist and paternalistic documentation, Chilean fiction politicizes the inclusion of Mapuche characters and epistemologies.

3

Lexis: Portrayals of linguistic topologies

Films that travel internationally and include indigenous languages are the first cultural artefacts/conveyors of Amerindian linguistic heritage that reach corners of the globe far away from Latin America. Most likely, the first movement of languages outside the region probably occurs through media and itinerant cultural artefacts. In positive ways, inclusion of indigenous languages in global mediascapes is a game-changing trend, as it contributes to linguistic revitalization projects, and the archival preservation of languages at risk of extinction. Conversely, the development in the last two decades in films, from an imagological perspective, prompts questions about the use of language as a social marker in the (re)presentations of identities, creating in the process linguistic ethnotypes. In this sense, as a medium of diffusion and circulation of ideas, films can be considered as platforms for the dissemination of linguistic stereotypes. A review of the role played by linguistic contrivances in the creation of any cultural artefact (i.e. films) ultimately becomes a discourse about the power structures behind the users of that language. In general terms, a major part of the cultural legacy of a community rests in their linguistic legacy, not only because it serves as an element of consensus and unification but because it reveals sensitivities. In the cinematic world, language can be used to denote, intensify, expand, confirm or foreshadow internal traits of characters or to infer reflections on power, status, difference and otherness (within and between groups). In films aligned with Western cinematic conventions, language has been entwined as an important marker of indigeneity (Carreño 2006). As such, it also operates as a token of authenticity and realism. With these considerations in mind, the first section of this chapter discusses the relation between linguistic realities, cinematic (re)presentation and framing through language, while the second section reviews the use of linguistic strategies in the quest for creating what are perceived to be authentic narratives.

Accented inclusion and vocative framing

After the introduction of sound, inclusion of language allowed for new possibilities of storytelling and strategies to use linguistic cues as part of the narrative. Silence and explanatory intertitles were replaced by the advantages of dialogues. Voices became sources of information not only about the storylines but also about the identity of the performers and narrators. Cinema was not able to mute languages, dialects and sociolects any longer. On the contrary, films became amplifiers of the cultural, political and social reality of the linguistic communities depicted in them. The nexus between images and sounds in media formats is complex, multilayered and symbiotic, nonetheless, in films, precisely because even silence has a meaning audiences recognize. Indigeneity is cinematically presented and represented in biased and subjective ways, and therefore is visually framed. Simultaneously, it is characterized and expressed through sounds that are equally biased and unneutral. Language in films, I argue, is vocatively framed.

While visuals have the capacity of erasing a sense of doubt about the (in)tangibility of a rumour, controversy or myth, images are convincing, seductive and polyvalent as they have many meanings, and are open for interpretation. Negating or opposing the veracity of images is difficult as they are not immediately assumed to be illusions or fabricated lies (half-truths). Visual framing revolves around the manipulation of images to focus public attention in a specific direction or to imply and emphasize connections that eventually convey a message or an idea. This framing happens through the deployment of cosmetic strategies (i.e. rendering attractive specific aspects, such as nature in *La Sirga*), aesthetic decisions (i.e. selecting the aspects that as a whole transmit the desired meaning, such as oblivion in *El destino*), enhancement (i.e. underlining aspects that contextualize an image, such as inclusion of kitsch elements in *La teta asustada*) and resonance (i.e. including aspects that validate the message that the image intends to express, such as the diaries in *La Distancia*). When language is added, framing becomes a vocative strategy that builds on descriptiveness (i.e. the capacity of the mono-/dialogues to narrate what is being seen, such as explaining the role of each character in *Könun Wenu*), relationality (i.e. formulating the links between the image, meanings and sounds, such as the dialogues between the workers of the factory in *Traspatio*), convertibility (i.e. turning linguistic codes into stimuli that reinforce the images being seen, such as the noises of the television in *La Tirisia*) and purposiveness (i.e. the capacity of framing through the symbolic inclusion or exclusion of language, such as the use of English in *También la lluvia*). Regardless of their motives, framing involves making choices that are ultimately informed by a set of facts. This implies that framing ultimately serves a purpose, or an agenda. To frame an image and a sound involves inflecting, imposing and reconfiguring elements in them so that the encoding and decoding processes align with each other.

Art makes it possible to transpose anxieties, sensitivities, emotions, attitudes and fears into audiovisual articulations. Since cultural repertoires are also translatable into combination of images and sounds, artists' main goal is to transmit their ideas, beliefs and views through representations that work simultaneously at many levels. The seductive nature of art activates the interest and emotions of viewers and has the capacity to distract them into believing what they see. Yet, truth and art have never been symbiotic. In fact, throughout human history, art has been the most common platform to create fictional scenarios. Alternatively, when an image is retrieved based in how its content is described, catalogued or systematized, it is through a conscious use of written language (actively visual and passively aural) on behalf of the searcher that visuals can be traced. It is through language that the general public expresses itself, discusses the images in question, exchanges thoughts about them and engages with visual representations, for instance, through comments in social media about the unauthenticity of dialogues in *Ixcanul*, or the lack of subtitles in *Magallanes*. It is through language that the general public is capable of searching for information in moments of doubt, uncertainty, outrage, indignation and fear. In today's media platforms, language plays a central role in labelling of images (i.e. *indio*), cross-referentiality of their content and materialization (even if only briefly) of the responses of users (general public), through comments or symbolic signs of support (e.g. likes, hearts), rejection (e.g. dislikes), outrage (e.g. angry faces) and so on. Focus on the importance of visuality of language and linguisticness of images is in itself an attempt to understand how cinema expresses real-life identity.

Linguistic reality/fiction

Language plays a key role in the way a film is told. As historic records attest, including literary outputs and cultural artefacts, languages have always been linked to social affiliations, sense of community, tools of cohesion and collectiveness. They have served as symbols of power and status, or else of denigration and exclusion. The power stowed in language is ultimately engrained in the affluence and influence of its speakers, language being a way to label, identify and unite those who use it. Across formerly colonized parts of the world, minor linguistic communities are relegated by the weight and size of the speakers of more relevant languages. Linguistic diversity, especially in the case of 'barbaric' languages, was never highly appreciated by colonizing superpowers, and eventually, neither by the newly established independent states of the twenty-first century. The dream of creating new states rested on the idea that a large spectrum of languages was counterproductive for the formation of homogeneous societies. Strategies such as the myth that Latin Americans belonged to a mestizo race were also embedded in the notion that, as race, the members of these new societies all shared a common language.

After the *República de Indios* (Indigenous Republics) were dismantled in c. 1840, in many countries across the region, new techniques were put in place to weaken and finally eradicate the use of indigenous languages. One of them was to exclude them from open and public spaces. Considering that education was one of the realms where harsh linguistic policies were applied, it comes as no surprise that disparities emerged among speakers of Spanish and disfranchised languages. The precarious economic situation of ethnic minorities has been perennially reflected in the economic and social repercussions of a systematic oppression against speakers of indigenous languages. This was due to the attempt to expunge their linguistic heritage, encompassing an attack against their culture, perpetrated by the lack of opportunities in terms of education access – a state that even further secured their social exclusion. As a direct consequence, by the end of the eighteenth century, failing to speak Spanish or Portuguese relegated individuals to the lowest tiers of society in Latin America, except in Paraguay. Until today, the social value attached to European languages across the Americas remains intact and can be felt across all areas of society, with media outputs offering clear examples of this. Although it may be tenuous to state that the absence of indigenous languages from mass communication is entirely linked to the precarious social status of their speakers, it has certainly had a negative impact. Barring linguistic diversity from public spaces is understood to exacerbate disenfranchisement and invisibility of minorities, as it accelerates pervasive processes of standardization implemented by authorities to amalgamate ethnically diverse communities into a uniform social fabric.

Along with disfavouring policies in education, media outputs are promoters of modernity and industrialization, which can contribute to the extinction of indigenous languages at an accelerated rate. Linguistic hegemony menaces diversity by facilitating spaces of diminishment and exclusion for less affluent and influential communities. In Latin America, this is threatening to vulnerable communities as speakers are more likely to turn away from their cultural heritage if their languages are repressed and undermined. As a result of the tight links between prestige, employment opportunities and inclusion, affiliation to a linguistic realm becomes a conscious decision. Remarkably, in contrast with their social reality, indigenous languages are nowadays recognized in many Latin American countries such as Bolivia, Ecuador and Guatemala, as part of their cultural heritage – at least from a legal standpoint. With Mexico, Peru and Bolivia leading the way, between the 1950s and 1970s, pressure from international academic circles and political involvement of ethnic minorities resulted in legal recognition of the linguistic diversity of native communities. However, in spite of laws endorsing use of Quechua in public contexts in Peru (1975), rendering mandatory the use of Guaraní at all levels of education in Paraguay (1992), encouraging the protection of Mexico's linguistic legacy (1992) and introducing bilingual programmes of education in Bolivia (1992), effective implementation is rarely enforced. As has been pointed out by sociolinguists, attitudes, orientations, preconceptions and sensitivities surrounding the use of these languages in social spaces need to change in order for them to thrive, for instance, in media spaces.[1]

Unfortunately, in most cases, inclusive linguistic policies aiming to safeguard indigenous languages stay at an ideological and symbolic stage. For instance, they hardly materialize in endeavours to increase the sense of belonging, prestige and status of Quechua (Andean countries), Tzotzil (Mexico) or Rapa Nui (Chile) speakers. There are particularly two aspects to consider in order to understand why policies fail to translate into tools for social inclusion of linguistic minorities. On the one hand, states do not enforce linguistic policies equally because, except for a few exceptions, members of government, officials, public services employees and/or school teachers are not conversant in those languages. On the other hand, European languages are regarded as vehicles of progress, modernity, internationalization and nationalism, while indigenous languages are thought to be vestiges of past civilizations, even by members of the communities that speak them. At many points, Amerindian heritage prompts sensitivities similar to those elicited by an antique statue in a museum, as opposed to the attractiveness of a computer screen or a modern airplane.

Central to any discussion on language and its role in cinematic narratives is to recognize that language is not only a tool to convey messages, ideas, emotions or thoughts. It is also a multidimensional space embedded in and foundational to sociocultural practices and extrinsically linked to processes of identity, recognition, prestige, discrimination, acceptance, isolation, inclusion, exclusion and ultimately power. Society is interwoven with language, not only because it is the most prominent tool in communication but also because it is usually one of the common traits shared cumulatively by its members. From this standpoint, languages are regarded as markers of collective cohesion institutionalized as symbols of sameness and homogeneity. From these processes of demarcation, ideologies surrounding language emerge as reflections of attitudes and standpoints about different linguistic groups. As Irvine and Gal (2000) observe, 'the alignment of language with ethnicity – understood as sub nationalism and reinforced by colonial policy – is a particularly important dimension of the representational process, though one that is hard to disentangle' (59). Wherefore, towards an outside world, language becomes synonymous with culture, a label and, often, a brand that is deployed for recognition and inclusion. In the case of cinema, inclusion of language has become a strategy to convey a sense of realism, verisimilitude and authenticity.

Due to historical processes, languages become entwined with visual characteristics of their speakers, their ethnicity, socio-economic background, affluence, influence, recognition and prestige. Languages face challenges comparable to those hindering the communities who speak them, both inside and outside media spaces. Attitudes towards one's language(s) and those of others illuminate, in many ways, worldviews about the sense of identity and the perception of other linguistic communities. In general terms, a major part of the cultural legacy of a society rests in their linguistic tradition, not only because it serves as an element of consensus and unification but because it evinces also historic, cultural and ultimately socio-economic processes. It is commonly believed that a community of language users can be categorized as a separate social group merely based on their linguistic heritage. Language as an entity on its own becomes incorporated in a system of symbolisms and preconceptions that are inferred about its speakers and these, in turn, elicit a set of assumptions and ideas (Urban 2004). Cinematic production reflects the anxieties and tensions that emerge in societies where language not only unites but also divides.

Arbitrarily, material wealth and social capital is thought to correlate directly with processes of recognition or erasure of a linguistic group (Fairclough 1989, 2013; Bourdieu 2001). This is not only because of the advantages that prosperity affords but also because of the access to platforms of diffusion and expansion to which languages of impoverished communities are denied. Spaces, such as television, radio, printed material, music and cinema, can serve to strengthen the position of a given linguistic group, while absence from these modes of dissemination can result in a group's language and existence being obscured, ignored or forgotten. In the case of Latin America, the dominance and supremacy of Spanish and Portuguese are unquestionable at all levels of social life across the continent.

Absence of languages spoken by native minorities is notable not only in media spaces but also in more formal settings, such as education, government and public services instances. It is therefore remarkable to witness the inclusion of minority languages in recent cinematic productions, such as Mixtec (Mexico) or Moqoit (Argentina). Notwithstanding, central to an analysis of cinematic narratives where, for instance, Guaraní (Paraguay), Kaqchikel (Guatemala) or Mapudungun (Chile) is included, is to establish to what extent the films in question reflect tangible social reconfigurations or the need to create more 'authentic' films. If a filmmaker chooses to include an indigenous language, even though only a small minority of cinemagoers speak Amerindian languages, it is worth asking what purpose it serves in a cinematic context. It could be argued that native languages enhance the sense of credibility and reality as audiences might assume that indigeneity unreservedly requires belonging to a different linguistic community. A language–ethnicity binary is present in many of the films reviewed.

It is then pertinent to ask whether including indigenous languages is done because they play the role of tokens of credibility, or whether this demonstrates an effort towards recognition and acknowledgement. Subsequently, this prompts questions about how indigeneity is linked to speaking an indigenous language, and whether a film character is presumed to retain his or her identity and indigeneity despite not being conversant in the language of his or her ancestors.[2] Arguably, inclusion of indigenous languages in cinema might also be understood as a vehicle to mark difference and strengthen a gap between mainstream society and ethnic minorities. After all, one of the manifestations of Otherness rests on linguistic affiliation. Along the same line, reviewing the addition of native linguistic traits in visual cultural artefacts animates inquiries about spectatorship, specifically how audiences, untrained in hearing these languages, react to narratives where 'unfamiliar sounds' play a key role. In the context of power, an important aspect to consider is the risk that linguistic legacy is manipulated, or even exploited. Lack of spaces for these languages renders them subaltern tools of communication as their speakers are ultimately positioned outside the hegemonic tiers of society. In cinema, due to power structures, filmmakers and film producers are unlikely to be speakers of minority languages. Likewise, most renowned actors and actresses are generally not members of indigenous communities, necessarily acquainted with Amerindian cultures or the complexities of their sociocultural status.

Linguistic (con)texts

A recent upsurge in the inclusion and acknowledgement of the pre-Columbian linguistic heritage of the continent is certainly positive. Out of the sixty-eight selected films, forty-four include conversations of various kinds and lengths in Amerindian languages; thirty-six use subtitles to translate these exchanges. Around 86 per cent of the films considered for this study include samples of their linguistic heritage, in the form of dialogues, songs or written text. A danger, notwithstanding, lies in not realizing that, for instance, Quechua has the potential to convey a sense of equality, preference, homage and recognition, while also having the potential to connote exoticism, prejudice, disinclination and, ultimately, difference and otherness. This is because language is embedded in cultural hierarchies of power. Although cinema neither causes social problems nor simply reflects them, its approach to language is far from neutral.

Visual homogeneousness (i.e. physical traits) is contested by vocal heterogeneity (i.e. uvular and glottal phonemes in some Amerindian languages). Peculiarities of non-native speakers of Spanish and Portuguese, or socially and geographically restricted varieties also serve as markers of identity. Accented Spanish spoken by an indigenous migrant in an urban space, as occurs in *La teta asustada* (Peru, 2009), denotes inequalities that a film has the capacity not only to problematize but also to strengthen and perpetuate. Audiences decode and contextualize visual representations from their own social reality standpoint. A human tendency to position images within familiar contexts helps one to understand the value attached to linguistic choices in motion pictures. Languages, speech styles and accents provide signals of social categorizations, such as the ethnicity, class and/or education level of their speakers. Invariably, they also operate on their own as sources of assumptions, stereotypes and preconceptions.

Both images and language serve as strategies to achieve more compelling, awe-inspiring cultural artefacts/productions that resonate with viewers' preconceptions of what the *indigenous* entails. In terms of linguistic inclusion, it becomes evident that filmmakers whose films incorporate histrionic excesses manipulate already oppressed means of communication. They possibly do so in order to ornament their productions, as *Play* (Chile, 2005) seems to do, to accentuate differences within a shared code, such as the use of stagy rural accents does in, for instance, *El niño pez* (Argentina–Paraguay, 2009), or to raise the sense of genuineness of a journey into the unknown in the manner shown in *El abrazo de la serpiente* (Colombia, 2015). Inconsequent use of Amerindian languages in films repeatedly denotes an attempt to garnish a story by creating linguistic ethnotypes, as one sees in *Caramuru* (Brazil, 2001), *Madeinusa* (Peru, 2005), *La teta asustada* (Peru, 2009) and *El facilitador* (Ecuador, 2013). More inclusive attempts include films like *Alicia en el país* (Chile, 2008), where silence is the common language, or *¿Quién mató a la llamita blanca?* (Bolivia, 2007), where an occasional gloss is provided. In more neutral approaches, both European and Amerindian languages play a vital role and exchanges anchored in unstaged, logistic, interactional and contextual patterns of human communication (e.g. *Dioses*, Peru, 2008; *Zona Sur*, Bolivia, 2009; *Yvy Maraêy: Tierra sin mal*, Bolivia, 2013). Throughout the large spectrum of films addressing indigenous topics, there are also examples of productions where Spanish or Portuguese replace altogether the native languages in order to reach wider audiences, like *Corazón del Tiempo* (Mexico 2008). The major downside to the increasing recognition of Amerindian languages in films is the tendency to exotify them.

Cinema is one of the formats that best articulates the entangled and multifaceted relation between the local and the global. This realization certainly becomes pertinent in the context of co-productions viewed and consumed by audiences outside of Latin America. A valid assumption is that exposing the global spectatorship to a more diverse set of languages facilitates the acknowledgement of previously unknown linguistic communities or, at least, opens spaces of contestation. It is not accidental that films such as *Qué tan lejos/How Much Farther* (Ecuador, 2006), *Madeinusa* (Peru, 2006) and *Dioses* (Peru, 2008) have included Quechua, while Aymara plays 'un papel protagónico' [a leading role] (Cisneros 2013: 53) in *Zona Sur* (Bolivia, 2009), and Guaraní is the only language spoken in *Hamaca paraguaya* (Paraguay–Argentina, 2000). In spite of signs of inclusion of indigenous linguistic heritage in cinematic spaces, it remains unclear what the shift has entailed. Tarica (2008) reminds us, for instance, that there is a long tradition of equating barbarity and proficiency in Quechua in literary texts. There seems to be a deep-rooted language–indigeneity dichotomy that deters any attempt to reconfigure long-established attitudes towards non-European linguistic communities in the region.

Textual and contextual dimensions of linguistic cinemascapes are best operationalized through the practice of translating spoken dialogues. For instance, in *Zona Sur* (Bolivia 2009), no subtitles are provided for scenes where interactions take place in Aymara. While this might have been regarded as a sign of reduction and devaluation some decades ago, today this is seen as the possibility of experiencing, rather than explaining. It can be argued that since dialogues in Spanish do not call for subtitles, providing translation for Aymara connotes lesser recognition and value. A way of interpreting the intentional absence of translation is that signs, gestures of fondness and nods of disaffection literally speak for themselves. The directors' choices of how their films approach language are not neutral, and preferences about accents, dialects or use of subtitles result from the ideologies held by filmmakers. When discussing her film, Chilean director Alicia Scherson (*Play*, Chile, 2005), for instance, observes in a televised interview that 'los mapuches urbanos no hablan una gota de mapudungun' [urban Mapuche communities do not speak a word of Mapudungun] and that the fact that the main character (Cristina) uses it is 'una mentira' [a lie] (Greene and Scherson 2015). In her own words, in the interview about the conceptual process of the film, she explained that she just 'quería usar subtítulos' [wanted to use subtitles] in her film. This information does not diminish the artistic value of Scherson's work in *Play*, but it certainly sheds light on the potential degree of manipulation behind the use of indigenous languages across Latin American cinematic spaces. Alternatively, one could also argue that the lack of subtitles throws non-indigenous audiences into the position of those who are monolingual in their indigenous languages. To a certain extent, it conveys a sense of the felt experience of those who lie outside the functional sphere of the language of power (even if only briefly).

Set in La Paz, *Zona Sur* might serve as a path to understand the complexities of a multicultural nation preoccupied with the reconfiguration of its social fabric in the aftermath of Evo Morales's ascension to power. This Bolivian film echoes concerns about the centrality of language precisely because 'a majority of Bolivians now have Spanish as their mother tongue; yet an even greater majority identify as indigenous' (Canessa 2007: 256). A shift in the perceived relation between language and identity raises questions about the connection that director Juan Carlos Valdivia makes between being Aymara and speaking Aymara, and to which extent this is a valid assumption. The *upsurge* of non-European linguistic elements in recent cinema might actually be evidence of an increased recognition of the traits commonly affixed to the Other, for example, accent, phonetic particularities/non-standard intonation. Alternatively, Aymara contributes to render the story more realistic, impress audiences, gain more acknowledgement in festivals and therefore increase revenues in the form of tickets sold. Filmmakers seem to assign languages an active role in the synergy between spectators, images and sound. Canons of representation appeal to the eyes and the ears.

In the case of *El niño pez* (Argentina–Paraguay, 2009), director Lucía Puenzo compares Guaraní with 'el canto de los pájaros' [the song of birds] (Carbonari 2010: 80). She alludes to how the natives bewitched the Spanish conquistadores. Set mainly in a well-to-do suburb of Buenos Aires, the story unfolds around the love story between Paraguayan maid Guayi (Mariela Vitale) and her employer's daughter, Lala (Inés Efron). Guayi has come to Argentina fleeing domestic violence and sexual abuse in her native country, but also escaping a difficult past that included having given birth to a son she conceived after her father raped her. A focal point is that Guayi's sense of displacement challenges some of the established tropes in the Argentine psyche, particularly in terms of social and natural orders. From a diasporic perspective, *El niño pez* is part of a group of New Argentine Cinema that suggests immigrants live happily ever after they have Argentinized (Medina 2007). Except, the ending of the film cannot unarguably be labelled as a happy one. After Lala poisons her father, Judge Bronté (Josep Munné), to death for demanding sexual favours from Guayi, the love affair of the young girls is jeopardized by the imminent consequences his death will have for both of them.

The story is told from an Argentine Spanish-speaking standpoint, while the figure being watched is the Paraguayan Guaraní-speaking character. Even if Guayi is a central character, her story is seen through Lala's eyes, and told through her empowered optic. Guaraní as a language is a focal point in the construction of the character of Guayi, especially when her musical abilities are underscored. The scenes where music plays a central role champion the notion that Guaraní is a more suitable language to express the young girl's pain and disappointment.[3] The linguistic choice seems to imply that certain sensitivities remain encrypted and are only expressible through channels that coincide with the preconceptions viewers have about the speakers of Guaraní, as opposed to those whose primary language is Spanish.

On this account, Guaraní comes to designate elements such as sensuality, supernaturalism and magic, and although they might have a positive value, they also convey the idea of being 'different'. After all, the Paraguayan intonation of the main character, Guayi, when she speaks Spanish, strengthens the perception that she is an immigrant and subaltern subject within the social hierarchy, working as a housekeeper for a well-to-do Buenos Aires family.[4] Whether or not she does it unconsciously, Puenzo is probably aware that Guaraní is often entwined with low socio-economic classes in Argentine urban settings. In the story, both Lala and her father, Judge Bronte, fall for the enticing foreign girl whose voice and sounds are difficult to resist. An imagological analysis of the use of Lala's songs demands questions about the ethnotype of an alluring Guaraní speaker who seduces with her *natural* charm. It seems problematic to regard the inclusion of Guaraní as a revalidation of Amerindian heritage in cinema if in fact its inclusion appears to be a strategy to tropicalize a character.

Transnationally, in many cases, *uncommon* languages alternatively evoke tropes of past civilizations, spellbinding geographies and captivating communities, all fruitful allusions in terms of acknowledgement, marketing, distribution and, as mentioned earlier, financial support. In this context, it becomes possible to argue that there is perhaps a link between funding and the use of Quechua in Claudia Llosa's *Madeinusa* (2005) and *La teta asustada* (2009), of Kaqchikel in Jairo Bustamante's *Ixcanul* (2015), and of Huitoto, Kubeo, Okaina and Tikuna languages in Ciro Guerra's *El abrazo de la serpiente* (2015). Amerindian languages operate as vehicles to confirm the ethnicity of the main characters and the provided subtitles act as a tool to enter their private, unknown world. Yet, along the line of the previously discussed viewer/tourist notion, one could argue that novel linguistic approaches enhance the journey and increase the sense of credibility. They become the movies' added value.

Inclusion of Amerindian languages vis-à-vis Spanish, or Portuguese in the case of Brazilian films, illuminates the entanglements between core and periphery. The phonetic qualities of a language are allegedly rare and alluring precisely because they belong to the realm of the unknown. In fact, many self-identified indigenous communities prefer using Spanish or Portuguese over their native languages in the production of films aimed for others. Why? They do not fetishize their own linguistic heritage, possibly as a testament to the recognition that languages are integral parts of epistemic systems. The ultimate goal is to communicate, not to confirm that the perceived, expected and assumed gap between Self and Other does sound different.

Caramuru: A invenção do Brazil (2001) confirms linguistic fetishization is often accompanied by other narrative strategies. Directed by Guel Arraes, the film stands out for presenting a tropicalized, eroticized pre-Columbian Brazil: a land inhabited by unsophisticated, childlike indigenous people who roam around free of any sense of responsibility, and believe a European man they encounter on the beach may actually be a god. Arraes builds on the myth that Brazil emerged from European inquisitiveness, chance and indigenous promiscuity, playfully presented as an unconventional practice, although not for the natives. *Caramuru* highlights the notion that there is no way to exotify the empowered subject (Portuguese), only the subaltern object (Indigenous Peoples). Their subalternity is stressed by their use of accented Portuguese, contrasted with a flawless continental version spoken by the newcomers. Although the film insists in being a parody of the encounter between two worlds and the creation of a nation, Arraes relies on outdated, fixed tenets that include the notion of the good savage, the erotic nude aboriginal woman and the naïve natives, which are paradigms entwining ethnicity, gender and alterity. As literature and films attest, indigenous women have been exotified for most of the time the Americas have been known to Europeans. *Caramuru* underscores this detrimental tradition.

The film basically 'argues that Brazil emerges from a sex triangle in which a European man and two Amerindian women 'eat' and subsequently incorporate part of the other' (Gordon 2009: 156).[5] This young European is Mello (Diogo Álvares Correia), an incautious painter who, almost by accident, is recruited to join an expedition to the Brazilian shores; the Amerindian girls are sisters Paraguaçu (Camila Pitangas) and Moema (Deborah Secco), daughters of chief Itaparica. The main storyline is that Mello has received the task of drawing a map of the newfound territories if he is to marry his fiancée back in Portugal; however, before boarding the ship, he had not expected to end up emotionally involved with one of the natives. It was not among his plans either to bring talented Paragauçu to Europe where she will become his wife.

Feather decorations, bikini-like garments, mystifying sounds and primitive lifestyles are seen in contraposition with an advanced, orderly Portugal. Central to the film is the depiction of *mestizaje* processes as arising from friendly encounters between sympathetic European explorers and receptive, easily available native women. Attempts to make the narrative frolic and playful can partly explain the clichés to which Arraes resorts. Paradoxically, though, it is mostly the indigenous visual and linguistic aspects that are mocked. Even if Diego is presented as weak and clumsy while Paraguaçu is depicted as determined and skilful, it is her culture that is ridiculed and derided. Out of the two worlds (Tupinambás/Portuguese), the caricature approach is only applied to the indigenous civilization. Arraes's parody confirms that even if race- and ethnicity-related matters in Brazil are only subtly articulated as cultural references, they frequently imply losses for the objectified party. *Caramuru* manages to show 'how the European *ego conquiro* and *ego civilizato* constructs a stereotypical identity for the *Other*' (Ayoh'Omidire 2010: 24), suggesting that the creation of an exotic figure could not be avoided, because after all, these were two worlds apart.

Voicing concerns vis-à-vis unspeakable realities

Alternatively, filmmakers are attentive to the universality of language to transmit and transpose unspeakable realities into sounds. It is only through the transcript of the dialogue on the screen in *Hamaca Paraguaya* (Argentina–Paraguay, 2000) that non-Guaraní-speaking audiences learn about the anxiety of two parents waiting for news about their son, who is fighting in the Chaco War (1935).[6] Directed by Paz Encina, the film persuasively presents time-images of absence, respite, sorrow and eventually grief. The sense of time is cleverly entwined with periods of silence and interaction in a language that is impenetrable for most international viewers. The use of Guaraní seems to complement the sense of violence, pain and marginalization in the story, possibly because as Encina states in an interview, 'all that is true is said in Guaraní, and the rest is said in Spanish' (López Medin and Encina 2021). The choice of not including Spanish resonates with the intimate character of the scenes. Through the interaction between Cándida (Georgina Genes) and Ramón (Ramón Del Rio), the film adumbrates many of the implications discursively attached to the notion of Otherness. The only other forms of communication are the barking of a dog and moments of silence. Guaraní in *Hamaca Paraguaya* corroborates Encina's attempt to reach innovative levels of cinematography. Bypassing conventional formulas conceived not to bore the spectators, Encina seeks to engage and transmit, rather than attract and translate. The Paraguayan director shows that Amerindian legacy does not need to be an instrument to elicit a sense of exoticism or tropicalism. She explains that the non-verbal has a political and a human side that bespeaks the ongoing presence of wars and dictatorships that still linger in the Paraguayan psyche (Losada 2010). This minimalist but contemplative film transmits the idea that Cándida and Ramón's dialogues unfold as natural sequences, rather than staged exemplars engineered to allure audiences thirsty for inaccessible but exciting sounds. Subtitles certainly facilitate the approachability to codes that otherwise most viewers would misread or simply fail to comprehend.

Contradictorily, the lack of intelligibility can also be a vehicle to secure the opacity of a situation or, as in *Brava gente brasileira*, to convey a sense of miscommunication. In this Brazilian film from 2001, the viewpoint is 'oposição em lugar de tradução: não se trata de traduzir o guaicuru para o português mas de afirmar a impossibilidade de entendimento' [opposition instead of translation: it is not about translating Guaicuru into Portuguese, but confirming the impossibility of understanding] (Avellar 2006: 57). The 103-minute-long film revolves around the clashes between Europeans and natives in the seventeenth century, and the opposing standpoints in a conflict where economic interests, sexual violence, interference of the Catholic Church and cultural differences that separate the Guaicuru people from the Portuguese troops seem endless. It is a story about love where words are not necessary but also where the lack of a common language leads to tragedy.

Director Lúcia Murat presents the indigenous perspective as the standard point of reference, contesting in the process obsolete European canons. Murat chose to have indigenous actors from the Kadiweu peoples to play the Guaicurus in the film, and not to gloss either their dialogues or gestures, in order to highlight the difference between the two worlds. Mental images about primitiveness come to mind when Ánote (Luciana Rigueira), the Guaicuru girl captured by the Europeans, kills her newborn baby. A situation that can reduce her to the figure of a savage – in the mind of viewers – recovers a new meaning once it becomes clear that infanticide is a Guaicuru practice to control population growth. The absence of a common language operates as an obstacle, both for the Portuguese troops and the audiences watching the film. Murat manages to obstruct the omnipresent, all-knowing stance that posits the centrality and authority of spectators, and demands a story to be self-explanatory, particularly when it involves 'distant' cultures. The lack of translation demonstrates her desire to problematize 'estranhamento como matriz de todos os processos interculturais e a violência, tanto física quanto simbólica, que deste emana inexoravelmente' [estrangement as a matrix of all intercultural processes and the violence, both physical and symbolic, that emanates inexorably from it] (Dos Santos, Tomaim and Valquiria 2013: 1213). The film does not seem to favour one viewpoint over the other, but shows opposition to the notion that a culture, and therefore a language, is ever to prevail or replace other ones. *Brava gente brasileira* demands audiences to look beyond their own process of enculturation. Therefore, the tradition of oppressive contexts in which indigeneity has a less prominent voice is challenged, and lack of translation is a key aspect in achieving this goal. In the world of *Brava gente brasileira*, both Amerindian and European languages have equal status, and audiences are expected to gain awareness about the implications this brings. The most obvious one is the lack of conversion between linguistic codes, which signal Murat's decision to mark boundaries and contest hegemony.

The artful use of language in order to elicit specific reactions among audiences does not always go unnoticed. In Peruvian *Magallanes* (2015), for instance, director Salvador del Solar recurs to untranslated Quechua in order to highlight indignation and outrage. In the last scene of the film, Celina (Magaly Solier) uses the indigenous language not only to express her exasperation about the abuses she has faced but also to reclaim her subjectivity after enduring all kinds of violence throughout her entire life. This episode closes the story of Harvey Magallanes (Damián Alcázar), a taxi driver who tries to make amends for the abuses he committed against her and her family during Peru's internal conflict two decades earlier. Psychologically scarred Celina, now settled in Lima, epitomizes how Peruvian cinema has started to acknowledge its history, diversity and implications of recent traumatic events (Barrow 2014). Quechua allows Celina to finally make a statement about her agency vis-à-vis injustice and remembrances of a silenced truth that she wishes to leave behind. Del Solar's decision to not offer subtitles for the final scene triggered strong reactions among viewers and critics. Through social media platforms like Facebook and Twitter, cinemagoers openly demanded that a translation be provided. National newspapers (e.g. *Capital*, *República*, *El Comercio*) covered the interest of the general public in deciphering Celina's monologue. Finally, several non-official translations started to emerge on the internet:

Celina: Dinero, qullqi, hamkunapa umaykichikpiqa qullqillam. Chay qullqiwanchu ñuqataqa hampiruwankichiq llapa ruwawasaykichita. Mamayta taytaytachu kawsarichimunkichiq kay qullqiwan. Untata munasqaykichikta ñuqawan rurarqankichiq dirichuykunatam saruparuwankichik. ¿Imanataq kaypi kachkani? Ah! ¿Imapaqtaq kaypi kachkani? Haykapikaman suyasaq. Dirichuykunatam sarupachkankichik kunanpas. Manañan manchakuykichichu qamkunataqa. Ni qamta, ni paytaq, ni pitaq / Money, money, in your head it's only about money, only money. Are you going to fix me from all that you have done to me by giving me this? My father, my mother, are you going to revive them with money? From the beginning, you have done whatever you felt like doing with my person. You have trampled on my rights. What am I here for? Ha? What am I here for? Until when am I going to wait? You are trampling on my rights, right now too. I am not scared of you all anymore, neither of you, nor of him, nor of anyone.[7]

The dramatic nature of the scene and Solier's unrivalled performative skills make clear that the episode is about empowerment and closure. Her choice of switching to Quechua is an attempt to protest against acts of injustice that viewers know well enough. From an imagological viewpoint, it is possible to conclude that even before the translation was made public, speculating viewers had guessed most of the contents of her monologue. After all, the film was based on a story that Peruvian audiences would recognize. De Solar's decision implies that the crudity of past and present abuse against native communities does not need translation because everyone knows it. Although the cinematic experience relies on imagery to create a plot, filmmakers rely upon sound in its various formats to mark the registers at play.

Examples of the creative use of sound include the above-mentioned use of a high-pitched tone to connote outcry in *Magallanes*, no speech at all in *Alicia en el país* in order to discourage ethnographic interpretation of the story, or enchanting songs of the sort used in *El niño pez*, *Madeinusa* and *La teta asustada*, as a way to externalize the inexpressible. Effectively, songs constitute a powerful mechanism for underscoring the ethnic background of many of the characters in indigeneity-oriented films. Peruvian director Claudia Llosa has stated that music is 'the way a community talks about its pain, and about the things it does not understand' (Peirano and Llosa 2010). Her observation explains the scene in *Madeinusa*, where the young girl evocatively sings as a way to express herself.[8] In like manner, through their songs, Fausta (*La teta asustada*) and La Guayi (*El niño pez*) reveal a fertile culture that differs from the depleted imaginaries of their oppressors, a practice of extracting and emptying that uncomfortably resembles the mechanics of exploitation behind commodities exchanges, or bioprospecting projects.

Directors Claudia Llosa and Lucía Puenzo seem to agree that an exotic song is a desirable element, in particular when they are combined with awe-inspiring lyrics, but not so an extended use of the native languages in more crucial dialogues. Singing for Fausta might be a more natural way to express her emotions than vocalizing them. Another possible explanation – a real-world truth – is that Quechua-speakers in urban settings, especially in Lima, are victims of stigmatization and marginalization, and that this diminishment causes them to forgo speaking their mother tongue in public areas. Analogously, the same ambiguity that speaking Quechua evokes in Lima is perceivable in the position Buenos Aires society assigns to Guaraní in *El niño pez*. Oppression and marginalization are central to many of the stories of indigenous migrants struggling to survive in Latin America's largest urban centres. Their subalternity translates into cinematic reflections where their linguistic performances become key pieces to create convincing characters, particularly through the use of dialectic peculiarities, thick accents and faulty language skills, elements that in imagological terms prompt the creation of ethnotypes. For instance, in *La teta asustada*, Llosa allocates Quechua a position within Lima's social ranking by linking it to the housekeeper and the gardener.

The reactions to their accents resemble the impressions that Los Tortolitos' sociolects elicit among nonrural Bolivian spectators watching *¿Quién mató a la llamita blanca?* In terms of the linguistic heritage of the communities portrayed in the story, Bellot succeeds in conveying a message of inclusion. Similar to the role of the commentator, each scene where words from Quechua are used includes explanatory texts about their meaning. Examples include *llocalla sonzo* [silly young man] (minute 27) and *c'haki* [hangover] (minute 39). At the beginning of the narrative, a thorough introduction into the lives of the characters makes clear that both Domitila and Jacinto were raised in La Paz, a piece of information that somehow justifies their preferred use of Spanish. The use of Quechua is reserved for moments of excitement, anger and intimacy, which coincides with the types of exchanges where code-switching between languages takes place, even in fiction.[9] Since the film works as a parody of what an ethnographic account should be, besides language, various indigenous elements are present throughout the narrative.

Alongside scenarios where adult migrants face the brunt of marginalization, it is impossible to ignore representations that address the obstacles by indigenous youth outside their linguistic communities. Through the social connotations attached to language, filmmakers manage to engineer convincing portrayals of culturally dissonant teenagers in *A terra dos homens vermelhos* (Italy–Brazil, 2008), abused child workers in *Nosilatiaj. La belleza*

(Argentina, 2012), and a monolingual Tzotzil boy attempting to travel illegally from his native Chiapas, all the way into the United States, in *La Jaula de Oro* (Mexico, 2013).

La Jaula de Oro is a reflection about the challenges faced by three teenagers on their path towards the so-called American dream. More importantly, the film offers a glimpse into the subaltern position indigenous societies endure, even among groups that are themselves victims of social exclusion. Besides his native Tzotzil, Chauk (Rodolfo Domínguez) can only utilize sign language and gestures in order to communicate with his travel companions, Sara (Karen Martínez Pineda) and Juan (Brandon López). In this way, *La Jaula de Oro* sheds light on the disavowal of Amerindian heritage within Ladino Guatemalan circles, and how this extends beyond the national borders. Juan embodies intolerance, while Sara represents the curiosity towards the suppressed Other. In this sample of social cinema, language stands out as a marker of distance and difference. Spanish director Diego Quemada-Díez manages to show how Chauk thrives in a part of the world where the colonized people are seduced to abandon their mother tongues.

The trio experiences unsavoury encounters with the Mexican border police, persecution from vicious gangs targeting Central American migrants and internal conflict between Chauk and Juan. After several days of travel, finding food becomes a matter of survival. In an episode where they attempt to catch a chicken, differences in cultural and linguistic backgrounds become quite evident:

Chauk walks to the chicken. Juan looks at him amused, hoping he will not be able to catch it. Skilfully, Chauk catches the animal, and caresses it.

CHAUK: *Jmet'ik banamil. Kolabal.* / *Mother Earth. Thanks*

Juan and Sara observe. The chicken stops clucking.

JUAN: *Este indio idiota, cree que la va a matar hablándole.* / *This stupid Indian, he thinks he is going to kill it by talking to it.*

Juan looks at Chauk with a sardonic smile and laughs at him. Chauk takes the animal's neck and twists it. Sara gets a bit scared; it is not a pretty image. Juan stops laughing, looks at Chauk surprised, there is a glimpse of respect in his eyes.[10]

Throughout the story, Chauk does not show any major improvement in Spanish, and this does not appear to be his main goal at any point. The film does not seem to imply that he is incapable of doing so either. Unexpectedly, he makes efforts to teach Sara some important words in Tzotzil, and in this sense, the narrative questions the prominence of Spanish, particularly in a context where borders erode. In the end, the story defends the notion that their common adversary is not a language barrier but an oppressive system that forces them to leave their homes and leads them to tragic events. Although essentialist in certain aspects, *La Jaula de Oro* is a sample of critical, rather than violent, cinema. After all, a calque of the same hegemonic order that prevents them from reaching their dreams demarcates the borders that they face on a figurative, physical, cultural and linguistic level.

A continuum of strategies including accents, various degrees of proficiency and songs are used to achieve this and reveal the diversity of approaches across national cinematic traditions, but also how heavily transnationalist tropes inform local filmmakers. Hence, shifts in the centrality of Amerindian linguistic heritage in films can easily be confused with attempts to intensify the sensibilities these productions evoke among Western(ized) viewers. In *El facilitador* (Ecuador, 2013), director Victor Arregui reserves close-up frames to show Elena's indignation (Maria Gracia Omegna) but not to show the pain of specific indigenous characters in the face of abuse (e.g. when an indigenous girl is beaten up by a soldier over a bucket of water). Close-ups and medium shots are also used to underline difference in some of the selected films. In *Play* (Chile, 2005), *Espiral* (Mexico, 2008), *El traspatio* (Mexico, 2009), *Climas* (Peru, 2014) and *Feriado* (Ecuador, 2014), the camera tends to focus on the face of indigenous characters while they speak in Amerindian languages – and not when they speak Spanish. Although contemporary films stand out for focusing on indigeneity from an individual rather than a group-oriented perspective, some films still resort to long shots or crane shots to approach the Others as a whole (e.g. *La Ciénaga* (Argentina, 2001), *El destino* (Argentina–Spain, 2006), *Los viajes del vientos* (Colombia–Germany–The Netherlands, 2009), *Xingu* (Brazil, 2012), *El verano de los peces voladores* (Chile, 2013)).

On a positive note, a number of films are genuine endeavours to champion the inclusion of indigenous languages into the cinematic landscapes of the continent. These are productions where language becomes a tool to contest marginalization and reclaim subjectivity. The common denominator among the above-discussed films is that language plays a key role in the creation of representations that echo the social reality of the continent, and tellingly, in the portrayal of indigeneity in cinema. Although away from a time where films mark the inability of 'Indians' 'to master the "civilized" language, recent Latin American films show a tendency to echo First World films in eliding, distorting, or caricaturing the "word of the other"' (Shohat and Stam 2014: 192). Through a Eurocentric lens, references to ethnic languages as less prominent vehicles of communication, mainly effective for evoking a sense of estrangement and nostalgia, abound in many of the region's films addressing indigeneity. In alignment with hegemonic ideologies, language is introduced in some cases as a means to complement, decorate and bolster the creation of 'authentic' indigenous characters.

(In)discernible sounds and authenticity

As a marker, language is a constant in heterogeneous (visual) narratives, not the least because it operates as an element that enhances the sense of realness, authoritativeness, nostalgia and credibility.[11] The social reality of characters is validated by realistic linguistic ideologies (Androutsopoulos 2012). Tactically, some Latin American filmmakers repeatedly turn to indigenous languages or accented Spanish or Portuguese as a means of rendering their stories more credible, convincing, engaging, alluring and authentic. Technology has enabled filmmakers to expand the use of language in their quest to create compelling narratives that engage spectators. The performative aspect of language becomes most evident when the focus shifts to the voices of the actors and their capacity to appear convincing. In numerous ways, 'genuine' portrayals/(re)presentations are intimately intertwined with vocal, verbal and linguistic aspects. For some filmmakers, brief exchanges in an Amerindian language seem to operate as antidote to possible criticism or scepticism about their 'realistic' approach.[12] To exemplify the quest for legitimacy, credibility and realism identified in indigeneity-oriented cinematic productions, the next paragraphs discuss the notion of the 'authentic' in the films *El abrazo de la serpiente* (Argentina–Colombia–Spain–The Netherlands–Venezuela, 2015) and *Pájaros de verano/Birds of Passage* (Colombia–Denmark–Mexico, 2018).

Exotic sounds and images draw attention, evoke associations and align with Eurocentric preconceptions, often used as eligibility requirements for financial support. The process through which Western viewership secures funding, and eventually more recognition is also evident in the popularity of *El abrazo de la serpiente*. Directed by Ciro Guerra (Colombia), the film revolves around the encounter of shaman Karamakate with two Westerners travelling into the heart of the Amazon rainforest, at separate times in history but with a similar goal. The first one is ailing German explorer Theodor Koch-Grünberg (Jan Bijvoet), who ventures into the Amazon basin in 1909 searching for the exceptionally scarce *yakruna* plant. Convinced that the flower could cure him of his unknown disease, he is willing to take any risk. The second one is American botanist Richard Evans (Brionne Davis), who seeks, under false pretences, advice and guidance from Karamakate three decades later (1940). With the aid of Manduca (Yaeunkü Migue), a local whom Koch-Grünberg saves from becoming a slave in a rubber plantation, he manages to persuade the sharp-witted but aggrieved shaman to lead him to the scarce flower. Although reluctant at first, young Karamakate (Nilbio Torres) agrees to help the German find a *yakruna*, even if he has plenty of reasons to mistrust white visitors. Being the last survivor of his clan, he represents the damage that external agents have caused along the Amazon basin.

As Chang (2015) notes, the story epitomizes how 'ravages of colonialism cast a dark pall over the stunning South American landscape' (para. 3), an observation reinforced by the intermittent sequences of encounters between an older Karamakate (Antonio Bolívar) and a deceitful Evans in 1940. Viewers witness how the American botanist manages to trick the elderly shaman into showing him unknown parts of the forest by pretending to be searching for *yakruna*. Soon enough, it becomes clear that Evans's real plan is to find plague-free rubber trees he can send back to the United States. However, what he does not know is that Karamakate has devoted his life to eradicate *yakruna*, to prevent anyone from using the (fictional) sacred plant in the wrong way. Different from Evans, he has nothing to lose now that his cultural legacy, the exceedingly rare flower and his memories are about to vanish completely. Complicating things further, the older Karamakate believes his *chullachaqui* (doppelgänger) wanders around in an unknown place and has lost any sense of hope. Visions, specifically hallucinations, prompt references to the use of entheogens among many pre-Columbian civilizations. The allusion to a serpent in the title of the film can be presumed to suggest a connection to a liana (e.g. *Banisteriopsis caapi*), used in concoctions for spiritual and healing purposes. Since bioprospecting is one of the themes in *El abrazo de la serpiente*, on this account, Guerra successfully hints at the implications that the war on psychoactive substances has had on indigenous populations.

That being said, Karamakate's character rekindles the ethnotype of the 'wise Indian'. His wisdom is such that viewers hardly question how he manages to survive on his own, for such a long time, in spite of a series of unfortunate events like a confrontation over Amazonian rubber plantations and malaria epidemics. When approached by Evans in 1940, it becomes evident that there have been technological advances in the 'outer' world compared to 1909, the year when he encountered Koch-Grünberg. Yet, besides marks of aging, Karamakate seems resistant to time, somehow entrapped in the past, or figuratively frozen on a forgotten page of an ethnographer's diary. In the end, there are many similarities between Guerra's well-structured scenes and what could be footage logs registered by an anthropologist doing fieldwork. *El abrazo de la serpiente* has the earmarks of a scientific narrative with ethnographic undertones. The film has the overall effect of wandering through a natural science museum, and prompts reflections on whose perspective is being favoured. Like being in an exposition hall, it is the viewers' viewpoint that explains the display of artefacts and their capacity to draw attention. If one is to agree that Guerra empathizes with the indigenous guide rather than championing the explorers' viewpoint, it is worth asking how this strategy does not perpetuate the stereotype of a defenceless but wise and childlike native. Modern devices in the form of Koch-Grünberg's compass, illogical creeds like a Portuguese fanatic cult – or just plain lies exemplified by Evans's false pretences – do not appear to test the allegedly hyperbolic naiveté of the Amazonia-based societies, according to the film. Guerra states that this is 'the story of an encounter between men from two worlds standing on each side of a river' (Zuluaga and Guerra 2015: para. 1). The question is how the narrative awakens and perpetuates the trope of the indigenous as stagnant figures of the past, dissociated from those gazing at them, and unable to understand them.

Although the film seems to be inclusive in terms of the linguistic heritage of the Amazonian communities, it is impossible not to wonder whether the use of indigenous languages (i.e. Huitoto, Kubeo, Ocaina and Tikuna) is actually a strategy to enhance the sense of credibility of the story, a fact Guerra has confirmed in several interviews when referring to the centrality of having filmed 'realistic' natives and their *natural* linguistic traits in order to make a genuine film. When interviewed by journalists, it becomes clear that some of the actors do not speak Spanish in their daily lives and that they celebrate the fact that Amerindian languages enter the realm of cinema. However, the conundrum lies in realizing that Guerra's main goal was not necessarily to delight Cannes or Los Angeles spectators with the sounds of Kubeo. Users of social media platforms, such as Facebook and Twitter, have commented on the fact that in *El abrazo de la serpiente*, 'los indios suenan a indios' [Indians sound like Indians do]. Viewers register an optical illusion with their eyes, and which is supported and enhanced by their ears. In this sense, the film offers an experience similar to the touristic venture into the jungle. Even if the phonetic landscape is dominated by Kubeo or Huitoto, they are embedded in a hierarchical structure that is ultimately put in place to entertain and surprise, not necessarily to reclaim or contest media spaces. The perspective remains Western in all its forms. The film, in essence, revolves around a German and an American venturing into the forest, and not about a Tikuna exploring the streets of Berlin or exploring New York's skyscrapers. Recalling Spivak (1988), can the subaltern speak, for instance, Dutch and roam around Rotterdam, looking for an endemic seed or animal to bring back to the Amazon?

The 125-minute-long film is mostly shot in black and white, and it corresponds to the criteria of Latin American films observed to be specifically tailor-made for international circuits of film festivals (Ross 2011; Middents 2013; Falicov 2017). As expected, the attention received from Cannes and a nomination to the Film Academy Awards (Colombian entry) secured an increase in the number of screenings in 'local' metropolitan Colombia. Yet, even though the film has an undeniable Colombian stamp, it is impossible to disregard the sources of funding that made possible its production. Besides receiving Argentine, Venezuelan and Spanish funds, this is the second time that the Dutch Hubert Bals Funds subsidizes a film directed by Ciro Guerra; the first one is *Los viajes del viento* (2009).[13] Among the criteria for the allocation of financial resources, Hubert Funds's conditions require that 'the story of the project should be rooted in the culture of the applicant's country' (IFFR 2016). *El abrazo de la serpiente* certainly complies with these guidelines, but it remains a matter of debate to what extent the film truly gives voice to the locals on the screen, rather than simply echoing the Western perspective of two characters facing many of the challenges of the rural corners of the so-perceived alluring Global South.[14] Unless the goal is to prompt a sense of exoticism and difference, it does not seem logical to recount the adventures and misfortunes of a German and an American in order to draw attention to Colombia's cultural and natural richness, evidenced through its indigenous people and Amazonian region. The fabulist nostalgia in *El abrazo de la serpiente*, particularly in terms of linguistic ethnotypes, and that have proved to be quite successful, is also present in the filmmaker's subsequent project.

Co-directed by Marcela Gallego, Guerra's third indigeneity-themed film, *Pájaros de verano*, relies on many of the techniques applied in *El abrazo de la serpiente*. Released in 2018, this Colombian-Danish-Mexican co-production is for the major part spoken in Wayuunaiki (also known as Wayuu/Wayúu or Guajiro). Dispensing with the inclusion of native speakers – except for one key performer – the film draws attention to a language rarely, if ever, included in films with such high production costs. The storyline invites the spectator to travel in time and space as the story is set in the 1960s–1980s in the arid northern part of Colombia (Guajira). The fiction feature offers subtle reminders of tumultuous moments in Colombian history but also of latent realities as it explores the involvement of Wayúu communities in drug trafficking. Gallego and Guerra's film underlines the marginalization experienced by communities almost forgotten by the state, and the onset of an industry that has scarred the social fabric of the nation, one still affecting thousands of Colombians. The co-production has been considered as an example of a 'new aesthetic-political programme' (Zuluaga and Muñoz 2018: para. 4) in which magic and realism are synthesized to present a relatable image of Colombia overseas. Indeed, *Pájaros de verano* stands out for carefully constructed images, scenes packed with surrealism, intense symbolism and stunning action sequences dotted with mysticism and set in ghostly locations. The figure of birds, perplexing dreams (mostly premonitions) and noises made by local instruments (e.g. sawawa) in the background add a magical touch to recurrent images of violence, which could be read in terms of Ochoa Gautier's (2014) politics of the aural. Since most dialogues in the film are (or intend, perhaps unsuccessfully, to be) in Wayuunaiki – hopefully intelligible for the native speakers – along with impeccable photography and dynamic action scenes, language is presumably one of the most distinctive elements of this fictional feature. Some of the performers have openly discussed how relieved they were when they heard Wayúu viewers understood their dialogues. Fictional scenarios remain within the realm of artistic expression and block any demands of authenticity. Yet, one cannot help wondering if, for instance, SnowGlobe, one of the funders of the film, would finance a production set in their local Copenhagen and spoken in a version of Danish that would hypothetically prompt the actors to ask audiences (at the premiere!) whether they understand the dialogues.

A valid observation is that the performativity of language as a marker of ethnicity is central to the portrayals of Zaida (Natalia Reyes), the main character of the story, in particular, because the film sprang from a need to depict 'Wayúu reality' in an authentic and realistic way, as Gallego and Guerra have expressed. In this context, the fact that Natalia Reyes acts using a language which is not her native tongue raises questions about the role of linguistic heritage in the creation of indigeneity-oriented films. In this respect, Gallego (2018) has noted that they actually wanted to work 'med professionelle skuespiller fra området, men der er ikke rigtigt nogen professionelle skuespiller, der taler Wayuu-sproget' [with professional actors from the region, but that there is not one single professional actor who speaks the Wayúu language].[15] Based on interviews with the team behind the *Pájaros de verano*, they sought to 'retratar' [portray], without 'copiar' [copying] (Berjón and Reyes 2018). Guerra asserts that 'para lograr una gran autenticidad, quisimos trabajar con el pueblo wayúu' [in order to achieve a major sense of authenticity, we wanted to work with the Wayúu people] (Olavarria et al. 2018).

Native speakers of the language, untrained actors willing to be part of the film, helped the crew to familiarize themselves with Wayúu culture and epistemologies. As Guerra explains, 'ninguno de nosotros habla wayuunaiki' [none of us speaks Wayuunaiki], but the cast was eager and curious to act in an unknown language (López 2018: para. 6). A valid observation is that the use of Amerindian languages is instrumental in the conception of a compelling story but becomes problematic when directors make claims about authenticity. Films are works of art and as such they grant their creators the freedom to conceive how characters should sound, that is, when to use a mixture of languages and how speech sets the tone of a sequence. Indigenous linguistic legacy, along with less-known languages, remains nevertheless more prone to be forgotten, or used in any conceivable manner. The absence of institutional entities or supportive states behind them possibly weakens their leverage. Through global cinema, these languages enter pancultural spaces where hybridity and mixture of themes, ideas, trends and genres is the norm.

Gallego and Guerra's fiction feature resembles an amalgam of *Cien años de soledad* (1967) by Gabriel García Márquez, a Viking saga, and a Shakespearian tale tinted with elements from Francis Ford Coppola's *The Godfather* (1972) and Andy Baiz's popular series *Narcos* (2015), produced by Netflix. It documents a historical moment in the long fight of Colombia against drug trafficking, and on this account, it makes an important contribution. *Pájaros de verano* is set during the so-called *Bonanza marimbera* ('Marijuana Rush'). This term refers to the period 1960–1980 when families in the Cesar, Guajira and Magdalena regions grew and sold marijuana illegally, still today romanticized as an unstrained period of time in the Colombian imaginary. Ursula (Carmiña Martínez) and her family demand that Raphayet (José Acosta) provide a considerable bride price for the hand of their daughter Zaida in marriage.

Moved by the interest of American hippies – apparently linked to Peace Corps volunteers stationed in the area – in the illicit plant, Raphayet and his friend Moises (Jhon Narváez) enter the marijuana trafficking business. Once married, Zaida and Raphayet find themselves at the centre of a ruthless war between the various parties involved in drug smuggling. *Pájaros de verano* implies that the community is progressively destroyed not only by the greediness of their members but also by the interest of foreigners in their natural resources (high-quality marijuana). Throughout the film, the difference between the Wayúu and *alijuna* (non-Wayúu) is made by their adherence to social codes, family interaction and, in the case of women, by their colourful, sumptuous dresses. In *Pájaros de verano*, speaking Wayuunaiki reveals their background, but also raises questions about the ways in which filmmakers define and portray the 'authentic' in the diegetic world of a fiction feature. After all, the main actors are not conversant in the language.

Reyes asserts that, prior to the film, her knowledge of the community she represents was limited. She explains that, as Colombians, 'todos temenos una mochila Wayúu, conocemos que hablan otro idioma' [we all have a Wayúu bag, we know they speak other language], but nevertheless, she adds, 'no es una cultura tan cercana' [it's not a closely related culture] (Berjón and Reyes 2018). The actress reflects on her four months in the region, and her extensive research as tools sufficient to portray a convincing Wayuunaiki speaker. Guerra explains that 'todo se escribe en español y hacer la traducción es un proceso final' [everything is written in Spanish and translating it is a final process] (López 2018: para. 6). As in his previous films, he experiments with language and manages to create a credible, well-received visual narrative. *Pájaros de verano* explores the intimate and quotidian life of a community, and its traditional, sacred and mystic aspects. Gallego and Guerra have stated on numerous occasions that it was important to approach the Wayúu culture with respect and consideration, but also to remain faithful to their cosmologies, worldviews and conventions. The role of Wayuunaiki is best epitomized in the character of Peregrino the Word Messenger (José Vicente Cotes), the one responsible for delivering messages between the various parties in times of conflict. Peregrino, a native speaker of Wayuunaiki, re-enacts his real-life occupation as conflict-mediator in the Guajira region. Gallego and Guerra resort to a real-life *pütchipü'ü* (messenger/palabrero) to acknowledge an important aspect of Wayúu culture, providing in the process an ethnographical/anthropological viewpoint on the screen. The inclusion of

Wayúu folklore, costumes, rituals, dances and history undeniably contributes to the authenticity Guerra mentions in several interviews. Consonant with this approach, casting Cotes as a *palabrero* seemed logical.

The fictional nature of cinema allows filmmakers to choose which elements from the 'real world' they wish to duplicate, and in what ways. Gallego and Guerra insist on how important it is to bring Wayuunaiki to the world's attention, but it is not clear for whom. In an interview with María Carolina Piña (Radio France Internationale) (2018), co-director Gallego observes that even if 'estabamos siendo repelidos todo el tiempo' [we were being repelled all the time] by the locals, *Pájaros de verano* manages to be 'una representación verídica' [a truthful representation] told from the Wayúu perspective. While Gallego adds that the 'gringos' are the catalysts of Colombian drug trafficking, Guerra expresses his annoyance with non-Colombian narco-dramas and how *Pájaros de verano* takes distance from any 'caricatura que hacen los extranjeros' [caricature made by foreigners] (Piña et al. 2018). As it appears, the quest for authenticity is closely linked to a sense of authority, self-censorship and a blurring of fact and fiction.

The mediatized fantasy in which films are embedded allows filmmakers, especially in international circles, to create fictional languages at will (e.g. *Avatar*, 2009, James Cameron), blend in different elements at different moments (e.g. *Vicky Cristina Barcelona*, 2008, Woody Allen), imply linguistic boundaries by manipulating accents (e.g. *The Pianist*, 2002, Roman Polanski), bypass historical accuracy (e.g. *Apocalypto*, 2006, Mel Gibson) or play with language in nuanced ways (e.g. *Lost in Translation*, 2003, Sofia Coppola). The central question is whether linguistic authenticity is only relevant insofar as it convinces audiences that the visual and audible dimensions of a film are equally authentic. Meticulous attempts to depict an unknown culture risk missing their goal if there is a disjunction between images and sounds. Alluring settings and awe-inspiring characters are surfaces, while monologues and dialogues uttered by actors convey a sense of depth and internalization. Nevertheless, the reality is that with less than 300,000 speakers – the majority of whom reside in Colombia and Venezuela – inaccurate, accented, flawed or broken Wayuunaiki is imperceptible to most viewers of the film (especially those outside the region).

Perhaps one of the most violent and yet subtle silencing strategies is probably the one in which a cultural artefact or creative work of art in any given format endorses silencing a linguistic community in its own language, its own territory and in a space that re-enacts a passage of its own (hi)story. *Pájaros de verano* privileges dialogues of non-Wayuunaiki speakers speaking (*a form of*) Wayuunaiki over episodes in which a member of a linguistic community in danger of extinction is offered a podium to, literally and figuratively, become the unheard voice of its own society. If one language dies every fourteen days, it is unlikely that humanity can afford to muzzle small linguistic societies much longer. It is difficult to imagine why cinematic productions should necessarily be armour-plated behind their status of works of art when the linguistic heritage of vulnerable communities is at stake. A valid observation is that Wayuunaiki is not one of Tolkien's elvish languages or Klingon, developed by Marc Okrand for the widely popular *Star Trek* science fiction franchise, at least not yet. As a living real-life language, its inclusion in a film that has circulated widely is a reason to celebrate, but also to remember the terms in which their speakers are approached, strategically visibilized, tactically replaced, conveniently translated and ventriloquized.

Gallego and Guerra aim to challenge lampooned portrayals of Colombia's illegal drug industry and its history. Yet, applying Guerra's same logic by which foreigners are not suited to create narco-narratives, for instance, about Pablo Escobar's emporium, would imply that Wayúu history should only be told by Wayúu directors. By the same token, only Wayuunaiki speakers would be suitable to bring their language to world audiences in an 'authentic' and 'authoritative' way. An analysis of the marketing campaign for the film reveals outright contradictions and inconsistencies. Much of *Pájaros de verano*'s advertising material and media coverage about the film shows that the use of spoken Wayuunaiki – an *exotic* language – is part of the promotional strategy of the film. In many ways, it is possible to draw conclusive connections between linguistic authenticity and higher levels of marketability of movies, predominantly in art house circles.

Films need to remain attractive to those audiences they intend to attract. In this context, language risks becoming a token of exoticism and allure rather than being an answer to the demands of communities facing discrimination and oblivion. Wherefore, linguistic diversity in films does not necessarily denote a more inclusive, all-encompassing, egalitarian approach to cinema, even though that might seem to be the case at first sight.

Conclusion

Imagology prompts questions about the use of language to mark characters who represent nations, creating in the processes linguistic ethnotypes. In films aligned with Western cinematic tradition, language is present as a salient marker of indigeneity (Carreño 2006). Since the colonization of the Americas, both at an economic and political level, indigenous languages have been excluded from any major arenas of participation. Mexico is simultaneously the nation with the highest number of Spanish speakers and the most diverse country in terms of multilingualism. Large waves of migration to wealthier regions of the country, particularly to urban centres, have resulted in dispersed and weakened linguistic pockets. Linguistic discrimination disguises itself in the distinction made between urban and rural accents. Due to historical processes, languages become entwined with visual characteristics of their speakers, their ethnicity, socio-economic background, affluence, influence, recognition and prestige. A close inspection at cinematic narrative from a linguistic standpoint needs to question in which ways, and for which purposes, cinema reflects tangible social reconfigurations or mere attempts to create 'authentic' productions through language. As this chapter has shown, languages are vocatively framed but are not necessarily acknowledged as a means of communication. Reviewing the addition of native linguistic traits in visual cultural artefacts evokes questions about spectatorship, specifically how audiences, untrained in hearing these languages, react to narratives where the languages play a significant role. In the context of power, an important aspect to consider is the risk that linguistic legacy is manipulated, or even exploited. The underlying notion is that filmmakers repeatedly turn to indigenous languages or accented Spanish or Portuguese as a means of rendering their stories more credible, convincing and alluring. Amerindian languages significantly feature in Latin American cinema, but from a tactical standpoint indigenous linguistic heritage is still used as a symbol/ornament that aligns with long-established linguistic ethnotypes of a nostalgic, alluring indigenous figure.

4

Emphasis: Embodiment of indigeneity

The realization that art has an organic and sensorial dimension draws attention to the fact that images stimulate perception by creating connections beyond the visual realm. Cultural artefacts mediate messages by communicating ideas and stimulating senses. During an interview with a Mapundungun-speaking informant in Santiago (Chile) on the inclusion of Mapuche elements in mass media, she shared her opinion that if cinema came with a smell, acacia would probably be chosen as the right fragrance to accompany a film about her community. At various levels and from various viewpoints, her insightful remark prompts a reflection about the capacity of art to contain the sensorial, the symbolic and the epistemic. Films do not smell or taste, but as this chapter argues, films do appeal to the senses by presenting references that ignite memories and connections (e.g. mental schemas). An image does not need to emanate any scent, for example, for it to prompt olfactory reactions and sensations. Visual narratives are canvases that capture representations of situations, oozing stimuli in the form of emotions. This is a fact filmmakers understand and apply. Central to this part of the book is to delve into the manifestation of indigeneity through repetitive visual codes devised to resonate ontologically and epistemically among target audiences. The main thesis is that cinema encapsulates the intertwined relation between nature, technology and the senses. Thematically, the first section, 'Nature–technology nexus as an ontological genre', argues that indigeneity-oriented films are a genre in their own terms, overrulingly identifiable by portrayals that depict indigenous societies as extension of nature, and foreigners to technology. The second section, 'Knowledge, sense and ethnicity', explores the epistemic and epistemological connotations of indigeneity-related narratives from a sensorial viewpoint. Both sections seek to review how indigeneity is embodied and contained in visual artefacts that use particular stimuli as a means to narrate and frame native societies.

Nature–technology nexus as an ontological genre

Indigeneity-themed films operate thematically as extensions of a longue durée tradition of visually articulating the idea that some societies are closer to nature than others. Reiterated aesthetic or narrative conventionalities define categories that viewers decode according to their cultural repertoire. Cinema conveys gesturally and expressively emotions based on the identification of the spectators with the images of storylines they choose to see. It is seldom the case that the audience does not know anything at all about the film they are about to watch. Looking closely at the corpus of films selected for this book, it becomes apparent that although the canvas might be blank at first, the palette of possibilities that filmmakers select when depicting indigenous figures cinematographically is quite limited/limiting. Revising the entire history of visual representation of pre-Columbian elements, cultures and languages, there is a clear, predictive set of elements that are present and notoriously absent. Even if many of the Latin American films reviewed in this volume might be considered, for instance, detective/mysteries (e.g. *El Traspatio*), survival adventures (e.g. *Cenizas eternas*), historical romantic comedies (e.g. *Caramuru*), biopics (e.g. *Evo Pueblo*), road movie films (e.g. *Cochochi*), ethnic family sagas (e.g. *Pájaros de verano*), rural dramas (e.g. *La Sirga*), satires (e.g. *¿Quién mató a la llamita blanca?*), coming-of-age dramas (e.g. *Nosilatiaj. La belleza*) or LGBTQ+ dramas (e.g. *Retablo*), few if any indigeneity-themed film also fulfils the precepts of, for instance, artificial intelligence dramas, musical comedies or superhero adventures.

Quoting again an insightful Aymara-speaking Lima-based informant, 'nadie hace películas con un Batman indígena, o cholo' [nobody makes films with an indigenous or *cholo* Batman in them], but there are plenty of cinematic productions where the connection is made between, for instance, indigeneity and the ability to communicate with nature. I argue that the reason is because cinematic productions revolving around indigeneity are in themselves a genre. On the one hand, the directors of the reviewed films do seem to follow canons of representation that coincide with the classical paradigms mobilized by art house cinema, and that position indigeneity in concrete ways that only partially deviate from archetypic stances. On the other hand, a salient overarching commonality observable in films focusing on ethnic groups is a tendency to interpret them, as this section intends to show, through the nature-vis-à-vis-technology filter.

Echoing Altman's (1999) discussion, genres are multilayered concepts that abstractly impose rubrics through which cinematic works are interrelationally conceived, scaffolded, fictionalized, presented and disseminated. From this standpoint, films about indigenous societies and cultures have constituted a genre for a long time. In terms of blueprint, one of Altman's canons, these visual narratives have specific formulas, rarely digressing from formats established even before cinema emerged as a medium. Although their structure varies in multiple ways, at their core, they also operate on an iconic and pictorial framework that seeks to express the materiality and physicality of an identity that (non-indigenous) filmmakers know only from a distance. Above all, label and contract are perhaps the most salient definitions of genre, out of those developed by Altman, that more emphatically distinguish films about indigenous peoples.

The films in the corpus are identifiable (label) precisely because exhibitors and distributors underline the inclusion of specific identities as a designation, but also an exhortation to the spectators about the plot, characters and cinematography. The films discussed in this book are here because they are advertised, to varying degrees and extents, as indigeneity-related movies. As they navigate across search engines, unhidden thanks to the magic of tags and dockets efficiently processed by algorithms, they find their way into screens of viewers. Cinematic difference sells, and indigeneity has the potential to engender it at best, without minimal benefit, or, on the contrary, at times, with damaging effect for the societies that are being represented. Indigeneity, I posit, is a popular genre.

Trained and untrained audiences seem to know what to expect (contract in Altman's words) and funding, exhibition and distribution networks encourage and facilitate the process of categorization of content. The contract is broken if audiences are not able to anticipate and predict. Filmmakers are aware that viewers' agency stems from the fact that genres provide certainty and predictability. Genres grant an extent of reassurance about the capacity of a story to provide visual pleasure; a film revolving around indigenous characters, at least in principle, *ought* to fit with potential spectators' preconceived models. Today's global cinematic landscape reinforces the standardization of genres that emerged in America to counteract and rule out unpredictability and box office loss. In her seminal work on Latin American road movies, Lie (2017) rightfully observes that a 'transnational dynamic explains why genres hitherto identified with US cinema have started to travel outside that geo-cultural domain' (4). This certainly applies to films produced in regions where cinematic industries depend on international financing and distribution networks.

Genres and generic labels evolve and subdivide into subgenres, but retain traits from the original blueprints that inform their basic formulas. Carreño (2006) asserts that indigeneity films are historical elongations and adaptations of westerns, of course, adapted to the reality of the region where the stories are set. Native communities (as they are imagined to be), vast territories, settlers–locals interaction, insularity and a scene dominated by a frontier where civilizations meet, classic western elements are aspects easily found in the corpus of representational films (see Table 1). Unfolding along parallel historical axes, indigenous renderings from an iconographic standpoint have been shaped by the ideological and political representativity of pre-Columbian legacy in the formation of Latin American nation states.[1] Pictorially, as Chapter 1 shows, European artistic and ethnographic conventions have informed the visuality of indigeneity at both sides of the Atlantic, and even beyond. Images do not cease to document and register the time of their creation. In the twenty-first century, the optic in indigeneity films – besides retaining traces of European canons of visual othering and American westerns' formulas – is normatively informed by identity politics, exoticism and environmental concerns (including greenwashing). The nature–technology dyad is crucial to understand the avoidance of artificiality that characterizes representational films and to contextualize the ontological dilemma that they pose in terms of iconic representativeness and political representativity. For unfranchised societies, identity politics is crucial for their recognition, but this often comes with idealizations about their role as natural beings or its ultimate defenders. This can become a problematic discursive practice when it reduces them to societies irrefutably decoupled from technical domains, technological advancements, futuristic milieus, machine-driven scenarios or, simply, the use of electric appliances.

Along this line, *Tiempos menos modernos* (Argentina–Chile, 2012), by director Simon Franco, gives a comic but in-depth account of a suspicious Tehuelche who suddenly receives a television set as part of a state programme to reach indigenous communities living in distant rural areas. Ramiro Payaguala (Oscar Payaguala), who has lived in isolation for most of his life, cannot bother to open the wooden box labelled with the government seals. Actually, it is the official connotations of the mysterious delivery that makes him doubt the contents of the package. It is his only friend, Chilean Felipe (Nicolás Saavedra), who convinces him of giving the newly arrived present the benefit of the doubt. The film manages to effortlessly point out the desolate conditions in which Argentine native communities live today. The picturesque landscapes and impressionist cinematography convey a sense of fiction, especially because the main character is an actor known in Argentina for his involvement in the struggle for the acknowledgement of the pre-Columbian cultural legacy of the country.

Gradually, viewers learn that Felipe tries to convince Payaguala to help him put up a show in his guesthouse so that tourists have an opportunity to see an 'ícono autóctono en vías de extinción' [an almost extinct autochthonous icon] (Frías 2012: para. 2). Yet, it is not Felipe but the new television set that really awakens the curiosity of the secluded man. Besides learning from exercise programmes and receiving updates about then-President Menem's ostentatious projects, Payaguala discovers the world of telenovelas. The nature of the melodramatic series and the beautiful actresses starring in them seduce Payaguala from the first day. *Tiempos menos modernos* chronicles the attempts at transforming, but also invading, distant topographies, at least from the perspective of the imaginary. Set in Patagonia, the film might be considered part of an early twenty-first-century tendency, described by Page (2009), to produce stories that experiment with new or reformed forms of nationalism and identity. Figuratively, the television set seems to suggest that, in spite of large distances, ideologically Argentina perceives, presents and disseminates itself as a unified whole. Through the materiality of the television set, and the tangibility of mass media in modern life, the film nevertheless preserves the idea that indigeneity and modernity are asynchronous.

In the same vein, with no clocks, no time and in a lost corner of the Andes, *Madeinusa* deserves special attention in its approach to indigeneity, described by Camps (2012) as a 'Greek tragedy translocated to the Andean region' (237). In doing so, the story of fourteen-year-old Madeinusa (Magaly Soler), who is to be deflowered by her father and town mayor, don Cayo (Juan Ubaldo Huamán), during the Holy Week festivities, is to remain within the realm of fiction. The diegetic world is carefully constructed, and the enhanced use of colour sharpens the exotic scenery, but also the outfits that the inhabitants of Manayaycuna wear during the festivities. The credibility of this portrait of Andean life, strengthened by the use of Quechua, is probably what renders the story so contentious. In many ways, the storyline might be read as an insensitive attempt to orientalize indigenous figures by portraying them as immoral and savage. Indeed, when it comes to representations constructed from an outsider's viewpoint, natives tend to be depicted as barbarians, victims or wise embodiments of Mother Nature (Hall 1996). In sync with similar depictions, dated mainly from the 1940s and 1950s, the village of Manayaycuna is depicted as a lost town, in terms of both space and time. For instance, instead of a clock, a sleepy man sitting in the main square turns around sheets of cardboard to mark the time, while drivers passing by avoid the town at all cost. Madeinusa has plenty of reasons for wanting to leave this world behind. Her desire to run away and her decision to offer her virginity to Salvador (Carlos de la Torre) – a geologist stopping by on his way to another town – rather than to her father operate as signals of submission to what is foreign or is antithetical to Manayaycuna. The notion that there is an *outside* world, which is opposite, or at least not parallel, to the inner core of an indigenous community prompts questions of how indigenous communities are perceived.

If a Greek tragedy can be understood as a fictitious story without reducing the Greeks to savages and uncivilized people, an Andean-based story can offer interpretations that are not unreservedly related to ethnicity. Cultural artefacts seeking to make demands on behalf of native peoples are prominent for highlighting the image of an exploited and humiliated *Indian* (Bedoya 2015). Considering this, Llosa's contribution is momentous as it presents a story where subjectivities emerge and develop. The film advances the notion of agency through the filter of abnormality and deviation. *Madeinusa* attests to the power of decision of this young girl, while it also embeds the story in a context where heavily drunk 'peasants' sexually assault their own daughters (Roca 2006). To alleviate its backwardness, the film seems to suggest that Manayaycuna is in need of moral guidance, according to modern, urban and Westernized sets of values (Pagán-Teitelbaum 2008).

Inherently, in varying ways, Salvador is presented as Madeinusa's saviour (Salvador means *saviour* in Spanish), even if he is not a free-willed, uncompelled one. He finds himself amidst an unfamiliar (rural) space outside his comfort zone, but inside a series of events where he symbolically embodies the urban figure within the narrative. Salvador facilitates Madeinusa's plan to ravage don Cayo's long-awaited night and serves as a reminder of the possibilities Lima might offer to the young girl. Her dream of leaving her hometown, more than anything to look for her mother, seems to become more latent in the presence of someone who embodies the city. Salvador is not an elongation of nature but an extension of a metropolis. Figuratively, Madeinusa seduces Salvador with the same intensity the city seduces her imaginary. Their sexual encounter is provoked by the girl, and orchestrated and carried out according to her wishes. Perhaps, this scene confirms Llosa's admiration for the ways in which José María Arguedas approaches intercourse in his literary works.[2] Coherently, besides being a key point of reference, his portrayals of sex as a form of attack have served as a framework for the filmmaker's depictions of lovemaking in her films.[3] Their encounter can be read as an attempt of the young girl to debunk the power structures in place, both from an ideological (male/urban/white vs. female/rural/indigenous) and physical (strength/freedom vs. weakness/imprisonment) standpoint.

Llosa proposes a portrayal of a contradictory subjectivity (a presumable victim takes control), while insisting on the possibility of Madeinusa's subversive agency. The use of Quechua in the scenes where Madeinusa and her sister Chale interact with each other conveys the notion that their mother tongue operates as a unifying element, a connector intimately related to their reality. The Amerindian language operates not only as a medium of ethnic expression but also as marker of woman- and sisterhood. Effectively, the old woman adjusting Madeinusa's dress utters a warning in Quechua once she notices traces of blood in her underwear. The linguistic choice in decisive moments of the narrative implicitly registers poignant coming-of-age stances. Vis-à-vis the inclusion of reductionist, distorted and derogatory traits, the film portrays a feminine subject who follows her own instincts. Different from her sister Chale (Yiliana Chong), Madeinusa is not particularly connected to Manayaycuna. Indigenist ideologies are based on the notion that indigenous communities are an extension of the lands they inhabit or where they were born.[4] Yet, young Madeinusa becomes undesirable for her community precisely because of her interest in other (unnatural or less nature-oriented) geographies and lifestyles.

The most crucial example of emancipation is probably Madeinusa's decision to poison her father for breaking her mother's earrings. If Manayaycuna is indeed a world ruled by irrationality, rituals and superstitions, the young girl ratifies her decision to ignore most of them, except perhaps the notion that *Tiempo santo* (Holy Time) is the time of liberation. After all, it was during the festivities that her mother left. It is a rite of passage to leave her home, but also to incarnate the Holy Virgin in the annual procession. Her evolution is given prime consideration throughout the narrative. Central to the film is to depict Madeinusa's urge to keep her surroundings clean (rat-free – nature-free), control over her own body (especially her braid) and, up until the right moment, her virginity. Certainly, her staged position as a procession virgin, and a to-be-lover of her father denotes perceived double standards and ideas about the syncretic nature of her culture (Monette 2013). There is nevertheless an intense sense of childishness, credulity, innocence and naiveté in her attitude.

The space and time of identity

Infantilized societies, easily tricked, have been part of the European iconographies about adventitious populations for centuries, particularly of those considered inferior. Childhood as an ontological and symbolical stage has historically occupied a particular place in films about indigenous societies, both across and outside Latin America. Unequivocally, the nature component is conjoined with allusions to ethnicity and age as stasis, but also part of a personal evolution. Presenting a variety of childhoods as different experiences (white, mestizo, indigenous) defined by social position, as opposed to a singular set of experiences equally available to everyone, is also a strategy to denounce alterity while exotifying the young Other.

Directed by Sergio Bloch and Tania Lamarca, the Brazilian trilogy *Tainá - Uma Aventura na Amazônia / Tainá: An adventure in the Amazon* (2001), *Tainá 2: A aventura continua/Tainá 2: A New Adventure* (2004) and *Tainá 3: A origem/Tainá 3: The Origen* (2011) explores the life of an orphan roaming around in the Amazon basin with few allies, one of which is Catu (a monkey). Tainá's story stands out not only for her heroic way of facing challenges, but also for being an embodiment of the jungle. Even if the trilogy aims to express concerns about the lack of ecological awareness among Brazilian younger generations, it does so by using outdated formulas. Tainá engages in dialogues with animals, using different codes, gestures and guttural sounds when she approaches a parrot, or a monkey. Her skilful use of spears and bows is unparalleled and, most notably, she can communicate with Mother Earth. In *Tainá 3*, when Tainá (Wiranu Tembé) encounters a blond young girl, a stranger Tainá describes as having 'cabelos do sol' [sun-like hair], the difference in childhood experience becomes tangible. Laurinha (Beatriz Noskoski) is fully dressed, lacks knowledge about nature, has caregivers and her future is secured. The notion that there is an indigenous version of childhood, as opposed to a mestizo or European variant, resembles other differentiations that the narratives make between characters based on their ethnicity.

Alternatively, *Alamar* (2009) proposes a reflection of indigeneity that is not explicitly inscribed either in indigenist or Indianist ideologies but rather in a hybrid, ennobled and respectful version of modern Mayan lifestyles. Director Pedro González-Rubio focuses on the special moments a five-year-old Natan (Natan Machado Palombini) shares with his father Jorge (Jorge Machado) on his fishing boat along the Chinchorro atoll reef. After his wife Roberta (Roberta

Palombini), bored with her enclosed life, decides to return to her native Italy, Natan is to follow her, but not before Jorge passes on to him some of the important lessons he has learnt about the sea and its mysteries. The Mexican-Italian co-production stands out for its elaboration on the problematic relation between humans and nature. With idyllic landscapes, the story is seductive for its simplicity but at the same time for the depth of its message about differences and coexistence. *Alamar* suggests that indigenous ways of living and interacting with the world do not necessarily oppose what is perceived to be a mestizo or European lifestyles and that the differences do not need to translate into quantifiable codes that presuppose one is superior to the other. Natan represents hybridity as another viable possibility, although linguistically his upbringing is European. His mother speaks to him in Italian while his father uses Spanish all along.

The last scene where Roberta is shown playing with her son on one of Rome's hills, wearing thick jackets and overlooking a clouded, urban but picturesque landscape does not convey the idea of comparison but rather of diversity. The child dwells in a space between a convoluted urban setting and a rudimentary natural state that articulate associations commonly made between childhood and innocence (Martin 2019). A source of inspiration for González-Rubio, in his own words, includes the 'purity of the landscape and the expansiveness of nature' (Jenkins and González-Rubio 2010). The Chinchorro reef differs from a European city in the same way that Jorge and Roberta have different expectations and desires. Jorge is portrayed as a father offering shelter, care and bonds, without implying that Mayan fatherhood is superior or inferior to European motherhood, or vice versa. *Alamar* connects the idea of realism and authenticity, suggesting that the child spontaneously moves in front of the camera, he does not perform (Martin 2019). Five-year-old Natan illustrates a tendency to focus on childhood in recent Latin American cinema and the central role that indigenous youth play in other films, such as *Cochochi* (2007), *La Jaula de Oro* and *Vaho* (2009).[5]

At the interface of infancy, kinetics and cultural heritage, highly acclaimed Esteban Larraín's *Alicia en el país* (2008) re-enacts the tumultuous journey of Alicia Esquivel, a Bolivian thirteen-year-old girl detained and deported in 2004, after attempting to enter Chile in search of work. Social issues such as forced migration, disparity, disruption and transmission of customs are at the core of the film that prompted Larraín to offer Esquivel (then fifteen), two years after the incident, to play the key role in a film intended to shed light on her own life. After learning about her journey in the newspapers, the prolific director was interested in exploring how Bolivian childhoods are shaped by economic hardships, millenary traditions and political conflicts at a regional level. Besides unfolding from real-life events, the story is constructed according to first-hand descriptions and is staged in the original settings where Alicia's journey took place. Dramatic landscapes of isolation, hardship and oblivion remind the spectator of the disavowal endured by indigenous communities across the continent. Besides a seemingly endless desert, salt flats, untouched nature and arid flat areas serve to introduce a sense of alterity to (inter)national audiences. Local viewers witness how Alicia makes her way into their country yearning for a brighter future. Larraín confronts the spectators with specificities of an intimate drama that prompt them to realize they cannot relate to the protagonist's journey. After all, the story of a lost childhood tarnished by an involuntary exodus is not how metropolitan Chileans – or most film festival attendees – imagine or remember their adolescence. The image of Alicia embodies aspects of difference that range from her early age, to her Quechua descent, and her illegal status as a potential migrant of indigenous roots. Figuratively, Larraín questions childhood as a period in one's life, by challenging ontological understandings of how human life is ideologically compartmentalized. Since the trail has been walked by Aymaras and Quechuas for centuries, the film epitomizes the centrality of knowledge transfers within communities, not necessarily conditioned by external definitions of space as property.

Poignantly, childhood is a state that dwells in places (e.g. ocean in *Alamar*, a trail in *Alicia en el país*) and that, in the case of rural topologies, raise questions about postcolonial complacency that struggles to place indigenous elements in urban contexts. Or else, a fixed imprisoning grid that refuses to indigenize the notion of metropolis, perhaps for fear of de-technifying its mere essence. Landscapes as articulations of nature, presented as allergic, immune or insular to any markers of modernity, scientific or technical presence seem to imply that pre-Columbian heritage and static-ness are perceived as synonyms. Unfortunately, it is an illusion as the destruction of ecosystems sadly demonstrates. The problematic aspect of this approach is that it positions indigeneity as a fossilized cluster of ethnicities with no future. Not because technology and future are the same, but because in the modern imaginaries, futuristic scenarios are entwined with one or the other form of technical artifices. As self-representational films discussed in the last chapter demonstrate, indigeneity, knowledge and technology are not necessarily discordant terms. The difference in frames of reference between, for instance, self-representational *Vestimenta Sapara: Una tradición en peligro/Sapara Clothing: A Tradition in Danger* (Ecuador, 2019) (see Chapter 7) and *La Sirga* (Colombia, 2012) is quite broad.

Directed by William Vega, *La Sirga* revolves around the arrival of Alicia (Joghis Seudin) to the impoverished, dilapidated and isolated inn her uncle Oscar (Julio Cesar Roble) runs with the help of Flora (Floralba Achicanoy). The nineteen-year-old is not welcomed, but her uncle knows that, as with millions of others, his niece has become victim of the internal displacements brought about by the various guerrilla groups operating in the country. The story takes place in La Cocha, a desolate, marshland village which Alicia fears will also be seized by the bands operating in the area. The beauty of the landscape makes up for the lack of glamour of the human dwellings and seems to conceal memories and whispers (Zuluaga 2012). As described by Vega, the locations are reminiscent of 'leyendas de pueblos, dioses, héroes y mártires indígenas alrededor de las lagunas, lugares de Los Andes por siglos epicentros de sabiduría, conservadas gracias a la tradición oral' [indigenous legends of towns, gods, heroes and martyrs dotted along the Andean lakes for centuries, epicentres of knowledge kept alive thanks to oral traditions] (Posso Gómez 2012: para. 2). The lake morpho-contextualizes an epistemic and ontological object that emanates the qualities of those that acknowledge it as a place of a specific kind. This assertion situates the notion of nature as an entity that defines human existence, and applies to those that abide by it. Simultaneously, it perpetuates the view that a natural being stays as such and that cannot be a technical/technocratic one. *La Sirga* pays homage to the history and natural state of a place where nature governs but also to the victims of a political state where nobody seems to govern.

The impressive scenery does not mask the broken dreams of Alicia and Oscar who have lost their loved ones in the armed conflicts, or the absence of tourists at an inn they insist on rebuilding, mostly with uneven pieces of wood. The imperfection and asymmetry remind the viewers that Colombia has been torn by war and that, like the inhabitants of La Cocha, Colombians understandingly struggle to reconstruct their country. Strong assets of *La Sirga* besides the evocative and dramatic landscapes include the pace of the narrative, and the tactful mention of details that remind spectators about the invisible but tangible violence that serves as backdrop to the story. The film echoes the processes by which violence has regrettably become a distressing and traumatic aspect of Colombian psyche. Towards the end of the story, the same forces that transmit a sense of uncertainty and ambiguity to audiences – just like the fog in the marshland – truncate the semi-romantic story that emerges between Alicia and the sailor/boatman/courier Mirichis (David Guacas).

Effectively, Vega addresses the scars and implications of a conflict at a micro- and macro-level, from a human and nature perspective. The topography that serves the film as stage invites spectators to relate the story to Andean peoples and their realities. In the booklet accompanying the released film and in interviews, Vega claims, without elaborating any further, that the characters of *La Sirga* are of indigenous descent (García Calvo 2012; Vega 2012). However, in the context of agency, appropriation and framing, this is a detail impossible to ignore. Although the story encapsulates rightfully the misfortune and isolation that affect many Colombian communities, it is not clear how the film epitomizes indigenous lived experiences in the present. Unless, of course, Vega refers to the effect of violence as a problem that affects indigenous societies across the region. Yet, it seems problematic to rely on ethnic passing as a strategy to increase marketability and appeal across international distribution networks and exhibition venues.[6] Vega explains that the location is 'holy land' and has been for centuries (García Calvo 2012: para. 3). Notwithstanding, *La Sirga* can hardly be understood as an homage to self-identified indigenous peoples as Vega claims it to be, based on the fact that the chosen location evokes nostalgic associations. As with other examples of Colombian cinema, the focus lies on imaginaries about ancient pre-Columbian elements.

It is unrealistic to expect accuracy to prevail over artistic freedom. However, legitimizing ahistoricism in the context of mis- and under-representation raises questions about objectification and manipulation. If the nature-vis-à-vis-technology canon is derived from Eurocentric readings and understandings of the world in relation to a dominant core, perhaps decentring it involves allowing the indigenous to invade the technological realm. As the next section suggests, expanding an understanding of knowledge might pave the way to less histrionic representations of indigeneity. But before that, cinema has to find ways of accommodating canons where epistemic and epistemological identities exist, escape and thrive beyond a universal benchmark of truth and knowledge.

Ethnicity, senses and knowledge

There is no cinema without stimuli being channelled through the transmission and elicitation of emotions that transpose information, and in the process, feed and activate imaginaries. Circulation of images and sounds is also the mobilization of strategies that appeal to the other three senses: smell, touch and taste. Widely accepted sensorial conditions, such as psychedelic-induced states of consciousness (e.g. use of peyote in *El sueño del Maraʼakame*), episodes that capture gustatory and haptic practices, such as eating with the hands (e.g. *El ombligo de Guieʼdani*), actions that arouse disgust, such as disposing rats (e.g. *Madeinusa*), create tension, such as preparing a rope to commit suicide (e.g. *Las niñas Quispe*), or consternation, such as stabbing oneʼs husband (e.g. *Dauna*), depict other ways of relating to oneʼs immediate environment. These are also effective strategies to expose audiences and engage them to witness other scenarios, sceneries and sensations. Indigeneity is expected to be cinematically represented through visual episodes that mark and offer a different array of stimuli, or that are at least capable of conveying the sense of fascination that surrounds the idea of a native Other. By default, these stimuli that sensorily seduce audiences operate as knowledge transfers that reconfigure what audiences *learn* about and from the societies being represented. Indeed, this knowledge is (de)contextualized according to each filmmakerʼs artistic decisions, sensitivities, fundersʼ recommendations, exhibitorsʼ input and so on. As confirmed by the 768 reactions of social media collected for this study, nevertheless, indigeneity-themed films are not experiences viewers easily forget. Some of them make waves and become controversial, securing a place in public discourse (e.g. *Roma*) and the archives of cinema for the decades to come.

Cutting the sprouts of a potato growing inside the protagonistʼs vagina as device against rape is one memorable episode of *La teta asustada* (Peru, 2009). In the film, Fausta (Magaly Solier), a lugubrious, traumatized girl, decides to take any measurement to avoid experiencing what her mother had to endure during her pregnancy: a haptic, graphic and symbolic practice Fausta learnt from her motherʼs stories.[7] Director Claudia Llosa suggests that the *earthly* is closely and intimately – literally – interwoven with the *indigenous*. Moulded by lack of opportunities, past traumas and seclusion, it is not difficult to read her presence as a sign of misplacement and foreignness, rather than as a statement of belonging and recognition. This feeling intensifies once her mother dies. Partly because of lack of resources, partly due to loneliness, Fausta decides to keep her un-embalmed corpse underneath the bed they used to share. Her plan is to bring it to their hometown. Through her uncle, Fausta manages to find a position as a domestic worker in service to Aída (Susi Sánchez), a recognized but eccentric pianist. But while Fausta is to collect the amount needed, she also contemplates transporting the corpse with her own hands, as a piece of luggage in the trunk of an intercity bus, an idea that produces a deep sense of disturbance and strangeness.

As clearly stated by the acclaimed female director, 'each movie has an audience, and it needs to be clear whom you are addressing before writing a story' (Peirano and Llosa 2010). The question that *La teta asustada* invites audiences to ask in the context of exoticism and alterity is whether the story seeks to shed light on the consequences of violence or agitate and stun audiences for whom the Andean region denotes a sense of distance and remoteness. The film depicts Quechua-speaking communities of individuals who bathe in asymmetrically hand-dug holes lined with plastic bags filled with water (swimming pools), store un-embalmed bodies in unthinkable places and, most importantly, resort to potatoes as protective shields against sexual violence. Even if one could defend the view that the *teta asustada* syndrome is metaphorical, or a condition acknowledged within indigenous epistemologies of specific communities, the fact is that Fausta is a central figure, but mainly because she tells a peripheral story.

In the film, her headmistress Aída is going through a difficult period in terms of artistic creativity, until she accidently overhears her new young maid singing an alluring lullaby. Fausta is not ready to share her song with anyone, but eventually gives in and agrees to sing for Aída, in exchange for pearls. Eventually, Aída presents Fausta's songs as hers in a public concert, while the defenceless, underprivileged maid has no means to denounce the plagiarism that has been committed. A figurative circle that reminds viewers of the colonization of the Americas closes. In a way, Llosa seems to be critical about the repercussions of cultural appropriation. After all, in the film, Fausta's song gained recognition only after Aída translated it into a solo concerto, a paradox given the fact that few musical instruments are as quintessentially Western as the piano. Yet, the question is whether Llosa herself is not guilty of appropriating a story of violence and suffering and adding to it exotifying elements in order to produce an outrageous, but popular film.

Curiously, during a press conference, Magaly Solier shared with the audience that Llosa had asked her once, 'Which animal would you like Fausta to be?' (Llosa and Solier 2010). Not knowing what to answer, Solier recalls spending time watching Animal Channel and finally deciding that Fausta's representation would be best expressed by the body language of hippopotami.[8] The shifting relation between an actress and a character and the process that lies behind the construction of a persona is imbued in the sensitivities and acting skills of each performer. However, here is the case of a film director/writer who believes a character she has written is best epitomized through the movements of an animal and advises the actress to imitate one in order to convey its essence. Her advice is not prompted by symbolism, for instance, resorting to an Andean animal like a condor, or even an animal representative of the region,[9] but any non-human creature that could be inspiring to the actress playing Fausta.

Llosa's elaborated *La teta asustada* revives the notion of the good savage by composing a story where an uncorrupted figure with primitive features is being idealized. As other savages, *good savages* are ultimately noble figures, 'defined either by what they lack or what they represent' (Wernitznig 2003: xiv). Fausta ostensibly represents an unfamiliar Other who has the potential to touch and even inspire audiences. For instance, in her doubly marginalized position, her decision to extract the potato from her body, in spite of her fears, is celebrated not only as a sign of accomplishment but also as the beginning of new ways of interacting with others, particularly with gardener Noé (Efraín Solís). The haptic practice of inserting and removing is certainly symbolically and evocative but also hierarchical. A doctor (embodiment of science) removes what the indigenous (perceived as embodiment of nature) has inserted. The young girl can be understood as a model for those who believe in the creation of urban, successful Andean societies, and that transitions, even from total isolation, are possible (Salinas 2016). Notwithstanding, it remains unclear to what extent a film that relies on elements of difference and even 'primitivism' (as defined by Western language dictionaries), such as the mother's corpse under the bed and the potato in Fausta's vagina, can be seen as an iconography that explains, rather than distorts, the understanding between two apparently distant worlds. The debates surrounding *La teta asustada* are evidence of the complex interplay between the national and international exhibition, funding, agency and role of cinema as platform to broadcast (preferably imperialist or exotic?) imagery. Rather than her own impressions, it could be argued that Llosa's approach exemplifies the sort of strategies to which filmmakers recur in order to stand out, specifically in the context of international festivals, competitions for funding and academic interest.

Otherness contributes to the expansion, acclaim, fame, prevalence and conclusively mediatized consumption of visuals, when films include shock value elements. Nonetheless, this does not mean that the social reality of indigenous peoples in the twenty-first century cannot be told through cinematic works that advance ethnotypes, while engaging with social commentary. In *A terra dos homens vermelhos* (2008), Chilean-Italian director Marco Bechis narrates the attempts of the Kaiowás to reclaim part of the land they consider as theirs, but which instead, at least officially, belongs to a soya bean producer who recursively resorts to violence rather than dialogue. After two members of the community take their own lives, Nádio (Ambrosio Vilhava) decides it is time to make an exodus to the land of his ancestors, even though this decision stirs up sensitivities within the Kaiowás. A series of confrontations reach a symbolic climax when Nádio' eats a handful of dust while arguing with the owner of the estate, Moreira (Leonardo Medeiros). It is an act of protest and desperation. Sensorily, this episode forces a reaction from the audiences, while it alludes to the idea that savoury tastes, pleasure from food and culinary sophistication are incongruent with Kaiowá values. At the same time, eating the reddish land reproduces the trope of the native as elongation of the territory they inhabit; they are one.

It is hard to question why Bechis chooses to articulate on the failed structures that Brazilian authorities have put in place to preserve its native population. In his own words, he desisted from making a film about an idyllic, imagined Amazon, to focus instead on the disturbing reality: 'When I met the Kaiowá just dressed in normal clothes, drinking alcohol and using mobile phones – even if they were never charged up because they don't have electricity – I said: "This is what Indians are today. This is the film"' (Phillips 2009: para. 4). One observation is that in his own view, certain beverages are ontologically excluded from the realm where the indigenous dwells and remains, an angle that eventually receives a place in the story, and which has accompanied the figure of the native for decades in the history of visual representation. It can be synthesized as the notion that practices of flavour and tastes are to be disciplined by colonialist assumptions about the peripheral body and what it consumes.

A terra dos homens vermelhos applies moderately political and ethnographic methods to sketch a chronicle of struggle and survival. Bechis uses metaphors and contradictions to show the ironies behind the methods implemented by the state to approach societies risking extinction. For instance, the Kaiowás work as actors playing 'true Indians' in order to entertain the tourists brought by Beatrice (Chiara Caselli), Moreira's wife, to do birdwatching. Bechis constructs a political statement by pointing out that this is the only alternative source of income the natives have, as opposed to being exploited in the fields. The light of hope in the story is embodied by the friendship between Osvaldo (Pedro Abrísio da Silva), a Kaiowá shaman trainee, and Maria (Fabiane Pereira da Silva), Moreira's daughter. As the narrative unfolds, the focus lies on the similarities between white and indigenous youths and suggests that future generations approach indigeneity less reluctantly.[10] This acclaimed reflection of the current state of affairs in the heart of the Mato Grosso region is nonetheless a portrayal carefully constructed from the perspective of 'a European', as Bechis describes himself (Phillips 2009: para. 3).[11] Alternatively and somehow paradoxically, directors from outside the region are participating in redrawing the panorama of canonical representations.

Catalan director Xavi Sala is tactful in his widely acclaimed portrayal of a Zapotec domestic worker who emigrates temporarily to Mexico City, bringing her teenaged daughter along. *El ombligo de Guie'dani/Xquipi' Guie'dani/Guie'dani's Navel* (Mexico, 2019) does not make concessions about the blatant racism that indigenous women face in urban households. The language plays a crucial role in the communication between mother (Érika López) and daughter (Sótera Cruz). Gue'dani is rebellious as she is critical about the hierarchies that define her position within the new household. Through their comments, Valeria (Yuriría del Valle), her husband, Juan Ríos (David), and her two teenaged children confirm Gue'dani's impressions. The family measures them according to their own standards. Sensorial stimuli play a dual role in the film. While the family reacts to the excessive amount of chili in the soup, their exchanges vocalize what their taste buds experience, and which transforms in a sense of pride or strangeness in Gue'dani's eyes. Audiences witness a Zapotec girl who hardly understands the overtly sensitive palates of her mother's employers. The kitchen is the epicentre of some of the most crucial moments of the film, nonetheless, because food is presented as an essential aspect of Gue'dani's culture, and yet a matter of critique and praise on behalf of the demanding members of the family. The steam billowing from the pots, the right way of preparing coffee, the excessively heavy trays, the questioning about the right portions and spices create a taste-oriented diegetic world. Meanwhile, they contextualize Gue'dani's nostalgia to go home, the place where her navel is buried, and is geologically identical to the handful of soil she keeps in a small plastic bag as a souvenir of her birthland. This doubly sensorial action of extracting and caressing a sample of sand with the hands and smell it during challenging times resonates with the idea that cinema is about the emotions that the senses elicit. This olfactory action is tactic, as it links the audiences to this memorable film, and Gue'dani to her roots, a land where her mother does not use English 'bye' as a greeting form.

Language is deployed as embodiment of the practices of exclusion of the family (e.g. speaking English to avoid being understood), a unifying force between mother and daughter, and a gesture of inclusion towards Maru (Mónica del Carmen), Gue'dani's only friend in Mexico City. In her position, as the daughter of a housekeeper living in the same street, their close relationship and camaraderie stems from having lived similar experiences. As Gue'dani teaches Maru words in Zapotec, the film reveals the sensorial intrinsicality of language and how it extrapolates sensitivities. The young neighbour's first vocabulary lesson begins with *xa'na'* (buttocks), *gui* (poo) and *xidxi* (breasts), followed by ways to ask someone's name and other pleasantries. Their friendship reaches a dramatic climax towards the end of the story, but from their conversations, it is possible to deduce how aware they are of their place within society. Anecdotes about receiving soap as Christmas presents to avoid corporal smell, sexual intimidation and invisibility, underline the physicality and embodiment of indigeneity in non-indigenous contexts. Sala's timely critique is a reminder of the variety of techniques and symbolism deployed across the region to construct visuals that stress alterity, appealing to the senses of the audiences, but also expanding our interpretation of what knowledge entails.

Contested and contained knowledges

Leaving behind monothematic approaches in terms of knowledge production and rebuttal of non-Western epistemic systems, contemporary filmmakers have embraced the addition of elements previously ignored, superficially addressed or framed as inferior or comical (e.g. ethnobotanical practices in *María Candelaria*, 1943). In the last two decades, cinema produced in the region has become more critical about established canonical understandings of knowledge, shedding light on the synergy between indigenous societies and their epistemic systems. Epistemic considerations, for instance, lie at the core of *La carga/The Load* (2016), a historical account directed by Mexican filmmaker Alan Jonsson and set in the sixteenth century. Using the timeline of one of Mexico's most renowned indigenous heroes, Caxcan insurgent leader Francisco Tenamaztle, it is easy to deduce that the story unfolds around the 1550s. It revolves around Painalli (Horacio García Rojas), a Tlamemeh porter/carrier, who is hired by Franciscan priests to transport Elisa (María Valverde) from the inner land to the coastal city of Veracruz in order for her to sail to Europe. She has the important mission of testifying against her father, Spanish commander Don Miguel de Ibarra (Eusebio Lázaro), for his crimes against indigenous communities and for trying to frame Tenamaztle. Painalli and his team are expected to literally carry her on their shoulders to her final destination, a difficult quest since her father and his army are set to do anything to prevent them from reaching their goal. Along the way, Painalli's traditional knowledge proves particularly useful in two crucial moments of the story. He uses medicinal plants from his immediate environment to prepare an ointment that can mitigate Elisa's wounds in her feet, but he also uses plants to poison the horses deployed by the Spanish army (Figure 3). In this sense, *La Carga* encourages viewers to question how to conceptualize ethnobotanical knowledge in these two contexts. Director Jonsson presents us with two sides of the natural world and the interface between legacy, knowledge, cure and toxicity.

As retaliation, the Spanish army burns Painalli's hometown, killing members of his family and destroying their homes. His son, Ollin, dies as well, but the story provides enough information to deduce he would have died anyway. The little boy is one of many of the thousand victims that smallpox caused in the Americas in the sixteenth century. Pile of bodies, scarred faces covered with pustules and unaffected Spaniards indicate the presence of a disease that only

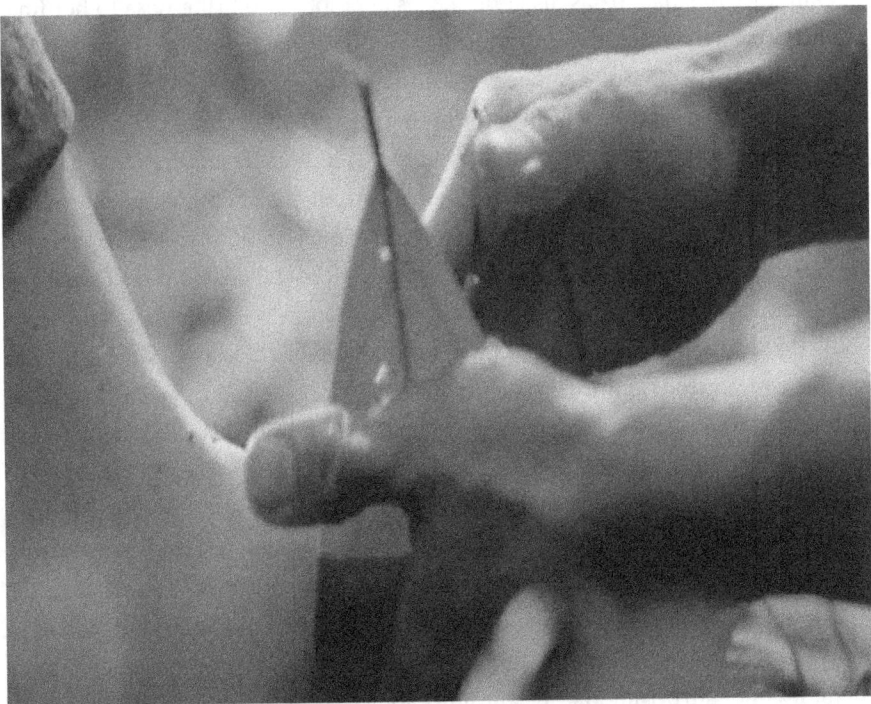

Figure 3 Screenshot of the film *La carga* (Mexico, 2016).

affects the natives. Although we do know that some Spaniard fell ill as well. Sensorily, the film articulates skilfully the visuality of decay through images that evoke ideas about cadaverine and putrescine smells.

The images of hopelessness of the child's grandmother as she cares for Ollin indicate this is a new disease unknown to them, a newly introduced ailment they have no plants for. The facial expression of Elisa when she sees Ollin suggests she knows what is affecting him and which terrible consequences this will have on him. Knowledge about this *hueyzahuatl* (the great leprosy), as for instance, the Aztecs came to know it, is passed from the Europeans to the indigenous communities. 'But what are you doing, don't you understand this could cost you your life?', says friar Valerio de Medina (Fernando Morán) to Painalli when he finds him praying in a hut specially designed for the most sorely stricken victims of the lethal virus. Smallpox is believed to be one of the main factors that made it possible for the Spanish Crown to conquer Mexico, as it decimated the population of adults, but above all, of children. One might ponder what smallpox is in the context of the colonization of the Americas, a present, an attack, an asset, a weapon?

Ollin dies of smallpox as his father keeps attempting to bring Elisa to her final destination. In the story, Vera Cruz is crucial for the young Spanish widow to travel back to Europe so that she can demand a fair trial for Tenamaztle, justice for her murdered husband and the crimes committed against indigenous peoples. Due to its geographical location, originally so-named Villa Rica de la Vera Cruz has had a long and strenuous history. Violent foreign armies, greedy pirates and atrocities against a large number of slaves from Africa have left a footprint in the city. But Veracruz was also an entry point of diseases from the so-called Old World, smallpox being one of them. Although in the case of Mexico, it was unintentional, we do know that further up, smallpox was weaponized as a biological warfare agent with terrible consequences for the native populations. Considering its global spread, its history and using scientific knowledge available today about this eradicated disease, particularly in the context of the corona health crisis, Jonsson's passages in *La carga* prompt us to reflect on what a virus really is. In light of the implications of human life, inflected by modernity, technological advancements and constant growth, it is worth asking if current human presence, just as smallpox, is a threat to the spaces humans occupy. Since the question of self-destruction and destruction of ecosystems transverses the definition of nature and the nature of those that inhabit them, it is not surprising that recent films approach indigeneity as an epitome of what is lost, as a source of knowledge and as hope for the future.

In Juan Carlos Valdivia's second film, *Yvy Maraêy: Tierra sin mal/Yvy Maraêy: Land without Evil* (2013), systems of knowledge and ontological considerations that acknowledge indigenous cosmovision are presented from a realization of the inescapability of one's positionality. Set in rural settings, this is Valdivia's second attempt to present a story where the mestizo or Eurocentric viewpoints do not presuppose superiority vis-à-vis indigenous epistemologies. Spoken in Guaraní, Quechua and Spanish, *Yvy Maraêy* follows the adventures of two friends, Andrés Caballero (Juan Carlos Valdivia) and Yari Timbuku (Elío Ortiz), through the dramatic Bolivian landscape. While Andrés operates as a reflection of Valdivia's alter ego, Yari embodies the rapidly disappearing Guaraní communities. Admiration, curiosity and a sense of being challenged by ancient epistemologies are the underlying reasons behind the main character's decision to embark on this road adventure. Andrés is looking for a story he can transform into a film, then he pauses and finds in a Guaraní girl's question the ontological synthesis of *Yvy Maraêy: Tierra sin mal*: '¿Cómo sabes de qué color miro yo las cosas?' [How do you know in which colour I look at things?] (Molina Ergueta 2010: 179). The Bolivian director skilfully conveys a story where indigenous and non-indigenous are equally important, while nature and the mysteries of the world (this one and the one hereafter) are the real obstacles.

Central to the film is the sincere friendship between two apparently different subjectivities and the promise of bonds that reflect a true sense of brotherhood. The name of the film alludes to *Yvy Maraêy*, a Guaraní myth about the hereafter. The legend has it that there is a final repository for those who die, or those privileged few who show enough bravery to enter it by bypassing their own death. The hope of a haven beyond the mundane world has prompted the imaginary of Guaraní generations, but also outsiders seeking a gate into this Promised Land. Valdivia does not idealize his characters. The film suggests that, even among subaltern groups, power disparities are widely found, and that compared to Aymara- and Quechua-speaking communities, the disenfranchisement of Guaraní and Ayoreo communities is unparalleled. Through creative flash-forwards, the story delves into the cosmovision of one of the least known indigenous societies in the Andes, in all its majesty.

The tradition of contemplating spaces as milieus to be absorbed and consumed by the external stimuli they evoke is not new in cinema, and this film is not immune to it. Aesthetically, Valdivia's film shares with other productions the use of vistas and impressive landscapes as mechanisms to draw attention and alert viewers about the newness of unknown and exotic geographies. A possible reading of the representativeness and agency of nature in *Yvy Maraêy* is that Valdivia proposes, without explicitly inferring it, that it is an unembodied entity. This is supported by the intentional attention devoted to artefacts, objects and abstract representations as parts of epistemic practices that confirm the convoluted relation each culture has with its immediate surroundings. The film subtly hints at the possibility that there is a multiplicity of knowledges, understood through sensorial systems that become accessible to those who are culturally, not necessarily, ethnically more receptible to them. Through a contraposition of visually arresting sequences, the film reflects on how exclusion and oblivion outwardly explain why communities maintain fervent adherence to their practices, worldviews, ontologies and knowledge systems.

Conclusion

The senses play a central role in the representation of indigenous societies, nonetheless, because they wrap strategies to embody the notions of ethnicity and difference in cinematic spaces. Images are constructed to evoke connections between touching, smelling and tasting, and, in the process, provide information about those being depicted. Facial expressions of disgust about too much chili in a soup, or gestures that are indicative of corporal odour are intended to bespeak stereotypes about strange culinary traditions, or lack of hygiene. Through the senses, cinema also allows for the expansion of ontological and epistemological understandings of the audiences. Knowledge production and recognition of peripheral forms of perceiving and interacting with the world are innovative approaches to narrate and present the indigenous. A need to present an imagined Other remains a constant in contemporary cinema nevertheless. The idea that indigenous childhoods are essentially different, for instance, is a trope identifiable in many recent films. New ontological considerations based on recycled formulations, or long-established schemas, confirm that indigeneity-themed films are a genre in their own right. Derivatives of Western cinema, indigenous peoples visual narratives are identifiable for a set of characteristics that set them apart. The most salient aspect is, above all, the convention of entwining native societies with nature and decoupling them with technology.

5

Axis: Identities and global imaginaries

By evaluating the prevalence of tropes, the intersectionality of ethnicity and gender as critical categories and the artistic production of the Other, this chapter aims at foregrounding the processes behind the conceptualization of histrionic indigeneity in Latin American cinema. Based on previously discussed shared and contrasting aspects of indigenous ethnotypes in films, this chapter discusses the taxonomy of paradigms of representations presented in the introduction. Furthermore, it examines how discourses of difference, either gender- or ethnicity-related, are embedded in the selected films, and how artistic tools are deployed by Latin American and 'global' filmmakers to create cinematic otherness.

Intersectional paradigms

This section considers how predominant patterns of representation emerge from long-established stereotypes and imagery resulting from sets of ideologies. Numerous factors, in particular power dynamics, have contributed to the set of paradigms applied to the portrayals of indigeneity in contemporaneous cinema. From a chronological perspective, long-established traditions have shaped the conceptual maps of both filmmakers and audiences. In many ways, cinema is a modern elongation of pre-established artistic practices in which the artists' worldviews reign. In the case of Latin America, ever since the start of European colonization, indigenous communities, vulnerable societies vis-à-vis dominant forces, have denoted a sense of exoticism, otherness and curiosity (Hall 1996; Stam 1997; Overing and Passes 2000; Ramos 1998; Bataille 2001; Carreño 2006; Hernández Castillo 2010; Mateus Mora 2012; Tompkins 2018). Historical accounts supporting ideologies of nationhood and sameness have also had an impact on the way that ethnicity has become a group marker. Visual representations emulate and replicate the conceptualizations of the filmmakers and how their cultural biases inform the assignation of traits to communities not widely recognized as part of a dominant majority.

Perceived attributes among in-groups determine their ideas and assumptions about out-groups (Fiske et al. 2002). Therefore it comes as no surprise that imagery in films about indigeneity reflects traits commonly ascribed to ethnic groups (ethnotypes). In this sense, based on the surveys discussed in the introduction, cinematic narratives focusing on ancient pre-Columbian civilizations might be likely to portray fierce, brave, industrious, loyal, honest and, above all, noble characters, who manage to survive in extreme conditions by displaying their superior intelligence, higher sense of freedom and warfare skills, as in *Erendira Ikikunari* (Mexico, 2006). Aesthetically, archetypes of representation dictate that they are colourfully dressed and staged in settings that agree with their unrestrained attitudes and well-preserved folklore, as is true in *Caramuru* (Brazil, 2001). Motion pictures about ancient indigenous societies, for instance, *El mito del tiempo* (Guatemala, 2008), include a certain degree of violence and hostility as we might expect and therefore agree with axiomatic traits. In the case of films enacting stories taking place in modern times, the spectrum of paradigms include loyal, industrious, honest and responsible characters, mostly willing to *adapt* to their environment, of the type seen present in *La Ciénaga* (Argentina, 2001), *Dioses* (Peru, 2008) and *Zona Sur* (Bolivia, 2009), but without giving up their unparalleled knowledge about forces of nature, as in *El abrazo de la serpiente* (Colombia, 2015), or embracing urban lifestyles too eagerly as is demonstrated in *La teta asustada* (Peru, 2009). In the context of the nation, characters framed in a positive way are those who are willing to accommodate and regard themselves as part of a country, contributing to its sense of legitimacy, as do the characters in *Evo Pueblo* (Bolivia, 2007), but without compromising their own culture as demonstrated by characters in *El destino* (Argentina–Spain, 2006). In varying ways, paradigms of representation obey stereotypical cultural matrixes. The idea that mental conceptualizations are embedded in culture becomes relevant when examining the current perception and image of the indigenous communities within society.

Topologies and perspectives

Even though it is not possible to affix the concept of validity and credibility to a specific identity, indigenous elements are considered pillars in the conceptualizations of *nation* across the region. It is therefore understandable that films might not always choose to endorse the idea that indigenous sovereignty lies above the boundaries established by the state, for example, *El Violín* (Mexico, 2005) or, as *Alicia en el país* (Chile, 2008) suggests, across national borders in general. As a matter of fact, although many of the films pertinent to this study problematize the power structures, for example, *El verano de los peces voladores* (Chile, 2013) or *Ixcanul* (Guatemala–France, 2015), none of the films set in modern Latin America reviewed for this study included a storyline rejecting the notion of country/state. Even though many endorse and encourage acknowledgement of indigenous societies, they do not challenge the sovereignty of the nation, understood as 'territorial groupings' (Stemplowski 2009: 284). A common aspect found in the films reviewed for this study is that the political undertone questions the lack of acknowledgement and inclusion on behalf of the state, a theme in *Dauna: Lo que lleva el río* (Venezuela, 2015), rather than the creation of separate, indigenous states of their own. Hence, support for the recognition of indigenous legacy in films is mainly cultural. Echoing the data collected by CDI (2006), Solano Acuña (2013), Genna and Espinosa (2012) Saiz, Rapimán and Mladinic (2008), Chirapaq (2015), and the interviews and surveys conducted for this study, an analysis of indigenous ethnotypes in sixty-eight films indicate filmmakers share many of the assumptions held by the audiences. Ethnotypes found in the selected films suggest filmmakers favour the idea of preserving indigenous cultures, languages and traditions, and regard these elements as key aspects of the national identity.

In terms of negative stereotypes, indigeneity is still denoted by images of enclosure, as presented in *A terra dos homens vermelhos* (Italy–Brazil 2008); peripherality, as *La niña santa* (Argentina, 2004) shows; disempowerment, central to *Ixcanul* (Guatemala, 2015); discordance with modernity, vital to *¿Quién mató a la llamita blanca?* (Bolivia, 2007); oblivion, a central theme in *Siguiendo las estrellas* (Panama, 2010); unrest, in the way *El facilitador* (Ecuador, 2013) illustrates; drunkenness, which informs *Madeinusa* (Peru, 2005); conformism, as at the core of *Tiempos menos modernos* (Argentina–Chile, 2012); and isolation, a key topic in *Distancia* (Guatemala, 2011). As these examples demonstrate, there is still a tendency to curtail indigeneity to a set of undesirable attributes and thereby recirculate archetypes observed in cinematic productions for decades. The relation between traits and representations is further complicated by a long-established propensity to exotify native peoples (Sánchez-H. 1999; Lienhard 1997, 2002; Segalen 1999; Hooker 2005; Eide 2011; Shohat and Stam 2014; D'Argenio 2020). The underlying notion is that narratives relying on an exotic Other resonate among audiences because viewers are widely acquainted with a nostalgic, but essentialist, imagery of indigenous societies. Historically, as Chapter 1 discusses, cinematic portrayals have considered the elements that underscore difference between indigenous characters and non-indigenous audiences.

Negative attributes ascribed to indigenous characters identified in the selected films ostensibly agree with previous critical analyses of cinematic portrayals (Nahmad Rodríguez 2007; Mateus Mora 2012; Flores 2014; Tompkins 2018). Canonical paradigms upheld during the 1960s, 1970s and 1980s, where ethnic communities are perceived as 'stereotypical minor characters – rural simpletons who provide comic relief or servants who cook, clean, and open the doors for the lighter-skinned protagonists' (Ramírez Berg 2002: 77), are still found in present-day films, although in less blatant form. Still today, the indigenous do not reflect in 'audience ratings' across media spaces unless the representations rely on stereotypes (Plascencia and Monteforte 2006). This might be explained by the importance that Eurocentric ideologies have in the cultural repertoire of both filmmakers and viewers.

In Bolivian cinema, films use an anthropological approach that only in the last decades has opened up spaces for agency and self-representation of the communities being represented. In the case of Venezuela, filmmakers focus mainly on the special bonds indigenous people allegedly have with their territories, their subaltern position in relation to urban characters and the distinct sense of aesthetics they evoke. Similarly, when moving to the Mexican screens, two different approaches can be found. On the one hand, characteristic traits of being indigenous are lack of education, deficient proficiency in correct Spanish and unwillingness to progress (Plascencia and Monteforte 2006). On the other hand, as this study confirms, filmmakers from Mexico seem to perceive their films as self-meditations about the discrimination and abuse these communities face. Similarly, although indigenous characters are not central in Argentine films, there have been recent attempts to highlight their place within the social fabric of rural areas, as well as in urban spaces where they are often overlooked.

As attested by the above considerations, motion pictures are conditioned by modes of representation that are difficult to challenge. Yet, it is clear that a central focus of many recent films is to present new manners of understanding indigeneity. These counter-stereotypic paradigms are built on the notion that indigenous characters are to be perceived individually, and not only as part of a larger collectivity. As in other media formats, cinematic spaces 'cannot generally present a full range of behaviours characteristic of a given group' (Schneider 2005: 416), but they can choose not to rely on generalizations and reductions. These alternative paradigms found in recent films advocate the idea that being indigenous does not override the sense of self, as one sees in *Corazón del Tiempo* (Mexico, 2008), nor does it negate the right to pursue one's dreams, in the way that *Erendira Ikikunari* (Mexico, 2006) portrays. Neither does an indigenous identity imply a fixed position within the social grid, as *Zona Sur* (Bolivia, 2009) shows, nor does it denote a sense of isolation for the characters in *Alamar* (Mexico, 2009). Newer portrayals depict subjects that contest abuse, as in the case of *Altiplano* (Peru–Belgium, 2009); oppose oppression in the manner portrayed in *El Violín* (Mexico, 2005); chase their dreams and inspire others, as happens in *La Jaula de Oro* (Mexico, 2013) and *Ixcanul* (Guatemala–France, 2015); and resist total subjugation, like the characters in *Alicia en el país* (Chile, 2008). These considerations indicate that the sixty-eight selected films approach indigeneity in diverse ways.

Besides the already mentioned individual-based approach, another salient shift in the imagery drawing upon indigenous topics is that indigeneity and modernity are no longer considered discordant notions. A recurrent observation is that changes in the Latin American social and political climate have prompted filmmakers to imagine new possibilities, in many cases departing from unexpected developments. For instance, *Evo Pueblo* (Bolivia, 2007) is the visual reflection of Evo Morales's trajectory from working as a farmer to become the first Aymara president of the country. The semi-fictional biopic focuses on the processes that this new state of affairs unveils and that the time has come for indigenous societies to be recognized. The film 'doesn't try to elevate Evo to a superhero, nor denigrate him as a person' (Carroll 2007: para. 3). Director Tonchi Antenaza exposes the multifaceted identity of Evo Morales while he forces viewers to avoid generalizations and reductions based on preconceptions about ethnicity. More importantly, he draws attention to the fact that indigenous societies are an integral part of present-day nations and that as such, they are fluid, shifting and evolving.

Furthermore, in recent depictions, modernity is presented through the lens of consumption, transnational interactions, progress and individual visibility. Along these lines, viewers witness an indigenous girl armed with a set of large headphones and her own wit carrying out an ethnography of her new city (*Play*, Chile, 2005), a Kuna fashion designer drawing attention to the weaving methods of her community in a fashion event (*Siguiendo las estrellas*, Panama, 2010), a diasporic young man relying on the power of art to mobilize his community (*El regreso de Lencho*, Guatemala, 2010), a Quechua activist who regards English as a tool of contestation (*También la lluvia*, Spain–Bolivia, 2010) and a Kaiowá woman who knows the power of technology to denounce abuse (*A terra dos homens vermelhos*, Italy–Brazil 2008). Although recent films do not propose that natives should renounce their traditional lifestyles, they do present communities interested in processes of industrialization (*El destino*, Argentina–Spain, 2006), or sceptical about them (*El verano de los peces voladores*, Chile, 2013), but never indifferent to the reorganization of economic structures. As an extension of modernity, urbanization is also widely discussed in recent films. The rural flight of indigenous groups to urban spaces is explored as a process in, for example, *Guaraní* (Paraguay–Argentina, 2015), a consequence in *La teta asustada* (Peru, 2009) or as a goal, as shown in *Madeinusa* (Peru, 2005).

Common conventions of representation from the 1960s, 1970s and 1980s have been replaced by new reformulations. Importantly, the transnationalism of Latin American cinema has brought about attitudes that resonate with the cultural repertoires of foreign spectatorship. Films made for international markets 'may latch onto stereotypes, either visual or narrative, that are embraced by audiences overseas' (Middents 2013: 155). In the process, they have contributed to reshape some of the most outdated, least favourable and reductionist renderings. Hence, in order to make sense of the taxonomy presented in the introduction, it is crucial to position it in the context of transnational processes, and not only in line with cultural, social and political changes across the region.

Newer portrayals of indigeneity are mainly narratives where major characters are central rather than peripheral, have complex personalities, show a broad range of traits and are portrayed as having a dynamic and fluid identity where ethnicity plays a major role but is not decisive. In present-day films, central characters have a sense of self and free will that does not necessarily reflect the attitudes, ideologies or epistemologies of their communities, and in fact, many narratives explore the conflicts they face when their individuality is in opposition with social conventions or a sense of collectivity. Contemporaneous imagery also focuses on the parallel, often discordant, position of indigeneity vis-à-vis modernity. An important aspect in these productions is that gender has become a central concern. The sixty-eight films reviewed in this study are imbued with impressions about the intersectional spaces between indigeneity and femininity, particularly brought to light by a considerable number of female filmmakers, as the next section discusses.

Intersectionality of ethnicity and gender

In order to engage in a discussion about gender and ethnicity as it is presented in films focusing on indigenous societies, it is necessary to consider the social dimension of both aspects. On the one hand, it requires acknowledging that gender has been highlighted and shaped as a social construct policed by normative structures, but, on the other hand, ethnicity has been entwined with historical, physical and biological considerations that have proven to be porous and inconsistent.[1] Hence, rather than reviewing intersectionality of two clearly defined notions, this section delves into the junction of conceptualizations, the boundaries of which are difficult to discern. They are approached simultaneously though because it is assumed that, either in real life or in artistic representations and expressions of this reality, gender- and ethnicity-based entanglements 'cannot be captured wholly by looking at the race or gender dimensions of those experiences separately' (Crenshaw 1991: 1244). Beyond cultural similarities, important aspects uniting the various groups labelled by the term *indigenous* are the shared experiences of disenfranchisement, abuse, cultural extermination, territorial plundering and violence. Thus, cinematic portrayals of indigeneity can be mainly assembled as visual spaces that meditate on communities that share a long history of discrimination, rather than images that confirm commonalities between pre-Columbian peoples. Ultimately, due to various processes, the common denominator among indigenous peoples is precisely their subaltern position face to face with a non-indigenous majority that believes it shares a common history, ancestry and set of values. It is conclusively the attitudes, sensitivities and impressions of filmmakers trained within 'mainstream' – not indigenous – canons that define how indigeneity is mediatized. Of course, this does not account for the recent contributions of indigenous filmmakers who are finding in cinema new platforms to tell their own stories from an insider's perspective.

In the case of gender, beyond the overtly simplified and recklessly condensed female/male binary, as a notion, it denotes fixations and inaccuracies that fail to explain the behavioural, cultural and political stances that the term seeks to denote. From a natural perspective, biology has been prioritized to determine the division between physical traits that distinguish a woman from a man, or vice versa. From a performative standpoint, gender as a trope has been regarded as a set of performative practices conditioned by processes embedded in social interaction, and persistently underlined by patriarchal institutions (Butler 1998, 2011; Segato 2007). In this sense, any artistic impression of society is expected to be inflected by female/male positioning. Due to the permeation and perpetuation of ideologies in cinematic discourses, gender, just as ethnicity, is a marker of agency and subjectivity that conflicts with, or subalternity and objectivity that reinforces, the masculine fixed stare (Mulvey 1975; McGowan 2003). Since audiences are assumed to acquire a '"masculine" position' as spectators, this raises questions about how indigenous women are depicted, and whether these representations seek to contest traditional canons. Stereotypes in Latin American cinema about women include century-old imagery of women depicted as lustful subjects or abnegated mothers (Garðarsdóttir 2005).

Furthermore, this study contemplates how the imagery of female characters also has been influenced by ethnicity, specifically a well-defined 'pigmentocracy' (Lipschutz 1944). Notably, the films depicting indigenous women have an additional focal point, the role of mestizo and white female characters. The selected films choose to portray non-indigenous women as part of a systematic structure of erasure, for example, *Ixcanul* (Guatemala–France, 2015); blatant racists like those portrayed in *El destino* (Argentina–Spain, 2006); unscrupulous employers as found in *La teta asustada* (Peru, 2009); distant and indifferent towards the less empowered, for example, *Dioses* (Peru, 2008); interested and respectful about indigenous cultures in the way of *Taínos: La última tribú* (Puerto Rico, 2005); integrated part of the indigenous communities, like *Cenizas eternas* (Venezuela, 2011) presents; willing to take risks to approach oppressed groups, a central theme in *A terra dos homens vermelhos* (Italy–Brazil, 2008); convinced about the relevance of supporting indigenous causes, for example, *El verano de los peces voladores* (Chile, 2013); and ultimate saviours, as found in *El facilitador* (Ecuador, 2013).

Conclusively, two patterns of representation of non-indigenous women emerge from this study. On the one hand, there is a clear tendency to imply that mestizo and white women can abridge the animosities between empowered and subaltern groups, and that their feminine condition enables them to recognize the condition of the oppressed segments of society in a more compelling way than men can achieve. On the other hand, filmmakers seem to suggest that a long-established oppressing plurality is also made up of women who regard indigenous communities as inferior and peripheral, although minimally when contrasted with men's regard for these same groups. Compared to accounts from previous decades, present-day representations realize that women are part of the social fabric of the indigenous communities, give them voice and advocate for their position within the internal (inside their communities) and external (in society at large) hierarchies. In Latin American cinema, indigenous women are depicted as silent but present, as in *El abrazo de la serpiente* (Colombia, 2015); nonconformist, like characters in *Madeinusa* (Peru, 2005); aware of the discordance between their cultural values and external factors, as in *Defensores de la vida* (Costa Rica, 2015); willing to fight back, as shown in *¿Quién mató a la llamita blanca?* (Bolivia, 2007); aware of their sense of self, as included in the storyline of *Corazón del Tiempo* (Mexico, 2008); and as women with full agency of the sort seen in *Zona Sur* (Bolivia, 2009).

Directed by Juan Carlos Valdivia, *Zona Sur* is, above all, an allegory to the times of transition ensued by Evo Morale's presidency. As discussed in Chapter 4, the narrative set in a wealthy area of La Paz explores the relationship between Wilson (Pascual Loayza) and the family for whom he works as a butler. Through telephoto shots, the story delves into the daily lives of an upper-middle-class family run by Carola (Ninón del Castillo), a divorced mother. The children are Andrés (Nicólas Fernández), who is ready to start school, and two insubordinate teenagers, Bernarda (Mariana Vargas) and Patricio (Juán Pablo Koria). Marcelina (Viviana Condori) and Erika (Glenda Rodríguez) are the other members of the inner core of the household, the maid and gardener, who serve to remind audiences of what older matriarchies used to be like. The family has many secrets between them but are also open about the levels of discretion each of them demands. Although the teenagers appear disconnected from the real world, they show acceptance of their role in an ever-changing society.

In his realistic portrait of contemporary Bolivia, Valdivia depicts a nation adjusting to a new state of affairs, an aspect he poignantly addresses in one of the last scenes. This is confirmed by some of the indigenous interviewees who observed that 'la rica termina siendo la Aymara' [the Aymara lady ends up being the rich one], and that 'el de las gafas sabe cocinar' [the character with the glasses knows how to cook]. Admittedly, these comments suggest that they have appreciated the diversity of storylines and characters, and the reconfiguration of hierarchies. Through a short pan of the camera, Valdivia depicts a doubtful Carola envisioning the possibility of selling her beloved house to a wealthy indigenous businesswoman, who is willing to pay a generous sum of money. The movement of the camera seems to indicate that her fixed position (social status) is being contested from sides she had not considered before. Bernarda does not hide her sexual inclination, just as Patricio is not shy about asking his mother to buy him condoms while they are having dinner. Little Andrés is also outspoken about his loyalty towards the Aymara servants, the chaos that his siblings cause and how absent their mother seems to be. The woman-household dichotomy is challenged in similar ways in *Erendira Ikikunari* (Mexico, 2006).

Erendira is set in Michoacan in the fifteenth century and the verbal track consists entirely of spoken Purepecha. The central character, young Erendira (Xochiquetzal Rodríguez), is considered only to be an obedient, stay-at-home, bride-to-be by her father and fiancée. Times are difficult for the Purepecha as they have just learnt a new race of invaders has landed in their territories from far away. Young chief Tangaxoan has the task to steer his people through the encounter with these unknown enemies (Europeans) who happen to possess a secret device (horses) that might afford them strategic advantages. A new direction is taken though once warrior Cuynierangari finds out that these new *tribes* are not interested in engaging in war but in being fed and eventually accumulating gold. The Purepecha people are divided into those willing to die rather than to accept a 'pacific' invasion and those who agree to befriend the newcomers. Erendira earns the respect of her community after she manages to steal one of the horses brought by the European expeditions and teaches herself to ride it.

As noted in the taxonomy of traits affixed to indigenous characters in cinema (see introduction), figures from historical accounts staged in previous centuries are widely regarded positively. Besides showing courage and tenacity, the young Purepecha girl affirms her sense of identity and agency by taking a stand, even though this means breaking with tradition and old codes of honour. The film advances the notion that the Europeans have a peculiar understanding of what is supposed, but morally questionably, to be valuable (gold). In terms of depictions of gender, the film presents a weak Tangaxoan (chief), a coward Nanuma (Erendira's fiancée) and a weak-minded Tishue (Erendira's secret admirer), who contrast with hordes of barefoot women bearing their children, but ready to fight for their community. In numerous ways, the film presents a juxtaposition of gender stereotypes, community roles and social status. In this film, director Mora Catlett suggests that the encounters between pre-Columbian civilizations and European colonizers took place under the terms of male chiefs and warriors on both sides, and that maybe women would have managed this historic episode differently.² The film explores the prohibition against indigenous women engaging in militant action, as well as the absence of European female explorers. This is a cinematic version of a renowned legend that raises questions about the invisibility of female warriors, leaders and civilians in both the European and indigenous chronicles. *Erendira* also questions the boundaries and definitions of gender, and of those practices that are prohibitive for women, in similar way to previously discussed films, for example, *Climas*, *Corazón del tiempo* and *El niño pez*.

In *El niño pez*, a sense of transgression is imbued not only in the patricide committed by Lala but also in the prolicide carried out by Guayi, the main character. The moral aspect of their actions invites the viewer to reflect on the vulnerability they face as women, and in Guayi's case, the challenges brought about by her less privileged, impoverished background.³ The discriminatory approach of the Argentine authorities towards Guayi resembles the treatment she receives at the Bronté's home. *El niño pez* depicts abusive fathers, absent brothers and biased policemen, while it allegorizes the female figure. Notwithstanding, it also overlooks the notion that not all females share the same experience of womanhood regardless of social constraints, such as class, race and ethnicity.

In fact, Lala seems to exotify and essentialize Guayi's ethnical roots, discounting that the same traits that she considers attractive and 'different' render her girlfriend subaltern; after all, one girl is to serve the other. Either out of naiveté or the comfort of her own position, these disparities seem at first glance to be invisible to Lala, but it can also be regarded as Puenzo's strategy to imply that ethnicity (with all that it entails) is secondary to gender. After all, their intimate moments are spaces where they allow themselves to dream about a shared future where external factors do not matter. If they manage to escape, Lala and Guayi have decided they want to go back to the Ypoá Lake (Paraguay), a common topic of conversation between them. The superimposed layers and depth of the lake are reminiscent of the social tiers, their complexities and the challenges they pose for the young couple.

The presence of Guayi and Fausta (*La teta asustada*) as domestic workers in a white or mestizo household reflects not only colonialist practices but also the complex interplay of class and gender. Even in narratives where the women take on the role of abusers, as in *La Ciénaga* (Argentina, 2001), *Nosilatiaj. La belleza* (Argentina, 2012), *Feriado* (Ecuador, 2014) and *Dioses* (Peru, 2008), the figure of an omnipresent, wandering indigenous maid is a common trope.

In the case of *La ciénaga*, Martel sketches how two sisters, Momi and Vero, can have different attitudes and sensitivities towards the less empowered. The film highlights Vero's racist attitudes towards Isabel, while it underscores Momi's affection for the domestic worker. Momi (Sofía Bertolotto) interacts with her environment through her inquisitive way of looking, mostly focusing on Isabel's chores. Somehow, her position suggests that closeness and fondness for the Other is to remain private and intimate. In fact, her profound devotion for Isabel is best exemplified by the significant role she plays in Momi's daily (and private) prayers; more than anything because Momi fears the young maid might leave the house. But Isabel does quit her job. Like in *Madeinusa*, the ending seems to suggest that it is the girls' agency which can ultimately serve to 'romper círculos fatales y destinos pre-señalados: la sirvienta en *La ciénaga* que escapa el orden bizarro de la quinta, Madeinusa partiendo a Lima' [break catastrophic and predetermined destinies: the maid in *The Swamp* escaping the dashing order of the villa, Madeinusa leaving to Lima] (Suárez 2014: 125).

Another possible form of escape is to conceal one's perceived indigenous background as a way to avoid social rejection and seclusion, as it is the case of Elisa (Maricielo Effio) in *Dioses* (Peru, 2008). Directed by Josué Méndez, the story unfolds around the protagonist's quest to hide her indigenous legacy from her new upper-class friends. After marrying Agustín (Edgar Saba), a wealthy entrepreneur, Elisa has decided to forget about her humble roots. She shares her new home with Agustín's self-indulgent youngsters, Andrea (Anahí de Cardenas) and Diego (Sergio Gjurinovic), who are constantly served by Inés (Magaly Solier), one of the Quechua-speaking domestic workers. As members of the household, they offer an ethnographic perspective of how this dysfunctional family interacts with each other, but also with a conceited environment where cacti from Madagascar, plastic surgeries and jewellery are of major importance. Rigid social structures not only apply to Elisa, as Méndez suggests. Agustín's children also feel compelled to renounce who they truly are and feel constrained. Ethnicity, just like class affiliation and fake pretentions, are presented as reflections of artificial social constructions that respond to practices, rather than to fixed realities. This satire offers a glimpse into the life of a woman who chooses to camouflage her identity with the same determination that a privileged young man (Diego) hides his romantic love for his sister (Andrea), who is about to be sent abroad by her father to cover up her unplanned pregnancy. *Dioses* offers a critique of the roles individuals assume, but it also sheds light on the set of ideologies behind the allocation of supposedly immutable positions.

The intersection of gender and ethnicity becomes evident in the way Elisa experiences her unfamiliar environment, as a wife, stepmother and member of a different social group. In like manner, the figure of Inés as a prototypical Quechua-speaking maid, contrasted with well-to-do European-looking Andrea, coincides with gendered and ethnicity-oriented paradigms. These characters are constructed on the premises that they play roles 'typically' assigned to women (subaltern or asymmetrical to male figures), whereas ethnicity dictates the degree of subalternity and asymmetry. The point at which the various axes affecting individuals' social order cross each other determines each character's social position (Crenshaw 1991). In this regard, there are significant gains to be accrued in determining how audiences perceive ethnicity- and gender-oriented imagery presented in widely consumed films, and how diversity is visually and narratively framed.

LGBTQ+ indigenous characters are central in *Antes o Tempo Não Acabava* (Brazil, 2016), directed by Fabio Baldo and Sergio Andrade; *Sueño en otro idioma* (Mexico, 2017), directed by Ernesto Contreras; and *Retablo* (2017), directed by Alvaro Delgado Aparicio. The question remains how gay, queer, and transgender and transsexual identities navigate through and across lived and fictionalized indigenous experiences, or whether this initialism and what it denotes encompass or fail to recognize realities beyond the metropolitan ideological spheres in which they are anchored. While the first film explores homosexuality from a spiritual perspective, the other two suggest that only heterosexuality is accepted within the imagined indigenous communities depicted in the films. In *Sueño en otro idioma*, the plot surrounds around the animosity between two former friends, Isauro (José Manuel Poncelis) and Evaristo (Eligio Meléndez), who happen to be the last surviving speakers of Zikril, a fictional Amerindian language. In spite of a number of attempts, the locals have accepted the idea that a reconciliation is not an option. Martín (Fernando Álvarez Rebeil), a researcher in linguistic revitalization, has a mission to reunite them, at any cost. He needs recordings of a conversation in Zikril, in order to decode the mysterious language. Martín ignores the two men having a past they are not willing to disclose publicly.

The intimate dimension of homosexuality is also central in *Retablo* (2017), the story of a son, Segundo (Junior Bejar), who accidentally discovers his father, Noé (Amiel Cayo), is secretly gay. The world of the fourteen-year-old boy, training to become an altar (story-box) maker, is inexorably changed in one day. Segundo does not want his mother, Anatolia (Magaly Solier), to find out about the indiscretions of his father, but in a patriarchal society, he loses any sense of respect for Noé. The family life crumbles and eventually, tension turns into physical violence. The intersectional dynamics of the films confirm new attempts to explore diversity at an individual level. One cannot ignore the films have been quite popular in festivals catering to LGBTQ+ audiences, and that *Retablo* was only possible because of crowdfunding campaigns.

A shift in recent portrayals of indigenous communities is evident from the increased inclusion of stories where female and gay characters are central, express their concerns, show agency and are determined to seek a change in the state of affairs. These are stories where they do not necessarily embody the soul of a community or a collectivity but rather narratives where their sense of identity resides on their own individual traits. Yet, there is a noticeable absence of lesbian characters. Contributions of female filmmakers such as Llosa, Martel, Murat, Puenzo, Said and Seggiaro stand out for expanding the spectrum of possibilities to which audiences, including indigenous ones, are exposed in terms of the imaginary. Indigeneity, just as gender, is an adaptable, fluid and shifting notion. Contemporary cinema makes attempts to encapsulate these fluctuations beyond canonical traditions of otherness.

Arrayed figures

This section assesses the similar approaches and tropes identified in indigeneity-oriented films conceived by Latin American (Global South) and Western filmmakers (Global North). Central to this review is to focus on the construction of ethnotypes and how these are designed to align with assumptions shared by 'glo(b)(c)al' audiences. As the introduction's evidence-based taxonomy of paradigms shows, the most common ethnotypes include the figure of impoverished, forgotten, natural and pure free spirits with a strong work ethic but also with a tendency to drink, be aggressive and lack formal education. Artistic freedom apparently allows for the creation of narratives where these ethnotypes are reinforced, reconfigured, replaced or discarded. Yet, as the next paragraphs suggest, this 'freedom' seems to be constrained by a number of other factors, beyond filmmakers' imaginary. As a matter of fact, even some of the shifts identified in recent feature movies appear to respond to 'glo(b)(c)al' processes and trends.

Global North vis-à-vis Global South

A film goes through processes of scripting, casting and editing, regardless of the dimension or quality of the project. The numerous ways those elements considered as 'indigenous' materialize in cinematic productions are evidence of the different sensitivities, ideas, approaches, preconceptions, conceptualizations, convictions and impressions these elements elicit. As should be clear by now, indigeneity-oriented motion pictures created by domestic and international directors seeking to attract the attention of transnational audiences – especially those supported by Western funding agencies – tend to result in exotifying narratives. Yet, at the same time, these films make important contributions by transmitting to the viewers the degree of precariousness and the potential for extinction to which indigenous communities are exposed. Through the conflicting duality of reality and fiction, by making films touching upon specific events that have affected indigenous peoples (e.g. dispossession of land, abuse of power and stolen children), filmmakers subvert imagined narratives by re-enacting concrete incidents. In varying ways, these portrayals appeal to the sense of empathy of audiences, who remain disturbed but also provoked by the abuse and injustice these stories condemn. Films addressing real events become tangible images that operate as repositories of testimonies and registered documentation of history. They become cultural products that denote the interplay between technology, history, society and art. Due to the nature of the imagery, these storylines become also studies of empathy as they retrospectively reflect on the structures of inequality that overburden those considered to belong to indigenous societies. In most cases, indigeneity-themed films have as premise that they are set in former colonized corners of the world. They are defined by the historical, geopolitical and ontological dimensions of indigeneity as a notion, and the global nostalgia surrounding it.

Since twenty-first-century cinema mingles the local and global without concessions, not surprisingly, a Hollywood studio or a Paris-based filmmaker can address topics that do not necessarily reflect their immediate surroundings without incurring accusations of cultural appropriation. Examples of films that have received accusations of this kind include *Amazon Forever* (France, 2004), *Apocalypto* (United States, 2006) and *También la lluvia* (Spain, 2010). Central to the subsequent review is an exploration of the ways this global interaction takes place, and what repercussions this process can have for less economically empowered regions, such as Latin America. Unavoidably, this leads to reflecting on the scenarios that emerge once foreign funding reconfigures the power dynamics within national and intraregional cinema industries (Ross 2010). The hypothesis is that external investors like the Hubert Bals Funds, the most prominent Dutch funding scheme, or Spanish Ibermedia exert direct or indirect influence on the artistic and, more importantly, the ideological framework of 'local' Latin American films (Villazana 2008). A point of concern in regard to this development is how these productions attempt to deliver the above-mentioned viewer/tourist contemplating approach. It is impossible to ignore the reality that externally funded films, just like tourism, tend to champion a transnational optic where 'the foreign "other" becomes an object of consumption, included in the price of the cinema ticket or the tour, with audiences / tourists encouraged to confuse seeing with understanding and knowing a country' (Shaw 2011: 19).

This observation is probably best exemplified by *Diarios de Motocicleta* (2004), a co-production financed by eight countries (Argentina, Brazil, Chile, France, Germany, Peru, United Kingdom and United States), and filmed in mainly touristic settings across the Andes. Directed by Walter Salles (Brazil), the film narrates Ernesto 'Che' Guevara's 1951 trip from his native Buenos Aires through deserts, mountains and jungles, all the way to Venezuela. Gael García Bernal (Mexico) plays the iconic Che, while Rodrigo de la Serna (Argentina) interprets charismatic Alberto Granado, his companion in this adventure to the heart of the continent. Salles offers a cartographical reading of the region, while suggesting connections between these geographies and specific social groups.

Although Che's original diaries of the trip, *Diarios de Motocicleta* (*Motorcycle Diaries*), posthumously published in 1995, discuss in detail his concerns about the Andean communities he encounters along the way, the film addresses them only in two episodes. The first one shows Che's reaction to the discrimination faced by wayfaring indigenous mine workers in Bolivia. The second one is an encounter with an elderly Quechua woman who did not have access to education because of her faulty proficiency in Spanish. It is impossible to ignore the fact that, besides a few lines in Quechua, the story does not include any linguistic elements of the pre-Columbian communities it allegedly 'favours'. This is particularly discouraging in light of the fact that there are at least six references to various language-related episodes in the original diaries.[4]

The film certainly serves as a useful tool to gain deeper insights into a lesser-known period in Che's life but does not give the indigenous communities the same consideration they receive in his notes. This reductionist approach prompts reflections on how filmmakers create marketable realities and simplify them.

It is worth asking whether Salles manipulates the narrative in order to comply with specific criteria or demands from the film's executive directors, which included Robert Redford. As Podalsky (2011) asserts, 'coproductions directed at multiple national markets' tend to 'minimize specific referential markers that might confuse audiences located "elsewhere"' (60). Pan-American *Diarios de Motocicleta* seems to focus mainly on presenting impressive landscapes, encounters in captivating venues and a glimpse into the lives of characters who are both chronologically and topographically far from the transnational audiences watching them, for instance, when mournful Ernesto sits down in Machu Picchu and wonders about the destruction of pre-Columbian civilizations at the hands of Spaniards, in spite of their advances in fields such as astronomy, mathematics and medicine. Yet the film itself does not champion the indigenous elements, expound on them or expand on the impression they left on Guevara, as his notes attest.

The story manages to explain the iconic leader's gradual change, and presents a compelling and convincing account of his youth. However, in many ways, it resembles more a two-dimensional travel brochure rather than an adaptation of one of the most inspiring moments in Guevara's life. Besides generating an upsurge in the number of tourists heading from Europe to South America, the film also drew attention from critics and audiences in film festivals worldwide. In fact, *Diarios de Motocicleta* was more popular outside Latin America than in 'local' cinemas, even if it is difficult to allocate the film to a single country. It is a reminder that the cinema produced in the region, in varying ways, relies on the support of external agents for funding and distribution and transnational spectators for acknowledgement and revenues. As previous chapters have shown, there have been significant adjustments in the representation of indigenous societies in recent Latin American films. These shifts echo important cultural and social changes, such as major recognition of indigenous groups, increased awareness about pre-Columbian heritage and an upsurge in political participation of indigenous communities. Yet, as this section intends to demonstrate, economic factors also play a role in the centrality given to indigenous themes in contemporaneous films. Narratives revolving around an exotic Other evoke the inquisitiveness of global (mostly Western) audiences and, in the process, increase their chances to secure a place within North American and European circulation networks. The competition to capture funding (through finishing/editing, training, distribution and promotion grants) is fierce. The production of (global) cinema for filmmakers from emergent economies often means to go through application processes that force them to render their projects more attractive (i.e. fundable according to the funder's criteria).

Scholars have addressed the entanglement of contents, funding and spectatorships, and underlined the connection between what audiences want to see, which funds are used and what filmmakers actually produce.[5] Their findings suggest that funding has quite an impact on the conception and creation processes of filmmakers. A valid claim is that filmmakers approach indigeneity or create a version of it that meets the criteria of co-production schemes, grants, festival juries and global audiences. A review of comments (N = 768) on social media platforms confirms indigeneity-oriented films evoke feelings of empathy, support, interest and acknowledgement. The presence of 'exotic' natives in cinematic spaces becomes a matter of eliciting certain attitudes and sensitivities among (predominantly Western) viewers, rather than offering genuine impressions about the communities being depicted. In many ways, films that resort to othering practices resemble invitations to expeditions into alluring, but unfamiliar destinations, where images and sounds, particularly native languages, decorate the setting. Informed by post- and neo-colonial ideologies, filmmakers risk harnessing the attention received by indigeneity to produce narratives that offer 'real' experiences through the spectacle of an (often overtly histrionic) Other.

Paradoxically, once these visuals have quenched the thirst for the unknown among Western viewers, they proceed to transform into validated samples of 'national' cinema.[6] For instance, *Ixcanul* (Guatemala–France, 2015), mainly funded with French resources and widely acclaimed at North American and European film festivals, was released in Europe long before there were any concrete arrangements to screen it in Guatemalan movie theatres, even though the film is marketed as a sample of Central American cinema. *Ixcanul*'s scenario supports the idea that Western economies (through their funding bodies of all sorts) might (in)directly foster non-Western cultural production as a means to diversify their repertoire of options, encourage a sense of cosmopolitanism and offer audiences new cinematic vocabularies and realities. A logical assumption thereupon is that there will be a strong correlation between the allocation of funds and the set of ideologies favoured in these narratives. In light of the impact foreign recognition has on dominant classes in Latin America, it can be maintained that indigeneity-oriented films operate as extensions of cultural neo-colonialism. For instance, *El abrazo de la serpiente* (2015), a co-production involving both Latin American and European countries

(Argentina–Colombia–France–Spain–The Netherlands and Venezuela), saw an increase in revenues after receiving the Art Cinema Award in Cannes and a nomination for the 2016 Academy Awards (Oscars). The sudden increase in the number of screenings of the film across the region – once the nominations were announced – suggests that the cultural filters of a dominant core, beyond production, exert influence on local audienceship.

In numerous ways, beyond funding, Western control manifests itself also in the marketing and subsequent popularity and consumption of these productions among 'local' audiences. It becomes difficult to pinpoint to what extent foreign-financed films catering mainly to Western viewers are samples of national cinema, not delocalized productions embedded in transnational cultural exchanges. To a certain extent, indigenous elements play a role in the attention that Latin America receives among certain cultural spheres, and which readily translate into recognition and media exposure. In this circle of production, portrayals of indigeneity serve to enhance the sense of exoticism traditionally ascribed to the continent, a response to the above-mentioned spectator–tourist pairing. The spectacle of the unknown, where a core visualizes a periphery, stands out as the common denominator. In the case of cinema, the question is how local and non-local filmmakers transmute Western financial support into narratives that fulfil the criteria of funding bodies, transnational audiences and ultimately 'local' spectatorship.

(G)lo(b)(c)al filmmakers

Reviewing some of the foreign films that include the continent's indigenous peoples, it becomes evident that the focal point is actually the core–periphery relation, not indigeneity as a notion on its own. In this sense, North American and European filmmakers noticeably direct their attention to the ways in which Western characters experience their encounter with entrancing peoples and landscapes, and thereupon develop an approach based on distance and alterity. Two major concerns behind this approach are the unbalanced core–periphery relation between Global South (Latin America) and Global North (Western countries), and the entangled power structures that lie behind representations of those considered subaltern (Spivak 2006). Fuelled by resources, foreign attention to the pre-Columbian heritage of the continent in the form of films has the potential to expound simplifications and reductions. Different from the case of films produced purely from within Latin America, these stories resonate with the expectations of the aimed-at audiences and are often endorsed by large studios embedded in well-connected distribution networks.

Perhaps the best example is Mel Gibson's *Apocalypto* (United States, 2006), a film that from its outset relied on box office revenues, not on restrictive grants or jury-based selection processes. Set in pre-Columbian Yucatan, this major American production revolves around the challenges young warrior Jaguar Paw (Rudy Youngblood) must face to save his young family after Maya soldiers destroy his village. The film stands out for its depiction of extreme acts of violence, even though the director claims he went 'light' in his portrayal of this 'culture of death' engaging in 'unspeakable' practices (Loder and Gibson 2006). Gibson resorts to elements and facts that have been widely discredited. Within academic circles, *Apocalypto* prompted strong reactions for being a gruesome misrepresentation. Beyond the inaccuracies though, the most important aspect to consider is the popularity of *Apocalypto* all over the globe and its capacity to generate revenues.

In spite of its disputable depiction of the Maya, the film ironically ranked as one of the most popular films among Mexican spectators in 2006. The paradox lies in the fact that a violent American epitome of pre-Columbian Yucatan told through the optic of an Australian is widely popular among Mexicans, in spite of accusations of historical imprecisions. Gibson has nevertheless claimed that the use of documented resources, the inclusion of *convincing* elements, including *real* indigenous faces (untrained actors cast according to physical features), and the *original* language strengthen *Apocalypto*'s value as a historical chronicle. Spoken in Yucatec Mayan, the film presents an all-indigenous world where in-groups and out-groups are defined by their group affiliations, not by an invasive outsider. From this perspective, Gibson conveys the idea that extreme violence was endemic and natural to the region prior to European colonization. Through a one-dimensional treatment of the characters, Gibson validates European attempts to civilize barbaric peoples in the Americas. Human sacrifices, sanguineous encounters, inhospitable nature and the use of actors who evoke an 'unsavoury feeling', quoting Gibson's words, serve to elevate the sense of exoticism of the story (Loder and Gibson 2006). Even if Apocalypto is fiction, widely consumed portrayals like those found in popular films have cultural value, particularly when these are touted to be accurate historical accounts.

There seems to be a preoccupation among Western filmmakers addressing indigeneity to insist in the importance of realism, authenticity and veracity. Like Gibson's *Apocalypto*, Jean-Pierre Dutilleux's *Amazon Forever* (France, 2004), as the credits announce, presents real 'tribes and rituals'. The French film revolves around the adventures of a young filmmaker, Nicolas (Aurelien Wiik), who joins a community living in the Toa Toari Reserve in their fight against loggers. This is the tale of a European in search of redemption, a sense of belonging and love, as he develops feelings for the chief's daughter. Yet, as it is clear from the point of reference of the narration, indigeneity does not really play a significant role in *Amazon Forever*, rather it focuses on how a young French man experiences an exuberating, alluring and distant world. Like Gibson, director Dutilleux asserts that indigeneity is the material, but Western artistic, ideological and interpretative practices are the instruments that eventually determine the final product. Ultimately, just as Gibson did, Dutilleux conceived a film primarily aimed at transnational audiences, mainly from Western countries, and offering a visual space for these viewers to contemplate a bewitching Other.

Spanish director Icíar Bollaín confirms this core–periphery relation in her Spanish-Bolivian-French-Mexican co-production *También la lluvia* (2010). Similar to *Amazon Forever*, this is the story of a filmmaker, Sebastián (Gael García Bernal), who ventures with his crew into 2000s Bolivia to shoot a 'historic movie' about the encounter of Columbus with the Taino people living on Hispaniola Island and the Tainos' subsequent revolt against the Spanish Crown. Sebastián's film within the film is possible thanks to transnational funding schemes that, as he mentions in the story itself, are highly interested in stories that involve 'Indians'. Sebastián and executive producer Costa (Luis Tosar) have chosen Cochabamba because they hope to be able to cast large numbers of low-paid (2 USD per day), nonspeaking, background actors. The casting process for Sebastián's movie is defined by the degree of exoticism of the candidates' physical features. Widely acclaimed Bollaín makes a film featuring indigenous actors while she problematizes within the narrative itself how actors are selected to play genuine indigenous roles, offering observations of observations. The sense of realism of the story manages to create a space of contestation between 'cine épico y cine social' [epic cinema and social cinema] (Paszkiewicz 2010: 239). The film within the film is an epic one, but the looming reality (the 2000's Cochabamba water riots) is social in all its aspects. In both cases, real-life Icíar and fictitious Sebastián face the pressing need of hiring large numbers of voiceless background performers as well as an outspoken indigenous leading actor. Bolivian actor Juan Carlos Adurivi interprets Daniel, a political activist who fights against the privatization of water, and whom Sebastián chooses to play Chief Atuey. Ironically, the Spanish director has explained that just as for Sebastián, her casting process revolved around finding the right 'cara' [face], even if the actor was not 'guapo' [handsome] or had a strange voice (Bollaín 2011).

In Bollaín's story, Adurivi is to embody a multidimensional personification of an indigenous leader engaged with his community, while for Sebastián, Daniel is to give life to the legend of an indigenous cacique who leads the Tainos to the uprising against Spanish oppressors. *También la lluvia*, seen from this angle, presents a two-sided frame with Daniel playing a key role in highlighting Sebastián's double standards. On the one hand, the young director insists on making a film about the oppressive practices of the first colonizers, while on the other hand, he underpays modern Bolivians to work as extras in his European-funded, exoticism-driven movie. Cochabamba's riots serve to highlight Bolivia's present-day challenges. Images of commotion also underscore how similar the roots of today's problems are to the dilemmas faced by indigenous societies five hundred years ago. This time, instead of a looting European kingdom, Bolivians need to contest the possible sell-out of their natural resources to a California-based firm.[7] On this account, Sebastián's Taino revolts resemble Cochabamba's riots.

The figure of Daniel stands out for offering the image of a modern, engaged, cosmopolitan Aymara (and English) speaker who makes audiences aware of the implications of colonization as an economic, historical and social process. In her film, Bollaín seems to present European expansion as a pervasive, ongoing project that extends beyond discernible boundaries and that has many faces. Ironically, one of them is cinema, a techno-cultural venture and enterprise, carried out in peripheral countries like Bolivia, with the economic support of influential and authoritative bodies in the form of funding schemes. The same apparatus she denounces for endowing Sebastián with tools to (ab)use a location and its people for his artistic goals gives her the tools to create *También la lluvia* and eventually *Kathmandu, A Mirror in the Sky*.[8]

Another example, *Altiplano* (Peru/Belgium/Germany, 2009), directed by Jessica Woodworth (United States) and Peter Brosens (Belgium), 'hypnotically braids strands of Incan mythology, Catholic voodoo, and campesino outrage to style a sympathetic outsider's portrait of South American mysticism' (Lanthier 2010: para. 1). The film is not only a denunciation of the abuses faced by indigenous societies but also a space in which to witness powerful Peruvian scenery. More importantly, the story focuses on the suffering of a renowned Belgian photographer who has recently lost her husband and an indigenous woman mourning her fiancé. The multilingual (Quechua, Farsi, French,

Spanish) narrative focuses on the encounter of these two women, Grace (Jasmin Tabatabai) and Saturnina (Magaly Solier), united by their losses but, as the viewers know, separated by their position within a world social hierarchy. The film has all the earmarks of transnationalism as Grace's husband, Max, dies during the protests organized by local villagers against the Europeans working in the nearby eye clinic.

Max becomes collateral damage when the anger of an indigenous community turns to violence. Their ignored demands about the mercury spills caused by excessive mining finally draw some attention. As an eye surgeon, Max becomes a 'victim' of a conflict he attempts to solve indirectly; after all, the locals need surgery because the pollution levels have reached hazardous levels. As the only solution to her grief and a life of destruction and dispossession, Saturnina commits suicide by drinking quicksilver from a bottle and films it, using Max's video recorder. The device becomes the repository of images of the young girl covered in silver-coloured poisonous chemicals that stream from her eyes and down her cheeks. An embodiment of technology (i.e. camera) serves as a tool to register the decentralization of transnational exchanges, but also the dependency of one disadvantaged part of the globe on the other privileged one. The problematic side of *Altiplano* resides in the use of specific histrionic codes that widen the distance between Grace and Saturnina and, in the process, aim to present Western audiences with disturbing Third World realities. The film operates as a cultural artefact that reflects how the Global North understands (or thinks it does) the realities of the Global South. In *Altiplano*, the conundrum lies in the lack of context behind these excessively staged images. Once the 'spectacle' is over, fictitious Grace, directors Woodworth and Brossens, and Western spectators can return to their position of contentment and security, while only the sense of appropriation, cultural reductionism and exoticism remain. In the same manner that a mercury spill pollutes nature, unbalanced interpretations risk tarnishing the representations of silenced groups. Furthermore, alluring vistas serve as background to a story that reminds critics that, just as tourism, cinema has also become an outlet that endorses 'la mercantilización de la cultura andina' [the commodification of the Andean culture] (Monette 2013: para. 28).

Locations such as the Amazon, the Andes, Yucatan, Cochabamba and Kathmandu (i.e. in the case of Bollaín's film set in Nepal) bring to mind the notion that films resort to strategies similar to those of tourism, at least in their need to watch a distant Other. These are stories that, similar to the experience and industry of travel, are carefully engineered to respond to the curious, adventurous and intrepid nature of audiences. Beyond their artistic intentions, a common aspect shared by films such as *The Great Match* (Gerardo Olivares, Spain, 2006), *The Fountain* (Darren Aronofsky, United States, 2006), *The Gift of Mother Earth* (Toshifumi Matsushita, Japan, 2008), *Postcards* (Josh Hyde, United States, 2010), *Blackthorn* (Mateo Gil, Spain, 2011) and *Lucifer* (Gust van den Berghe, Belgium, 2014) is a sense of self-bestowed freedom and self-imposed compromise. Empowered with economic resources (mainly Western funding) and technology, filmmakers seem to feel free to meander around distant locations, particularly rural areas, 'play the tourist' and approach otherwise forgotten subjects like indigenous communities, customarily in unrestricted settings where locals celebrate the received attention. The compromise lies in their commitment to produce visuals that confirm the distance between a wealthy transnational West and distant, so-perceived convincing characters, set in far-flung geographies (from the venue where the films are screened) and inflicted by 'local' realities.

Conclusion

Latin American and 'global' filmmakers create cinematic otherness by deploying either gender- or ethnicity-related discourses of difference. Films emulate and replicate the conceptualizations of their conceivers, and hence, canons of representation obey long-established stereotypical formulas. Data collected by several surveys conducted across the region and an analysis of the corpus of films suggest directors and audiences have similar ideas about indigenous communities. Ethnotypes reflect traits commonly ascribed to ethnic groups from a collective perspective. A taxonomy of traits identified in the sixty-eight films indicates indigenous characters are often portrayed not only as convincing, pure, intelligent and relatively free but also impoverished, forgotten, abject and remarkably different. Motion pictures created by domestic and international directors seeking to attract and seduce global audiences result in exotifying narratives. These offer portraits of indigeneity that resonate with (g)lo(b)(c)al viewers' preconceptions of what the *indigenous* entails. Transnational networks of production and distribution favour storylines that align with Western cultural repertoires. Cinema across the region emphasizes the connection between spectacle, indigenous societies and images of exclusion (e.g. *A terra dos homens vermelhos*), poverty (e.g. *La niña santa*), lack of education (e.g.

Ixcanul), discordance with modernity (e.g. *¿Quién mató a la llamita blanca?*), oblivion (e.g. *Siguiendo las estrellas*), unrest (e.g. *El facilitador*), drunkenness (e.g. *Madeinusa*), conformism (e.g. *Tiempos menos modernos*) and isolation (e.g. *Distancia*). The cinematic landscape of the region is conditioned by traditions of representation that are difficult to challenge, and that seem to apply to productions directed by international filmmakers. Yet, there have been attempts to problematize and contest the social category of the indigenous as a canonical notion (e.g. *Corazón del Tiempo*, *Erendira Ikikunari*, *Zona Sur*, *Alamar* and *Roma*). In films informed by counter-stereotypic paradigms, individuality of characters is championed over ideas of collectivity and passivity. These are also productions where indigeneity and modernity are no longer considered as mutually conflicting and contradictory. In this respect, attention has focused on gender. In fact, most recent indigeneity-oriented films pay special attention to the intersectional spaces between ethnicity and femininity.

6

Catalysis: Paradigms and disruption

Central to this chapter is the discussion of paradigms of representation and how they have disciplined the ways in which indigeneity-related and -inspired narratives are told. Invisibility or visibility, according to a lens that privileges audiences and favours filmmakers, not the societies being depicted, is then contrasted with the disruptive point-of-view approach introduced by *Roma* (Mexico–United States, 2018). Reflecting retrospectively on the films reviewed in the previous chapters, the first section, '(In)visibility and representation', reviews canons of representation not only as visual and ethnicized strategies but also as evolving sites for negotiation and inclusion. The second section, '(Re)drawn blueprint', focuses on Alfonso Cuarón's groundbreaking work and explores how the film redraws the blueprint for representations of indigeneity in cinema. As this chapter shows, *Roma* does not stand out for being aspirational or entirely counter-stereotypical in certain aspects but for changing the conversation about the focus of stories where indigenous figures are presented and represented but not seen.

(In)visibility and representation

Canons of representation, understood as traditions of categorizations, reflect the perspective of the representers, not of those being represented. They retain their value though, as they inscribe, document and register how unfranchised peoples are viewed, and will be viewed for decades or centuries to come. Dominant iconic representations are linked to networks that mobilize images and ideas efficiently and have the capacity to obscure, silence and eclipse peripheral visual externalizations of the same (imagined) reality. So far, the favoured point of view in films about native peoples, partly informed by the intimate relation between science, politics and art, is the Western optic, even if we recognize that the West, as such, is a contended term, seldom scrutinized, but in fact a trope built on rather unsubstantial or, at times, randomly intertwined premises, more tightly linked to a potpourri of ethnicity, religion and, above all, transfers of knowledge, objects, technologies and practices, than to an actual common history (Appiah 2019). Paradoxically, but not coincidentally, both the West and the Indigenous are born as encompassing terms for quite diverse nations, clustered in groupings, overlooking their diversity for the sake of digestible conceptualizations.

Positioning Western traits on top of an iconic hierarchy, followed by a set of peripheral Others, has been part of cinema (originally a European medium) since its onset. The invention of symmetrical and asymmetrical figures is not new. Many of the films analysed in this volume implicitly or explicitly suggest that there is a divisor line between a producing centre and a (mis)/(under)/(re) presented periphery. Latin American cinema has retained a model in which European elements are considered enactments of an aspirational Self. This instant coveted Self is assumed to respond to latent processes. It is embedded in the national psyche and collective assumptions, strongly linked to racialization, otherness and systems of power. Central to understanding how this unravels and manifests in films is a consideration of the psychological aspects of visual narratives. Both at a conscious and subconscious level, the figure of the indigenous has a symbolic value. Informed by an imperialist androcentric positioning and colonialist canons, retained in various degrees up until now, films tend to exotify indigenous elements. This is still perceivable in present-day films, even if 'the concept of indigeneity has clearly transformed over time, bringing us today's plurality of meanings' (Landzelius 2004: 17). Through a strategic arrangement of various elements, visual narratives can create a sense of separation between what audiences perceive as a mainstream, central Self, a peripheral Other – in this case, a native Other – even if these are not clear-cut positionalities either.

A long tradition in cinema of associating indigenous societies with non-aspirational traits resides in the self-bestowed authority and artistic freedom of filmmakers to bypass the fact that identity is not an empty canvas. Reduction, simplifications, omissions and erasures ultimately create an imaginary tabula rasa. Visual representations are not factual products that necessarily seek to portray a culture, society or someone's lived experience accurately. They do not have to be. Artists' freedom must prevail. Notwithstanding, filmmakers cannot expect members of the depicted communities or viewers not to question their position vis-à-vis those they represent. The tangibility of tools, connections, financial resources and technology weighs heavily on pieces of art that grant their makers but not their 'objects/subjects of inspiration' any benefit, especially if these are societies, still today, facing major challenges. Films rely on strategies to beautify or obscure whom and what they metaphorically and figuratively depict. Internal and external traits of a character are part of the creation of a cultural artefact that ultimately seeks to seduce. Following conventions, cliché enactments of native peoples as naive beings unable to harm anyone, or as submissive sages who witness their own destruction are still quite common. Externally, otherness encompasses superficial embodiments of ethnicity, race and nation by ultimately associating characteristic physical features with specific assumptions and attitudes.

Filmmakers use certain techniques in order to enhance the appeal of images of indigeneity, characters of ethnic descent, sceneries associated with pre-Columbian cultures or emotions entwined with nostalgic ideas about native communities. Indeed, 'in spite of different backgrounds, careers, and agendas, U.S., European, and Latin American filmmakers share a common goal when they address nativeness: representing the indigenous difference through the fictional construction of the "Indian" that will convey their understanding of "authentic" nativeness' (Quispe-Agnoli 2011: 95). Despite the polyvalent nature of an ethnically diverse region, embedded in a mestizo context, the extended effects of ideologies of otherness are deeply engrained across the continent. After all, although there are exceptions, most of the viewers watching an internationally promoted story about marginalized communities are probably not members of ethnic minorities themselves. One can always wonder how different the storylines and aesthetic approaches would be in *La teta asustada*, *Taina* or *Caramuru* if the filmmakers identified themselves as indigenous.

Even if there are no unambiguously binary, black or white, representation, but an ocean of shades, hues and tints, discourses of otherness do tend to revolve around the notion of a civilized and elaborated core surrounded by an undeveloped, unfinished and subaltern periphery. Following the path traced by literature, paintings and photography, cinematic works, as a format, operate as sources of information encapsulated in cultural artefacts that travel and gain new meaning across their journeys. They inform others about their makers' social, cultural and epistemic systems. Seeking to attract attention in an era where human-eyes-attention span is capitalized, images of the unknown are enhanced to foster fascination. It is an old tradition but it has evolved. Although films by indigenous filmmaking projects are increasing in number, they remain small, compared to industrial cinema. Consequently, third parties who do not belong to ethnic minorities are those producing widely screened portrayals of the indigenous. Through exaggeration of features, both on internal and external scales, difference is marked. Inequity is a key aspect to understand the perpetuation of artistic strategies that categorize and simplify, and avoid challenging and questioning. Discourses of difference are still deployed to mark dominance and privilege.

Cinema empowers filmmakers to enhance the dividing line between their own community and other groups according to their orientations and sensitivities. Expression of emotions and ideals is the purpose of optical narratives, as any form of art, so the arbitrariness of the medium relegates roles to those depicted, attending mainly to the viewpoint of the storyteller. It therefore becomes pertinent to observe whether contemporary productions focusing on indigeneity seek to encourage awareness about disenfranchised groups, or whether they are simply realistic reflections of a remodelled state of affairs. Here, a key point to bear in mind is the relation between producers and consumers. Exhibition and distribution of feature films are intrinsic parts of the industry of production and are largely correlated with their content, both on- and offline. Media technologies can allow excluded groups to enter a realm where they can be seen and heard, but hardly in an unbiased, straightforward and indifferent way.

Indigeneity as part of the social fabric of Latin America has been converted into images and constructed following filmic precepts to serve a purpose within a narrative. Based on economic power ideals, the region is commonly considered as a subaltern realm, and so is its cinematic production, also at a local level. Attendance rates confirm that most Latin Americans prefer foreign, mainly North American, feature films over regionally produced ones. The region is part of a common global visual culture market. By extension, Latin Americans are not immune to the implications of globalized cinematic industries, recognizable for the 'interconnectedness of cinematic practices' (Dennison and Lim 2006: 6). As expected, national cinema is scrutinized based on international standards. Although national productions expose situations with which local communities relate, they are in peril of becoming imperfect counterparts of popular narratives precisely because of their sense of perfection.[1] On the other hand, since Latin American cinema has been regarded as refreshing, realistic, extrinsic, but mainly different, filmmakers from the region risk crafting narratives and images aiming mainly at quenching the thirst for exoticism among Western audiences in film festivals (Falicov 2019), or subscription content platforms. After a major hit (mainly signalled by box office numbers and accolades), the most successful directors eventually move on and capture funding for so-perceived *mainstream* films in collaboration with *mainstream* studios.

From the onset of filmic representations of native societies, cinema has tended to suggest that a collective Other suffices to understand differences within difference. A plurality-oriented approach has glossed over the complexities that a singularity-oriented methodology can expose. Although the horizon is changing, for most of the history of Latin American cinema, indigenous characters have been depicted as part of a group defined by a perceived sense of sameness. Audiences are encouraged to adopt the ethnographical tradition of observing 'tribal' behaviour as a means to experience unfamiliar societies. Films such as *Diarios de Motocicleta*, *El facilitador*, *Los viajes del viento*, *Siguiendo las estrellas* and *Tainá* trilogy suggest that binary associative traits explain taxonomic connotations that assemble individuals in easily identified clusters. Cinema tends to avoid zooming into the identities of those depicted to be different unless their difference is actually a theme in the storyline. In *El verano de los peces voladores*, *Dioses*, *Feriado*, *La mujer sin cabeza* and *Xingu*, ethnicity serves a similar purpose to the scaffolding around a building, or the pane around a window. It provides a structure and access, but is not the focus. The above-mentioned films include a victim of a hit-and-run accident, abused and ignored employees, silenced members of communities and casual extras used as human background. They are important to the narrative to understand the microscopically addressed lives of the central figures. Yet, they are evidence that representation, visibility and inclusion are not necessarily synonyms. An imagined native still dwells in narratives where generalizations prevail over singularity and distinctiveness.

Processes of self-association are embedded in a natural desire to observe, relate and co-create, ultimately with the goal of recognizing traces of Self in the Other, or alternatively spurning the Other for being different from our Self. Meanings are created in correlation to the set of codes deployed in a film and the emotions they provoke. Tension emerges between a spectrum of selective Selves in contrast with a range of imagined Others. The point of view in a film matters because it positions the observer and contextualizes the space, time and line of events of the story. A vantage point offers also vistas that have a social and symbolic value, beyond the diegetic world. Indigeneity in some films instigates tensions, for instance, when characters are racialized (e.g. *El niño pez*), or reduced to caricatures sketched from a tropicalist viewpoint (e.g. *Caramuru*).

Bearing in mind that films are not monologues, they are presumed to enter a dialogue with the audience in which the authority in question can be the filmmaker, production company, supporting state, ideological system or the film itself. Since the film is not produced in a vacuum, a social background is used as a point of reference in regard to the narrative and the external factors inherent to it. Similarly, a given point in time and some quality of the characters are arbitrarily, but not unfoundedly, chosen to situate the narrative. As the controlling figure in charge of reconfiguring paradigms evolves, so does the dialogue in which audiences and producers engage, regardless of their factual similarities or differences with the actual state of affairs. Shifts in perspectives and meanings do not need to reflect discernible changes, beyond the need of hegemonic systems to portray others differently, always based on their own discourse. Canons historicize content and, hence, become identifiable connectors between formulas audiences know and updated approaches to century-old archetypes. Filmmakers follow predetermined criteria naturally because cultural repertoires are encyclopaedic compendiums of tropes with which viewers will be familiar. In this sense, a good onlooker (e.g. *Defensores de la vida*), fabulism (e.g. *Los ojos azules*), mysticism (e.g. *Los viajes del viento*), postcolonial nostalgia (e.g. *Taínos: La última tribu*) or the visual need to have subtitles as graphic materializations of difference (e.g. *Play*) all become acts of an *homo depictor*.

Networks of funding, distribution and exhibition retain their position as filters that define whether such messages ever reach any spectator at all (Ross 2010). Even if a film endorsing equality is produced with the goal of reclaiming mediatized space for minorities, it is only by reaching the spectators that it can ever have any social impact. While funding determines the feasibility of a project, endorsement and distribution secure its eventual dissemination. Social divisions and power structures have given birth to systems of cinematic representation that reflect one-sided perspectives embedded in fixed and reductive interpretations (histrionic indigeneity). Yet, as this chapter shows, there is hope. Similar to the evolution in paradigms of audiovisual representation of ethnic communities in literature and fine arts, cinema has also changed its formulations and understanding of how indigeneity is presented, mostly prompted by social shifts and cultural reorientations.

Canonical turn

Particularly noticeable in the second decade of the twenty-first century, emphasis has been placed on the aural aspect of cinema, resulting in the inclusion of Amerindian languages, even imaginary ones (e.g. *Sueño en otro idioma*). Underlining the points raised in Chapter 3, the presence of indigenous linguistic heritage in mainstream/festival films is reconfiguring Latin American cinematic landscapes. Languages are intrinsic to identity, inundate spaces, structure communication and operate as concatenations across constellations that rule one of the five human senses. The language choice, with or without subtitles, does not go unnoticed. In the corpus of films reviewed in this volume, language has one main function: marking and making identity. This is a common pattern throughout all the films, and as the next chapter shows, a similar – although not identical – situation occurs in self-representational film projects. In contemporary cinema, the indigenous figure does not need to hide her/his sounds in any context and that is a reason to celebrate. Linguistic heritage is managed and deployed to articulate, express and contextualize, for instance, silenced individuals (e.g. *El regreso de Lencho*), temporality of legacy (e.g. *Vaho*), indeterminacy (e.g. *El destino*), inclusion (e.g. *Cenizas eternas*), loyalties (e.g. *Guaraní*) or continuity (e.g. *Burwa dii ebo*). Sonorous elements acoustically frame a story in similar ways as colour and granularity moderate the aesthetic composition of an image. The melody of a sawawa (e.g. *Los viajes del viento*) bespeaks the presence of an identity. Symbolically, the sound of a body being run over by a car also signals interaction with a subject that does not need to speak to be heard (e.g. *La Ciénaga*), although the individual remains invisible nevertheless. Cinema registers points of contact between standard hegemonic languages and tangential linguistic realities in unprecedented ways.

Other important changes in the paradigms of representation include the bold decision of some filmmakers of following their own criteria. Self-introspection and the capacity to create spaces for the Other in equal terms (e.g. *Yvy Maraêy: Tierra sin mal*) challenge the tradition of avoiding the exposure of masses to films that are ideologically critical but commercially not profitable. Some contributions are questioning economies of production of stories that aim to preserve a machinery where power is indiscriminately bestowed to the dominant, albeit usually minority, segments of society. Consequently, they are instigating social advancements as they promulgate new forms of sketching indigenous elements in cinema and prompt conversations about real-life issues, such as blatant discrimination (e.g. *¿Quién mató la llamita blanca?*, *Nosilatiaj. La belleza*, *Alicia en el país*, *Antes o Tempo Não Acabava*, *Dauna: Lo que lleva el río*, *Distancia*, *El traspatio* and *La Sirga*).

Presenting indigenous realities as part of mainstream societies without spectacularizing their existence is another positive development in recent films.

Distancing from a canonical dynamic in which a viewer/tourist wanders around and observes the world of a distant Other (Urry 2002) has also dismantled the sense of enchantment linked to (mostly rural) specific topologies. Avoiding the tendency to use the diegetic world as a journey into unknown geographies, and exotic realities, a practice observed in festival films produced in the region (Shaw 2011), the focus is placed on lived experiences. Demands for reconfigurations in the social order (e.g. *Zona Sur*), examples of subjects retaking control of their lives (e.g. *Magallanes*) or individuals finding common grounds (e.g. *Tiempos menos modernos*) are recent attempts to look beyond ethnicity labels.

Instrumentalizing and managing ethnicity has been the backbone of the creation of nations that amalgamate diversity. Moving attention to some of the strategies used to create meaning and endorse a national identity quickly leads to the concept of *mestizaje*. Upholding the idea that 'people are not white or black, but rather, they are whiter than or darker than others' (Moreno Figueroa 2013: 139), as a practice, has strengthened ethnic hierarchies in the region. As a policy, *mestizaje* has blocked the recognition of ethnically subordinated groups that caused the institutionalized notion that all members of society should identify with the new symbols of the nation. This understanding comes from the fact that identity across Latin America has been construed through processes of amalgamation and standardization that have failed to recognize other identities. Considering that emancipation of audiences in terms of equality is believed to be attainable through images encouraging ethnic diversity and inclusion, recent aspirational portrayals of indigenous figures are paradigm-changing.

Syntonic with and in syntony with new times, indigenous figures are endowed with qualities that, until now, with some exceptions, were mostly assigned only to non-indigenous characters, such as agency and dexterity (e.g. *Erendira Ikikunari*), courage and intelligence (e.g. *El Violín*), and loyalty and talent (e.g. *Retablo*). The idea that the Other's perspective is rooted in a cosmovision and set of values and principles that is as valid as any other is also a noticeable addition (e.g. *Brava gente* and *Corazón del Tiempo*). Cinematic storylines concerned with individual identity are a novelty as well, allowing for more diversity of indigenous character (e.g. *A terra dos homens vermelhos*) and different lifestyles (e.g. *Alamar*). An indigenous life is shown in the context of microcosmic experiences of common human dilemmas that resonate across larger societies (e.g. *Cochochi*, *Erase una vez en Bolivia* and *La Jaula de Oro*).

In *Cochochi* (2007), for instance, directors Laura Amelia Guzmán and Israel Cárdenas follow the adventures of two brothers commissioned by their grandfather to deliver medicines to an elderly couple. In each scene of this cautionary tale, real-life brothers Evaristo (Evaristo Lerma Batista) and Luis Antonio, colloquially called Tony (Antonio Lerma Batista), show how different they are from each other. Discipline and obedience do not appeal to Tony, whereas Evaristo feels compelled to act responsibly and has a high sense of duty. Luis Antonio's apparent and, at times, callous indifference stands in stark contrast with Evaristo's interest and outlook towards the future of his family and community. Now that they have completed the compulsory phase of their education at the local primary school, Tony is excited about not having to study anymore. Despite receiving a scholarship that would allow him to enrol in high school, Luis Antonio, in his own words, does not 'care' about those things. In fact, he does not attend the graduation ceremony in which the grant is awarded.

Through a flat plane and a single shot, the camera focuses on Evaristo as he explains to the school principal that Tony is absent. While Tony wants to enjoy each moment, Evaristo sees the value of education to creating a bridge between the Raramuri/Tarahumara- and Spanish-speaking communities. Throughout the film, differences in their character traits become progressively more evident in their approach to the task they are expected to complete. At the onset of their journey, the brothers disagree on which means of transportation they could use. Evaristo is hesitant about Tony's idea of taking the best horse of the stable against their grandfather's instructions. After losing the horse in an unknown location, not being able to hand over the medicines clearly worries one of the boys more than the other. Dotted with comic passages and free of overtly intense or violent episodes, *Cochochi* presents a credible portrayal of indigenous childhood in rural Mexico. Guzmán (Dominican Republic) and Cárdenas (Mexico) structure a narrative thread that allows audiences to witness the emergence, negotiation and naturality of an enmeshed identity.[2]

Evaristo and Tony are children, belong to the Raramuri/Tarahumara community, are bilingual and pay allegiance to the Mexican flag. They presumably grew up together in a corner of the state of Chihuahua, cared for by their grandfather and in close contact with a landscape that has informed their sense of belonging, but without standardizing their outlook towards the world that surrounds them. These brothers are two quite different characters and *Cochochi* is a space to witness variety within diversity and the negotiation between the general and the particular. The contextualization of personal identity within a community, a larger society and the inescapability of global forces is a new and bold stance in the Latin American cinematic panorama, nonetheless, because of the soft power of images that travel across nations, regions and continents.

Masses consume media and are fed with orientations and ideas and, hence, free from physical coercion, the soft power of media lies in being able to attract audiences and expand ideologies merely by luring and seducing. This type of power, 'exerted mainly through influence and culture, as opposed to "hard power", coercive or military' (Martel 2012: 482), affords media producers the ability to present, promote, favour, endorse, ratify, disperse and promulgate beliefs, ideas, values and forms of perceiving the world, ourselves and others. The power of films, therefore, lies in their potential to become platforms of social coercion. Indigeneity in fiction can be depicted in any conceivable way, regardless of reality, because venturing outside the materialistic world is precisely what consumers of entertainment seek. Artistically, the creation of otherness presumably relies on the manipulation of those constituents that ultimately come together to create a final product: the film. The use of the camera plays a significant role, as it controls and steers the viewer's perspective, defines the focal points and enhances or makes opaque elements of the mise-en-scène, according to the message the filmmaker wants to transmit. Yet, whose point of view is favoured in the context of mis- and under-represented communities matters even more. As I argue in the next section, Cuarón in *Roma* disrupts the paradigmatic representation of indigeneity in fictionalized films.

Although in terms of language, the inclusion of Mixtec in *Roma* resembles, in many ways, the strategic use of Amerindian languages identified in many other films, Cuarón introduces some novelty in this respect as well. By magnifying the scale at which cinema depicts the human experience of those perceived to be indigenous, Cuarón demonstrates that an intimate unfragmented representation is the reverse approach to iconic ethnotypes.

(Re)drawn blueprint

Roma (Mexico, 2018) is a catalyst for change in the use of stereotypes in Latin American visual culture, as it presents a syntonic, rather than a histrionic, approach to indigeneity. Above all, it deranges the convention of showing from a distance the point of view of those being represented. Inspired by his own childhood, Cuarón not only shows that indigenous and exotic are not necessarily synonyms but also that memory consists of images, as much as sounds. With an overriding concern to portray accurately and authentically a crucial moment in his life (1970–1), the Mexican director brings *Roma* to life with a plethora of sounds endemic to his hometown. Although the high-cost cinematic production, endorsed and distributed by Netflix (United States), is allegedly fictional, the black-and-white film is in most aspects autobiographical. Cuarón tried to remain at all times faithful to his memories and those of Liboria Rodríguez, his real-life nanny and inspiration for the story. The main character, Cleo (Yalitzia Aparicio), is a young Mixtec girl employed by Sofía (Marina de Tavira), who impersonates Cuarón's mother, and Antonio (Fernando Grediaga), his conspicuously absent father.

The story focuses mainly on Cleo's routine in her position as domestic worker, but also as an important figure in the upbringing of Sofía's children, Sofi (Daniela Demessa), Paco (Carlos Peralta), Pepe (Marco Graf) and Toño (Diego Cortina). The interaction between the members of the family, particularly between Cleo and 'Señora Sofía' (Mrs. Sofía), serves as reflection and critique of the highly hierarchized Mexican society in which they live. Other members of the household include Sofía's mother, Teresa (Verónica García), Cuarón's grandmother, and Adela (Nancy García), Cleo's co-worker, roommate and confidant. At all times, the story is told from Cleo's perspective, and not from Paco's, the character who represents Cuarón as a child. In fact, except for brief episodes, Paco remains in the background as a minor character throughout the entire film. Even if there are many indigenous women who are employed as domestic workers in Mexico, the notion of ethnotypes does not seem to apply in the case of *Roma*. The fact that the narrative focuses on an individual in a compelling, subtle and yet multilayered manner operates as an antidote to clichéd or stereotypical depictions. Cuarón zooms into the life of Cleo to a level of detail that there is no room for generalizations. As the following paragraphs argue, Cleo's indigenous identity is mainly marked by her Mixtec roots and linguistic ancestry. While this Mixtec background is not presented as an ornament, an exotic addition or an improvised strategical twist, it signals Cleo's and Adela's background, a tactic widely identified in indigeneity-oriented films.

Identity ma(r)ker

Dialogues in Tu'un Savi/Mixtec signal Cleo's and Adela's ethnic identity throughout the film; both the opening and the closing dialogues are in the Amerindian language. The opening sequence offers a glimpse into what it seems to be an average day in Cleo's life as a domestic worker. The first scenes also provide clues about the sociolinguistic dynamics at play. Cleo speaks to Borras the dog, in Spanish, alternates between Mixtec and Spanish when she interacts with Adela and addresses the family members in Spanish. The initial episodes include a moment in which Pepe, the youngest of the children, exhorts Cleo and Adela with a pleading tone to 'ya no hablen así' [stop talking like that]. The brief interaction is evidence that Spanish is not the only means of communication in the house, and that Pepe feels excluded. Linguistic spontaneity is visibly determined by the surroundings.

Mixtec is reserved to have private conversations, share secrets, discuss delicate family matters, preserve intimacy and exchange opinions and gossip. As an exception, Cleo uses a lullaby in Mixtec to put Sofi to bed and wake her up in the morning. Sofía's only daughter mumbles along and is clearly pleased by a daily musical ritual that denotes intimacy and affect. The scenes in Sofi's bedroom remind viewers of the possibilities of childhood as a period of time in which connection, attachment and emotions transcend the boundaries of ethnicity, class and language barriers. Mixtec operates in the film as the most salient marker of Cleo's ethnic background. Her social status and subjectivity are explained by her ancestry and ethnicity, inherently linked to external aspects (her physical traits), and internal ones (her presumably native tongue). On screen, Cleo externalizes her identity through brief but meaningful dialogues that Aparicio utters, despite not being fluent in Mixtec.

Aparicio notes that she is the daughter of a Mixtec speaker (Raúl Ismael Aparicio), who refused to pass on his linguistic heritage to his children 'porque él temía que fuéramos discriminados por no poder hablar bien el español' [because he feared that we would be discriminated against for not speaking Spanish properly] (Sánchez 2018: para. 5). These remarks confirm that traditionally, in Mexico, indigenous languages are given a lower social status than mainstream Spanish. While Mexican media devote limited or no attention to the linguistic diversity of the country, the biographical nature of *Roma* forces the film to publicly acknowledge it. In line with Cuarón's desire to portray the multilingual reality of Mexico City as he remembered it, the leading role needed was to be able to speak Tu'un Savi/Mixtec. After a lengthy process of casting, Aparicio was chosen as main actress and was eventually encouraged to bring a Mixtec-speaking friend that could play Adela, but someone who could also assist her with the dialogues scripted in Mixtec. Aparicio (Cleo) and García (Adela) know each other from their formative years as preschool teachers, and in her position as teacher, García becomes Aparicio's language coach throughout the making of the film. Their bond as confidants and friends seen on screen reflects their real-life friendship. García and Aparicio come originally from the State of Oaxaca, a requisite to be selected for the film so it would coherently match with Libo's background. Not speaking Mixtec in real life denotes a performative aspect of Aparicio's interpretation of Cleo, but her variant of Mexican Spanish, in terms of pronunciation and prosody, is in line with Cuarón's quest for authenticity. Cleo's speech becomes a trait that accentuates the dividing line between the metropole (Mexico City) and the surroundings (State of Oaxaca).

Reflecting on films such as *El Violín/The Violin* (Mexico, 2005) and *El corazón del Tiempo/Heart of Time* (Mexico, 2008), it is worth observing that there are examples of visual narratives in which language is not necessarily used to imply difference. The exchanges between Cleo and Adela denote code-switching patterns that not only reflect their sociolinguistic reality but also raise questions about the connections between levels of proficiency in Mixtec, Mixtec identity and 'Mixtec-ness'. At many moments in the history of the cinematic (re)presentation of indigenous societies, language has been used as a token of authenticity. While *Roma* has undoubtedly increased levels of visibility and prominence within spaces rarely devoted to indigenous cultural themes, the language–ethnicity binary remains problematic. A case in point is the Mixtec sentence, 'In tiu'n ntav'i' [A star is born], used by the highly esteemed fashion magazine *Vogue Mexico* (December 2018 edition) to complement/decorate a picture of Aparicio on its cover. Bearing in mind the invisibility of certain segments of Mexican society in media spaces, *Roma* is evidence of the cultural vibrancy of soft power. Yet since Aparicio does not speak Mixtec, introducing, presenting and promoting her as an indigenous woman reveal inconsistences if the language–ethnicity binary was applied. As it appears, the popularity of Cleo, hence *Roma*'s, is, in many regards, linked to Aparicio's 'Mixtec-ness' and, by default, her linguistic heritage.

Aside from this, *Roma* challenges the approaches to Amerindian linguistic heritage in Latin American films in two senses. On the one hand, Cleo is not depicted as a less eloquent speaker of Spanish, epitomized, for instance, in the way she corrects Pepe's mistaken use of past tenses. On the other hand, Mixtec is not portrayed as less worthy of the spectator's attention than other languages present in the story. As far as the first aspect is concerned, although power hierarchies are at play at all times and Pepe is a child – therefore his language skills are less developed – Spanish is shown as part of both Cleo and Pepe's cultural patrimony. The scene opens with a close-up of a half-eaten breakfast, Pepe sits at the table while Cleo stands next to him.

The child wears a school uniform, while his caregiver wears a uniform that for practical and indexical reasons signals her occupation.

The camera focuses on Cleo's hands maneuvering a spoon, and Pepe's crossed arms.

PEPE: *Cuando yo era grande, tú estabas ahí pero eras otra.* / When I was old, you were there, but you were someone else.

Cleo uses a spoon to crack a boiled egg open and places it in Pepe's cup.

CLEO: *¿Cuándo eras?* / When you were?
PEPE: *Sí.* / Yes.

The camera changes focus and now a medium shot shows both Cleo and Pepe, almost at the centre of the scene.

CLEO: *¿O cuándo seas grande?* / Or when you get old?
PEPE: *No, cuando eras* / No, when I was old.

Cleo pours salt in the egg and mixes it.

CLEO: *Sí, ¿Y cuándo fuiste grande?* / And when were you old?
PEPE: *Cuando no había nacido.* / Before I was born.

Pepe takes the salt container from Cleo, adds more salt to his egg and even more once she goes back to the kitchen. The breakfast routine offers glimpses of the power structures at play, but also the didactic and formative role of Cleo.

The second aspect to consider is the position of Mixtec within the narrative, particularly in respect to other languages in the film. Bearing in mind that attention has been paid to every detail of this elaborated fiction feature leads to believe that the opening of the film has a symbolic meaning. Within the first ten seconds of *Roma*, the acclaimed director discreetly presents cues about his own views on language. Before the opening credits, the logo of Esperanto Filmoj, the California-based producing company owned by Cuarón, is spelled out in changeable letters and characters from different alphabets that resemble a split-flat display. It then reads in Esperanto – the constructed language invented by Ludwik Lejzer Zamenhof to foster peace among nations – 'Filmo produktita de Esperanto-Filmoj' [Film produced by Esperanto Films]. This is followed by a practical explanation: 'Diálogos en Mixteco subtitulados. Otros idiomas no están subtitulados' [Subtitles are provided for dialogues in Mixtec. No subtitles are provided for other languages]. The announcement is brief, but it sets the tone for the story that is about to start. From its onset, the film champions Amerindian linguistic identity over languages commonly considered as more prestigious; the other languages briefly included in the film are Japanese, English and Norwegian. By the same token, Cuarón conveys the notion that conversations and songs in Mixtec are relevant for audiences to understand and confirms the centrality of Cleo's perspective as main referent.

While the surreal, almost allegorical, inclusion of the Norwegian hymn *Barndomsminne frå Nordland* (also known as *Å eg veit meg eit land*), sung by Mr. Larsen (Kjartan Halvorsen), marks the climax of an important sequence in the film, the New Year Eve's fire, no translation is provided. I suggest that the last line of the song, 'Å eg minnest, eg minnest so vel dette land!' [Oh I remember, I remember so well this land!], is symbolically paired with Cleo's lines in the subsequent scene: 'Sabes, se parece a mi pueblo. Claro allá está seco pero se parece' [You know, it feels like my village. It's drier there, but it feels like it]. Both lines presumably allude to the sense of nostalgia all humans share, regardless of linguistic, ethnic, social or cultural differences. Mr. Larsen is head of the Larsens, a Scandinavian family that, along with the Matos and the Richards, celebrates New Year's Eve with the Cuaróns in a hacienda out of town, owned by the Bárcenas family. Exchanges in English between the members of the families add a sense of transnationalism to Cleo's environment, but serve also as referents of the aspirational psyche of upper middle classes across the region.

Language remains a marker, epitomized at best in the question Benita (Clementina Guadarrama), the main hacienda housekeeper, asks Cleo in the basement where the workers celebrate New Year's Eve on their own terms: '¿Ya hablas inglés o qué?' [So what, do you speak English now?]. This question follows Benita's previous remarks about the snob attitude of some of the nannies working for urban families, and Cleo's reluctance to drink alcohol during her pregnancy. In the version of *Roma* streamed on the English-speaking platform of Netflix, the question is not translated. A tactical move that resembles the initial decision of the American media powerhouse of providing subtitles in peninsular Spanish for those living in Spain; later on, dropped after the decision proved controversial. The interplay of artistic sensitivities, reality and authenticity, in terms of representation and linguistic approach remain unresolved issues. Paradoxically, when choosing the characters to play the Larsens, Cuarón could not remember whether they were Swedish or Norwegian, and whether the last name was Larsson instead of Larsen. Since it had to be either, he decided to portray them as Norwegian (Nordseth 2018). Perhaps, the most authentic aspect of memories are the emotions they evoke, rather than their accuracy, both in terms of images and sounds. There are reasons to believe that more (re) constructed moments and sounds in *Roma* resemble Cuarón's past as much as Norway resembles and still deviates from Sweden. Cuarón's *Roma* is an ode to a specific person whose identity includes indigenous linguistic ancestry, but more importantly, many other traits that captivate and remind audiences that humans are very similar to each other and sound similar as well.

Cloned ethnotypes

Across the previous chapters, a common denominator has been to attempt to assess how the indigenous figure is portrayed, and to address the problematic aspects of (re)presentation in fictional features. As has been noted, in contexts where exoticism, skewed economic structures and a notorious Self–Other interplay dictate the criteria for (g)lo(b)(c)al filmmakers, long-standing ethnotypes, even if modified, easily become the norm. Filmmakers as photograph artists have the option of correcting an image by cloning it, thus reproducing almost identical images modified according to personal taste. Similarly, cinematic ethnotypes evolve according to sensitivities of each filmmaker. Major visibility of ethnic communities and political participation of self-identified indigenous groups across the region have resulted in more inclusive cinematic depictions. Often though, reconfigured patterns of representation disguise many aspects such as cultural canons, economic interests, thematic trends linked to transnational proclivities, remodelled attitudes, international demand and expectations of World Cinema spectators. Conclusively, cloned representations are more likely to succeed through the various stages of revision of a film project.

Latin American films, although more visible than ever before, remain confined to more reduced circles than cinema produced in English, starred in by international celebrities, designed to present relatable 'Western realities' or engineered to seduce or impress through an unparalleled use of visual and narrative effects. In an interconnected cinema landscape, the films that (re) present the region beyond its borders align with aesthetic codes imposed by widely recognized festivals and distribution networks. The local cinema consumed by local spectators, locally produced and distributed, and invisible in international settings, emerges from a need to entertain, rather than to provide glimpses into hypnotizing, shocking and distant episodes of Global South realities. At a national level, directors are aware of their need to produce consumable visual narratives. The disjuncture between internationally and nationally oriented fictional features is evidence that spectators have different tastes and interests, but also that funders and distributors have a considerable impact on the themes and approaches championed by films they fund and distribute. Despite the contrivances of a competitive, centralized and traditional cinematic landscape, important reconfigurations in the depiction of Amerindian characters and cultures have been charted in Latin American films produced since the turn of the century. The most notorious change lies in the portrayal of the indigenous as an individual, as opposed to an anonymous member of a community. Simultaneously, filmmakers have become more aware that ethnic differences do not suppress personal traits and that depicting is not the same as ostracizing or idealizing. Another recent change is signalled by films that explore the intersection of gender and ethnicity, and the diversity across both markers of identity.

A valid observation throughout the critical analysis of the films reviewed in this project has been the relatively limited attention most of these cinematic productions receive. Since the majority are readily labelled as samples of art house cinema, outside specific circles, in many cases, their resonance among (inter)national audiences is limited, brief and short-lived. Usually, the cultural, mediatic and economic vibrancy of indigeneity-oriented films, especially if they are spoken in indigenous languages, is intrinsically linked to international awards. As has been discussed, recognition of cinematic works in widely acclaimed film festivals (e.g. Cannes) or nominations – even short listings – for highly esteemed accolades (e.g. Oscars) are status symbols or badges of authority that warrant acknowledgement in the (co-)producing countries. Out of the sixty-eight representational films reviewed in the previous chapters, *Roma* stands out for becoming what many consider an iconic masterpiece set to transcend time and space, and for providing a reconfigured blueprint for cinematic portrayals of indigeneity (Diagram 2).

After the turn of the century, almost two decades have seen an increased number of productions that challenge clichéd portrayals or question established archetypes in various ways, from different angles and set in different times. Allowing for new ways of understanding the continent, filmmakers have explored, among other themes, the crisis experienced by an adopted girl who is reunited with her father (*Distancia/Distance*, Guatemala, 2011), the insecurity

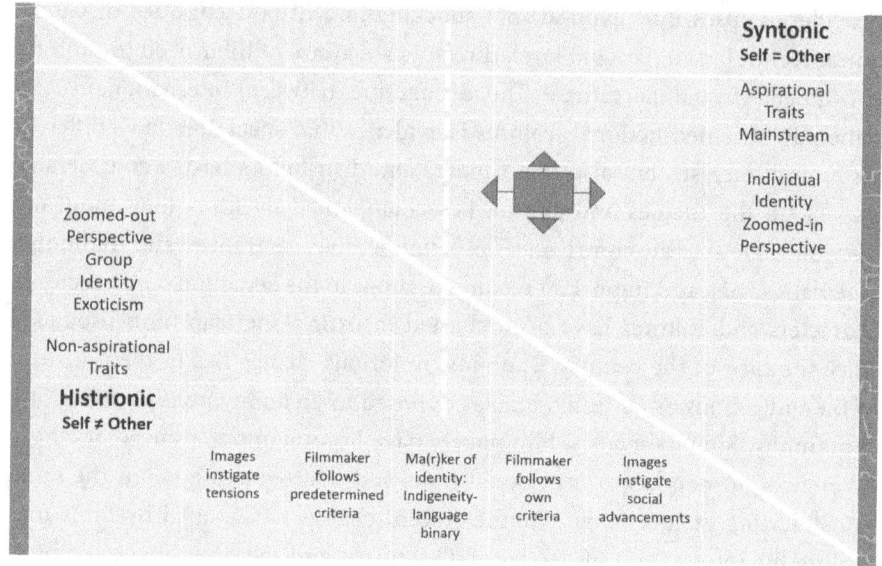

Diagram 2 Position of *Roma* (Mexico, 2018) within a (re)drawn blueprint for indigenous ethnotypes.

of a gay teenager in love with a Kichwa car mechanic (*Feriado/Holiday*, Ecuador, 2014), the anxiety of three former classmates scarred by an agonizing sense of guilt (*Vaho/Becloud*, Mexico, 2009) and the history of a national park in the heart of the Amazon basin (*Xingu*, Brazil, 2012). For almost two decades, filmmakers have compiled stories where main and secondary characters are depicted as presidents, activists, fashion designers, violinists, factory workers, hairdressers, anthropologists and most commonly domestic workers. The approach to this occupation is quite diverse, and often it has been informed by narratives where the focal point seeks to witness and present rather than to express and recognize the contrivances and implications of this line of work. In this respect, *Roma* adds new dimensions to the question of representation.

Roma confirms an observation made by Rony (1996) more than two decades ago about cinema not only being technology but a 'social practice with conventions' (8), bound to adhere to the cultural repertoire of the viewers. The film reconfigures the aesthetics of a common stereotype, the figure of the indigenous domestic employee. From beginning to end, the story does not intend to convey the idea that Cleo is set to change profession or expand her horizons beyond the household where she works and lives. Neither does Cuarón attempt to disguise the fact that a large number of domestic employees in Mexico City and other urban centres are of indigenous descent, and as such, subject to strict hierarchized social circles. In various ways, the film does reduce the distance between on- and off-screen reality and dislocates the borders that comfortably separate fictionalized characters from audiences. It has also encouraged a national debate about race, ethnicity, domestic workers' rights, class divisions and social hierarchies in its native Mexico. The film has inspired conversations at national and international level, become the subject of academic debates, encouraged the interest of audiences in Tu'un Savi/Mixtec heritage and language, and, at a more superficial level, attracts tourists to the Roma neighbourhood (Figure 4).

In terms of visibility, the popularity of *Roma* confirms the impact, effectiveness and coerciveness of soft power, but also that repeatedly cloned ethnotypes might not be de rigueur elements in order to create compelling visual artefacts. From the opening credits, Cuarón's film is an ode to a person, and a portal to follow human subjectivity through small but perceptible details. Endorsed by Netflix, a mediatic powerhouse of sizeable global outreach, *Roma* chronicles a decisive moment from Cuarón's childhood, the difficult year in which his parents divorced, his siblings almost drowned and his nanny's pregnancy ended in tears. Set between 1970 and 1971, the point of reference is the set of experiences lived by Cleo, his nanny, during these memorable months. In her position as domestic worker and caregiver of four children, the film shows Cleo's interaction with her employer, the children, her boyfriend – eventually a source of betrayal and pain – Fermín (Jorge Antonio Guerrero) and a city, Mexico City. Clearly inspired by Italian neorealism, Cuarón forces viewers to pause and recognize that daily chores, as simple as collecting dirty clothes or turn off the lights, are rituals of everyday life. In a comparable way, the city and its noises remind audiences that there is a parallel world to the universe that encompasses Cleo's life. The mundane becomes important and the gestures recover meaning.

The film forces a reconfiguration of what the terms domestic and indigenous entail. It uses affect and emotions to convince spectators that the axiomatic enumeration of traits that belong to each category is diffused and somehow unproductive. An ethnotype is a canvas in the process of being drawn with infinite possible combinations of traits that are affixed to groups based on their ethnic background, group affiliation or ancestry. The result is a referential set of stereotypes that simplify our understanding of the surroundings and reduces them to fractions. Indigenous societies 'have been mythologized by anthropologists and ethnographers, by tourists and the tourist industry,

Figure 4 Film location of *Roma* (Mexico, 2018) in Mexico City.

and through art and literature … images have changed through time, with portrayals of vanishing Indians, primitives, half-breeds, squaws, warriors, and militants taking their turn in the foreground during various historical periods' (Bataille 2001: 4). Through *Roma*, Cuarón overhauls the blueprint for cinematic archetypes of indigenous characters in Latin American visual landscape. More importantly, the film deploys emotions and affect as strategies to recalibrate how audiences relate to a common stereotype (clone), and to prompt a social reflection on the subject.

Syntonic representation

Roma suggests new ways of understanding the figure of indigeneity, specifically from a feminine perspective. It suggests that space and physical distance play a vital role as catalysts in Cleo's evolution along and beyond the axes of affect where she dwells. As a putative family member, Cleo epitomizes the fluid division between labour and connection, and between vocation and dexterity.

Interactions between Cleo and the children are marked by tokens of intimacy, respect and an unspoken maternal bond. *Roma* highlights the ways in which the relationship between the domestic workers and employers develops into an intimate symbiotic alliance – the Cuaróns needed her, and she needed the Cuaróns. The invisible ties that connect her to Sofía's children are difficult to dissolve.

The symbolism of the home as a space of affect, and as an affecting space, increases as the camera focuses upon old objects, corners, furniture, inhabited untidy rooms and decorated walls, where it is easy to imagine Cleo spends hours. Each scene in the courtyard, kitchen, on the staircase, in bedrooms, living room, dining room and in the room Cleo shares with Adela intensifies the feeling that her domain encompasses every part of the physical space. Cleo makes the beds, cleans the floors, feeds the children and removes the droppings left by Borras, the dog, on the floor of the courtyard. The privacy of the home is gendered and stratified when a clear correlation can be traced between the role of each room and the bodies that inhabit them, but also when the practices and routines that take place in these spaces follow an indigenous/non-indigenous, feminine/masculine, top/down taxonomy. The Cuaróns approach Cleo according to a schematic allocation of tasks that link her position primarily to the kitchen, courtyard and roof. A cartographical reading of the mansion situates her at the social and spatial periphery. As with the laundry room, her bedroom and bathroom are located in a separated part of the house. Implicit in *Roma* is the emphasis on the agency and subjectivity of women whose occupations demand high levels of confidence and trust. The original layout of the Cuaróns' house follows a map of a space in which experiences materialize. The bedroom Cleo shares with Adela is an austere room, not precisely flooded with light or with carefully chosen furniture. Two small beds next to each other are complemented by a modest table, and an overtly full wardrobe.

The storyline and imagery challenge the assumption that characterizations of domestic workers/nannies serve only to present a contrast to the other members of the household. In varying ways, *Roma* presents the figure of the house as a space supported not just by walls but also by intense, convoluted, long-established relations between those who share their most intimate, personal and private space. The fact that a domestic worker is bound to amalgamate her personal life with her occupation irrevocably magnifies the affective dimension of this profession. Despite the low prestige that this remunerated activity has, it ironically demands a level of skill, sacrifice and commitment not commonly found.

Roma does not romanticize Cleo's work, but it does align with the canonical practice in Latin American visual culture of typifying and defining the indigenous according to their occupations (see Chapter 1), traces of a pattern of representation identified by Moriuchi (2018) in *Costumbrismo*, and that have been adopted and preserved as part of the cinematic vocabularies since the arrival of the medium in the region. Yet, in *Roma*, the optic deployed does not seek to justify the distance between the observer and the observed. Cuarón does not imply this is de rigueur state of affairs (i.e. indigenous are meant to occupy low-status lines of work), and that contrasts with an outmoded tradition of explaining characters by their places in society, or overlooking individual differences between those having the same occupation.

A point of reflection is the character of Adela. The film implies that even though they share commonalities in terms of ethnic background, social status, age and gender, their work ethos and attitudes towards the family are different. Adela lunches while Cleo serves lunch to the family, she also sighs when additional requests are made by a member of the family. Through a scene in the bedroom shared by the domestic workers, the camera focuses briefly on the mirror of the wardrobe that shows Adela sleeping while Cleo wakes up and starts working. Cleo takes on the role of caring for each member of the house, including her co-worker, Borras the dog and the birds kept in two cages next to the staircase that leads to her bedroom. Through the contrast between both employees, Cuarón insists that each member of the house, as an individual, is different. At the same time, the message in *Roma* is also that the sense of difference others produce in us translates into indifference and disdain. Interactional patterns in the house reflect social stratum at all times. Many sequences convey the lack of acknowledgement that Cleo faces. One of them is marked by the layered position of the family when they welcome the father in the courtyard in a symbolic array. The mother and the children are in the front row, while somewhere in the picture, in the shadow, Cleo bends slightly forward to hold Borras and prevents him from jumping and ruining the celebratory moment. Mr Antonio (Fernando Grediaga), Cuarón's absent father, walks into the house without saying anything.

In cinematic representations of domestic labour one can distinguish three affective/affecting aspects of the representations of this line of work. The first is from the perspective of the employee, the second from that of the employer and the third from the viewpoint of audiences witnessing the parallel, hierarchized and mechanized routines. Thematically, Cuarón sheds light not only on the commodified exchanges of salary/labour and closeness/trust, but also on the privacy and intimacy binary experienced by both employer and employee. The abstract nature of chores and childcare materializes in wages but also in more elaborate family structures. The popularity of the widely acclaimed co-production (e.g. *Golden Lion* at Venice Biennale) rests on its subtle but effective narrative style. One can hope these awards encourage other filmmakers to apply a socially engaging optic. *Roma* explores the hierarchies of households as reflections of society at large, while exalting the centrality of female subjectivity. A sense of verticality animates the scenes that take place inside the house, but a sense of horizontality reigns in the kitchen and courtyard.

From an intimate standpoint, the Mexican director engages audiences to explore how agency and subjectivity can be realized and articulated through human emotions such as rejection, betrayal, loneliness, isolation and uncertainty. The narrative challenges assumptions that a cinematic portrayal of domestic work can only be achieved through one-sided demeaning, patronizing images. *Roma* sheds light on the affective axes of an interiorized, nostalgic conceptualization of the home. Cleo and the Cuaróns' relationship can be regarded as an example of the process by which motion elicits emotion (Bruno 2002). The main idea is that spaces (e.g. a house or the streets of Mexico City) can be understood through actions and movement (e.g. making beds or walking to the cinema), actions that eventually materialize in reactions, effects and emotional links – central aspects to the sense of (com)motion that the film has inspired on- and off-screen.

Roma today still seduces spectators, critics, festival juries and media commentators, and even more so when it was released. The international press reacted in line with their own interpretations of Cleo's story and of her background. A newspaper from South Korea observed, for instance, that the 'Indians in the movie work in the land in their hometowns, like Cleo's mother, or kill time in their poor neighborhood, like Cleo's boyfriend' [[영화 속 인디오들은 고향 땅에서 농사를 짓거나 (클레오의 어머니) 열악한 빈민촌에서 시간을 죽이고 (클레오의 남자 친구)]. In other countries, the press was fascinated not only by the photography or the sound but also by the social commentary. In Italy, for example, the film was praised for its capacity to challenge 'canoni della cultura bianca' [the canons of white culture], whereas in the Netherlands, Aparicio's nomination was described as a truly equity success story.

Before seducing the world, Cuarón had to seduce Netflix first, the company behind its production and exhibition. In many ways, it is historical that one of the most renowned media companies lies behind the production of a 'Mexican film in black and white, in Spanish and Mixteco, that is a drama without stars' (Cuarón 2018b). Therein lies the off-screen realistic facts that surround the production of *Roma*, but also what this film as a visual artefact signifies in a bigger context. Cuarón paves the way for visual productions conceived beyond hegemonic ideologies, but without seeking to contest core–periphery structures either; after all, Netflix would never invest in a film with no future.

Conclusion

This chapter outlines how the canons of tradition explain the range of representations and degrees of visibility in indigeneity-themed films. In order to explain inclusion of minorities in feature films from a social standpoint, a key aspect is to explore to what extent viewers perceive cinematic reality as different from their tangible world. The underlying notion is that motion pictures are narratives conceived to fit audiences' expectations and secure entertainment by retaining an acknowledged state of affairs, caricatures and stereotypes. And yet, indigeneity-themed films as a genre are continuously evolving in response to social changes. One film, in particular, stands out.

Roma has recalibrated the optic used to depict ethnic societies cinematographically in films made by non-indigenous directors. Central to *Roma* is an emphasis on the agency and subjectivity of women whose occupations demand high levels of engagement. Spectators witness Cleo investing the most valuable years of her life raising someone else's children and taking care of a home on behalf of her employer. Cuarón's autobiographical narrative takes place in his native Mexico City in 1970–1 and addresses the social inequality of societies in which ethnicity is linked to privilege. Cuarón's approach to the life of a live-in maid creates a space to remember that violence, political unrest and poverty are part of Mexico's collective memory. Cleo, the Mixtec-speaking domestic worker who serves a well-to-do family in *Roma*, is played by Yalitza Aparicio, the daughter of a Mixtec speaker with no formal training as an actress. Dialogues in Mixtec signal Cleo's and Adela's ethnic identity throughout the whole film. At the same time, the film challenges the notion that indigenous characters are not eloquent in Spanish and favours Mixtec over other languages used in the film. The opening as well as the closing dialogues are in the Amerindian language. *Roma* explores the hierarchies of households as reflections of society at large, while exalting the centrality of female subjectivity and sense of identity. In this sense, the film operates as a catalyst for change in the blueprint for ethnotypes in Latin American cinema. Cuarón concentrates on Cleo to a level of detail that there is limited room for generalizations. The underlying notion is that the film presents a syntonic, rather than histrionic approach to indigeneity and that it explores the psychological and physical divisions of the spaces where the private/public dichotomy acquires new meanings.

7

Wääjx äp: Epistemic and ontological repositioning

In a Facebook post placed on 24 November 2017, Ayuujk linguist Yasnáya Elena Aguilar Gil proposed *Wääjx äp* as a potential Mixe translation of the name of the widespread communication application WhatsApp. With a symbolic comment, the insightful scholar and activist reminds her followers of the importance that media spaces play in the visibility, awareness and acknowledgement of indigenous cultures and languages. Her post encourages to reflect on the problematic assumption that ethnic minorities are not active members, participants, producers and consumers of media content. Despite the challenges and limited support and resources, effectively, self-representational cinema is finding its way across mass communication outlets. Gradually, films have become important platforms of outreach, dissemination and cultural exchange for communities who identify themselves as indigenous.

An upsurge in the number of Indigenous Cinema productions has closely been followed by a parallel development. Andean filmmakers mainly based in rural areas (predominantly in Peru), and not necessarily self-identified as indigenous, are becoming noticeable, outside their immediate communities, for their widely popular motion pictures, many of which include Amerindian characterizations and elements, or indigeneity-oriented themes. Both are irruptive and equalizing formulations defined by the kinetic aspects of self-representational films conceived outside conventional centres of production and inscribed across and through cybernetic spaces and practices. These stories not only voice the concerns of directors and collectives usually spoken for but also serve as outlets to express the creativity, imagination and first-hand experiences of under-represented communities. Above all, they are epistemological objects that prompt a reflection about cinematic ontologies, knowledge production/transfer and materialize the interface between art, politics and technology in unprecedented ways.

Whereas the first section, 'The cybernetics of self-representation', explores the themes addressed in films conceived by indigenous collectives through the lens of knowledge production, transfer and dissemination, the second one, 'Screen(ed)/(ing) intimacy and clusivity', focuses on *Cine regional* (Regional Cinema) works produced in Peru. In both cases, this chapter seeks to present an overview of approaches, not to assess their validity, aesthetic qualities or cinematography.

The cybernetics of self-representation

While webs of commercialization of objects have (un)efficiently encapsulated exchanges of capital, the circulation of artefacts with cultural value has involved the expansion and dissemination of ideas at a more abstract level. Systems of systems (i.e. festivals, platforms, post-production, publicity, press conferences) move cultural artefacts (i.e. DVD, posters, promotional photos, soundtracks) across global screens, anticipating and responding to the engagement of audiences. This feedforward–feedback dynamic creates a loop where content emerges, evolves and circulates, but within the limits of the business model that steers it. Representational films (hetero-images) are switchable in the sense that they are supported by networks that gatekeep their content. Self-representational films, on the contrary, navigate across unswitchable webs, such as YouTube, Vimeo, DVD markets on the street, piracy sites, emails and, indeed, as the name of this chapter indicates, WhatsApp messages. This is not a question of size but stature. Auteur cinema, festival-driven productions are industrial projects, fed and retroactively interlinked by nods that secure their circulation across venues, platforms and archives. Indigenous Cinema remains mostly outside these spaces. It is partly a matter of logistics and cultural identification, but mainly of control of a line of production that is financially unsustainable unless profits can be secured.

Cultural products have the capacity to operate as venues to articulate a group's identity, to contest invisibility or to claim agency in terms of self-representation. Throughout the history of cinema in Latin America, non-indigenous filmmakers have produced most of the films that portray Amerindian societies and their cultures. Since the introduction of cinematography in the region, foreign and local directors have felt tempted to tell narratives that include indigenous characters or pre-Columbian cultural heritage, despite the ethical and political implications thereof. In the last three decades, Indigenous Cinema has entered the scene. These are films commonly conceived by collectives and directors who identify themselves as indigenous, and who present their work as cultural artefacts that envision aspects of their communities that only their members can express (Schiwy 2009; Córdova 2011; Gleghorn 2019). The political, contestatory and symbolic character of this type of cinema explains why indigenous elements are emphasized. Authorship of these productions is linked to private, intimate and personal processes, such as self-identification and a need to reach indigenous audiences beyond their own communities.

Lack of resources and democratization of technology have paradoxically created the optimal terrain for indigenous cinematographers to produce their own media without the same degree of external interference. There is certainly input in the form of support, collaborations, technical assistance and networking (i.e. via NGOs), but it can hardly be comparable in size and scope to the resources granted to commercial, festival-bound, industrially produced cinema. In a media ecosystem, elements and functions result in a multifaceted outcome, anticipated by the interaction of processes and unexpected combinations (Fuller 2005). Indigenous Cinema epitomizes human–machine co-production, and it is conditioned by it. Self-representational cinema emerges from the human need to articulate, express, transmit and communicate one's story from a peripheral position, often with only one tool (i.e. basic camera). In her important work on cybernetics and cinema, Ute Holl observes that the human-apparatus dynamic, even in the case of decolonialized bodies, 'cannot become visible in any other way than by means of those films which also decentre the observer' (2002, 2017: 284). In contraposition, indigenous filmmaking depends on its capacity to decentre the dominant optic, ontologically readjusting what cinema means across spaces *lived*, not just visited by producers of cinema.

Since the turn of the century, films by indigenous directors have increased in number, and Indigenous Cinema has emerged as a genre. Its mere existence confirms 'the need to stage an audiovisual "duel" between the repertoire betrothed by colonialism and the proposals generated by those who have been racialised by instruments of power' (Gleghorn 2019: 95). Even if indigenous films rarely reach large numbers of spectators outside their own communities, overtly interested viewers or specifically tailored venues such as indigenous film festivals or academic gatherings, they retain their value as cultural artefacts within the producing communities. Financial constraints and government support at a regional and national level vary considerably. There is a stark contrast between Indigenous Cinema produced in the Global North (e.g. United States) and Global South (e.g. Ecuador).

In the specific case of Latin America, a tradition of codifying 'the indigenous world for the comprehension of an urban public' (Richards 2011: 11) has fossilized hierarchies of representativeness and cinematic praxis. Even if the landscape has changed in the last twenty-five years, as Ginsburg (1995) has observed, indigenous communities do not belong to producing networks and hence their productions are mostly small-case projects, primarily directed at local audiences, almost without exception with limited economic resources. Indigenous media makers are 'in a conflicting position, in which they fight against – while sometimes unintentionally reproducing – the imagery and practices of display that commodify, exoticize or spectacularise indigeneity' (Zamorano Villarreal 2014: 91). Although indigenous visual cultural artefacts risk becoming an extension of 'metropolitan discourses' that seek to co-opt 'indigenous cultures as exhibiting qualities that underline the uniqueness of the national culture' (Canessa 2007: 4), auto-images and hetero-images differ predominantly in two aspects.

On the one hand, knowledge production and knowledge transfer are central for indigenous directors/collectives at all stages of the conception, execution, exhibition and dissemination processes. Whereas an imagined flower is central in *El abrazo de la serpiente* (2015), and a historically researched medicinal practice is included in *La carga* (2016), for instance, in self-representational *La flor que vive/The Living Flower* (2015), transmitting knowledge about the applicability of ethnobotany is the main drive. Logically, the format defines the content, and both *El abrazo de la serpiente* and *La carga* are fictionalized semi-historical adaptations, whereas *La flor que vive* is a documentary. The comparison holds if the focus remains on the representativeness, agency and approach of media production when mis- and under-represented societies and epistemologies are involved. The core issue remains that indigenous filmmakers invest in preservation of knowledge in all its forms, whereas non-indigenous filmmakers are predominantly interested in artistic expression and engagement of audiences. The urgency of remaining epistemically present differs from the goal of materializing aesthetically seductive works of art.

On the other hand, auto-images in the case of unfranchised communities, kept at the periphery of national discourses in the countries to which they belong geopolitically, are not *just* images or media content.

From its Fourth Cinema stasis, Indigenous Cinema is 'a place where "material reparation" is made, "political autonomy" is fought for as "state sovereignty" is simultaneously challenged, and through that challenge, the very myths undergirding settler nationhood are dismantled' (Thornley 2017: 202). Peripheral visual externalizations become evidence of the ontological dilemma that identity poses in the relationship between colonial enactments and first-person narrations of ethnic minorities. Focusing on the classification of indigenous films as documentaries, animation or fiction misses the point. These are artefacts embedded in networks that grow, adapt and react to input (i.e. viewers) and stimuli (i.e. oil projects), but also tools, for political and pedagogical goals, vessels of information, history and worldviews, and systems of their own, spreading across self-structured axes that include the deployment of artisanal and homemade techniques for distribution and accessibility. In fact, the absence of institutionalized databases or archives prompts the diversity of systems, networks and strategies of circulation devised by indigenous media producers. Effectively, the stories told through these cinematic productions can be considered as 'electronic collective memory' (Plascencia and Monteforte 2006: 31) that communicates and narrates in first person. Indigenous authors have tools to invert the distortive 'folklorizing' (Ajxup Pelicó 2015: 41) optic that has defined them visually, but heuristically, their goal is to address specific situations, cases and topics. Scripted, directed and acted, either entirely by indigenous collectives/filmmakers or collaborative/commissioned projects, these media projects reflect the involved communities in terms of outset and vantage point. The topic, structure and participation are, in most cases, a matter of agreement at a communal level; exceptions include individual film projects derived from workshops.

In recent years, self-representational films are also emerging in the form of highly elaborated, excellently orchestrated works of cinematography, and *Mala Junta/Bad Influence* (Chile, 2016), is perhaps the best example thereof. Symbolically addressing the friendship between rebellious Tano (Andrew Bargsted) and withdrawn Cheo (Eliseo Fernandez), director Claudia Huaiquimilla manages to weave a powerful reflection of what conflict, prejudice and unspoken truths actually mean. *Mala Junta* is not an elegy or idealization, and in fact, the film examines and self-examines Mapuche identity and what it means in Chile today.[1] From a fictionalized perspective that engenders the viewpoint of a cosmopolitan director committed to her ancestry, *Mala Junta* can be, in many ways, considered a self-referential representational film.

The other productions discussed in this section offers a glimpse of the various themes most commonly addressed in indigenous filmmaking across the region: injustice and environment concerns, gender, tradition, history, cosmologies and intracultural relations. Across digital spaces, these thematic approaches define their retrievability, findability and categorization, according to the cataloging protocols of the specific interfaces in question. Hence, algorithms and artificial intelligence in social media (e.g. Facebook) and search engines (e.g. Google), even if randomly and not necessarily intentionally, co-inscribe, co-disseminate and co-communicate minor-scale indigenous filmmaking projects throughout their platforms. Integrated systems, for instance documentary works made in Bolivia, are examples of spaces that 'privilege knowledge made invisible by conventional channels' (Archibald 2011: 173). But they are also examples of human (indigenous nations)–machine (virtual sites) frameworks that expand the richness of indigeneity-oriented content across the internet. Discerned categories, based on content, create micro-systems, as many of them are screened in the context of knowledge sharing settings, while they also establish systems that question other systems.

Many films of various formats and sizes focus, for instance, on inequality in the legal, judicial, law enforcement and military systems. Their creators express concerns and share personal experiences about abusive treatment, illegality of natural resources projects on their territories and invisibility. Documentaries and fiction voice their opinion about issues that mainstream media might not consider relevant, among other things, because of the economic interest of private and public instances. In this sense, these low-budget productions operate as portals that register and document overlooked aspects and points of view, and simultaneously systems that question how other systems operate. *Cuidado/Paktara/Attention* (Ecuador, 2008) delves into corruption, *Los descendientes del jaguar/Puma chirikuna/The Jaguar's Descendants* (Ecuador, 2012) into transnationalism of resources, *Mari Mari* (Chile, 2011) into oil revenues, and *Por la tierra vivimos/We Live for the Land* (Mexico, 2012) into hypocrisy fed by economic interests within governmental institutions.

A representative example of networks that emerge as response to the operationalizations of other networks (i.e. ministries) includes the transnational reaction of audiences to the documentaries *¡Y siguen llegando por el oro!/And They Keep Coming for More Gold!* (Colombia, 2012), *Razón de estado/The State's Reasons* (Chile, 2009), *Justicia sin palabras/Mute Justice* (Mexico, 2011), *Hidrofractura: El agua, el aire, la tierra ... la muerte/Hydrofracture: Water, Air, Land ... Death* (Argentina, 2012) and self-representational *Vestimenta Sapara: Una tradición en peligro/Sapara Clothing: A Tradition in Danger* (Ecuador, 2019).

Colombian *¡Y siguen llegando por el oro!* depicts the attempts of multinationals to start mining projects in the region of North Cauca. Reminiscent of older days when Spaniards came searching for gold, the Nasa communities seek to denounce the greediness of both foreign companies and local authorities. This documentary directed by Harold Secué uses historical references and a parodical undertone to question the complex circulation of natural resources. Along this line, director Guido Brevis presents a social critique of the ongoing conflict between the Chilean state and its Mapuche minority in *Razón de estado/The State's Reasons*. This intense documentary from 2009 questions the irregular treatment ethnic minorities face in the Chilean judiciary system, the stigma affixed to these communities within legal stances and the vulnerability of ethnic minorities once they enter the country's carceral system.

Lack of acknowledgement within legal frameworks is also central to *Justicia sin palabras/Mute Justice* (Mexico, 2011), one of the most screened self-representational documentaries from Mexico. In this compelling story, director Sergio Julián Caballero sheds light on the unfair treatment of monolingual indigenous detainees in the Mexican judiciary system. From various angles, he illustrates the invisibility of those who do not speak Spanish, once they are detained. This is by far the first attempt to explore the disadvantageous position of a social group that is discriminated simultaneously on grounds of its ethnicity, affiliations, social status and linguistic heritage. *Justicia sin palabras* explores the power of media to denounce abuse against individuals trapped in an intersectional system of difference; that is, a position in which various inseparable elements contribute to strengthen the degrees of discrimination (Crenshaw 1991). In the context of indigenous monolingual prisoners, carceral spaces can be defined as the topological materiality of social disparities of exclusion within exclusion-based networks. An assessment of how institutional structures work illuminates broader questions and ontologies pertaining to the role of cinema as reflection of malfunctions.

The versatility of indigenous filmmaking allows for the creation of films that lie at the intersection of knowledge transfer, political denounce, self-ethnography and environmental justice. *Vestimenta Sapara: Una tradición en peligro/Sapara Clothing: A Tradition in Danger* (Ecuador, 2019) and *La flor que vive/The Living Flower* (Peru, 2013) embody collaborations with foreign support that, even if minor, contribute to the preservation of epistemic practices, and render visible localized realities. While the Sapara in *Vestimenta Sapara: Una tradición en peligro* explain the use of *llanchama*'s bark (*Poulsenia armat*) to fabricate textiles,

Pelagia Gutiérrez Vega, director and narrator of *La flor que vive*, gives details of the medicinal properties of several plants from the High Andean region. In both cases, their stories harness the ecology of media networks to synthesize and contextualize concrete first-hand experiences and traditional knowledges in documentaries that question geopolitical structures inflected by capitalism, environmental pollution and cultural standardization.

In the same vein, Olinda Muniz Wanderley addresses the interconnection between economic interests, geopolitics and the degradation of ecosystems in *Equilíbrio/Equilibrium* (Brazil, 2020). Invoking and embodying the figure of Kaapora, the Tupinambá filmmaker stages a visual rebuke about the various factors that have contributed to the current environmental and sanitary crises. Images of a Japanese whaling vessel, fires in the Amazon, the Usinsk oil spill and the radioactive waste repository in Morsleben, all courtesy of Greenpeace, serve as background to a reprimand about how and thanks to whom humans might face their own extinction. The film discusses the position of indigenous communities as collateral damage of power dynamics and unsupervised deployment of science and technology. Muniz Wanderley touches upon the paradox of intelligent creatures who dig their own grave. *Equilíbrio* uses comparison as a tool to denounce the ontological dilemma that mostly non-indigenous societies face: not realizing all organisms (including *Homo sapiens*), in Muniz Wanderley's words, are 'hóspedes' [guests].

Alternatively, *La flor que vive* is a self-representational production, set out to dissect indigenous epistemologies primarily from within. In this Peruvian documentary, Pelagia Gutiérrez Vega shows fragments of her life, practices and motivation as a Quechua-speaking healer who sees the impending necessity of disseminating ethnobotanical knowledges about medicinal plants. 'These plants exist since the time of our ancestors and are not extinct yet' is the explanatory opening sentence, pronounced by Pelagia. These words have a sense of warning, in the context of the current crisis we face and of the lack of commitment that is needed to prevent the ecosystem where these plants grow to be affected by it. The community of San Martín de Hercomarca, which is geopolitically part of the Peruvian territory, is also geopolitically part of a world community impacted by the indivisibility of a common planet and a common destiny. Many, if not all, of the plants Pelagia uses to heal herself and those surrounding her will disappear if no action is undertaken. In the short documentary set in Vilcashuamán, she also reflects on her journey to rediscover the medicinal practices of her parents and ancestors after one of her kids fell ill. Her despair grew as she sold in vain some of the few belongings she had to buy expensive medicines to save the life of her daughter. It was ultimately these medicinal plants, Pelagia stresses, that really cured her.

Maraysera is mentioned as one of the rare plants only found in the highest part of the hills. It's special as it cannot be found everywhere, while *remilla* is also mentioned as a common remedy for nausea, and also to bathe newly born babies. Infants can also benefit from the properties of *qenwa*, against diarrhoea, she adds. In her kitchen, she explains that preparing the right ointment for pain and discomfort in hands and feet requires the previous selection of warm plants, to which pieces of sheep brain are added, used for its fat content. While Pelagia sieves the unwanted pieces, she reflects on the incursion of industrial ointments in the life of her community. It is impossible to ignore that the aliments she mentions do not necessarily overlap with diseases we can easily relate to the repertoire of afflictions most commonly cited and used in Western medicine. She mentions *susto* (fright), sometimes defined as a pre-Hispanic cultural disease comparable to modern anxiety, and *calambre de los pies* (feet cramps) as ailments that need to be treated. For many viewers, these are rather classified as symptoms of other conditions. But does disease differ according to our systems of knowledge or how we sieve the wanted from the unwanted pieces of data or observation? Perhaps, in Pelagia's epistemic system, symptoms are the treatable aspects of a disease or those worth being treated. Is it possible that the lack of understanding of the environmental crisis as a disease, but above all, of all its signs, is what explains our lack of understanding? The ontological implications of defining what we observe ultimately condition how we react and respond. Are we perhaps missing a vocabulary that allows us to speak of and see symptoms as signs that action needs to be undertaken?

In January 2018, five years after the release of this documentary and its eventual exhibition regionally and internationally, Pelagia unfortunately died in a car accident, fifty-six years of age. For her, documenting stories about her cultural identity, legacy and epistemologies was a way to preserve them, but now she is gone. That documentary remains indeed as an effective tool to archive and preserve the knowledge Pelagia wanted to pass on to future generations. Films as repositories of knowledge, rites, customs and history from an insider's perspective challenge commercial cinema approaches. Since the turn of the century, some of the documentaries exploring these themes and that have circulated most widely include *Apaylla* (Ecuador, 2011), *El conflicto en el sueño mapuche/Pewma jadkulu/Conflict in the Mapuche Dream* (Chile, 2000), *Inacayal* (Argentina,

2011), *Kotkuphi* (Brazil, 2012), *La limpia/Chiqui Pichay – Wayrachirina/The Purging* (Ecuador, 2012), *Minkakuy* (Peru, 2014), *Q'uma chuyma/Clean Heart* (Bolivia, 2013), *Raíz del Conocimiento/Jiisa Weçe/Raíz del Conocimiento – Roots of Knowledge* (Colombia, 2010), *Varayuqkuna/Ancestral Authority* (Peru, 2015) and *Wachikua: Nuestra Historia/Wachikua: Our History* (Colombia, 2014). The portrayal of crucial elements of pre-Columbian heritage is central to works resulting from communal decisions and reflect the necessity to document traditional aspects that risk extinction. In parallel, communities are also interested in assembling visual projects that pay homage to figures who have played a vital role in their survival and in reframing dominant historiography.

Visual cultural artefacts also become breeding grounds for self-critique across, within and throughout media-producing communities and beyond. Initiatives stemming from collective projects have resulted in critical junctures that explore the positionality of gender within indigenous societies through cinematic output of various sorts and lengths. Many have circulated widely across film festivals, special international events, gender-themed screenings and LGBTQ+ networking sessions. Some of these include highly acclaimed *Atempa, sueños a orillas del río/Atempa: Dreams by the River* (Mexico, 2013), *Cholitas con fútbol de altura/Cholitas and Football at High Levels* (Bolivia, 2014), *El día de las comadres/The Godmothers' Day* (Argentina, 2013), *Palabras de agua/Ga tëya sziaya co'c/Words of Water* (Colombia, 2012), *Txêjkhô khâm mby – Mulheres guerreiras/Warsome Women* (Brazil, 2018) and *Zhamayama: Nuestra música/Zhamayama: Our Music* (Colombia, 2012). These are productions that illustrate the complex layers of difference to which women belong, as members of disfranchised ethnic minorities, and simultaneously in their allegedly subaltern condition, compared to men. Within this theme, the most salient aspect is the desire of filmmakers to portray how and why women seek to free themselves from the social systems that oppress them, both inside and outside their communities, from perspectives that range from forbidden love affairs to the practicalities of gendered roles. Issues of representation of gender lie at the core of auto-images, offering visceral renderings that dislocate assumptions more commonly found in hetero-images.

Directed by Mixtec filmmaker Edson Caballero Trujillo, *Atempa, sueños a orillas del río* is a particularly enlightening documentary as it explores the *muxe* identity at the heart of Zapotec society. By shedding light on the naturalized presence and social acknowledgement of a third gender, Caballero Trujillo demonstrates the subtleties and complexity of gendered indigenized and indigenized gendered corporeality. Embodied in Tino, a young *muxe*, Raciel, an adult *muxe* and mentor figure to Tino, and Maira, a female political activist, *Atempa* is an intimate portrait of distinctiveness. Sánchez Cruz (2018) asserts that the film can be conceived as a vehicle to witness how *muxes* in fact 'se des-identifican' [de-identify] (27) and negotiate ways of building a future beyond markers. After all, Tino dreams of being the honouree of a memorable *quinceañera* (fifteenth birthday) celebration, but also of leading a life beyond that point, perhaps following some of Raciel's advice. When the long coveted moment arrives and throughout its preparation, the community shows support. If a *muxe* is inscribed in the epistemological system of a society, the link to the reverberations etched in each of the LGBTQ+ letters does not seem to hold. Self-representational films, on this account and many more, force viewers to acknowledge the situatedness of ontological considerations. Additionally, self-representational cinema registers the workings of gender as intersectionally traversed by traits and categorizations that, in the case of indigenous communities, involve their linguistic reality. Indigenous filmmaking has become a tool to reshape the internal conversation about the position of women as females, as members of ethnic minorities and bi- or monolingual citizens within Spanish- or Portuguese-speaking contexts.

An important aspect to consider is that denigrated elements, such as so-perceived 'substandard' languages, find a platform to be recognized and validated. In varying ways, self-representational cinema is an outlet to contest the linguistic hegemony that defines the position of minorities' languages under the rule of European languages (Hearne 2012). Commonly, auto-images do not seek to manipulate this legacy to exotify or enhance the effect of authenticity. Indigenous languages are widely used in these films because they are mainly crafted to be consumed locally. The limited economic resources and access to networks of distribution of Indigenous Cinema do not necessarily mean that these productions are not screened and seen outside the producing communities, but the dynamic of dissemination does not seem to affect the linguistic choices of the producers. A major difference between non-indigenous filmmakers and indigenous directors is that language is not used as an ornament but as a vehicle of communication. While the dominant language is used when the films emerge primarily from workshops where the main goal is to share these productions with other indigenous communities – Spanish or Portuguese being the most practical tools of communication – there also seems to be a convention of 'not speaking on behalf of' a third party, likely stemmed from the fact that indigenous communities have been silenced for centuries.

Media productively stage encounters between producers and consumers of content, and this certainly applies to indigenous cinematic productions. The engagement of audiences with the narratives of indigenous filmmaking provides insightful cues about indigeneity as a concept, and the processes by which content (heritage) and social categories (ethnicity) used descriptively as referents determine the ways in which identities are emphasized or parenthesized. Even if orality plays a pivotal role in the dissemination of communal projects, interaction between spectators and authors on virtual spaces is evidence of feedback episodes. Confirming its cybernetic nature, self-representational films, in contrast with commercial productions, react to the comments of their audiences and implement changes or additions accordingly; feedback introspectively defines content. A synergy between the network-producers and users is best epitomized by the role of social media sites as systems that not only circulate the films but also facilitate input–output–input contact moments.

Using a corpus of 508 entries posted by viewers of Indigenous Cinema in Facebook, YouTube and eight blogs, the most salient aspect is the sense of acknowledgement (93 comments), pride (78 comments), self-pride (69 comments), support for their cause (61 comments) and interest in other facets of their cultures (30 comments) expressed by spectators. The majority of negative comments are aimed at governments on the basis of their policies (98 comments), peppered with a sense of shame on behalf of non-indigenous viewers (5 comments). Through this interaction, indigenous directors/collectives receive feedback and advice about their filmmaking skills (12 comments), their political approach (8 comments) and future implementations to solve the issues addressed in the films (19 comments). Except for 11 negative comments about indigenous peoples, the feedback provided by spectators is intended to encourage the production of more films on the same topic, a similar issue, another aspect of the authors' worldviews and other possible locations. Córdova (2017) insightfully asserts that 'access to internet technology is itself socially and culturally stratified and when audiences turning to such platforms for entertainment can be fickle (amid an endless array of choices) and even unpredictable' (174). Yet, given the circumstances of unfranchised communities, virtual spaces do prompt access to networks and materialize in retrievable outlets for the mobilization of self-representation visualizations that decentre hegemonic mono-dimensional validation and understandings of knowledge production.

Ultimately, filmmaking based on personal accounts and first-hand experience of belonging to an ethnic minority aims to reflect life at a private and communal level. The necessity of presenting an 'autoverdad' (self-truth) (Karakartal 2006: 13) runs alongside the selected stories. This is particularly the case of those that focus on rites and customs from a reflective point of view, but also as a response to the desire of documenting cultural practices. Many of the above-mentioned films stand out for proposing spaces where meaning can be negotiated. The selected samples of self-representational cinema seem to challenge traits of one-sidedness in a format and content that distinguish between heterogeneous representations. A valid and reliable strategy to review how ethnic minorities are depicted in mediatic spaces, such as cinema, is to assess the axis of power in relation to the ideas being conveyed. Undeniably, Indigenous Cinema not only is a source of new messages but is also an important contribution to the conservation, growth and future of ethnic minorities within multicultural contexts. Indeed, these are films that enter a dialogue with visual narratives conceived by non-indigenous film directors. One of the aspirations they seek to fulfil in this continuous exchange of ideologies is to correct misunderstandings, misrepresentations or manipulated accounts of a story. Access to filmmaking technologies, hampered by economic resources for decades, paradoxically provides a path towards a more diverse media ecosystem. Unfranchised ethnic groups are effectively using existing networks to communicate and disseminate their media content, by proxy, establishing networks that bypass the centralized systems behind the production of commercial and industrial cinema. For indigenous communities, a cybernetic incursion means to occupy digital spaces that serve their needs as communities, opening up channels, even if not autonomous, for communication of knowledge, interaction and visibility. Knowledge reforms understanding, but is also inscribed in practices that are inherently gestured by markers only specific audiences understand. Auto-images have an intimate in-group dimension, as the next subsection shows.

Screen(ed)/(ing) intimacy and clusivity

Self-representational cinema prompts reflections and sets forth questions about the ontology of cinema, representation, identity and the circulation of images and ideas about ethnic labels and categorizations. Filmmakers in remote and small-scale urban areas across the Peruvian landscape are finding ways to express their realities, without positioning themselves or their works along political, cultural or identity-oriented axes. In *Cine regional* (Regional Cinema) works, it appears that the inclusion of elements that could be labelled as 'indigenous,' 'Andean' or 'autochthonous' (e.g. Amerindian rites) is not considered as ideological or strategic components of the story, tokens of authenticity or key pieces to position a narrative in relation to other productions. Neither are they extensions of processes with self-identity connotations that seek to equate (mis)representation. Ideologically, *Cine regional* has as main goal to entertain and engage with its intended audience – even if non-Andean viewers have access to these movies, they are neither the referents nor the envisioned addressees. The complex interplay between public and private, and inclusion and exclusion explains the sense of social clusivity that informs the production, exhibition and reception of these narratives. Here I draw on clusivity, a term used in linguistics to make a grammatical distinction between inclusive and exclusive first-person pronouns. By applying this concept, I reflect on the fact that *Cine regional* films are cultural artefacts made for specific audiences and screened in settings where filmmakers and viewers interact with each other in their own ways.[2]

These films have an intended 'inclusive we' approach. Socially, they operate as cultural artefacts inherently linked to notions of inclusion or exclusion, based on the perspective, conceptualization, association and identification of the viewers. The conceptual distance, in many ways entwined with the geographical one, contributes to the creation of a category that positions them at the margin of established, Lima-based centres of production. Implicitly, Peruvians are not told to actively seek indigenous elements in *Cine regional* productions because these films are not supposed to be indigenous. The label, thus the category, is *regional*; sometimes *provinciano/provincial* is also used, even if it has a pejorative connotation. Yet, content-wise, they share undeniable commonalities with other films predominantly mobilized as indigeneity-themed movies, or presented as Indigenous Cinema productions. Self-reliantly, *Cine regional* widens the stylist and thematic gulf between Lima-based filmmakers and (mostly) unsupported directors based in less affluent areas across the country.

The distinct optic that distinguishes Indigenous Cinema from *Cine regional* raises ontological questions that oddly add to the problematic positionality of indigeneity-themed films as contextual processes or decontextualizing cultural artefacts, even if indigenous filmmaking and *Cine regional* are both rooted in a communal need to articulate a group's identity, to contest invisibility or to claim agency, differing drastically from commercial and industrial works, semi-commissioned or at least conditioned by canonical approaches and international constraints (representational cinema). Nevertheless, they are different. As previously discussed, authorship of Indigenous Cinema is linked to private, personal and communal processes, such as self-identity and self-concept. The authenticity, verisimilitude and position of films conceived from an in-group standpoint is seldom scrutinized, precisely because indigenous film projects operate according to codes that resonate with its objectives. The conundrum lies in understanding films where locations, actors and worldviews are assembled to create stories, told from an insider's point of view, that express Amerindian lives, but without allusions or self-referential reflections in terms of their indigenous contents. Hence, Peruvian *Cine regional* fluctuates across a continuum in terms of indigenous contents, use of Amerindian languages and Andean cosmologies, perspectives and beliefs, but there is a subtle avoidance of indigenous self-referentiality.

The practice of making cinema outside centralized networks of production and distribution has increasingly grown since the first movie, *Lágrimas de fuego/Tears of Fear*, directed by José Gabriel Huertas and Mélinton Eusebio, was released in 1996. Counting over 217 titles, produced mainly in Ayacucho, Puno, Junín and Cajamarca, most *Cine regional* films are believed to share certain commonalities (Bustamante and Luna Victoria 2017). These include not only a diverse range of approaches, themes, formats and subgenres but also a lack of external funding, inaccessibility to mainstream exhibition venues, limited attention from mass media, critics, academics, government institutions and filmmakers based in the capital city. Two currents are commonly identified within this type of cinema, heavily influenced by oral tradition. On the one hand, there is a considerable number of widely popular horror and melodramatic films, predominantly produced in Puno, Ayacucho, Junín and Cajamarca. On the other hand, there is an active but less circulated production of documentaries, short films and experimental films. Both currents are reminiscent of Bolivian sociologist Silvia Rivera Cusicanqui's (2015) observations that the *subaltern* comes only to the surface when the representations are done 'en sus propios términos' [on their own terms] (88).

Even if they are staged in overtly sentimental or phantasmagorical scenarios, the storylines emerge from the daily problems, obstacles, victories and occurrences audiences perceive personally, and settings where their everyday life takes place. The clusivity aspect of the circulation and circulating practices of and around *Cine regional* films are best exemplified by the reactions of viewers.

Some of the comments shared by social media users include: 'Todo fue grabado en nuestro pueblo' [everything was recorded in our village], 'Profesor, ya he visto su película' [Teacher, I have seen your film], 'Mi vecino hace de policía' [My neighbour plays a cop]. Filmmakers travel from town to town exhibiting their movies in venues, such as communal meeting rooms, diverse types of schools, squares and modest ballrooms. They engage with audiences at a personal level in exhibition sessions that allow ample opportunities to receive feedback. Peruvian peripheral cinema stands out for its intimate character vis-à-vis the authoritative, corporate and centralized Lima-based film industry. Ethnicity is not a recurring theme, probably because it is entwined with the identity of producers and consumers; neither of them needs to explain who the other is or what is special about them. Exceptions include the figure of elderly people and shamans, who are referred in most cases as *nativos* (natives). Films in this category are evidence that indigenous, non-indigenous, mestizo and non-mestizo are contended terms in media spaces – as much as in a real-life ABCD Continuum – but irrelevant to motion pictures where defined ethnical ascriptions are not a focal point.

A number of stereotypes and archetypes are certainly found in *Cine regional*, but they do not seek to create the figure of an Andean subject beyond the characterizations local actresses, actors and extras offer of themselves. As the next paragraphs intend to show, cultural traits, considered from a hegemonic perspective as quintessentially indigenous, emerge naturally in most of these narratives. Through a review of the important number of extended interviews conducted by Bustamante and Luna Victoria (2017), it is possible to assess that filmmakers' in-group standpoint scape the essentialist, divisive and arbitrary conceptualizations commonly used to approach the topic of indigeneity. Their references and anecdotes confirm that they mostly seek to produce cinematic spaces that echo their immediate surroundings and their sounds.

Reflecting on the discussion on language in Chapter 3, Spanish and Portuguese, or other European languages, are not instrumental enough to transmit the notion of difference needed to secure the level of verisimilitude or credibility desired by the filmmaker in hetero-images. In *Cine regional*, Aymara and Quechua are partially or entirely spoken in some of the movies and there are examples of films where Spanish dialogues are noticeably inflected by Quechua semantic, pragmatic and dictional elements. Accented Spanish or subtitles do not appear to be strategies to render the film more exotic or to highlight linguistic diversity, among other things, because a number of filmmakers, actors, producing teams and locals, involved in the productions as extras, actually use Amerindian languages in their daily communication. Inclusion of words, mainly from Quechua, in dialogues and structural aspects of the conversational exchanges conveys the idea that actors' diction and speech style are not manipulated. *Cine regional* is popular because it presents realities audiences recognize as theirs. It approaches language in similar ways as Andean communities make use of it in real social contexts. The excerpt of an interview conducted by Marisol De la Cadena (2006), where she asks a *campesino* about his linguistic attitudes presumably gives an idea of how communities on fringe zones experience language:

> Don Mariano sonrió cuando le pregunté si una mezcla de castellano y quechua sería una tercera manera de hablar; él gentilmente dijo: ¿Por qué? Por supuesto que estas categorías híbridas – «raras» a los sentidos dominantes – portan la materialidad de la historia y las políticas [Don Mariano smiled when I asked if a mixture of Spanish and Quechua would be a third way of speaking; he gently replied: Why? Obviously, these hybrid categories – 'strange' to the dominant senses – carry with them the materiality of history and politics]. (78)

Don Mariano moves within a space where hybridity is not explained or dissected. Audiences of films such as *Qarquacha, el demonio del incesto/Qarquacha, the Devil of Incest* (2002), *El Pecado/The Sin* (2007) and *El destino de los pobres/The Fate of the Poor* (2011) relate to life experiences where their language choice, mixed linguistic heritage, bilingual or monolingual scenarios and natural pronunciation are part of their identity, and of a spectrum of Selves contained in their minds. Visual artefacts that reflect this reality present stories that are unlikely to script dialogues that only focus on an aspect of the communities they intend to show.

Cine regional films apply the intimate approach to language, to more external aspects of characters, for instance, clothes, practices, rituals, norms, values and the scenarios where their lives take place. The realistic execution of the films is logically linked to the lack of resources and artisanal character of this relatively new type of cinema. Family members and friends are involved as main actors, extras, technicians, support and communication staff, often on an unpaid basis unless the film generates revenues, once it is released. The condition in which the films are made certainly limit the possibilities filmmakers have to articulate their ideas, but do not subdue the effect these stories have on audiences, either paying to see the film or to obtain a (pirated/homemade) copy of it on the street (Figure 5). Directors, actors and audiences meet during informal and

Figure 5 Homemade copy of *El Pecado* sold in a market in Cuzco.

formal screenings, and as the previous paragraphs indicate, there are more commonalities than differences between the producers and consumers of these visual cultural artefacts. Conversations, in physical and virtual spaces, from an input and output end inform subsequent productions, and in this sense, *Cine regional* cybernetically enacts Andean oral tradition.

Melodramatic narratives with strong social critique and pedagogical nuances are one of the most popular genres, the other being horror films. Common themes in socially inspired dramas include the impact of the armed conflict (*Sangre inocente/Innocent Blood*, 2000; *Frágil/Fragile*, 2007; *Secuelas del terror/Terror After-Effects*, 2010), social unrest of all sorts (*Vicio maldito/Wicked Vice*, 2000; *Marcados por el destino/Cursed by Fate*, 2009; *Trampas de tu lado oscuro/Traps of Your Dark Side*, 2013) and orphanhood or relationships between parents and children (*Triste realidad/Sad Reality*, 2004; *Madre, una ilusión convertida en pesadilla/Mother, an Illusion Turned into a Nightmare*, 2009; *Niños pobres/Poor Children*, 2009; *El hijo del viento/The Son of the Wind*, 2009; and *El destino de los pobres/The Fate of the Poor*, 2011). Family as a trope is a constant in Peruvian cinema produced outside Lima, with a focus on the idealized figure of each member of the family.

El pecado/The Sin (2007), directed by Palito Ortega Matute (1967–2018), considered by many as a key exponent of *Cine regional* and a major figure within Peruvian cinematic circles, stands out for the characterization of Padre (Reynaldo Arenas). This is an affectionate, tolerant and caring member of the Pampa Pira community, who decides to stand by his transsexual son, despite his sexual inclinations being highly stigmatized throughout the Andean region. From an early age, Eduardo (Dany Cabezas) fantasizes with becoming a woman, despite the rejection and marginalization this can bring along. Bullied and repetitively assaulted by his brothers, Serafín (Gustavo Cerrón) and Esteban (Irving González), Eduardo decides to escape to Lima, where his transformation into Yahaira takes place. This biopic features Eduardo 'Yahaira' Córdova, whose life serves as a source of inspiration for the film. Yahaira is presented as a hybrid figure with Andean roots, underlined by iconic Quechua elements, even if her choices contradict the status quo of the community that fails to acknowledge her. Beyond the social critique it advances, *El pecado* reframes the morphology, plasticity and authority of cinema produced from the periphery. Yahaira's oblique story and her embodiment of Andean identity adumbrate that *Cine regional* works have the capacity to operate as cultural processes, social advancement projects and visual abstractions that prompt open conversations. This triple role came to the test during the screening of *El pecado* in school ballrooms, squares and small-scale concert halls in rural Peru.

Adversity remain a common theme, reflecting sustained and systemic social issues. Directed by Jaime Huamán Berrocal, *El destino de los pobres/The Fate of the Poor* (2011) takes place during the armed conflict and focuses on the challenges faced by impoverished communities in rural areas of the Apurímac Region. Juana Robles (Fiorela Lloclla) has lost her husband and is left alone with her two children, Sarita (Sol de Lucero Calderón) and Julián (Jeferson Sotomayor). Due to her debilitated health condition, Juana is forced to seek medical aid away from the village, leaving the children in custody of her brother, Valentín. Not willing to endure his abuses, the siblings decide to escape and search for their mother in the nearby cities. Although the task proves to be insurmountable, they are willing to find Juana at any cost. In the process, Julián goes blind and Sarita sees herself forced to steal in order to provide food for her younger brother. Only at the end of the movie, they manage to find their mother in a moribund state, confirming what audiences have suspected from the beginning. Long and medium shots run uninterrupted, at times, with no sound. Untrained performers and mistakes in the editing phase reveal the lack of resources Huamán Berrocal had at his disposition, but also the plurality of *Cine regional*. As a format and genre, it manages to contextualize a plot, integrating internal narrative and visual vocabularies that attract and captivate audiences. One valid question is why and how audiences react or do not react when parts of the film are mute, curiously lingering to know more once the accidental hiatus ceases. Perhaps, films at the periphery are forms of engagement where relations between audiences and content are not built on preconceived schemas. Maybe soundless episodes are appreciated for their rawness and accidentality, symbolically reminiscent of the characters' destinies.

In *Cine regional*, language matters. *El destino de los pobres* is in Spanish, except for dialogues in Quechua between members of older and younger generations. In line with other Peruvian films, the shaman in the story only speaks in an Amerindian language. Juanita and Valentín are presented as bilingual characters on a fringe zone between tradition and modernity. The film does not convey a miserabilist scenario, but the social critique is evident. An inefficient state has forgotten to safeguard children, widows and the sick. The second part of the film, *El destino de los pobres II*, released in 2017, explores the lives of the siblings in the streets and emphasizes the unrelenting grip of violence and neglect the most vulnerable segments of the population face.

Cruelty, bloodthirstiness and fierceness are also present in films focusing on mythical creatures, monsters and zombies, but in most cases, the perpetrator is not human. Horror-oriented films have become important exponents of Peruvian *Cine regional* and rank among the most popular titles among audiences in rural areas. Narratives with the capacity to startle the viewers are mostly based on Andean figures audiences recognize. Some of these include *uma* (flying witch head); *aya tullu*, a ghost with deformed bone structure; and *jarjacha*, also known as 'qarqacha, qarqaria' or 'jarjaria', reputably 'a monstrous two-headed llama (sometimes represented with three heads)', who used to be human until it engaged in 'incestuous sexual relationships' (Eljaiek-Rodríguez 2018: 210). Another variant of *jarjacha* is the figure of *kharisiri*.

Promoted in the trailer as 'el personaje siniestro más temido en el mundo Aymara' [the most feared sinister figure in the Aymara world], *El misterio del Kharisiri/Kharisiri's Mystery* (2004) is a version of the legend transposed to the cinema by Henry Vallejo Torres, a filmmaker based in Puno. The plot surrounds the challenges Paúl (Waldo Callo) needs to face in order to find Mariela (Jesica

Riviera), a journalist gone missing in strange circumstances. The film focuses on the adventures of an urban reporter in an unknown geography where Andean epistemologies rule, and where a coca reading ritual performed by a shaman is the key to resolve the mystery. Vallejo Torres admits that a film about Kharisiri requires permission from the local shamans (Ramos 2012). An interpretation of the film is that the story symbolically suggests ancestral culture struggles against dominant foreign powers.

Audiences relate to *El misterio del Kharisiri*, mainly based on their own beliefs and first-hand experiences, as they assert on virtual spaces: 'Kharisiri existe de verdad' [Kharisiri really exists], 'qué miedo' [how scary] and 'ten cuidado' [pay attention]. Some ask the director for a sequel, to make a trilogy, or simply to reveal details of the story they do not understand. *Kharisiri* is the term used by Aymara-speaking communities to refer to the same creature commonly known as *pishtaco* by those who speak Quechua. Different versions of the myth surrounding *pishtaco* are the focal points in films produced, in Ayacucho, such as *Pishtaco* (2003), directed by José Antonio Martínez Gamboa; *Nakaq* (2003), directed by José Gabriel Huertas; *Sin sentimiento/Without Feelings* (2007), directed by Jesús Contreras Matias; and *Jarjacha vs. Pishtaco: La batalla final/Jarjacha vs. Pishtaco: The Final Stand-off* (2011), directed by Nilo Escriba Palomino, and in Huancayo, *Sangre y traición/Blood and Treason* (2005), directed by Nilo Inga Huamán. All films on the topic are based on the widespread belief that *kharisiris/pishtacos* behead their victims in order to steal their adipose tissue. In terms of outset, scope, content and, to certain degree, aesthetics, *Cine regional* is informed by trends and fluxes across the global cinematic horizon. Recalling fights between Hollywood-inspired superheroes, a final stand-off between two Andean cosmovision figures oddly and counterintuitively indicates a need to align with mainstream approaches. Notwithstanding, references to external sources do not eclipse the well-defined epistemologically oriented undertone of *Cine regional* films. Heritage, cosmovision and mysticism are fixed, paramount points of reference.

Directed by Puno-based Javier Cáceres Saravia, *La leyenda del Ekeko/Ekeko's Legend* (2010) is one of five titles that have been made about Ekeko, the Tiwanakan deity. The other four, *El plan Papanoel/Santa Claus Plan* (2005) (Dir. Álvaro and Diego Loayza), *Si acaso en Chuquiago/If ever in Chuqiago* (2009) (Dir. Daniel Moya and William Camacho Año), and *Illa* (2015) (Dir. Matio Camacho) are Bolivian productions varying in format and approach. In Cáceres's version, a connection is drawn between knowledge of herbal lore and the pre-Columbian roots of the Ekeko's legend. Germán Cuno Escobar (Ekeko) epitomizes a practitioner of good magic who ventures into the countryside, undoing the evils wrought by Awqa (Percy Viza Parillo), a black magic conjurer who has sworn to take over the planet. Quechua is used mainly for magical words that signal contact moments with supernaturality, while changes in the colour of the diegetic world highlight the moment otherworldly forces are invoked. Awqa's attempts to destroy happy marriages, enslave locals and even murder peasants are prevented by the heroic and intuitive Ekeko. Cáceres sheds light on the figure remembered and worshipped every year during the Alasitas fair in La Paz, but he does not specifically address Ekeko's symbolism as the god of prosperity and good fortune. In contrast with an iconic image of a man carrying banknotes, jewellery, bags of food, this version of Ekeko is embodied in an average 'campesino'.

Andean mythology is also camouflaged in narratives that seek to convey a frightening and eerie atmosphere but also operate as warnings about undesired behaviour (e.g. incest). In all cases, the popularity of the films appears to be connected with the inclusion of legends and myths couched in the cultural repertoire and imaginary of locals, but also in their ties with their past. Reviewing the interaction between audiences and films, based on entries on social media platforms, the level of identification with the themes of the films is high.

Besides a sense of recognition, nostalgia and acknowledgement, audiences identify in *Cine regional* films poignant moral statements. Comments such as 'hay que aprender' [one has to learn] or 'hay q valorar a nuestros padres' [we have to [sic] appreciate our parents] indicate the movies are interpreted as narratives from which viewers can learn life lessons or be instructed about societal aspects unknown to them. Another example of the intimate relation viewers develop with these films and their filmmakers is messages on social media venues of those aspiring to act in them. Spectators identify themselves in the narratives and its proximity to their lives. Comments such as 'invita, no?' [open invitation, right?], 'puedo ser tu actor?' [can I be your actor?] can be found, for instance, in promotional posts of the film *La leyenda del Ekeko/Ekeko's Legend* (2010) in Facebook.

The virtual dimension of home-grown Peruvian cinema proves influential in the promotion of the films among social media users encouraging others to attend the screenings or buying the DVDs. Since low-budget productions are excluded from most conventional advertisement venues, directors find ingenious ways of publicizing their work. *Wiñaypacha* (2017), for instance, managed to secure additional screenings thanks to word-of-mouth advertisement, complimentary reviews in blogs and recommendations across social media platforms (Reyna 2018), although the qualities of this promising film, directed by Óscar Catacora, and a number of important awards, both at national and international level, would have sufficed to ensure its lasting popularity.

Wiñaypacha (2017) is set to make a dent in the history of Peruvian cinema for several reasons. It is considered as the first feature movie locally produced, entirely spoken in Aymara, but also one of the most widely screened *Cine regional* productions. Catacora's film excels in terms of the number of viewers, exposure in national and international media, special attention given by critics and reception among urban and rural audiences. The plot surrounds around an elderly couple, Phaxsi (Rosa Nina) and Willka (Vicente Catacora), who lives in an isolated, inhospitable and frigid corner of the Andes and tries to survive in spite of their lack of resources: an honest portrayal of oblivion, abandonment and the cyclicality of human life and the natural world; a conscientious story that 'privileges crafting individual over collective identities' (D'Argenio 2020: 151).

Catacora is Aymara and the main actor of the film is his grandfather. The diegetic world aligns with their own lived experiences, and the story emerges from his desire to draw attention to the suffering and poverty older generations face in rural areas, often, due to large migration waves of their children to the cities. The young director explains that the film is artistically inspired by the desire to articulate an Aymara reality but through the means of codes borrowed, among others, from Italian neorealism, European existentialist schools and movies by Yasujiro Ozu (Tsang 2018). The story explores the daily challenges faced by Phaxsi and Willka, an elderly couple living in an idyllic but hostile topography. Life without their son is difficult and they wait for him to return from the city before it is too late. Often alternating between extreme long and long shots, snow-capped mountains envision the story takes place closer to heaven than to the city where a forgetful son has gone in search of a new life. Crude scenes such as the destruction of their home in a fire, the loss of their animals and finally Willka's death are complemented with different hues, anticipated by foreshadowing tones. Audiences foresee some of the most dramatic moments of the story. In this sense, the predictable aspect of the plot positions it closer to other artisanal Peruvian titles.

Catacora admits his surprise not only about the reception of audiences but also of Lima-based distribution networks, willing to allot prime screening times to a film, otherwise commonly considered as 'regional' (Reyna 2018).

Yet, in their detailed review, Bustamante and Luna Victoria (2017) do note that urban audiences respond differently when the artistic approach of *Cine regional* productions resembles arthouse projects. *Wiñaypacha* combines styles but remains faithful to Aymara epistemologies and cosmovision; in fact, the title is often translated as *Eternity* or *Eternal Space*. Pratt (1992) notes that 'autoethnography involves partial collaboration with and appropriation of the idioms of the conqueror' (7), but it is difficult to discern who the 'conqueror' and 'conquered' are in *Wiñaypacha*. Intimate stories of realities in the fringe zones, and of subjects dwelling along 'borderlands' are evidence of a change. Cinema is entering a phase where filmmakers recognize that hybridity is in itself an identity (Anzaldúa 1987), that indigeneity as a categorization can have a political and scholastic, rather than a unifying, dimension (Ouweneel 2018) and that 'in the Andes, essentialized differences between people are produced through cultural processes' (Canessa 2005: 21).

Wiñaypacha is the portrait of a fictionalized version of an Aymara director's childhood, involving family members (real people), in an auto-ethnographic setting, meticulously executed to fulfil (inter)national cinematographic standards, while offering a poignant moral. This is achieved without purposefully entwining ethnic differences, essentialist traits or exotifying symbolisms with the characters of the story, or the background of the director. The story allows audiences to catch a glimpse of the daily life of a couple merged in their natural surroundings, not expecting to evoke complex assessments or conceptualizations of their identities. Catacora[3] creates a space, not ontologically defined by a specific function or category, where self-representation seeks external codes to present an intimate story, submerged simultaneously both in reality and in fiction, but resisting to become a political statement, or to encourage reverential approximations. Screen(ed)(ing) intimacy assumes audiences are acquainted with the proximal and innermost contexts of a character, united by a sense of clusivity and adhesion, and hence, they rarely seek to provide self-definitions. A discernible private sphere serves as backbone in *Cine regional*. Although some viewers express their concerns about poor acting skills, substandard editing facilities, lack of resources, incoherent plots and home-grown cinematographic methods, this does not distract audiences from appreciating a cinema that reflects them, without analysing them.

Cinema reproduces and mobilizes long-established ideas about the indigenous, but in a paradoxical way, it also mirrors the blurred, ambiguous and fuzzy boundaries of the term 'indigeneity'. *Cine regional* filmmakers parenthesize indigenous heritage rather than emphasize it. As a result, these films problematize the concepts of identity and ethnicity and raise questions about intimacy and affiliation at a micro- and macro-level.

Conclusion

Self-representational cinema has differed from visual narratives made by non-indigenous filmmakers, biased in form and content, informed by hegemonic ideologies and embedded in media frames of reference that have never given prominence to the issues that matter to unfranchised social groups. Gradually, films have become important platforms of communication, dissemination and cultural exchange for communities who identify themselves as indigenous, and filmmakers mainly based in rural areas (predominantly in Peru). These directors do not necessarily identify themselves as indigenous, but nevertheless create stories that articulate the Amerindian soul and psyche. They seek and disseminate stories that have not been heard before, to draw attention to topics that are ignored and more importantly, they attempt to create their own visual narratives, often in their own languages and disseminated through cybernetic pathways. Feedback from audiences and the interaction between producers and viewers explains why it is important for under-represented communities to present their own version of their social and cultural reality, contesting a well-established tradition of representation in the process. The main findings of this study are that Indigenous Cinema creates films that thematically differ from the visual narratives produced by directors that do not belong to the community they seek to portray, and that the films have an impact beyond the target group.

Alternatively, Peruvian *Cine regional* filmmakers create stories that offer intimate renderings of Amerindian worldviews, but bypassing self-referential reflections in terms of their indigenous perspective. Ethnicity is not a recurring theme, probably because it is entwined with the identity of producers and consumers; neither of them needs to explain who the other is or what is special about them. Their references and anecdotes confirm they mostly seek to produce cinematic spaces that echo their immediate surroundings and their sounds. Peruvian *Cine regional* stands out for its intimate character vis-à-vis the authoritative, corporate and centralized Lima-based film industry. Fiction is used as a format to expose narratives inflected by a high sense of clusivity that target audiences understand.

Synopsis: Conclusion

The next paragraphs are intended to conclusively present the findings of this book, but also to provide a synoptic survey of how these conclusions have been reached. In the Latin American case, films are embedded in processes of enculturation that include not only how the indigenous is understood but also to which category it is perceived to belong. As this book has demonstrated, there are certain commonalities but also notable differences in the way recent films (2000–20) approach indigeneity. Ethnotypes serve as the backbone of many of the fictional films, produced in the region, focusing upon ethnic communities, pre-Columbian legacy, and Amerindian cultures and languages. Contemporary films mirror assumptions shared by, on the one hand, respondents and informants of interviews, and, on the other hand, users of social media (approached through digital ethnography) on the portrayal of indigenous characters in mediated spaces. Mental schemas informed by preconceptions, clichéd images and sensitivities reflect attitudes among Latin Americans towards the indigenous components of their culture, history and memory. Reinforced by a visual tradition in which ethnotypes are a cornerstone, modern visual arts across the continent mirror a perceived division between a mainstream Self (mestizo culture) and a secluded Other. Paradigms of representation identified in sixty-eight representational films (hetero-images) selected for study confirm that there is a strong tendency to ascribe specific traits to those depicted as indigenous. After considering the production and reception of indigeneity-oriented visual narratives, the use of imagery in the staging of identity/otherness, and global processes (looking at the particular through a universal lens) linked to the production of cinema, it must be acknowledged that core–periphery hierarchies are still quite common.

From a formalist perspective, indigenous ethnotypes, as reviewed here, are constructed through visual strategies and elements of a storyline. As evidenced in this analysis, films are illustrations that aim to emulate, remodel, enhance or present intangible possibilities, mostly by appealing to our senses and sensitivities. Films have the potential to adumbrate or reconfigure assumptions about the indigenous Other and to repeat or avoid rhetorical and visual strategies to mark difference. Through visual codes, movies deploy ethnotypes and portray societies, often by recurring to fixed formulas and tropes. I argue that indigeneity films are a genre, based on a close inspection of the deployed repetitive patterns and conventions, consistency of labels used to describe the films for distribution and marketing purposes and the contract between audiences and producers – viewers consume based on formulas they know. From a longue durée perspective, it could be said that the cinematic figure of the native is almost as old as cinema itself, first, through ethnographic footage, eventually moving on to incipient encapsulations of fictionalized indigenous lives. Indigenous presence has political, social and ideological connotations and cinema spaces have recognized that fact from early on. Even before films emerged as formats, the visuality of native communities in works of art foreshadowed the convention of presenting them as naturalized beings, foreigners to artificiality. Preconceiving them as fossilized societies appears to block any attempt of imagining them in futuristic terms. The nature–technology dyad, I suggest, serves as sine qua non criteria of films revolving around indigeneity, enhancing the notion that they constitute an identifiable genre. Pre-Columbian legacy, ethnicity, linguistic diversity and self-representational cultural artefacts, I posit, are more than a 'subject', 'source of inspiration', 'topic' or 'trend' (terms often used in this context). Indigeneity films are a genre (at least, a subgenre, for sure) in continuous evolution, as other genres are.

Until recently, indigenous characters in films tended to be depicted mainly as superficial, relatively stable and mono-dimensional. Most indigenous actors were allocated short dialogues, if any at all, or were presented only from a single perspective, in this way preventing audiences from relating to their stories or feeling empathy for their plight. To simplify matters, directors frequently opted for group scenes, giving the impression that there were not individual differences between indigenous characters, or at least not differences worth exploring in detail. Exclusively and persistently, for a long time, actors belonging to under-represented communities were assigned secondary roles. The particular interest and willingness shown by contemporary non-indigenous filmmakers to focus on indigenous themes in recent feature movies is therefore considered a remarkable change.

Throughout history, elites at a regional and global level have resorted to pictorial (re)presentations in order to entice masses. In his analysis of the first representations of natives in European art, Rubiés (2009) observes that in the context of Renaissance representations of the 'New World', 'no representation could fully substitute direct experience [and that] without that experience, it was difficult to fight against cultural prejudices and against self-interested lies' (123). Imagination has steered the paintbrushes of artists, the photo cameras of photographers and, as this volume has intended to show, the cameras of filmmakers. An important aspect of how a dominant group depicts less powerful communities lies in the images put forward. As Ouweneel (2018) asserts, the cognitive noble savage schema (CNSS), recurrent in many of the films analysed in this review, 'consists of an ethnotype designed about the indigenous people in the West, seen from Europe, long before the Americas had been integrated into the Spanish Empire' (23). Throughout history, the convention of sketching the indigenous as noble savages, leading 'an uncorrupted, natural way of life close to nature in an egalitarian state' (123), has foregrounded their (in)visibility. These realizations shed light on the ethical, political and propagandist aspects of representations; hetero-images (images of out-groups) do not necessarily intend to reflect reality or being inspired by it.

An undeniable legacy of the arbitrary systems of representations introduced in contemporary cinematic spaces is their use of ethnotypes, stereotypes linked to ethnicity. Ethnotypes are based on mental representations and preconceived ideas couched in cultural repertoires. Across the region, several studies confirm that Latin Americans perceive indigeneity in negative ways. Inclusion of indigenous ethnotypes in cultural artefacts, even when it is done through strategies that involve an appreciation and exaltation of the senses, has the power of undermining and harming communities perceived as subaltern. This is particularly relevant in the case of portrayal of women. Affixation of traits, even if their goal is to beautify, might instigate vulnerable viewers to understand these societies in a given way, as it is often the case with films catering to younger generations, or inexperienced viewers. Additionally, they have the potential to become points of reference for audiences who have never before come into contact with self-identified indigenous communities. The actual truth is that most Latin American films touching upon indigeneity do not aim at indigenous viewers. On the contrary, they cater to mainstream and increasingly more diverse global audiences.

Filmmakers impose specific meanings on viewers according to preconceived orientations in order to create a sense of alterity (Stam 1997). This is possibly the case of films such as *Caramuru* (Brazil, 2001), *Diarios de Motocicleta*

(Argentina–Brazil–Chile–France–Germany–Peru–UK–United States, 2004), *Play* (Chile, 2005), *La teta asustada* (Peru, 2009) and *Los viajes del viento* (Colombia–Germany–The Netherlands, 2009). Power structures are thus easily linked to the crafting of an alternate, opposite subaltern who is different from the viewing *We* as a means to reinforce, elevate and promote the sense of security of a universal, dominant, normative Self. To an extent, languages play a significant role in the deployment of power as they denote who belongs to the core and who belongs to the periphery.

There are commonalities but also striking differences in the optic Latin American filmmakers apply to the inclusion of indigeneity in recent films. Mexican cinema highlights the importance of identity, whereas Andean directors seem to apply indigenist practices reminiscent of previous decades. In the case of Brazil, natives are still depicted through tropicalist and tropicalized renderings, and historical accounts are chosen over stories staged in present-day times. Across the Southern Cone region indigeneity is positioned as a relatively recent re-encounter with forgotten topologies, or as notion waiting to be redefined in light of social acceptance or state-promoted acknowledgement. Central American and Paraguayan films including indigenous themes and characters are limited, primarily due to a lack of resource or state-related oblivion.

Echoing previous decades, Mexican filmmakers stress the centrality of agency espousing individuality rather than a sense of collectivity. Local filmmakers are punctilious in their self-effacing portrayals and yet, they adhere to romanticized indigenous representations. Although reductionist, outdated and mono-dimensional characterizations are present in Mexican cinema, the figure of the indigenous is embedded in narratives where diversity is recognized and validated. Indianist views, in contrast to indigenist frames of reference, are present, for instance, in *El Violín* (2005) and *Corazón del Tiempo* (2008). In these films, resistance vis-à-vis agents of an oppressor state is celebrated. While indigenism is concerned with paternalistic attitudes (Tarica 2008), indianism advocates the absolute independence of indigenous peoples (de la Peña 2005), both can be found in Mexican portrayals of indigeneity. In neighbouring Guatemala, social unrest, long-term effects of civil war and economic disparities serve as elements to expose the subaltern positionality of indigenous peoples – diverse and numerous and yet subject to inequality, discrimination and abuse. The production of *El regreso de Lencho* (2010), *Distancia* (2011) and *Ixcanul* (2015) is testament to the difficulties faced by Guatemalan directors.

Across the Andes, indigenist iconography remains a by-product of the socially engaged cinematic scene that flourished in the twentieth century. Over many decades, indigenist ideologies informed the formation of national identities, and have become a common theme in cinema until now. A connection is made between territories, ethnicities and knowledges, prioritizing on the primacy of the mestizo figure as a reconciling element. In this context, language is a marker of identity, intimacy and unity, but also an indicator of cultural boundaries and distance. Hence, some of the films suggest that Amerindian languages are endemic to rural areas, or characteristic of isolated geographies.

Two recurrent tropes are noticeable in the cinematic portrayal of Peru's ethnic composition. On the one hand, the extolment of autochthonous cultural elements, embodied in a championed recognizable mestizo, praised and idealized for containing indigenous elements underneath the surface. On the other hand, indigenist approaches in Peruvian cinema show a tendency to highlight the sense of intrinsic tellurian nature of Andean communities. Claudia Llosa, the director of controversial *Madeinusa* (2005) and *La teta asustada* (2009), deserves special credit for creating spaces for women filmmakers from the region, increasing the visibility of Latin American female-centred narratives.

Bolivian, Ecuadorean and Peruvian cinema focuses on the points of connection between urban settings and indigenous epistemologies, in particular when 'rural' characters establish strong bonds to their significant environments. Ecuadorean films, such as *El facilitador* (2013) and *Feriado* (2014), explore the inconsistencies experienced by urban upper-class youth once they are confronted with the reality of the Andean world. In similar ways, Bolivian filmmakers explore the encounter between past and modernity and the intersection of urban and indigenous lifestyles in films such as *Evo Pueblo* (2007), *Zona Sur* (2009), *Erase una vez Bolivia* (2011) and *Yvy Maraêy: Tierra sin mal* (2013). As for Colombian cinema, a commonality among the selected films is to suggest the figure of the indigenous belongs to insulated corners of the country, often in complete isolation. Indigenous ethnotypes are easily found in films directed by Ciro Guerra, which remain nevertheless memorable cinematographic works, such as *Los viajes del viento* (2009), *El abrazo de la serpiente* (2015) and *Pájaros de verano* (2018). Although widely acclaimed by critics and audiences, *El abrazo de la serpiente* has the attributes of an ethnographic visual project and an overall effect of a carefully curated museum hall, inevitably casting doubt on whose point of view is being presented.

Moving attention to the Southern Cone region, there seems to be two dominant approaches. On the one hand, indigeneity-oriented cinema from Argentina appears to portray indigenous characters as part of newly rediscovered rural geographies. Hence, indigenous ethnotypes align with notions, such as periphery, emigration, hierarchy and distance, both at a social and cultural level. Effects of colonization, cultural clashes and displacement are common tropes in *El niño pez* (2009), *Tiempos menos modernos* (2012), *Nosilatiaj. La belleza* (2012), *La Ciénaga* (2001), *La niña santa* (2004), and *Zama* (Argentina, 2017), while retaining paternalistic attitudes (metropolitan European narrates stories of indigenous rurality). Spatial constraints are also key features of Chilean depictions of indigeneity. *Play* (2005), *Alicia en el país* (2008), *Könun Wenu: La entrada al cielo* (2010), *El verano de los peces voladores* (2013) and *Las niñas Quispe* (2013) explore identity and tradition without overlooking the reverberations of social hierarchies. On the other hand, Chilean directors use the screen as a platform to reflect on the identity crisis that the notion of modernity sparks in the context of, for instance, the relation between the state and Mapuche communities.

In the case of Brazil, tropicalism emerges as a prevailing pattern in recent narratives, predominantly in films based on historical events. Both Brazilian and foreign productions about native communities in the Amazon basin equate the notions *Índio* (indigenous) and *selva* (jungle), deploying the sets of ideas linked to these terms. Examples include *Brava gente brasileira* (2001), *Caramuru* (2001), *Tainá* (2001), *A terra dos homens vermelhos* (Italy–Brazil 2008) and *Xingu* (2012). During the first two decades of the century, Paraguay has entered, at least partially, into the cinematic landscape of the region, mainly as a point of reference (i.e. *El niño pez*), intersectional space (i.e. *Guaraní*) and historical site (i.e. *Hamaca Paraguaya*). The use of Guaraní as a connector between Amerindianness, past and present, denotes the role of language in indigeneity-oriented films produced since the turn of the century.

Throughout the films reviewed in this study, European languages stand out as the norm, even in situations where indigenous languages would realistically be used as the means of communication. In fact, the use of 'exotic' sounds appears to be a strategy to stress difference and otherness. Inclusion of Aymara, K'iche or Tupi denotes not only recognition and acknowledgement but also attempts to enhance a sense of genuineness that does not necessarily serve to contest the subalternity of these languages. A review of the role played by linguistic contrivances in the creation of any cultural artefact (i.e. films) ultimately becomes a reflection about the users of that language. In films aligned with

Western cinematic tradition, language signals indigeneity (Carreño 2006). Inclusion of indigenous languages in cinema might also be understood as a tool to enhance a sense of difference. While forty-four out of the sixty-eight selected representational films (hetero-images) include dialogues in Amerindian languages, thirty-six use subtitles to translate these exchanges. Around 90 per cent of the films considered for this study include samples of their linguistic heritage, either in the form of dialogues, songs or written text. As a marker, language is a constant in heterogeneous cultural artefacts, not the least because it operates as an element that enhances the sense of realness, authoritativeness and credibility. As has been observed, the visibility/invisibility of certain cultural elements, such as Amerindian languages or oddly accented Portuguese and Spanish, plays a role in how cinematic indigeneity is constructed. Use of languages for ornamental reasons (i.e. *Play*) supports the notion that besides audiovisual instances, filmmakers also use linguistic strategies to epitomize and fabricate ethnotypes. At a transnational level, as is often the case, these languages risk operating as tokens of authenticity, capitalizing on intangible cultural legacy for the sake of acknowledgement, distribution, marketing and, ultimately, financial support. Filmmakers seem to assign languages an active role in the synergy between spectators, images and sound. Inclusion of Amerindian languages vis-à-vis Spanish, or Portuguese in the case of Brazilian films, sheds light on the dynamics between core and periphery. In varying ways, acknowledgement of linguistic diversity is also a vehicle for reinforcing sociolinguistic hierarchy.

The audible qualities of films contribute to its sense of credibility, reception and capacity to engage spectators. In the majority of films assessed in this project, the figure of an 'authentic' Amerindian subject is linked to non-European linguistic ancestry, or a dual sociolinguistic identity that confirms pre-Columbian rootedness. In *Roma* (2018), Alfonso Cuarón follows the steps taken by other Latin American filmmakers in the casting processes of their films, for instance, Alicia Scherson (*Play*, 2005), Lucía Puenzo (*El niño pez*, 2009) and above-mentioned Ciro Guerra (*Pájaros de verano*, 2018). The performers are not necessarily speakers of the languages their characters speak on screen. Linguistic nativeness in an Amerindian language becomes secondary, probably because of the limited size of the linguistic communities in question. However, this does not seem to apply to films that include widely spoken languages, for instance, Quechua (*Retablo*, 2015) or Guaraní (*Guaraní*, 2015). This practice risks silencing linguistic communities at risk of disappearing, or denied from entering cinema as a format to render their languages visible and audible.

Beyond language, artistically, filmmakers rely also on sensorial experiences and stimuli to transmit specific ideas. Images that appeal to haptic, olfactory and palatal processes and practices are simultaneously sources of information about the indigenous figure. Ontologies and epistemologies of the senses are semiotically engendered in gestures and small details that in combination with hues and tonalities allow many of the selected films to stage the sense of difference they seek to convey. It is common across contemporary cinema to imply that indigeneity is linked to bright colours (e.g. *Espiral*, Mexico, 2008; *Defensores de la vida*, Costa Rica, 2015), excessive facial and corporal make-up (e.g. *Caramuru*, Brazil, 2001; *Cenizas eternas*, Venezuela, 2011) and noticeable accessories (e.g. *Tainá – Uma Aventura na Amazônia*, Brazil, 2000; *Xingu*, Brazil, 2012; *Dauna: Lo que lleva el río*, Venezuela, 2015; *El abrazo de la serpiente*, Colombia, 2015). Elements predominantly associated with indigenous characters include herbs, dead animals, fire, shamanic tools, feathers, objects endowed with mystical properties and semi-humanized animals (e.g. *El niño pez*, Argentina–Paraguay, 2009; *Los ojos azules*, Mexico, 2012; *El Facilitador*, Ecuador, 2013; *Defensores de la vida*, Costa Rica, 2015). A distance is marked not only by the senses but also by the knowledges, cultures and topologies that are favoured.

Difference is underlined, nonetheless, because the images are commercialized through international networks where exoticism is a product. Urban, Eurocentric, highly acclaimed (trans)national productions remain the norm, especially when they are endorsed by international production and distribution networks. Foreign funding operates as a strategy to support and encourage the production of images of a distant periphery (Latin America) that resonates with a dominant core (Europe and North America). Some of the films produced in the region resemble portals that allow viewers to experience alluring peoples and geographies from the comfort of their chairs.

Foreign-funded films that address indigenous themes from an exotifying perspective include, for instance, *Madeinusa* (Peru–Spain, 2005), *El niño pez* (Argentina–France–Paraguay, 2009), *Cenizas eternas* (Venezuela, 2011) and *Antes o Tempo Não Acabava* (Brazil, 2016). These are stories where outdated stereotypical portrayals or long-established tropes of difference serve as the backbone to media spaces where the indigenous is presented as subaltern. Alternatively, in light of social shifts that have registered across Latin America since the turn of the century, there are a number of films that seek to reconfigure long-established ethnotypes. Films such as *Brava gente brasileira* (Brazil, 2001), *La Ciénaga* (Argentina 2001), *El violín* (2005, Mexico), *El destino*

(Argentina–Spain, 2006), *A terra dos homens vermelhos* (Italy–Brazil, 2008), *Espiral* (Mexico, 2008), *Alamar* (Mexico, 2009), *Zona Sur* (Bolivia, 2009), *Distancia* (Guatemala, 2011), *Nosilatiaj. La belleza* (Argentina, 2012), *La Jaula de Oro* (Mexico, 2013) and *Yvy Maraey* (Bolivia, 2013) put forth questions about the effects of mainstream societies on fragile, disfranchised communities. Furthermore, they operate as visual venues to disseminate notions of equality and acknowledgement.

In real life and in fiction, ethnicity and gender are social categorizations with enormous implications for individuals, and in particular, for ethnic minorities and women. Lipstchutz observed that 'pigmentocracy' is a de rigueur qualifier across the region and cinema registers the implications thereof. Throughout most of the selected narratives (e.g. *La Ciénaga*, Argentina, 2001; *Siguiendo las estrellas*, Panama, 2010; *Nosilatiaj. La belleza*, Argentina, 2012), a hierarchy is evident where female characters rank according to Eurocentric canons in terms of prestige, social position and beauty. As this study has shown, there are still well-stablished paradigms of representation in the depiction and creation of indigenous characters in cinema, especially female ones, a convention of placing women in subaltern positions. In terms of representation, the predominant tendency throughout the continent is to contest the dichotomy that pits indigeneity against collectivity. Through different strategies, most of the sixty-eight films reviewed in this study portray complex indigenous characters, not merely one-sided members of a group, as was the case in previous decades. Youth, rural flight, LGBTQ+ issues and transnational movements are among the range of recurrent approaches identified in recent films. Individuality is gaining resonance in films focusing on indigenous peoples.

On a positive note, many of the films assessed in this study seem to favour feminine figures, and hence contest a social hierarchy dictated by gendered difference. Partly, the number of female directors whose contributions are reshaping the cinematic landscape of the region may explain this. Consequently, female main and secondary characters are tonally depicted not only as individuals with a high sense of subjectivity and agency but also as individuals with a marked sense of ethnic identity and social responsibility. As I have shown, there have been some major shifts in the representation of Latin American indigenous women.

Newer portrayals of indigenous women, such as the figure of Cleo in *Roma* (Mexico, 2018), redefine and recalibrate the spaces allocated to women in cultural spaces. Realistic, compelling and multilayered depictions of indigenous female characters presumably reconfigure how audiences perceive women of indigenous descent. In terms of gender, one identifiable change in recent fictional works is that they reject the idea that femininity/masculinity and heterosexuality/homosexuality are fixed binaries. In fact, contemporary productions (e.g. *Retablo*, Peru, 2017) redraw the heterosexual indigenous ethnotype and expose sexual diversity across and within indigenous communities, an approach rarely seen in films produced before the turn of the century.

Yet recent films still portray differences between wealthy, European-appearing, powerful characters and dark-skinned figures who are framed as the least important members of society. In films in which the main character is not an indigenous woman, the inclusion of additional female indigenous characters is, from the outset, fragmented, short-lived, superficial and ultimately secondary. They are often portrayed as marginal characters identified by their low-paid occupations and unfavourable social status. *Roma*, directed by Alfonso Cuarón, stands out for championing the perspective of a domestic worker, problematizing social hierarchies within and beyond the diegetic world of the film. Ultimately, though, in the grammar of representation applied to cinematic spaces, spectators are encouraged to use ethnicity, beauty and socio-economic status as cues to interpret the position of characters using references from their cultural repertoire.

As attested throughout this review, a salient trend among filmmakers is to suggest that a bricolage of convincing indigenous elements elevates and secures the veracity of a story and epitomizes the depicted communities conclusively. The core–periphery dichotomy becomes clear in the fact that the stories are told through a Eurocentric angle. Indeed, the preceding discussion about films by foreign and Latin American filmmakers addressing indigeneity reveals that there are common aspects found in co-productions, festival-tailored films and productions endorsed by large studios.

Repetitive formulas (characteristics of a genre) show that indigeneity is depicted in similar ways in films made by foreign directors, like those of Darren Aronofsky (*The Fountain*, United States, 2006), Gust van den Berghe (*Lucifer*, Belgium, 2014), Mateo Gil (*Blackthorn*, Spain, 2011), Josh Hyde (*Postcards*, United States, 2010), Toshifumi Matsushita (*The Gift of Mother Earth*, Japan, 2008), Gerardo Olivares (*The Great Match*, Spain, 2006), and Latin American directors, the likes of Sergio Bloch (*Tainá – Uma Aventura na Amazônia*, Brazil, 2000), Ciro Guerra (*Los viajes del viento*, Colombia, 2009; *El abrazo de la serpiente*, Colombia, 2015), Cao Hamburger (*Xingu*, Brazil, 2012), Claudia Llosa (*Madeinusa*, Peru, 2005; *La teta asustada*, Peru, 2009), Alicia Scherson

(*Play*, Chile, 2005), and that the same parameters appear to exert influence on both groups of filmmakers. The departing point is that financial pressure in the form of funding, combined with recognition, exemplified by prizes and interested/interesting viewers among Western audiences can unveil strategies of Western – mainly European – interference in the creation of cinema across Latin America. Funding filmmaking in peripheral regions might be regarded as a European project to support the creation of exotic images that entertain their cinephile audiences, but that might fail to produce visuals that genuinely mirror filmmakers' interests, viewpoints and concerns. More importantly, this core–periphery relation can result in a spectacle of the exotic that aims at transnational spectators and, eventually, after gaining recognition, at 'local' audiences (Middents 2013). An analysis of 786 entries in digital platforms shows indigeneity-oriented films evoke feelings of empathy, support, interest and acknowledgement among global and local viewers.

The most noticeable shift in paradigms, compared with previous decades, is the centrality of individuality and self-identity. In films produced between 2000 and 2020, indigenous characters can be well-rounded, complex, multifaceted and free to contest the rules of their communities. In fact, ethnic affiliation does not denote opposition to modernity or isolation. Although filmmakers perpetuate the long-established propensity of portraying the indigenous as an alluring figure, reconfigured canons allow for stories where indigeneity can be understood from different viewpoints. Assessing the registers at play, it becomes evident that the social subalternity of Latin America's self-identified indigenous groups still serves as background to stories where alterity is highlighted, or even staged. This is confirmed by indigenous and non-indigenous audiences interviewed for this book.

Filmmakers consciously know that in many cultural repertoires, particularly in Western countries, Latin America as a notion prompts images of remote landscapes inhabited by picturesque peoples. Indigenous ethnotypes and themes inherently serve as points of reference in the imaginary of inquisitive audiences holding preconceptions that certain motion pictures seem to confirm, rather than contest or problematize. As has become clear, language has increased in importance in recent cinema, and on that account, it seems fruitful, in future research, to review how linguistic elements render stories more 'credible' and 'convincing'.

Since indigeneity has become more visible in Latin American productions in the last decades, it could be speculated that visual narratives are simply reflecting shifts in social order. From a theoretical perspective, another alternative is to assume that no major shifts have taken place, but that filmmakers have chosen to exotify their narratives to render them more attractive to foreign audiences. This assumption would be particularly relevant in the context of an increasingly globalized world. A third viable option is that indigenous ethnotypes are in the process of becoming part of mainstream discourses in media spaces without necessarily being linked to social reconfigurations, and that media are actually deploying new paradigms as tools to facilitate this process. Finally, a fourth reflection urges that if indigeneity is depicted through new patterns, these patterns might be prompted by a shift in the array of meanings needed by hegemonic discourses.

As discussed earlier, the global entanglements of an under-supported film industry and a need to supply imagery that resonates with outdated cultural repertoires might explain the continuity of this tradition. Usually endorsed by funding bodies, there are ample examples of cultural artefacts where otherness is stressed or highlighted by means of exaggeration. In this way, some of the sixty-eight films reviewed in this study resort to indigenous peculiarities in order to accentuate what is seemingly 'characteristic' of these 'beautiful' but 'divergent' communities. In the end, this book reiterates anew that the term 'histrionic indigeneity' can be used to refer to the type of cinematic indigeneity that results from portrayals that decorate and manipulate. It is therefore worth asking whether contemporary attempts to include indigeneity in cinema instead of reflecting social changes are actually examples of soft power, understood here as the ability of Global North to exert influence on Global South without coercion. Among the most illuminating insights that emerged from the interviews with indigenous respondents was their desire to see more 'versions' of indigeneity; in particular, because ethnic minorities do not commonly possess comparable tools (access to studios, distribution networks, editing facilities) to contest *mainstream* representations.

Reflecting retrospectively on the films reviewed throughout this study, I suggest that *Roma* in December 2018 convincingly signals the beginning of a paradigm shift in the representation of indigenous characters across the region. By zooming into the human experience of an indigenous individual, Cuarón shows that an intimate portrait challenges iconic ethnotypes. Understanding 'syntonic' as 'responsive to and in harmony with the environment so that affect is appropriate to the given situation' (Oxford Dictionary 2016), I suggest that *Roma* can be regarded as a syntonic – as opposed to histrionic – cultural artefact.

Cuarón's film syntonically rejects recycled interpretations. Most importantly, the Mexican-American co-production has proven effective in leading certain media outlets to recognize and reconfigure new understandings of ethnic diversity beyond entertainment-oriented portrayals, or partially inclusive approaches. My sense is that there are lessons to be learned from Cuarón's approach, in terms of visibility, identity politics and soft power. I anticipate that *Roma* will reconfigure levels of plasticity of cinematic spaces, although the future of indigeneity, I would argue, lies in self-representational filmmaking.

In terms of self-representation, under-represented communities show respectable attempts to enter media spaces and to produce films that fit their canons of production, both in terms of aesthetic paradigms and content. Through their cinematic outputs, self-identified indigenous societies make contributions that contest the ways in which indigeneity is portrayed in motion pictures made by non-indigenous groups. In this sense, media works produced by self-identified societies have the capacity of challenging stereotypes, fabricated realities and biased impressions, often common characteristics of heterogeneous representations.

Indigenous cinema allows (under)/(mis)represented societies to create platforms where they can raise awareness among themselves, among other indigenous communities in similar situations and among mainstream audiences who are rarely acquainted with issues that hegemonic channels of dissemination are reluctant to favour. The central aspect of cinematic production emerging from self-identified indigenous filmmakers/collectives is the acknowledgement and inclusion of their epistemic systems as valuable vessels and repositories of knowledge. Although non-indigenous filmmakers have become more aware of the mono-dimensional epistemic regimes their own films risk favouring, as I have shown, the approach and target are different. Auto-images intend to disseminate knowledge, as it is understood, used and preserved by the producing communities. Hetero-images accommodate, adapt and include indigenous forms of knowledge, but the seductiveness of the narrative remains the main goal. Self-representational films create and travel across systems (i.e. websites) where epistemic systems establish nods of contact with other systems. For example, a film resulting from a collaboration of an indigenous collective and filmmakers to denounce extractivism (e.g. *Hidrofractura*), eventually posted on YouTube to reach others, is a digital cultural artefact where three systems interact (social, judicial and digital). Auto-images facilitate the process by which indigenous communities can become epistemically present. In the process, they alert or, at least, prompt viewers to consider that not all societies are ontologically consonant. Moreover, the creation of films is the creation of repository of memory and evidence that might strengthen their position vis-à-vis dominant forces.

Indigenous cinema is closely being followed by exponents of *Cine regional* (Regional Cinema). These are Andean filmmakers (collectives, less so) from rural regions in Peru, problematizing the definition of self-representation and representation of those perceived to be indigenous. This is a cinema where mostly untrained actors, unstaged locations and unscripted worldviews are assembled to create narratives that articulate Amerindian worldviews. The focus lies on the need to create cinema and, hence, identity politics is not a common theme. The popularity of the *Cine regional* is not affected by the absence of economic means, or what for many viewers appears as poor editing and acting skill, improvised plots and artisanal cinematographic methods. Unlike city-based cinematographic production, Andean filmmakers engage with local audiences (on- and offline) in digital platforms or exhibition sessions, where they receive feedback, creating cybernetic landscapes similar to those constituted by Indigenous Cinema networks. No ethnic labels are used, probably because the viewers are conversant in the vocabularies deployed in the film, and active participants in their dissemination. A sense of intimacy and hence social clusivity informs the dissemination of these productions as self-representational cultural artefacts.

Following the interaction between audiences and films across social media, it is clear that audiences appreciate media spaces that escape the regimes imposed by ethnic labels (i.e. indigenous, non-indigenous mestizo, non-mestizo and *cholo*). *Wiñaypacha* (2017) stands out not only for its artistic qualities but also for its number of viewers, exposure at a national and global level and positive reception. The undefined, contestable and problematic boundaries where groups allegedly 'end' are usually not an object of study or serve as inspiration in *Cine regional* productions. An analysis of films produced by indigenous filmmakers/collectives leads me to conclude that they refuse to use ethnotypes as referents for their works. On this account, recent visual narratives produced in the region are agential attempts to reclaim media spaces. Self-representational films serve as reflective accounts of how self-identified indigenous communities understand themselves. The absence of ethnotype-based conventions commonly found in Eurocentric cinematic productions is evidence of how these films operate in a space parallel to conventional visual systems. Thematically, self-identified indigenous filmmakers/collectives recur to films as vehicles to share stories and their epistemologies, mainly with other indigenous communities. The image of the 'noble savage' is replaced by visual abstractions of their worldviews, or realistic portrayals of their daily lives. Indigenous Cinema does not have transnational canons of an imagined Other as referent. Compelling personal or collective stories affecting the producing communities are also central to many of the self-representational films produced in recent decades. The intimate character of these stories and a total freedom from any economic constraints (those needed for large-scale ambitious projects) possibly explain their ideological approach. In most cases, self-identified indigenous filmmakers are mainly interested in the message, rather than the format. Another important aspect is that the films are engineered to be consumed by audiences that understand the mechanisms of production behind the stories. As a medium and space of communication, cinema is popular among groups interested in creating collaboration networks and outlets to express themselves. The use of ethnotypes is not intentionally avoided, but it does not serve a purpose within circles where being the Other is celebrated, rather than avoided or ostracized. On the whole, the major difference between 'mainstream' and Indigenous Cinema in Latin America is the absence of visual strategies, aesthetic conventions, agendas (i.e. reputation) and commercial endeavours. At the intersection of art, entertainment, technology, ethics and politics, cinema has different meanings for different producing communities. This study by no means questions, assesses or scrutinizes self-identification and identity processes, or affiliation of those who consider themselves indigenous. Abetting the monopoly of images, and restrictive production and distribution networks, indigenous and Andean cinematic production are finding its own outlets and dissemination platforms.

Stereotypes about those perceived to be different confirm there is a tension in the way identity is imagined and understood. Cinema reflects and documents this tension. In future productions, the figure of the imagined indigenous Other might be replaced by the creation of visual narratives in which Self and Other are one.

Notes

Basis: Introduction

1. Sandra Xinico Batz is a Kaqchikel anthropologist, primary school teacher and columnist, recipient of the Gisella Paz y Paz and Jorge Rosal Award and active member of the Education Network for Sustainable Development in her native Guatemala. Attempting to answer this question is a focal point in her article 'El síndrome de Ixcanul: ¿entre realidad y película?' (The Ixcanul Syndrome: Between reality and film?), published in three parts in the Guatemalan newspaper *La Hora* in September of 2016.
2. See De Valck (2014).
3. Mesa Gisbert (1985); Ramírez Berg (1992); Lienhard (1997); Stam (1997); Gamboa (1999); de Tacca (1999); Virdi (2003); Lusnich and Cuarterolo (2005); Quispe Escobar (2007); Nahmad Rodríguez (2007); Wilson and Stewart (2008); Schiwy (2009); Taylor (2009); Maturana (2010); Mouesca (2010); Villazón (2010); Rodríguez (2011); Mateus Mora (2012); Cisneros (2013); Cupples (2013); Alba (2015); Tompkins (2018); Barrow (2018); D'Argenio (2020).
4. See Schiwy (2009); Shohat and Stam (2012); Cisneros (2013); Barrow (2018); D'Argenio (2020).
5. See de Pury-Toumi (1997) and Zavala (2011).
6. Pratt convincingly points out that 'although party A (the indigenous) are marked as having *priority* in relation to party B (the invaders), what in fact has priority is B's (the invaders') temporality' (Pratt 2007: 398).
7. This was a large-scale research project conducted by the CDI (Commisión Nacional para el Desarrollo de los Pueblos Indígenas/National Commission for the Development of the Indigenous Peoples) (2006) and involving 1,550 Mexican informants.
8. This study, also carried out in Chile, was a reproduction of one conducted by Saiz in 1991, identical in scope and methodology but slightly different in terms of outcome. In the previous study respondents did not mention negative traits such as 'extremist' and 'unfairly privileged'.
9. See Merskin (2011); Davis (2013).

10　Term coined by Estelle Tarica to refer to a cultural production created by a social group about another group and that is inherently destined to present a fragmentary dimension (Tarica 2008).

11　Defined by Wade as the ideology that favours 'whiteness and devalue blackness and indigenousness, and in more recent ideologies of multiculturalism, which tend to limit the nature of the space blackness and indigenousness can occupy' (Wade 2005: 255). For representations where the pigmentation of skin is a trope in cinema and a reflection of the social implications of race, see Young (1996).

12　Early examples include: *Desayuno de indios* (1896), *Danse indienne* (1898), *El suplicio de Cuahtémoc* (1904), *Aus der leben der Taulipang in Guayana* (1911) and *La voz de su raza* (1914).

13　See Ramírez Berg (2002) and Lie (2012) on stereotypes.

14　This project is a product of my reflections as a mestizo man, having lived my childhood and part of my adolescence in Latin America, but most of my adulthood and certainly all my academic life in Europe. As it is based on an unfunded doctoral and postdoctoral project, no economic interests are derived or had an impact on the thoughts put into this book.

15　Subtitles are provided in the English-speaking version of the film.

16　*Zona Sur* is further discussed in Chapter 5.

1 Mimesis: Circulation of ideas and images

1　Other important cartographical documents that maintained their informative value but served also to circulate ideas about the Americas and its inhabitants included *Atlas Lopo Homem-Reineis* (1519) and *Carte geographique de la Nouvelle France* by Samuel de Champlain (1612).

2　*Costumbrismo* as a movement focused on creating visual typifications of traditions, occupations, ethnicities and social realities from the standpoint of *creole* ruling classes. An image out of context was imaginatively the reflection of a new social order in which all subjects had a place (Olson 2014).

3　The number of categories identified in artworks varies according to the focus and criteria of each study. In his detailed analysis, Nicolás León (1924) identified fifty-three *castas*.

4　Many of these photographers led itinerant careers or had previous experience in other far-flung destinations, such as Brehme in the German colonies in West Africa (i.e. Cameroon and Togo) and Lumholtz in Australia.

5　Interestingly, while Lumholtz's first work was entitled *Among Cannibals: An Account of Four Years' Travels in Australia and of Camp Life with the Aborigines of Queensland*

(1889), his second book bore the title *Unknown Mexico: A Record of Five Years' Exploration among the Tribes of the Western Sierra Madre, in the Tierra Caliente of Tepic and Jalisco, and among the Tarascos of Michoacan* (1902), which gives an idea of how rapidly paradigms and attitudes evolved in the academic circles at the time.

6 Based on data gathered by Beatriz Bermúdez Rothe (1995).

7 Images that have apparently remained unchanged if one considers that although they 'have been broadly adopted to generalize misrepresentations of all indigenous peoples' (Iseke-Barnes and Danard 2008: 28), they are, for instance, still easily found on the internet nowadays. Some examples include websites promoting tourist destinations, New Age music and healing products.

8 Besides Veyre, another prominent figure was German ethnologist Theodor Koch-Grünberg who made several contributions to the visual representation of Brazilian, Guyanese and Venezuelan peoples in his travel logs, photography and clips (e.g. *Aus der leben der Taulipang in Guayana/Of the Lives of the Taulipang in Guyana*, 1911).

9 His most notorious pieces of work include: *El amor que huye/The Fleeing Love* (1917), *Los amores de Amparito/Amparito's Lovelife* (1917), *Triste Crepúsculo/Sad Twilight* (1917), *Costumbres mayas/Mayan Customs* (1918), *Las ruinas de Uxmal/Uxmal's Ruins* (1918), *Fiestas de la reina de belleza en Yucatán/Beauty Pageant Celebrations in Yucatan* (1918) and *El cultivo del henequén/Henequen's Crops* (1919) and *Venganza de bestia/Beast's Revenge* (1919) (Mateus Mora 2012).

10 Based on the poem bearing the same name and written by Juan Zorrilla de San Martín, this film produced by México S.A. is notorious for being the first Latin American attempt to transpose a written literary piece focusing on indigeneity into the world of cinema.

11 *De raza Azteca* (1921) is a modern tale of a couple attacked by a gang of criminals and fiercely rescued by a young indigenous man who evokes his Aztec background to gain strength and overrule the attackers (Mino 2012).

12 Many of his productions were based on research and demonstrated an academic approach, comparable to modern ethnological documentaries, and were well received among domestic audiences and abroad (Stam 1997).

13 Many of the actors in the film were actual members of the community who took part in the revolt in 1904.

14 See Wood (2006).

15 From early days, films in this Andean country have been highly politicized and have not avoided touching upon the 'most familiar "problem" of modern Bolivia, locating the place of indigenous people' (Lucero 2009: 261).

16 The idea that a film showed a contemporary Aymara man and a European elite woman having an affair instigated Bolivian authorities to confiscate the film and burn it (Córdova 2007).

17 In *Wara Wara*, genders have been inverted in comparison to *La Profecía del Lago*, and the setting is the Conquest of the Americas.
18 Local newspapers praised it for being a state-of-the-art 'superproduction' (Villazón 2010), after its national premiere at Teatro Princesa of La Paz.
19 To a great degree, cinema was used to serve as a 'register of the modernization of the nation-state' (Himpele 2008: 107) while avoiding allusions to points of 'contemporary contention' (Lucero 2009: 261).
20 Based on data gathered by Beatriz Bermúdez Rothe (1995).
21 Some of these include *Janitzio* (1934), *El Indio/The Indian* (1938), *La bonita india/Beautiful Indian* (1938), *Rosa Xochimilco* (1938), *Signo de muerte/Sign of Death* (1939) and *La noche de los Mayas/The Night of the Mayas* (1939).
22 Although not actually feature films, *Él es Dios/He Is God* (1965) and *Semana Santa en Tolimán/Holy Week in Tolimán* (1966) are still regarded as two important documentaries on the notion and understanding of God and how indigenous elements are interwoven with Catholicism.
23 Examples of this trend include *La Virgen Morena/The Brunette Virgin* (1942), *María Candelaria* (1943), *Río Escondido/Hidden River* (1947), *Maclovia* (1948), *Rebelión de los Colgados/The Rebellion of the Hanged* (1954), *Las Rosas del Milagro/The Miracle Roses* (1959), *La Serpiente Emplumada/The Feathered Serpent* (1962), *Fiestas de San Francisco en Magdalena/San Francisco's Celebrations in Magdalena* (1969), *La pasión de Cristo/Passion of Christ* (1970), *Las manos del hombre/The Man's Hands* (1976) and *Jornalero/The Day Laborers* (1977).
24 The film depicts the love story between a Maya cacique's daughter and a white explorer traversing the Yucatan Peninsula. As expected, this relationship is not well thought of by the community and provokes the wrath of the gods who punish the community with long-standing drought. Witchcraft and unnatural phenomena are used to glorify the connection between the Maya and nature, but the film also includes allusions to their autochthonous justice system. In a tragic sequence of events and as a result of their unapproved affair, both lovers end up dead and order is re-established.
25 Influence of *indigenismo* (indigenism) extended into academic, artistic, literary and visual circles. A focal point of this movement was the recovery of lost indigenous traditions and themes, and the acknowledgement of oppressed cultural outlets. A common aspect thread in indigenist works is the centrality of indigenous characters but viewed through a mestizo optic.
26 On this account, Barbash and Taylor (2007) observe that 'in the act of consuming indigenista fiction, [the audience] virtually accompanies the pseudo-ethnographer across a threshold, swept up like a vicarious participant observer on a fictional fieldwork expedition' (26).

27 The film served to reaffirm Carlos Navarro, its director, as one of the most acclaimed filmmakers in Mexico (Standish and Bell 2004). For many, the onset of the Golden Age in cinema in the country coincides with the release of *Janitzio* and other large productions that elevated the status of cinema by applying sound technology and the new options it afforded. Actors reclaimed their voices and gained new opportunities to promote their work.
28 See Tierney (2007).
29 Known as *ethnobiography* (Colombres, 2005), this technique was developed by Prelorán during the years he worked for the University of Tucuman as ethnographer and documentarist (1963–9).
30 These influential filmmakers are known for advocating the use of militant cinema as a platform to contest hegemonic interests, subjugation of lower classes and political underrepresentation. Essentially, their political standpoint was oriented towards an increased participation of audiences. They saw cinema as a platform to encourage masses to stand against any sort of imposed imperialism and class oppression, evidently mirrored in films such as *La hora de los hornos/ The Hour of the Furnaces* (Chile, 1968) or *Los inundados/Flooded Out* (Argentina, 1962).
31 The narrative revolves around Hermógenes, an indigenous artisan living with his wife in a small village in the region of Puna, struggling to survive and support his family amidst precarious conditions. Since he earns his living by making wooden religious artefacts, Prelorán allows viewers to explore how syncretism is embedded in the daily life of indigenous communities (Korstanje 2010).
32 See Chanan (1996).
33 In the film, Sebastiana Kespi, the twelve-year-old main character, plays out her daily life in front of a camera and so do the other characters without any training as actors. The film contributed to enhance the visibility of Uru Chipaya culture.
34 Other measures against director Sanjinés included confiscation of the equipment used to make the film, termination of contracts and other sanctions (Carreño 2005). General René Barrientos, in spite of his indigenous ancestry, responded promptly and aggressively to the de-colonizing ideology on which Sanjinés built his narrative (Félix, Kohl and Farthing 2011).
35 In terms of outreach and ideological impact, other salient productions released during these critical years for Bolivian cinema included *Yawar Mallku* (1969), *El coraje del pueblo/People's Courage* (1971), *La gran tarea/The Great Task* (1972) and *Chuquiago* (1977) (Birri 2013).
36 The community of Kaata, the town where *Yawar Mallku* is set, showed hostility to the filmmaker and his crew at first. Feeling downtrodden and forgotten by the central government, locals saw Sanjinés and his crew as a group of intruders from the capital city, La Paz (Giukin 2015). Due to the geographic isolation of the

location, realistic characters and external settings added a sense of credibility to the film. Up until today, this production is still highly regarded in terms of social impact, outreach and de-colonization of cinema. Since the coca plant is easily entwined with subversion, backwardness and religion, it comes as no surprise it performs an important role within the story. Being central to the cosmology of most Andean civilizations, images of coca leaves seem to symbolize an urge to transgress and challenge imperialist and colonialist canons (Murra 1970).

37 See Schroeder Rodríguez (2016).
38 At that moment in history, late 1960s–1970s, filmmakers across the continent felt the need to encourage masses to participate actively in reshaping their relatively young democracies. They sought to create awareness about the distribution of power, criticize social inequity, inspire spectators to take action against oppressive governments and unmask those exploiting their communities. Central to these narratives were characters fighting against abuse, inequality and violence. These were stories that would raise consciousness and resonate among audiences living under conditions of violence and injustice, primarily to stimulate them to engage politically. The social climate across the region translated into fictional discourses aimed to spur viewers to reclaim a reconfiguration of their social order.
39 Auteurism refers to the notion that filmmakers attach their signature, reading strategy, personality and techniques of self to their work (Staiger 2003).
40 Along with Gerardo Vallejo, Solanas and Getino founded Grupo Cine Liberación (Liberation Film Group) towards the end of the 1960s. The movement sought not only to open up spaces of contestation and militancy in films but also to make films tools to voice political concerns anonymously without facing repression from the Argentinean state.
41 Once speech became an option, Bolivian cinema entered a new stage in terms of diffusion, social impact and cultural value (Himpele 2008).
42 Renamed FUNAI in 1967. In spite of accusations of abuse and violence against indigenous communities, the SIP had a positive influence in the production of visual material on the cultural heritage of isolated groups in remote corners of the country (Burns 1975).
43 It is worth noting that School of Cusco had primarily produced documentaries and short ethnographical films, all with the goal of mirroring the ethnical diversity of the country. Some of their productions included *Corpus del Cusco/Corpus Christi in Cusco* (1955), *Carnaval de Kanas/Scenes from the Kanas Carnival* (1956), *Lucero de nieve/Qoyllur Riti/Snow Star* (1956), *Misa Indiana/Indian Mass* (1961), *Jarwi/Ballad* (1967), *Puente de Ichu/Bridge over Ichu* (1970), *Los hombres del agua/Men of Water* (1973), *Pastores de los Andes/Shepherds of the Andes* (1975) and the feature film *Los perros hambrientos/The Hungry Dogs* (1977).

44 Other films notable for this approach included *Los Warao del Delta del Orinoco/The Warao from Orinoco Delta* (1968), *Atabapo* (1968), *Los Guaicas/The Waicas* (1968), *Paraíso amazónico/Amazonian Paradise* (1970), *Curare* (1970), *Cuivas* (1971), *Los últimos guajiros/The Last Guajiro* (1973), *Zonas de Refugio/Shelter Zone* (1974), *Suumain Wayúu* (1975), *Yanomama* (1976), *Kariña* (1977) and *Yo hablo a Caracas/I Address Caracas* (1970).

45 The film was known outside Ecuador as *The Sons of Tupac Amaru*.

2 Metropolis: Production of audiovisual cultural artefacts

1 See Cajas (2013) and Durón (2014).
2 Hybridity is understood as a process that 'involves the fusion of two hitherto relatively distinct forms, styles, or identities' or the 'cross-cultural contact, which often occurs across national borders as well as across cultural boundaries' (Kraidy 2005: 5). Although the term is problematic and open for discussion, Kraidy's definition seems applicable to the Latin American context.
3 See Hernández Castillo (2010).
4 Mexican neo-realism distinguished by the intentional focus on daily life 'commonplace details' (Ramírez Berg 2015: 188).
5 See Tarica (2008).
6 For the conceptual evolution of this ideology, see Stabb (1959); Cornejo-Polar (1989); Tarica (2008); Favre (2009).
7 Due to its militant nature, films produced by Sanjinés and his Group Ukumau are commonly considered as productions aimed to contest hegemonic and imperialist ideologies. Some of his films include *Yawar Mallku* (1969), *El enemigo principal* (1973) and *Fuera de aquí* (1976).
8 After eight decades, in the depiction of Colombian indigenous peoples 'un élément récurrent se présente: le stereotype' [a recurring element is present: stereotypes] (Mateus Mora 2012: 236). As subsequent chapters will demonstrate, recent films from the country appear to approach indigeneity through a lens of otherness and indigenism, mainly endorsed by current cinematic economies and their ties to globalized audiences. Ciro Guerra's *Los viajes del viento* (2009) and *El abrazo de la serpiente* (2015) is reviewed in light of the impressions their films have evoked among audiences, experts and academics.
9 See León (2010).
10 See Cornejo-Polar (1989); Lauer (1997); De la Cadena (2001); Tarica (2008); Tompkins (2018).

11 See Dirección General de Estadística, Encuestas y Censos Dirección General de Estadística (2002).

3 Lexis: Portrayals of linguistic topologies

1 See Grenoble and Whaley (2009) for a discussion about linguistic revitalization.
2 Chapter 6 offers a discussion about the use of Mixtec in *Roma* (2018).
3 Similar to other films from the last decade, such as *La teta asustada* (Peru, 2009), *¿Quién mató a la llamita blanca?* (Bolivia, 2007) and *Magallanes* (Peru, 2015), the mother tongue in *El niño pez* is presented as the only viable instrument for women to express emotions, possibly because it presupposes their connection to an inner core and their roots.
4 Argentine actress Mariela Vitale had an on-site dialect coach to instruct her how to sound 'Paraguayan'.
5 Arraes's film 'de-centres the literal variant of *comer* (to eat)' underscoring the sexual implication of this term with two scenes in the film where the tradition of cannibalism (allegedly ascribed to the Tupinambás) is shown (Gordon 2009: 156).
6 *Hamaca Paragauaya* has been included on the corpus on the ground that the film is entirely spoken in an indigenous language, rather than its focus on characters specifically depicted as indigenous.
7 The unofficial translation from Quechua is by Antonio Muñoz Monge.
8 Madeinusa 'sings as a way to meditate, to pass the time as she engages in her chores, to remember the past, maybe even to grieve her absent mother in the lonely *Waychawcituy* song in the beginning of the film (*waychaw* being magpie in Quechua)' (Kroll 2009: 120).
9 See Barnes (2012) for a discussion about code-switching.
10 Original script in Spanish: Chauk llega hasta donde está la gallina. Juan lo observa divertido, esperando que no pueda atraparla. Hábil, Chauk atrapa al animal, la acaricia.

    CHAUK: *Jmet'ik banamil. Kolabal. Madre Tierra. Gracias.*

Juan y Sara observan. La gallina deja de cacarear.

    JUAN: *Este indio idiota, cree que la va a matar hablándole.*

Juan mira a Chauk burlón, se ríe de él. Chauk toma el cuello del animal y lo truena. Sara se asusta un poco, no es una imagen bonita. Juan deja de reír, mira a Chauk sorprendido, algo de respeto se asoma en sus ojos (Quemada-Díez, Portela and Carreras 2015: 30).

11 The creator of the narratives belongs to a different social group than the one he or she intends to portray (Tarica 2008).
12 Possible examples include Diego Araujo (*Feriado*, Ecuador, 2014), Victor Arregui (*El facilitador*, Ecuador, 2013), Carlos Carrera (*El traspatio*, Mexico, 2009), Cao Hamburger (*Xingu*, Brazil, 2012), Alicia Scherson (*Play*, Chile, 2005), Augusto Tamayo San Román (*Bien esquivo*, Peru, 2001).
13 The film received a script grant of € 10,000 (IFFR 2016).
14 The majority of funding schemes share the same criteria for the allocation of funds, also within Europe.
15 This answer was given by Gallego during her visit to Copenhagen, the hometown of SnowGlobe, the Danish production company that co-produced the film (Gallego 2018: 7).

4 Emphasis: Embodiment of indigeneity

1 See Chatterjee (2020).
2 José María Arguedas (1911–1969), a renowned Peruvian novelist prominent for literary works where he explores the clashes between indigenous and Eurocentric epistemologies. He is known for writing in Quechua and Spanish, and juxtaposing both languages to convey a sense of utopian unity, for example, *Agua/Water* and *Warma kuyay/Child's Love*.
3 These are Llosa's observations during an interview (Peirano 2010).
4 Conventionally, Arguedas's works (Llosa's point of reference) denote 'a political and aesthetic tradition of thought that points to a natural connection, of an almost sacred order, between the land and its inhabitants' (Tarica 2008: 37).
5 See Podalsky (2011); Rocha and Seminet (2014); Martin (2016, 2019); Randall (2017); Soledad Paz-Mackay and Rodriguez (2019).
6 Understood as an opportunistic approach embedded in 'a continuous and enduring historical phenomenon that opens a wide window onto larger issues about inconstant racial definition' (Hobbs 2014: 25).
7 Her decision is mostly driven by a condition known as *la teta asustada* (the frightened tit), which is allegedly common among the offspring of women who were victims of sexual abuses during the 1980s and 1990s in Andean Peru.
8 From a transcript of her answer during the press conference: 'I began with movements of animals. I watched Animal Planet and it's from there that I extracted Fausta's movements when she comforts herself, when she picks up the pearls, when she looks up, her way of looking is taken from the hippos' (Solier 2010).

9 A notable exception is the hippopotami that Pablo Escobar used to keep in his private zoo, and that after his death, have settled in the Magdalena River (Colombia).
10 A valid observation is that recent cinematic portrayals envision younger generations as more inclusive, embracing and sympathetic to ethnic and cultural diversity. Both as producers (filmmakers) and consumers (audiences), younger generations seem to have fewer prejudices than their parents do (did).
11 Ample scholarship has drawn attention to the impact of foreign (mainly European) involvement, notably in terms of financial support, either artistically or in relation to the canons that resonate with Western audiences, but also emerging trends in deterritorialized transnational cinematic praxis (Bedoya 2002; Shaw 2007; Pinazza 2011; Leen 2013; Middents 2013; Falicov 2017; Nagib 2020).

5 Axis: Identities and global imaginaries

1 See Connell (1987); Glenn (1999); Smedley and Smedley (2005); Segato (2007); Butler (2011).
2 The figure of *La Malinche* comes to mind in the context of womanhood, indigeneity and foreign invasion. The story of a woman serving as translator, counsellor, intermediary and lover of a European conquistador (Hernán Cortés) has served as backbone to narratives and myths about treason, but also about empowerment. As González Hernández (2002) observes, the 'símbolo de la traición' [the symbol of betrayal] and 'entrega al poder extranjero' [surrender to foreign power] (171), can also be read as a natural response to a state of chaos without a political or cultural unity.
3 See Forné (2017).
4 According to the diaries, Ernesto Guevara and Rodrigo de la Serna encounter monolingual Aymara-speaking farmers and fishermen on two occasions (Chile and Bolivia), meet a member of the Yagua people and eventually visit his community (Peru), are allocated a monolingual Quechua-speaking guide (Huancarama) and come in contact with speakers of various indigenous languages in Huambo leprosarium (Guevara 2005).
5 See Villazana (2008); Pinazza (2011); Ross (2011); Middents (2013); Shaw (2014); Falicov (2017).
6 As Middent (2013) points out, 'the "made for export" films play fantastically well to international audiences, and recognition abroad then circles back to affirm status as higher art among upper-class audiences at home' (155).

7   Even if 'the Water War protesters' principal leaders and coordinators were not predominantly indigenous', the most affected social groups were largely ethnic groups (Canessa 2007: 253).
8   Set in the Himalayas, this Spanish production from 2012 revolves around a Spanish teacher who fights against the Nepalese caste system and the lack of education among the most impoverished communities.

6 Catalysis: Paradigms and disruption

1   This refers to the competition with mass production and organized distribution systems of large production hubs like Hollywood.
2   See López (2015) for a broader discussion on the representation of ruralness in the film and Lie (2017) on road movies and how the horse is epitome of a buddy in *Cochochi*.

7 Wääjx äp: Epistemic and ontological repositioning

1   Confirmed by *Mis hermanos sueñan despiertos/My Brother Dream Awake* (2021), Huaiquimilla's work cannot be possibly addressed in detail in this volume.
2   For a detailed discussion of clusivity in political discourse, see Wieczorek (2013).
3   Sadly, during the revision stage of this book, Óscar Catacora passed away. His untimely death constitutes an irreparable loss. Catacora's passing reinforces the strength of his cinematic legacy and the place of Wiñaypacha [in italics] in Latin American cinematic tradition.

Bibliography

Acuña González, G., Díaz González, J. A., Alfaro Orozco, E., Chacón Araya, K., Mora Izaguirre, C., Solís Bastos, L., ... & Mora Solano, S. (2016). Percepciones acerca de las relaciones entre Costa Rica y Nicaragua. https://repositorio.una.ac.cr/handle/11056/14129. Accessed on August 2021.

Adare, S. (2005). *'Indian' Stereotypes in TV Science Fiction: First Nations' Voices Speak Out*. Austin: University of Texas Press.

Aguilar Gil, Y. E. (2017). Ëëts, atom: Algunos apuntes sobre la identidad indígena. *Revista de la Universidad de México*, 18, 17–23.

Aguilar Gil, Y. E. (2020). *Ää: manifestos sobre la diversidad lingüística*. Mexico: Almadía-Bookmate.

Ajxup Pelicó, V. (2015). Contexto social, político y económico de la dinámica guatemalteca actual. *Revista Análisis de la Realiad Nacional*, 69(4), 38–44.

Alba, María D. C. N. (2015). La narrativa indigenista en Argentina: Una doble denuncia. *Anales de Literatura Hispanoamericana*, 44, 403–22.

Altman, R. (1999). *Film/Genre*. London: British Film Institute.

Amado, A. (2004). Velocidades, generaciones y utopías (a propósito de La ciénaga, de Lucrecia Martel). *ALCEU*, 6(12), 48–56.

Androutsopoulos, J. (2012). Introduction: Language and Society in Cinematic Discourse. *Multilingua*, 31, 139–54.

Anzaldúa, G. (1987). *Borderlands – La Frontera: The New Mestiza*. San Francisco, CA: Aunt Lute Books.

Appiah, A. (2019). *The Lies That Bind Rethinking Identity, Creed, Country, Color, Class, Culture*. New York: Liveright Publishing Corporation.

Archibald, P. (2011). *Imagining Modernity in the Andes*. Lanham, MD: Bucknell University Press.

Arevalo, L. (Interviewer) and Vega, W. (Interviewee) (2015). *La Sirga*. Retrieved from: https://www.youtube.com/watch?v=_uvbkQuJw7M. Accessed on December 2018.

Avellar, J. C. (2006). O som do silêncio/Le son du silence. *Cinémas d'Amérique Latine*, 12, 39–59.

Ayoh'Omidire, F. (2010). Globalization and Identity Discourse in Latin America: Caramuru vs. the Brazilian Foundation Myth. *Global South*, 4(1), 7–30.

Banegas Flores, C. (2008). Cine e Identidad: La construcción de la identidad cultural nacional en tres periodos del cine boliviano. *Iberoamerica Global*, 1(4), 71–95.

Barbash, I., and Taylor, L. (2007). *Cross-Cultural Filmmaking: A Handbook for Making Documentary and Ethnography Films and Videos*. Berkeley: University of California Press.

Barnes, L. (2012). The Role of Code-Switching in the Creation of an Outsider Identity in the Bilingual Film. *Communication*, 38(3), 247–60.

Barrow, S. (2014). Out of the Shadows: 'New' Peruvian Cinema, National Identity and Political Violence. *Modern Languages Open*. Retrieved from: http://eprints.lincoln.ac.uk/view/creators/2655.html. Accessed on August 2021.

Barrow, S. (2018). *Contemporary Peruvian Cinema: History, Identity and Violence on Screen*. New York: I.B. Tauris, Bloomsbury Collections.

Bataille, G. (Ed.) (2001). *Native American Representations: First Encounters, Distorted Images, and Literary Appropriations*. Lincoln: University of Nebraska Press.

Baud, M. (2003). *Intelectuales y sus utopías: Indigenismo y la imaginación de América Latina*. Amsterdam: CEDLA.

Baud, M. (2010). Ideologías de raza y nación en América Latina, siglos XIX y XX. In E. de Rezende Martins and H. Pérez Brignoli (Eds), *Historia General de América Latina*, volume XI (pp. 175–93). Madrid: Ediciones UNESCO.

Bedoya, R. (2002). Nuestro cine: Una historia intermitente. *Libros y Artes*, 6, 14–17.

Bedoya, R. (2015). *El cine peruano en tiempos digitales*. Lima: Universidad de Lima.

Beller, M. (2007). Perception, Image, Imagology. In M. Beller and J. Leerssen (Eds), *Imagology: The Cultural Construction and Literary Representation of National Characters* (pp. 3–17). Amsterdam: Rodopi.

Bellido Gant, M. L. (2002). Fotografía latinoamericana: Identidad a través de la lente. *Artigrama: Revista del Departamento de Historia del Arte de la Universidad de Zaragoza*, 17, 113–26.

Berjón, J. C. (Interviewer), and Reyes, N. (Interviewee) (2018). *#Entrevista Natalia Reyes*. Retrieved from: #Entrevista Natalia Reyes | Actriz "Pájaros de verano" - YouTube.

Bermúdez Rothe, B. (1995). *Pueblos Indígenas de América Latina y el Caribe: Catálogo de cine y video*. Caracas: Editorial Biblioteca Nacional.

Bigenho, M. (2015). Embodied Matters: *Bolivian Fantasy* and Indigenismo. *Journal of Latin American Anthropology*, 11, 267–93.

Birri, F. (2013). Las Banderas de Jorge Sanjinés: Ukamau (1966). *Nuevo Texto Crítico*, 26(1), 7–15.

Bollaín, I. (2011). The Oral History of Hollywood. Retrieved from: https://www.youtube.com/watch?v=oliHeIto8PM. Accessed on October 2018.

Bourdieu, P. (2001). *Langage et pouvoir symbolique*. Paris: Editions Fayard.

Brading, D. (2008). Manuel Gamio and Official Indigenism in Mexico. *Bulletin of Latin American Research*, 7(1), 75–89.

Bruno, G. (2002). *Atlas of Emotion: Journeys in Art, Architecture, and Film*. New York: Verso.

Burns, E. B. (1975). *Latin American Cinema: Film and History*. Los Angeles, CA: UCLA Latin American Center Press.

Bustamante, E., and Luna Victoria, J. (2017). *Las miradas multiples: El cine regional peruano* (vols 1–2). Lima: Fondo Editorial, Universiad de Lima.

Butler, J. (1998). *Subjects of Sex/Gender/Desire*. Oxford: Oxford University Press.

Butler, J. (2011). *Gender Trouble: Feminism and the Subversion of Identity*. London: Routledge.

Cajas, C. (2013). Perfil del cine nacional en Guatemala. *Razón y palabra*, 17(1–82), 148–70.

Camps, M. (2012). Madeinusa. *Chasqui*, 41(1), 236–7.

Canessa, A. (Ed.) (2005). *Natives Making Nation: Gender, Indigeneity, and the State in the Andes*. Tucson: University of Arizona Press.

Canessa, A. (2006). 'Todos Somos Indígenas': Towards a New Language of National Political Identity. *Bulletin of Latin American Research*, 25(2), 241–67.

Canessa, A. (2007). Who Is Indigenous? Self-identification, Indigeneity, and Claims to Justice in Contemporary Bolivia. *Urban Anthropology and Studies of Cultural Systems and World Economic Development*, 36(3), 195–237.

Canessa, A. (2012). *Intimate Indigeneities: Race, Sex, and History in the Small Spaces of Andean Life*. London: Duke University Press.

Carbonari, P. (2010). Entre la pluma y la cámara/Entre la plume et le caméra. *Cinémas d'Amerique Latine*, 18, 78–83.

Carreño, G. (2002). Fotografías de cuerpos indígenas y la miras erótica: reflexiones preliminares sobre algunos casos del confín austral. *Revista Chilena de Antropología Visual*, 2, 133–53.

Carreño, G. (2005). Pueblos Indígenas y su Representación en el género documental: Una mirada al caso Aymara y Mapuche. *Revista Austral de Ciencias Sociales*, 9, 85–94.

Carreño, G. (2006). Pueblos originarios en el cine chileno: Reflexiones sobre la construcción de dispositivos visuales. *Boletin del Museo Chileno de Arte Precolombino*, 11(1), 33–43.

Carretero, M., and Kriger, M. (2011). Historical Representations and Conflicts about Indigenous People as National Identities. *Culture and Psychology*, 17(2), 177–95.

Carroll, R. (2007, June 6). After Evita – Evo, the Movie, puts Bolivia on Map. *The Guardian*. Retrieved from: https://www.theguardian.com/world/2007/jun/06/film.filmnews. Accessed on January 2019.

Castillo, D. A. (2019). Trafficked Babies, Exploded Futures: Jayro Bustamante's *Ixcanul*. In J. Gómez Menjívar and G. E. Chacón (Eds), *Indigenous Interfaces: Spaces, Technology, and Social Networks in Mexico and Central America* (pp. 119–40). Tucson: University of Arizona Press.

Chanan, M. (1996). New Cinemas in Latin América. In G. Nowell (Ed.), *The Oxford History of World Cinema* (pp. 740–9). Oxford: Oxford University Press.

Chang, J. (2015). Film Review: 'Embrace of the Serpent'. *Variety*. Retrieved from: http://variety.com/2015/film/festivals/film-review-the-embrace-of-the-serpent-1201510916/. Accessed on December 2018.

Chatterjee, P. (2020). *I am the People: Reflections on Popular Sovereignty Today*. New York: Columbia University Press.

Chicangana-Bayona, Y. A. (2008). El nacimiento del Caníbal: un debate conceptual. *Historia Crítica*, (36), 150–73.

Chirapaq, Centro de Culturas Indígenas del Perú (2015). *¿Quiénes son los indígenas? Estereotipos y Representaciones Sociales de los Pueblos Indígenas en el Perú*. Lima: Jesús Bellido M.

Chirix, E. (2015, February 6). ¿Colonialismo en el feminismo blanco? Comunidad de Estudios Mayas [Web log entry]. Retrieved from: http://commaya2012.blogspot.nl/search/label/Ensayo. Accessed on March 2019.

Cisneros, V. (2013). Guaraní y quechua desde el cine en las propuestas de Lucía Puenzo, *El niño pez*, y Claudia Llosa, *La teta asustada*. *Hispania*, 96(1), 51–61.

Colombres, A. (1985). *Cine, antropología y colonialismo*. Buenos Aires: Ediciones del Sol.

Comisión Nacional para el Desarrollo de los Pueblos Indígenas [CDI] (2006). *Percepción de la imagen del indígena en México: diagnóstico cualitativo y cuantitativo*. Ciudad de México: Imprenta CDI.

Connell, R. W. (1987). *Gender and Power: Society, the Person and Sexual Politics*. Stanford, CA: Stanford University Press.

Contreras, S. M. (2008). *Blood Lines: Myth, Indigenism, and Chicana/o Literature*. Austin: University of Texas Press.

Córdova, A. (2011). Estéticas enraizadas: Aproximaciones al video indígena en América Latina. *Comunicación y Medios*, 24, 81–107.

Córdova, A. (2017a). Ixcanul. *NACLA Report on the Americas*, 49, 114–15.

Córdova, A. (2017b). Following the Path of the Serpent: Indigenous Film Festivals in Abya Yala. In H. Gilbert, J. D. Phillipson and M. H. Raheja (Eds), *In the Balance: Indigeneity, Performance, Globalization* (pp. 163–81). Liverpool: Liverpool University Press.

Córdova, V. (2007). Cine Boliviano: del indigenismo a la globalización. *Revista Nuestra América*, 3, 129–46.

Cornejo-Polar, A. (1989). Indigenist and Heterogeneous Literatures: Their Dual Sociocultural Status (S. Casal-Sánchez, Trans). *Latin American Perspectives*, 16(2), 12–28.

Coronado, J. (2009). *The Andes Imagined: Indigenismo, Society, and Modernity*. Pittsburgh, NE: University of Pittsburgh Press.

Cortés, M. L. (2010). El inesperado auge del cine centroamericano. *Escena*, 33(67), 83–90.

Crenshaw, K. (1991). Mapping the Margins: Intersectionality, Identity Politics, and Violence against Women of Color. *Stanford Law Review*, 1241–99.

Cuarón, A. (2018a). *Roma, behind the scenes: Cutting to Emotion.* YouTube. Netflix Channel. Retrieved from: https://www.youtube.com/watch?v=c1foOyAAjDI. Accessed on April 2019.

Cuarón, A. (2018b). Golden Globe Winner Full Press Room Speech. *Hollywood Reporter.* Retrieved from: https://www.youtube.com/watch?v=5I2SvaQ46mA. Accessed on March 2019.

Cupples, J. (2013). *Latin American Development: Routledge Perspectives on Development.* London: Routledge.

Da Fonseca, V. A. (2010). Eus e olhares sobre os outros: relatos de Hans Staden e suas releituras cinematográficas. Outros Tempos–Pesquisa. *Foco-História*, 7(9), 100–15.

Dagrón, A. G. (1982). *Historia del Cine en Bolivia.* La Paz: Editorial Los Amigos del Libro.

D'Argenio, M. C. (2013). A Contemporary Andean Type: The Representation of the Indigenous World in Claudia Llosa's Films. *Latin American and Caribbean Ethnic Studies*, 8(1), 20–42.

D'Argenio, M. C. (2020). Wiñaypacha (2017) by Óscar Catacora: Overcoming Indigenismo through Intimacy and Slowness. In S. Barrow and C. Vich (Eds), *Peruvian Cinema of the Twenty-First Century: Dynamic and Unstable Grounds* (pp. 143–59). Cham: Palgrave Macmillan.

Dávalos Orozco, F. (1989). *Summa fílmica mexicana: hacia una filmografía crítica del cine mexicano* (Dissertation). UNAM.

Davies, S. (2016). *Renaissance Ethnography and the Invention of the Human: New Worlds, Maps and Monsters.* Cambridge: Cambridge University Press.

Davis, P. (2013). *Cognition and Learning: A Review of the Literature with Reference to Ethnolinguistic Minorities* (2nd edn). Dallas, TX: Summer Institute of Linguistics (SIL). Original version, 1991.

De la Cadena, M. (2001). Reconstructing Race: Racism, Culture and Mestizaje in Latin America. *NACLA Report on the Americas*, 34(6), 16–23.

De la Cadena, M. (2006). ¿Son los mestizos híbridos? Las políticas conceptuales de las identidades andinas. *Universitas Humanística*, (61), 51–84.

De la Cadena, M., and Starn, O. (2007). *Indigenous Experience Today.* Oxford: Berg.

Dennison, S. and Lim, S. H. (2006). Introduction: Situating World Cinema as a Theoretical Problem. In *Remapping World Cinema: Identity, Culture and Politics in Film* (pp. 1–18). London: Wallflower Press.

De Valck, M. (2014). Film Festivals, Bourdieu, and the Economization of Culture. *Canadian Journal of Film Studies*, 23(1), 74–89.

Dirección General de Estadística, Encuestas y Censos Dirección General de Estadística (2002). *Encuestas y Censos. Censo Nacional de Población y Viviendas.* https://www.ine.gov.py/. Accessed on October 2018.

Dos Santos Tomaim, C., Tomaim, R. and Valquiria, R. (2013). O estranhamento como matriz estética em Brava Gente Brasileira, de Lúcia Murat. *Dialogos*, 17(3), 1193–215.

Durón, H. (2014). *New Central American Cinema (2001–2010)* (Doctoral dissertation). University of Kansas. Retrieved from: https://kuscholarworks.ku.edu/handle/1808/14530. Accessed on June 2018.

Eide, E. (2011). *Down There and Up Here: Orientalism and Othering in Feature Stories.* New York: Hampton.

Eljaiek-Rodríguez, G. (2018). *The Migration and Politics of Monsters in Latin American Cinema.* London: Palgrave.

Escajadillo, T. (1990). *La narrativa indigenista: dos estudios.* Lima: Editorial Juan Mejía Baca.

España, Rafael de (2006). La conquista de México en el cine: El caso de la Virgen de Guadalupe. *Boletín Americanista*, 66, 29–49.

Fairclough, N. (1989). *Language and Power.* New York: Longman.

Fairclough, N. (2013). *Critical Discourse Analysis: The Critical Study of Language.* London: Routledge.

Falicov, T. (2010). Migrating from South to North: The Role of Film Festivals in Funding and Shaping Global South Film and Video. In G. Elmer, C. H. Davis, J. Marchessault and J. McCullough (Eds), *Locating Migrating Media* (pp. 3–22). Lanham, MD: Lexington Books.

Falicov, T. (2017). Film Funding Opportunities from Latin American Filmmakers: A Case for Further North-South Collaboration in Training and Film Festival Initiatives. In M. M. Delgado, S. M. Hart and R. Johnson (Eds), *A Companion to Latin American Cinema* (pp. 85–98). Chichester: John Wiley & Sons.

Falicov, T. (2019). *Latin American Film Industries.* London: Bloomsbury.

Farago, C. (2010). On the Peripatetic Life of Objects in the Era of Globalization. In M. Sheriff (Ed.), *Cultural Contact and the Making of European Art since the Age of Exploration* (pp. 17–42). Chapel Hill: University of North Carolina Press.

Favre, H. (2009). *Le movement indigéniste en Amérique Latine.* Paris: L'Harmattan.

Félix, M. P. F., Kohl, B. and Farthing, L. (2011). *From the Mines to the Streets: A Bolivia Activist's' Life.* Austin: University of Texas Press.

Ferreira, R. (2015). Cuatro películas peruanas frente a la violencia política: Los casos de Lombardi, Eyde, Aguilar y Ortega. *Lienzo*, 36, 151–65.

Fiske, S. T., Cuddy, A. J. C., Glick, P. and Xu, J. (2002). A Model of (Often Mixed) Stereotype Content: Competence and Warmth Respectively Follow from Perceived Status and Competition. *Journal of Personality and Social Psychology*, 82, 878–902.

Flores, S. (2013). *El Nuevo Cine Latinoamericano y su dimensión continental. Regionalismo e integración.* Buenos Aires: Imago Mundi.

Flores, S. (2014). Sujetos en el margen: Representaciones de los indígenas en la pintura y el cine latinoamericano. *Questión*, 143, 116–29.

Forné, A. (2017). Hidrografías del devenir en *El Niño Pez* de Lucía Puenzo. *Revista Iberoamericana*, 83(261), 837–44.

Fowler, W., and Lambert, P. (2006). *Political Violence and the Construction of National Identity in Latin America*. Basingstoke: Palgrave Macmillan.

Franco, J. (1993). High-tech Primitivism: The Representation of Tribal Societies in Feature Films. In J. King and A. M. López (Eds), *Mediating Two Worlds: Cinematic Encounters in the Americas* (pp. 81–94). London: British Film Institute.

Franco, J. (2013). *Cruel Modernity*. Durham, NC: Duke University Press.

Frías, M. (2012, March 29). El Amplio alcance de una historia minima: 'Tiempos menos modernos'. La vida de un baquiano patagónico cambia por una TV. *Clarín*. Retrieved from: http://www.todaslascriticas.com.ar/pelicula/tiempos-menos-modernos/criticas. Accessed on March 2019.

Fuller, M. (2005). *Media Ecologies: Materialist Energies in Art and Technoculture*. Cambridge, MA: MIT Press.

Gallego, C. (2018, November 19). Trækfugle en film af Cristina Gallego and Ciro Guerra. Øst for Paradis. Retrieved from: http://distribution.paradisbio.dk/log/film/Traekfugle%20(310-1)/pressemateriale_birds%20of%20passage_dansk.pdf. Accessed on February 2019.

Gamboa, A. (Ed.) (1999). *El cine de Jorge Sanjinés*. Santa Cruz: FEDAM.

García, G. (1999). In Quest of a National Cinema: The Silent Era. In J. Hershfield and D. Maciel (Eds), *Mexico's Cinema: A Century of Film and Filmmakers* (pp. 5–16). Wilmington: Scholarly Resources.

García Calvo, C. (2012). William Vega, director de la 'Sirga'. *LatAmCinema*. Retrieved from: https://www.latamcinema.com/entrevistas/william-vega-director-de-la-sirga/. Accessed on September 2018.

Garðarsdóttir, H. (2005). Kvenlegar ásýndir Rómönsku Ameríku. *Ritið*, 2(5), 63–80.

Garðarsdóttir, H. (2014). Subjectivities in the Making. In C. Rocha and G. Saminet (Eds), *Screening Minors in Latin American Cinema* (pp. 105–18). Lanham, MD: Lexington Books.

Garza, A. de la (2010). Diversity, Difference and Nation: Indigenous Peoples on Mexican Screen. *National Identities*, 12(4), 413–24.

Genna, K. and Espinosa, A. (2012). Identidad, etnicidad y bienestar social en un contexto socialmente excluyente. *Psicologia & Sociedade*, 24(1), 84–93.

Getino, O. (2007). *Cine Iberoamericano: Los desafíos del nuevo siglo*. Buenos Aires: Ediciones CICCUS.

Ginsburg, F. (1995). Mediating Culture: Indigenous Media, Ethnographic Film, and the Production of Identity. In L. Devereaux and R. Hillman (Eds), *Fields of Vision: Essays in Film Studies, Visual Anthropology, and Photography* (pp. 256–61). Berkeley: University of California Press.

Giukin, L. (2015). *Small Cinemas in Global Markets: Genres, Identities, Narratives*. Lanham, MD: Lexington Books.

Gleghorn, C. (2013). Revisioning the Colonial Record: La Relacion De Michoacan and Contemporary Mexican Indigenous Film. *Interventions – International Journal of Postcolonial Studies*, 15(2), 224–38.

Gleghorn, C. (2019). Subverting Racist Imagery for Anti-racist Intent: Indigenous Filmmaking from Latin America and the Resignification of the Archive. In P. Wade, J. Scorer and I. Aguiló (Eds), *Cultures of Anti-Racism in Latin America and the Caribbean* (pp. 73–100). London: University of London Press, Institute of Latin American Studies.

Glenn, E. N. (1999). The Social Construction and Institutionalization of Gender and Race. In M. M. Feere, J. Lorber and B. B. Hess (Eds), *Revisioning Gender* (pp. 3–43). Thousand Oaks, CA: Sage.

Goffman, E. (1959). *The Presentation of Self in Everyday Life*. Edinburgh: University of Edinburgh, Social Sciences Research Centre.

González Hernández, C. (2002). *Doña Marina (La Malinche) y la formación de la identidad mexicana*. Madrid: Ediciones Encuentro.

González Manrique, M. (2009). Reivindicación de lo indígena en el cine mexicano. In E. Media García, J. Marcos, M. Gómez Ullate and D. Lagunas Arias (Eds), *Fronteras, patrimonio y etnicidad en Iberoamérica* (pp. 205–19). Sevilla: Signatura.

Gordon, R. A. (2009). *Cannibalizing the Colony: Cinematic Adaptations of Colonial Literature in Mexico and Brazil*. West Lafayette, IN: Purdue University Press.

Graham, L., and Penny, G. (2014). Performing Indigeneity: Emergent Identity, Self-Determination, and Sovereignty. In L. Graham and G. Penny (Eds), *Performing Indigeneity: Global Histories and Contemporary Experiences* (pp. 1–31). Lincoln: University of Nebraska Press.

Greene, R. (Interviewer) and Scherson, A. (Interviewee) (2005). *Alicia Scherson, la ciudad y las alcachofas*. Retrieved from: http://www.bifurcaciones.cl/2005/12/la-ciudad-y-las-alcachofas/. Accessed on March 2018.

Grenoble, L. A., and Whaley, L. (2009). *Saving Languages: An Introduction to Language Revitalization*. New York: Cambridge University Press.

Guevara, E. (2005). *Diarios de motocicleta* (3rd edn). Buenos Aires: Planeta.

Gutiérrez Chong, N. (Ed.) (2007). *Women, Ethnicity, and Nationalisms in Latin America*. Aldershot: Ashgate.

Gutiérrez Chong, N. (2017). The Study of National Identity. In A. Dieckhoff and N. Gutierrez Chong (Eds), *Modern Roots: Studies of National Identity* (pp. 3–21). New York: Routledge.

Gutiérrez Chong, N., and Valdés González. L. M. (2015). *Ser indígena en México. Raíces y derechos*. Mexico DF: UNAM.

Gutiérrez Usillos, A. (2017). Transgresiones y marginalidad: El arte como reflejo de la visión del 'otro'. Modelos europeos para los cuadros de castas: Ter Brugghen y Wierix. *Libros de la corte*, 5, 185–208.

Guzmán, T. D. (2013). *Native and National in Brazil: Indigeneity after Independence.* Chapel Hill: University of North Carolina Press.

Hacking, I. (1983). *Representing and Intervening: Introductory Topics in the Philosophy of Natural Science.* Cambridge: Cambridge University Press.

Hall, S. (1996). Cultural Identity and Cinematic Representation. In H. Baker, M. Diawara and R. Lindeborg (Eds), *Black British Cultural Studies: A Reader* (pp. 210–22). Chicago: University of Chicago Press.

Hart, Stephen M. (2004). *A Companion to Latin American Film.* Woodbridge: Boydell and Brewer.

Hearne, J. (2012). *Native Recognition: Indigenous Cinema and the Western.* Albany: State University of New York Press.

Hedrick, T. (2003). *Mestizo Modernism: Race, Nation, and Identity in Latin American Culture, 1900–1940.* New Brunswick, NJ: Rutgers University Press.

Hernández Castillo, R. A. (2010). Indigeneity as a Field of Power: Multiculturalism and Indigenous Identities in Political Struggles. In M. Wetherell and C. Talpade Mohanty (Eds). *The SAGE Handbook of Identities* (pp. 379–402). London: Sage.

Hershfield, J., and Maciel, D. (1999). *Mexico's Cinema a Century of Film and Filmmakers.* Wilmington, DE: Scholarly Resources.

Himpele, J. D. (2008). *Circuits of Culture: Media, Politics, and Indigenous Identity in the Andes* (vol. 20). Minneapolis: University of Minnesota Press.

Hobbs, A. (2014). *A Chosen Exile: A History of Racial Passing in American Life.* Cambridge, MA: Harvard University Press.

Holl, U. (2002). *Kino, Trance & Kybernetik.* Berlin: Brinkmann & Bose.

Holl, U. (2017). *Cinema, Trance and Cybernetics.* Trans. Daniel Hendrickson. Amsterdam: Amsterdam University Press.

Hooker, J. (2005). Indigenous Inclusion/Black Exclusion: Race, Ethnicity and Multicultural Citizenship in Latin America. *Journal of Latin American Studies*, 37(2), 285–310.

IFFR Site, Hubert Bal Funds (2016). https://iffr.com/en/hubert-bals-fund. Accessed on December 2018.

INDH (2018). *Resultados de la IV Encuesta Nacional de Derechos Humanos.* Santiago: ClioDinamica Consulting.

INEGI – Instituto Nacional de Estadística y Geografía [INEGI] – Consejo Nacional para Prevenir la Discriminación [CONAPRED] (2018). *Encuesta Nacional sobre la Discriminación 2017.*

Inter-American Development Bank (2020). *Percentage of Indigenous Populations in Latin American Countries.*

International Work Group for Indigenous Affairs (IWGIA) (2020). *Country Profiles.*

Ipsos (2018). *Encuesta Nacional: Percepciones sobre Diversidad Cultural y Discriminación Étnico-racial.* Mexico: IPSOS.

Irvine, J. T., and Gal, S. (2000). Language Ideology and Linguistic Differentiation. In P. V. Kroskrity (Ed.), *Regimes of Language: Ideologies, Polities, and Identities* (pp. 35–84). Santa Fe: School of American Research Press.

Iseke-Barnes, J., and Danard, D. (2008). Indigenous Knowledges and Worldview: Representations and the Internet. In L. E. Dyson, M. Hendriks and S. Grant (Eds), *Information Technology and Indigenous People* (pp. 27–9). Hershey, PA: Information Science.

Izquierdo Iranzo, P., Martínez Pastor, E. and Galmes Cerezo, M. (2017). La representación étnica en la publicidad argentina, brasileña y méxicana (2012–2014). *Prisma Social*, 17, 241–67.

Jenkins, D. (Interviewer) and González-Rubio, P. (Interviewee) (2010). Pedro González-Rubio discusses 'Alamar'. *Time Out*. Retrieved from: https://www.timeout.com/london/film/pedro-gonzalez-rubio-discusses-alamar-1. Accessed on May 2017.

Johnson, R., and Stam, R. (Eds) (1995). *Brazilian Cinema*. New York: Columbia University Press.

Karakartal, E. (2006). Réinventer un cinéma comme espace de libération et de réappropriation de soi: Récit de l'expérience de l'Atelier Tokapu à Villa El Salvador (Pérou). *Cinémas d'Amérique Latine*, 14, 3–22.

King, J. (2000). *Magical Reels: A History of Cinema in Latin America* (2nd edn). London: Verso.

Korstanje, M. (2010). Reseña de 'Hermógenes Cayo: Un Análisis Cinematográfico Contemporáneo' de Prelorán, Jorge (director)'. *Andes*, 21, 349–53.

Kraidy, M. (2005). *Hybridity, or the Cultural Logic of Globalization*. Philadelphia, PA: Temple University Press.

Kroll, J. A. (2009). Between the 'Sacred' and the 'Profane': Cultural Fantasy in Madeinusa by Claudia Llosa. *Chasqui*, 38(2), 113–25.

Landzelius, K. (Ed.) (2004). Introduction: Native on the Net. *Native on the Net: Indigenous and Diasporic Peoples in the Virtual Age* (pp. 1–42). New York: Routledge.

Lanthier, J. (2010). Altiplano. Slant Magazine. Retrieved from: https://www.slantmagazine.com/film/review/altiplano. Accessed on April 2017.

Lauer, M. (1997). *Andes imaginarios. Discursos del indigenismo*. Cusco-Lima: Centro de Estudios Regionales Andinos Bartolomé de Las Casas-Sur.

Leen, C. (2013). The Silenced Screen: Fostering a Film Industry in Paraguay. *Monografías*, 323, 155–80.

Leerssen, J. (2007). Imagology: History and method. In M. Beller and J. Leerssen (Eds), *Imagology: The Cultural Construction and Literary Representation of National Characters* (pp. 17–32). Amsterdam: Rodopi.

Leerssen, J. (2016). Imagology: On Using Ethnicity to Make Sense of the World. *Iberic@l*, 10, 13–31.

Leerssen, J. (2017). A Summary of Imagological Theory. *Imagologica*. Retrieved from: http://imagologica.eu/theoreticalsummary. Accessed on September 2019.

León, C. (2010). *Reinventando al otro: El documental indigenista en el Ecuador*. Quito: Consejo Nacional de Cinematografía.

León, N. (1924). *Las castas del México colonial o Nueva España: Noticias etno-antropológicas*. México: Talleres gráficos del Museo Nacional de Arqueología, Historia y Etnografía.

León Frías, I. (1996). Peru. In T. Barnard and P. Rist (Eds), *South American Cinema: A Critical Filmography 1915–1994* (pp. 275–91). New York: Garland.

Lerer, D. (2017, Oct 20). Lucrecia Martel on Location with Zama: 'All That Heroic Past and Brave Macho Stuff Makes Me Ill'. *BFI, Film Forever*. Retrieved from: http://www.bfi.org.uk/news-opinion/sight-sound-magazine/interviews/lucrecia-martel-interview-zama. Accessed on November 2020.

Leyva Solano, X. (2005). Indigenismo, Indianismo and 'Ethnic Citizenship' in Chiapas. *Journal of Peasant Studies*, 32(3–4), 555–83.

Liano, D. (2015). Distancias Geograficas, distancias visuales. *Oltreaoceano: rivista sulle migrazioni*, 9, 149–61.

Lie, N. (2012). Stereotypes and Identity Construction: Concepts as Tools. *Interférences littéraires/Literaire interferenties*, 9, 183–91.

Lie, N. (2017). *The Latin American (Counter-) Road Movie and Ambivalent Modernity*. Cham: Palgave.

Lienhard, M. (1997). Of Mestizajes, Heterogeneities, Hybridisms and Other Chimeras: On the Macroprocesses of Cultural Interaction in Latin America. *Journal of Latin American Cultural Studies*, 6(2), 183–200.

Lienhard, M. (2002). La noche de los mayas: representaciones de los indígenas mesoamericanos en el cine y la literatura, 1917–1943. Mesoamérica, 23(44), 82–117.

Lipstchutz, A. (1944). *El Indoamericanismo y el problema racial en las Américas*. Santiago: Editorial Nascimiento.

Llosa, C. and Solier, M. (2010). *La teta del exito: Mujeres Peruanas, Academy Award Ceremony* [Press conference recording]. Retrieved from: https://www.youtube.com/watch?v=lD40GyC0rI8. Accessed on March 2019.

Loder, K. (Interviewer) and Gibson, M. (Interviewee) (2006). *Mel Gibson Tells Some Brutal Truths about the Amazing 'Apocalypto'*. Retrieved from: http://www.mtv.com/news/1548104/mel-gibson-tells-some-brutal-truths-about-the-amazing-apocalypto/. Accessed on February 2019.

López, A. M. (2015). Cartographies of Mexican Cinema in the 21st Century. *Rebeca-Revista Brasileira de Estudos de Cinema e Audiovisual*, 4(1), 36–51.

López, J. (2018, November 7). 'Pájaros de verano', el narcotráfico, la familia y lo femenino. *Digital Noticias 22*. Retrieved from: https://noticias.canal22.org.mx/2018/11/07/pajaros-de-verano-el-narcotrafico-la-familia-y-lo-femeninoo/. Accessed on January 2019.

López Medin, S. (Interviewer) and Encina, P. (Interviewee) (2021). An Always Open Circle. *Post: Notes on Art in a Global Context*. MOMA. Retrieved from: https://post.moma.org/an-always-open-circle/. Accessed on December 2021.

Losada, M. (2010). Hamaca Paraguaya. *Chasqui*, 39(1), 204–5.

Lucero, J. A. (2009). The Lion King vs. Evo Morales? Adventures in the Andean Vision World. *A Contracorriente*, 6(2), 258–67.

Lusnich, A. L., and Cuarterolo, A. (2005). *Civilización y Barbarie: En el cine Argentino y Latinoamericano*. Buenos Aires: Editorial Biblos.

Luzuriaga, C. (2014, August 11). La indutria ecuatoriana del cine: ¿Otra quimera? *El Telégrafo*. https://www.eltelegrafo.com.ec/noticias/carton/1/la-industria-ecuatoriana-del-cine-otra-quimera. Accessed on April 2019.

Macdonald, G. M. (1994). Third Cinema and the Third World. In S. C. Aitken and L. E. Zonn (Eds), *Place, Power, Situation, and Spectacle: A Geography of Film* (pp. 27–45). Lanham, MD: Rowman and Littlefield.

Malik, K. (1996). *The Meaning of Race: Race, History and Culture in Western Society*. London: Macmillan.

Mandler, S. (2012). Paper Dove/Paloma de papel, 2003. In I. M. Queipo (Ed.), *Socio-Critical Aspects in Latin American Cinema(s)* (pp. 119–22). Frankfurt: Peter Lang.

Martel, F. (2012). *Mainstream: a guerra global das mídias e das culturas*. Sao Paulo: Civilização Brasileira.

Martin, D. (2016). *The Cinema of Lucrecia Martel*. Manchester: Manchester University Press.

Martin, D. (2019). *The Child in Contemporary Latin American Cinema*. New York: Palgrave Macmillan.

Martínez San Miguel, Y. (2011). Taíno Warriors? Strategies for Recovering Indigenous Voices in Colonial and Contemporary Hispanic Caribbean Discourses. *Centro Journal*, 23(1), 197–215.

Martínez Sotelo, G. (2012). Cine mexicano y su representación periférica: La representación de las luchas armadas contemporáneas. *Teatro: Revista de Estudios Culturales*, 25, 55–70.

Mastodonte, Proyecto (2006). La llamita desafiante de Bellott [Web log entry]. Retrieved from: http://proyectomastodonte.blogspot.nl/2006/08. Accessed on March 2019.

Mateus Mora, A. (2012). *L'Indien: images et conflits*. Paris: L'Harmattan.

Maturana, F. (2010). Nutuayin Mapu y el cine indígena en Chile. El cine de Carlos Flores. *La Fuga*, 412 (n.p.).

Maxwell, J. M., and Nelson, B. C. (October, 2018). Ixcanul [sic]: A Commentary from Oxlajuj Aj. *Publications*. Latin American Research Center. University of Calgary. Retrieved from: https://larc.ucalgary.ca/publications/film-review-ixcanul-sic-commentary-oxlajuj-aj. Accessed on December 2021.

McGowan, T. (2003). Looking for the Gaze: Lacanian Film Theory and Its Vicissitudes. *Cinema Journal*, 42(3), 27–47.

Medina, M. (2007). Orgullosamente (no) argentinos: la estética de la migración y de la identidad en el cine argentino contemporáneo. In V. Rangil (Ed.), *El cine argentino de hoy: Entre el arte y la política* (pp. 103–17). Buenos Aires: Biblos.

Merry, S. (2016, August 25). Jayro Bustamente offers an unforgettable portrait of Mayan life in 'Ixcanul'. *The Washington Post*.

Merskin, D. (2011). *Media, Minorities and Meaning: A Critical Introduction*. New York: Peter Lang.

Mesa Gisbert, C. D. (1985). *La aventura del cine boliviano, 1952–1985*. La Paz: Editorial Gisbert.

Mesa Gisbert, C. D. (2010, February 4). *Zona Sur: El éxito de Juan Carlos Valdivia en el Sundance*. Retrieved from: https://carlosdmesa.com/2010/02/04/zona-sur-el-exitro-de-juan-carlos-valdivia-en-del-sundance/. Accessed on November 2018.

Middents, J. (2009). *Writing National Cinema: Film Journals and Film Culture in Peru*. Hanover, NH: Dartmouth College Press.

Middents, J. (2013). The First Rule of Latin American Cinema Is You Do Not Talk about Latin American Cinema: Notes on Discussing a Sense of Place in Contemporary Cinema. *Transnational Cinemas*, 4(2), 147–64.

Mino, G. F. (2012). Los indios que forjaron una patria. Comunidades indígenas y el mito nacional: el caso de María Candelaria. *Montajes: Revista de Análisis Cinematográfico*, 2, 107–33.

Minority Rights Groups International (MRGI) (2020). *World Directory of Minorities and Indigenous Peoples*.

Miquel, A. (2006). Panorama del cine mexicano contemporáneo. *Inventio, la génesis de la cultura universitaria en Morelos*, 2(4), 81–6.

Molina Ergueta, M. C. (2010). Zona Sur: ver y no mostrar. *Fotograma*, 1(4), 27. https://issuu.com/carlosfidelintriago/docs/fotograma_revista_de_cine_4. Accessed on November 2018.

Molina Ergueta, M. C. (2014). Lo más bonito y sus mejores años. Cine boliviano de los últimos 50 años (1964–2014). *Ciencia y Cultura*, 32, 153–82.

Monette, M. E. (2013). Negociaciones entre la cultura andina y la cultura urbana limeña en *Madeinusa* y *La teta asustada* de Claudia Llosa. *Revista Nuevo Mundo, Mundos Nuevos*. Retrieved from: http://journals.openedition.org/nuevomundo/65640. Accessed on March 2019.

Mora Catlett, J. (1989). *Mexican Cinema: Reflections of a Society 1896–1988*. Berkeley: University of California Press.

Mora Catlett, J. (2009). Eréndira Ikikunari: Celebrating Indigenous Cultural Heritage. *Revista Harvard Review of Latin America*. Retrieved from: https://revista.drclas.harvard.edu/erendira-ikikunari/. Accessed on September 2018.

Moreno Figueroa, M. (2013). Displaced looks: The Lived Experience of Beauty and Racism. *Feminist Theory*, 14, 137–51.

Moriuchi, M.-Y. (2018). *Mexican Costumbrismo: Race, Society and Identity in Nineteenth-Century Art*. University Park: Penn State University Press.

Mouesca, J. (1998). *Cine y memoria del siglo XX: Cine en Chile, cine en el mundo, historia social y cultural de Chile, historia social y cultura mundial, cuadros sinópticos (1895–1995)*. Santiago de Chile: LOM Ediciones.

Mouesca, J. (2010). El cine chileno y la historia nacional. *Cinémas d'Amérique latine*, 18, 17–22.

Mulvey, L. (1975). Visual Pleasure and Narrative Cinema. In M. G. Durham and D. M. Kellner (Eds), *Media and Cultural Studies: Keyworks* (pp. 342–52). Oxford: Blackwell.

Muñiz, C., Serrano, F. J., Aguilera, R. E. and Rodríguez, A. (2013). Estereotipos mediáticos o sociales. Influencia del consumo de televisión en el prejuicio detectado hacia los indígenas mexicanos. *Global Media Journal México*, 7(14), 93–113.

Muñiz, C., Marañón, F. and Saldierna, A. R. (2014). ¿Retratando la realidad? Análisis de los estereotipos de los indígenas presentes en los programas de ficción de la televisión mexicana. *Palabra Clave*, 17(2), 263–93.

Murra, J. V. (1970). Current Research and Prospects in Andean Ethnohistory. *Latin American Research Review*, 5(1), 3–36.

Nagib, L. (2006). *A utopía no cinema brasileiro: matrizes, nostalgia, distopias*. Sao Paulo: Editora CosacNaify.

Nagib, L. (2020). *Realist Cinema as World Cinema: Non-cinema, Intermedial Passages, Total Cinema*. Amsterdam: Amsterdam University Press.

Nahmad Rodríguez, A. D. (2007). Las representaciones indígenas y la pugna por las imágenes. México y Bolivia a través del cine y el video. *Revista de Estudios Latinoamericanos*, 45, 105–30.

Native American Films Site (2012). Retrieved from: http://www.nativeamericanfilms.org/mexico1.html. Accessed on October 2021.

Noboa, W. G. (1995). *El Cine silente en Ecuador: (1895–1935)*. Quito: Editorial Casa De La Cultura Ecuatoriana.

Nordseth, P. (2018, December 5). Slik fikk en norsk professor filmdebutere i Netflix' nye sotrfilm. *Filter, film og tv*. Retrieved from: http://filterfilmogtv.no/slik-fikk-en-norsk-professor-fildebutere-i-netflix-nye-storfilm/. Accessed on January 2019.

Ochoa Gautier, A. M. (2014). *Aurality: Listening and Knowledge in Nineteenth-Century Colombia*. Durham, NC: Duke University Press.

Ojeda Llanes, F. (2007). *Decodificando el Tepeyac*. New York: IVE Press.

Olavarria, É. (Interviewer), Gallego, C., and Guerra, C. (2018) (Interviewee) (2018). Ciro Guerra y Cristina Gallego hablan de sus 'Pájaros de verano'. Retrieved from: http://www.youtube.com/watch?v=XrmuDIQSN_w. Accessed on April 2019.

Olson, C. J. (2014). *Constitutive Visions: Indigeneity and Commonplaces of National Identity in Republican Ecuador*. University Park: Pennsylvania State University.

Online Etymology Dictionary (2017). Retrieved from: https://www.etymonline.com/. Accessed on December 2021.

Ouweneel, A. (1996). *De vergeten stemmen van Mexico een reeks ontmoetingen in de achttiende eeuw*. Amsterdam: Amsterdam University Press.

Ouweneel, A. (2018). *Resilient Memories: Amerindian Cognitive Schemas in Latin American Art*. Columbus: Ohio State University Press.

Overing, J. and Passes. A. (Eds) (2000). *The Anthropology of Love and Anger: The Aesthetics of Conviviality in Native Amazonia*. New York: Psychology Press.

Oxford English Dictionary (2017). Retrieved from: http://www.oed.com. Accessed on November 2021.

Pacheco de Oliveira, J. (2005). The Anthropologist as Expert. In B. de l'Estoile, F. Neiburg and L. Sigaud (Eds), *Empires, Nation and Natives, Anthropology and State-making* (pp. 223–47). Durham, NC: Duke University Press.

Pagán-Teitelbaum, I. (2008). El glamour en los Andes: la representación de la mujer indígena migrante en el cine peruano. *Revista Chilena de Antropología Visual*, 12, 1–30.

Page, J. (2009). *Crisis and Capitalism in Contemporary Argentine Cinema*. Durham, NC: Duke University Press.

Pan-American Health Organization (2020). https://www.paho.org/en. Accessed on November 2021.

Paszkiewicz, K. (2010). Del cine épico al cine social: el universo metafílmico en También la lluvia (2010) de Icíar Bollaín. *Lectora: revista de dones i textualitat*, 18, 227–40.

Peirano, L. (Interviewer) and Llosa, C. (Interviewee) (2010). *Presentación guión La teta asustada*. Retrieved from: https://www.youtube.com/watch?v=OBY_tY5FKGQ. Accessed on January 2019.

Peña, G. de la (2005). Social and Cultural Policies towards Indigenous Peoples: Perspectives from Latin America. *Annual Review Anthropological*, 34, 717–39.

Phillips, T. (2009, September 11). Birdwatchers: A Tribe's Fight for Justice. *The Guardian*. Retrieved from: https://www.theguardian.com/film/2009/sep/11/birdwatchers. Accessed on November 2021.

Piedras, P. (2012). Argentina. In I. M. Queipo (Ed.), *Socio-critical Aspects in Latin American Cinema(s)* (pp. 33–9). Frankfurt: Peter Lang.

Piña, M. C. (Interviewer), Gallego, C. and Guerra, C. (Interviewee) (2018). *Pájaros de verano*. Retrieved from: http://www.youtube.com/watch?v=ufUyHXZv5PI. Accessed on April 2019.

Pinazza, N. (2011). *Globalisation and the National Imaginary in Contemporary Argentine and Brazilian Cinema* (Doctoral dissertation). University of Bath.

Retrieved from: https://birkbeck.academia.edu/NataliaPinazza. Accessed on January 2018.

Pizarro Gómez, F. (1997). Identidad y mestizaje en el arte barroco andino: La iconografía. *Colección Aalten*, 159, 196–213.

Plascencia, C. G., and Monteforte, G. (2006). El cine y video en los pueblos indígenas: acciones y Reflexiones. *Cinémas d'Amérique Latine*, 1, 30–4.

Podalsky, L. (2011). *The Politics of Affect and Emotion in Contemporary Latin American Cinema: Argentina, Brazil, Cuba, and Mexico*. New York: Palgrave.

Posso Gómez, A. (2012, August 8). La Sirga, del caleño William Vega, llega a las salas de cine. *El país*. Retrieved from: https://www.elpais.com.co/entretenimiento/la-sirga-del-caleno-william-vega-llega-a-las-salas-de-cine.html. Accessed on November 2018.

Pratt, M. L. (1992). *Imperial Eyes: Travel Writing and Transculturation*. London: Routledge.

Pratt, M. L. (2007). Afterword: Indigeneity Today. In M. De la Cadena and O. Starn (Eds). *Indigenous Experience Today* (pp. 397–404). Oxford: Berg.

Pratt, S. (2009). Truth and Artifice in the Visualization of Native Peoples: From the Time of John White to the Beginning of the 18th Century. In K. Sloan (Ed.), *European Visions: American Voices* (pp. 33–40). London: British Museum.

Pury-Toumi de, S. (1997). *De palabras y maravillas: Ensayo sobre la lengua y la cultura de los nahuas*. Sierra Norte de Puebla: Centro de estudios mexicanos y centroamericanos.

Quemada-Díez, D., Portela, G., and Carreras, L. (2015). La Jaula de Oro. *Las cuadernos de Cinema*. Retrieved from: http://cinema23.com/cuadernos-de-cinema23/. Accessed on January 2019.

Quispe-Agnoli, R. (2011). Elusive Identities: Representations of Native Latin America in the Contemporary Film Industry. In D. Cummings (Ed.), *Visualities: Perspectives on Contemporary American Indian Film and Art* (pp. 95–118). East Lansing: Michigan State University Press.

Quispe Escobar, A. (2007). La imposibilidad mestiza en La nación clandestina. Construcciones emblemáticas en el cine de Jorge Sanjinés. *Punto Cero*, 12(15), 51–8.

Rabasa J. (1993). *Inventing America: Spanish Historiography and the Formation of Eurocentrism*. Norman: University of Oklahoma Press.

Ramírez Berg, C. (1992). *Cinema of Solitude: A Critical Study of Mexican Film, 1967–1983*. Austin: University of Texas Press.

Ramírez Berg, C. (2002). *Latino Images in Film: Stereotypes, Subversion, and Resistance*. Austin: University of Texas Press.

Ramírez Berg, C. (2015). *The Classical Mexican Cinema: The Poetics of the Exceptional Golden Age Films*. Austin: University of Texas Press.

Ramos, A. R. (1998). *Indigenism: Ethnic Politics in Brazil*. Madison: University of Wisconsin Press.

Ramos, L. (2012, February 17). Cine puneño: recordando 'El misterio del Kharisiri', de Henry Vallejo. *Cine Encuentro*. Retrieved from: https://www.cinencuentro.com/2012/02/17/cine-puno-peru-recordando-el-misterio-de-kharisiri-henry-vallejo/. Accessed on April 2019.

Randall, R. (2017). *Children on the Threshold in Contemporary Latin American Cinema: Nature, Gender and Agency*. Lanham, MD: Lexington Books.

Rappaport, J. (2014). *The Disappearing Mestizo: Configuring Difference in the Colonial New Kingdom of Granada*. Durham, NC: Duke University Press.

Rasch, E. D. (2008). *Representing Mayas. Indigenous Authorities and the Local Politics of Identity in Guatemala* (Doctoral dissertation). University of Utrecht. Retrieved from: https://www.academia.edu/804607/Representing_Mayas_Indigenous_Authorities_and_the_Local_Politics_of_Identity_in_Guatemala. Accessed on March 2022.

Reyna, R. (2018, May 7). Director de 'Wiñaypacha': 'Esta película nos ha dado una gran lección. Rpp Noticias. Retrieved from: https://rpp.pe/cine/peru/director-de-winaypacha-esta-pelicula-nos-ha-dado-una-gran-leccion-noticia-1121043. Accessed on January 2019.

Richards, K. (2011). *Themes in Latin American Cinema: A Critical Survey*. Jefferson, NC: McFarland.

Ríos Gastelú, M. D. (2006). Cultural: ¿Quién mató a la llamita blanca? *Boliviscopio*. Retrieved from: http://boliviscopio.blogspot.com/2006/09/culturalquin-mat-la-llamita-blanca.html. Accessed on March 2019.

Rist, P. H. (2014). *Historical Dictionary of South American Cinema*. Lanham, MD: Rowman and Littlefield.

Rivera Cusicanqui, S. (2015). *Sociología de la imagen*. Buenos Aires: Tinta Limón.

Roca, P. (2006). Madeinusa o el insulto hecho al cine. *Centro de Medios Independientes*. Retrieved from: http://peru.indymedia.org/news/2006/09/35352.php. Accessed on April 2019.

Rocha, C. and Seminet, G. (Eds.) (2014). *Screening Minors in Latin American Cinema*. Lanham, MD: Lexington Books.

Rodríguez, A. (2011). La trama, la historia y la política en 'El último malo'. *Dossiers Cine y Política*, 8(2), 162–72.

Rodríguez, M. C. (2015). The Island Image and Global Links in Puerto Rican Cinema of the 21st Century. *Imaginations: Journal of Cross-Cultural Image Studies*, 6(2), 26–35.

Rony, F. T. (1996). *The Third Eye: Race, Cinema, and Ethnographic Spectacle*. Durham, NC: Duke University Press.

Ross, M. (2010). *South American Cinematic Culture: Policy, Production, Distribution and Exhibition*. Cambridge: Cambridge Scholars Publishing.

Ross, M. (2011). The Film Festival as Producer: Latin American Films and Rotterdam's Hubert Bals Fund. *Screen*, 52(2), 261–7.

Rossi, J. J. (1987). *El cine documental etnobiográfico de Jorge Preloran*. Buenos Aires: Ediciones Búsqueda.

Rubiés, J. P. (2009). Texts, Images, and the Perception of 'Savages' in Early Modern Europe: What We Can Learn from White and Harriot. In K. Sloan (Ed.), *European Visions: American Voices* (pp. 120–1300). London: The British Museum.

Rueda, A., Vargas, F., and Saint-Dizier, A. (2006). Encuentro con Francisco Vargas. *Cinémas d'Amérique Latine*, 14, 166–75.

Saiz, J. L., Rapimán, M. E. and Mladinic, A. (2008). Estereotipos sobre los mapuches: Su reciente evolución. *Psykhe*, 17(2), 27–40.

Salas Zamudio, S., and Atilano-Villegas, R. Y. (2020). Fotografía Porfiriana: La intencionalidad y la mirada en la revista El Mundo Ilustrado. *MAGOTZI Boletín Científico de Artes del IA*, 8(15), 63–70.

Salinas, P. (2016). El mar en la representación cinematográfica de la migración interna en el Perú: de Gregeorio a La teta asustada. *Confluencia*, 31(2), 113–27.

Sánchez, J. (2011). La primera visión europea estética de los indoamericanos en la invasión de América. *Anuario Americanista Europeo*, 9, 81–99.

Sánchez, A. P. (2018). Cómo descubrió Alfonso Cuarón a Yalitza Aparicio para Roma. *Vogue*. Retrieved from: https://www.vogue.mx/agenda/cultura/articulos/yalitza-aparicio-roma-alfonso-cuaron/14111. Accessed on April 2019.

Sánchez, H. J. (1999). *The Art and Politics of Bolivian Cinema*. Lanham, MD: Scarecrow.

Sánchez Cruz, J. (2018). *Subcultural Politics: Sexual Dissidence, Sickness and Subversion in Chile and Mexico, 1986–2013*. University of California Riverside. Retrieved from: https://escholarship.org/uc/item/6dd5q3kj. Accessed on December 2021.

Sandoval García, C. (2002). *Otros amenazantes: los nicaragüenses y la formación de identidades nacionales en Costa Rica*. San José: Editorial Universidad de Costa Rica.

Schiwy, F. (2009). *Indianizing Film: Decolonization, the Andes, and the Question of Technology*. New Brunswick, NJ: Rutgers University Press.

Schmorak Leijnse, A. (2009). Esteban Larraín – Alicia en el País. *Cineciritc.biz*. Retrieved from: http://www.v2016.cinecritic.biz/index.php/es/entrevista/19-categorie-es-es/entrevistas/122-abril-mayo-2009-entrevista-a-esteban-larrain-alicia-en-el-pais. Accessed on February 2019.

Schneider, A. (2007). *Appropriation as Practice: Art and Identity in Argentina*. New York: Palgrave Macmillan.

Schneider, D. J. (2005). *The Psychology of Stereotyping*. New York: Guildford Press.

Schroeder Rodríguez, P. A. (2016). *Latin American Cinema: A Comparative History*. Los Angeles: University of California Press.

Schwaller, R. (2016). *Géneros de Gente in Early Colonial Mexico: Defining Racial Difference*. Norman: University of Oklahoma Press.

Segalen, V. (1999). *Essai sur l'Exotisme*, 1978. Paris: Gallimard.

Segato, R. L. (2007). *La nación y sus otros: raza, etnicidad y diversidad religiosa en tiempos de políticas de la identidad*. Buenos Aires: Prometeo Libros Editorial.

Seggiaro, D. (2012, February 7). 'Una historia real sobre la cultura wichí competirá en el Festival de Berlín.' Interview by Agency Télam. *Clarín*. Retrieved from: https://www.clarin.com/cine/nosilatiaj-la-belleza-festival-de-berlin_0_SJuWhqvnvQx.html. Accessed on December 2018.

Shaw, D. (2003). *Contemporary Cinema of Latin America: Ten Key Films*. New York: Continuum.

Shaw, D. (2007). *Contemporary Latin American Cinema: Breaking into the Global Market*. London: Rowman and Littlefield.

Shaw, D. (2011). Babel and the Global Hollywood Gaze. *Situations*, 4(1), 11–31.

Shaw, D. (2014). Fonds de finnancement Europeens et cinema Latino-Americain: alterisation et cinephilie bourgeoise dans *La Teta asustada* de Claudia Llosa. *Diogène*, 245, 125–41.

Shaw, D. (2017). Intimacy and Distance – Domestic Servants in Latin American Women's Cinema: *La mujer sin cabeza* and *El niño pez*. In D. Martin and D. Shaw (Eds), *Latin American Women Filmmakers: Production, Politics, Poetics. World Cinema* (pp. 123–48). London: I.B. Tauris.

Sherman, S. R. (1998). *Documenting Ourselves: Film, Video, and Culture*. Lexington: University of Kentucky.

Shohat, E., and Stam, R. (2012). *Race in Translation: Culture Wars around the Postcolonial Atlantic*. New York: New York University Press.

Shohat, E., and Stam, R. (2014). *Unthinking Eurocentrism: Multiculturalism and the Media*. New York: Routledge.

Signorelli Heise, T. (2012). *Remaking Brazil: Contested National Identities in Contemporary Brazilian Cinema*. Cardiff: University of Wales Press.

Smedley, A., and Smedley, B. D. (2005). Race as Biology Is Fiction, Racism as a Social Problem Is Real: Anthropological and Historical Perspectives on the Social Construction of Race. *American Psychologist*, 60(1), 16–26.

Solanas, F., and Getino, O. (1970). Toward a Third Cinema. *Cineaste*, 4(3), 1–10.

Solano Acuña, A. S. (2013). Percepciones y actitudes de la población costarricense hacia la población indígena costaricense [sic. costarricense]. https://repositorio.una.ac.cr/bitstream/handle/11056/7328/Percepciones%20y%20actitudes%20de%20la%20poblaci%c3%b3n%20costarricense%20hacia%20la%20poblaci%c3%b3n%20ind%c3%adgena%20costaricense%20%5bsic.%20costarricense%5d-Pulso58.pdf?sequence=1&isAllowed=y. Accessed on April 2019.

Soledad Paz-Mackay M., and Rodriguez O. (Eds) (2019). *Politics of Children in Latin American Cinema*. Lanham, MD: Lexington Books.

Spivak, G. C. (1988). Can the Subaltern speak? In C. Nelson and L. Grossberg (Eds), *Marxism and the Interpretation of Culture* (pp. 271–313). Urbana: University of Illinois Press.

Spivak, G. C. (2006). *In Other Worlds: Essays in Cultural Politics*. London: Routledge.

Stabb, M. (1959). Indigenism and Racism in Mexican Thought: 1858–1911. *Journal of Inter-American Studies*, 1(4), 405–23.

Staiger, J. (2003). The Practices of Authorship. In D. Gerstner and J. Staiger (Eds), *Authorship and Film* (pp. 27–60). New York: Routledge.

Stam, R. (1997). *Tropical Multiculturalism: A Comparative History of Race in Brazilian Cinema and Culture*. Durham, NC: Duke University Press.

Stam, R., and Spence, L. (1983). Colonialism, Racism and Representation. *Screen*, 24(2), 2–20.

Standish, P., and Bell, S. (2004). *Culture and Customs of Mexico*. Westport, CT: Greenwood.

Steagall, L. (2009). Arts Innovator: Rodrigo Bellot, Bolivia. *Quarterly Americas*. Retrieved from: http://www.americasquarterly.org/rodrigo-bellot-bolivian-filmmaker. Accessed on April 2019.

Stemplowski, R. (2009). *On the State of Latin American States: Approaching the Bicentenary*. Krakow: Krakowskie Towarzystwo Eduk.

Suárez, J. (2014). Le déclin du mélodrame: les cinéastes contemporaines et la transformation du genre. *Cinémas d'Amérique latine*, 22, 114–27.

Tacca, F. de (1999). A imagem do índio entegrado/civilizado na filmografia de Luiz Thomas Reis. *Resgate: Revista de Cultura*, 8(1), 19–44.

Tarica, E. (2008). *The Inner Life of Mestizo Nationalism*. Minneapolis: University of Minnesota Press.

Taylor, A. (2009). *Indigeneity in the Mexican Cultural Imagination Thresholds of Belonging*. Tucson: University of Arizona Press.

Thornley, D. (2017). ImagineNATIVE Film + Media Arts Festival: Colaborative Criticism through Curatorship. In S. Tascón and T. Wils (Eds), *Activist Film Festivals: Towards a Political Subject* (pp. 199–213). Bristol: Intellect.

Tierney, D. (2007). *Emilio Fernández: Pictures in the Margins*. Manchester: Manchester University Press.

Tompkins, C. M. (2018). *Affectual Erasure: Representations of Indigenous Peoples in Argentine Cinema*. Albany: State University of New York Press.

Tsang, J. (2018, April 9). 'Wiñaypacha': Una cámara entre el cielo y la tierra. *El Comercio*. Retrieved from: https://elcomercio.pe/luces/cine/impreso-winaypacha-cine-peruan o-aimara-camara-cielo-tierra-noticia-510652. Accessed on October 2021.

United Nations (2021). *Permanent Forum on Indigenous Issues*.

Urban, W. M. (2004). *Language and Reality: The Philosophy of Language and the Principles of Symbolism*. New York: Routledge.

Urry, J. (2002). *The Tourist Gaze*, 2nd edn. London: Sage.

van Groesen, M. (2008). *The Representations of the Overseas World in the De Bry Collection of Voyages (1590–1634)*. Boston: Leiden.

Varas, P., and Dash, R. (2000). (Re)imaginando la nación argentina: Lucrecia Martel y La ciénaga. In V. Rangil (Ed.), *El cine argentino de hoy: Entre el arte y la política* (pp. 191–208). Buenos Aires: Biblos.

Vega, W. (2012). La Sirga – Detrás de Cámaras de Dirección. Retrieved from: https://www.youtube.com/watch?v=NSYLXYWFk5Y. Accessed on October 2021.

Villazana, L. (2008). Hegemony Conditions in the Coproduction Cinema of Latin America: The Role of Spain. *Framework*, 49, 65–85.

Villazón, F. V. (2010). *Wara Wara: La Reconstrucción de una película pérdida*. La Paz: Plural, Cinemateca Boliviana y CAF.

Virdi, J. (2003). *The Cinematic ImagiNation* [sic]: *Indian Popular Films as Social History*. New Brunswick, NJ: Rutgers University Press.

Vogue Mexico (2018). Mexico City: Condé Nast.

Wade, P. (2005). Rethinking Mestizaje: Ideology and Lived Experience. *Journal of Latin American Studies*, 37(2), 239–57.

Wernitznig, D. (2003). *Going Native or Going Naïve? White Shamanism and the Neo-Noble Savage*. Lanham, MD: University Press of America.

Wernitznig, D. (2007). *Europe's Indians, Indians in Europe*. Plymouth: University Press of America.

Wieczorek, A. E. (2014). *Clusivity: A New Approach to Association and Dissociation in Political Discourse*. Newcastle upon Tyne: Cambridge Scholars Publishing.

Wilson, P., and Stewart, M. (2008). *Global Indigenous Media: Cultures, Poetics, and Politics*. Durham, NC: Duke University Press.

Wilt, D. E. (2004). *The Mexican Filmography: 1916 through 2001*. Jefferson, NC: McFarland.

Wood, D. (2006). Indigenismo and the Avant-Garde: Jorge Sanjinés' Early Films and the National Project. *Bulletin of Latin American Research*, 25(1), 63–82.

World Bank Group (2019). https://www.worldbank.org/en/home. Accessed on October 2021.

Xinico Batz, S. (2016, September 17, 24 and October 1). Kemonïk ch'ab'äl/Tejer voces. El síndrome de Ixcanul: ¿Entre realidad y película? Parts I, II and III. *La Hora*. Retrieved from: http://lahora.gt/sindrome-ixcanul-realidad-pelicula-parte-i. Accessed on September 2021.

Young, L. (1996). *Fear of the Dark: 'Race', Gender and Sexuality in the Cinema*. New York: Routledge.

Young, R., and Cisneros, O. (2011). *Historical Dictionary of Latin American Literature and Theater*. Lanham, MD: Scarecrow.

Zamorano Villarreal, G. (2014). Crafting Contemporary Indigeneity through Audiovisual Media in Bolivia. In H. Gilbert and C. Gleghorn (Eds), *Recasting Commodity and Spectacle in the Indigenous Americas* (pp. 77–95). London: School of Advanced Study, University of London.

Zavala, A. L. R. (2011). INDIO/INDÍGENA, 1750–1850. *Historia Mexicana*, 60(3(239)), 1643–81.

Ziyasheva, D. (2015). Director's Statement. *World Film Presentation*. Retrieved from: http://worldfilmpresentation.com/. Accessed on September 2021.

Zuluaga, P. A. (2012). A propósito de La Sirga, película de William Vega: Noche y niebla. *Razonpublica.com*. Retrieved from: https://www.razonpublica.com/index.php/cultura/3247-a-proposito-de-la-sirga-pelicula-de-william-vega-noche-y-niebla.html. Accessed on July 2021.

Zuluaga, P. A. (Interviewer) and Guerra, C. (Interviewee) (2015). *Tenemos que hablar*. Retrieved from: https://www.youtube.com/watch?v=jKUAHsIPqW8. Accessed on March 2019.

Zuluaga, P. A., and Muñoz, G. (2018). Contemporary Colombian Cinema: The Splintered Mirror of a Country. *Icónica* (December 17, 2018). http://revistaiconica.com/cine-colombiano-contemporaneo-el-espejo-astillado-de-un-pais/. Accessed on April 2019.

Filmography

Aguilar de la Cruz L. (Producer) and Huertas Pérez, J. G. (Director) (2003). *Nakaq* [Motion picture]. Peru: Luis Aguilar de la Cruz.

Alcove Entertainment (Producer) and Cárdenas, I. and Guzmán, L. A. (Directors) (2007). *Cochochi* [Motion picture]. Mexico-Canada: Buena Onda Pictures.

Alcove Entertainment (Producer) and Cárdenas, I. and Guzmán, L. A. (Directors) (2007). *Cochochi* [Motion picture]. Mexico-Canada: Buena Onda Pictures.

Almodóvar, A., Almodóvar, P., Corsi, T., Cura, V., García, E., Martel, L., Petrillo, C., Piñeyro, E., Razzini, V. and Slot, M. (Producers) and Martel, L. (Director) (2008). *La mujer sin cabeza* [Motion picture]. Argentina-France-Italy-Spain: Aquafilms-El Deseo-RandC-Slot Machine.

Alomoto C. A. (Producer and Director) (2012). *Chiqui Pichay – Wayrachirina* (La Limpia) [Documentary]. Ecuador.

Amador, F. (Producer) and Solar del, S. (Director) (2015). *Magallanes* [Motion picture]. Peru-Spain: CEPA-Nephilim-Proyectil-Tondero.

Angueira, M. (Producer and Director) (2011). *Inacayal* [Motion Picture]. Argentina: INCAA.

Antezana, T., Ranvaud, D., Rodas, H. and Sardi, S. (Producers) and Antezana, T. (Director) (2007). *Evo Pueblo* [Motion picture]. Bolivia: Prodecine and Silvio Sardo Communications.

Anteza, T., Ranvaud, D., Rodas, H. and Sardi, S. (Producers) and Antezana, T. (Director) (2007). *Evo Pueblo* [Motion picture]. Bolivia: Buena Onda.

Apurimac Films (Producer) and Huamán Berrocal, J. (Director) (2011). *El destino de los pobres* [Motion picture]. Peru: Apurimac Films.

Aridjis, E. (Producer and Director) (2012). *Los ojos azules* [Motion picture]. Mexico: Producciones Noche Oscura.

Aronson, L., Tenenbaum, S. and Wiley, G. (Producers) and Allen, W. (Director) (2008). *Vicky Cristina Barcelona* [Motion Picture]. United States-Spain: The Weinstein Company, Mediapro, Gravier, Antena 3 and TV3.

Arnillas, L., Meier, E. and Vallve, E. (Producers) and Figueroa, L., Nishiyama, E. and Villanueva, C. (Directors). *Kukuli* [Motion Picture]. Peru: Kero Films.

Asociación Civil Yakarí and Alfarería Cinematográfica (Producers) and Crespo, M. (Director) (2015). *Dauna: Lo que lleva el río* [Motion picture]. Venezuela: Cines Unidos.

Attar, N., Cordova, P. and Gosalvez, P. (Producers) and Cordova, P. (Director) (2011). *Erase una vez en Bolivia* [Motion picture]. Bolivia: Cine Artesanal-Pucara Films.

Ávila H., R. (Producer) and Toro, F. (Director) (2010). *Könun Wenu* [Motion picture]. Chile. Imaginaria audiovisual.

Barata Ribeiro, A., Berlinck, B. and Meirelles, F. (Producers) and Hamburger, C. (Director) (2012). *Xingu* [Motion picture]. Brazil: Globo Filmes-O2 Filmes.

Bautista García, A., Figueroa García, D. and Mueller, M. (Producers) and Jansen, I. (Director) (2018). *Tiempo de lluvia* [Motion picture]. Mexico: Lista Calista Films and Fidelio.

Berman, S. (Producer) and Carrera, C. (Director) (2009). *El traspatio* [Motion picture]. Mexico: Berman-BURSA.

Brevis, G. (Producer and Director) (2009). *Aniceto. Razón de estado* [Documentary]. Chile.

Briones, I., León, M. and White, M. J. (Producers) and León, M. (Director) (2019). *Canción sin nombre* [Motion picture]. Peru: La Vida Misma Films, La Mula Producciones, Bord Cadre Films, Mgc Marketing and Torch Films.

Bustamante, D. and Ruiz, O. (Producers) and Vega, W. (Director) (2012). *La Sirga* [Motion picture]. Colombia-Mexico-Argentina: Contravía Films.

Bustamante, D. and Gallego, C. (Producers) and Guerra, C. (Director) (2009). *Los viajes del viento* [Motion picture]. Colombia-Germany-Argentina-The Netherlands: Ciudad Lunar-WCF-ZDF-Arte-Razor Films.

Bustamante, J. and Matheu, G. (Producers) and Bustamante, J. (Director) (2019). *La Llorona* [Motion picture]. Guatemala: Ministerio de Cultura y Deportes de Guatemala, La Casa de Production and Les Films du Volcan.

Caballero, S. J. (Producer and Director) (2011). *Justicia sin palabra* (Mute justice) [Short film]. Mexico: Ojo de Agua Comunication.

Caballero, T. E. (Producer and Director) (2013). *Atempa* (Sueños a orilla del rio) [Documentary]. Mexico: Infraterra productions.

Cáceres Saravia, J. (Producer and Director) (2010). *La leyenda del Ekeko* [Motion picture]. Peru: Peligro Producciones.

Cadenas, M. (Producer and Director) (2011). *Cenizas eternas* [Motion picture]. Venezuela: Antoni Films.

Calasich (Producer and Director) (2007). *Las bicicletas de los Huanca* [Motion picture]. Bolivia: Calasich Producciones.

Camacho W. (Producer) and Moya, D. (Director) (2009). *Si acaso en Chuquiago* [Short film]. Bolivia: Tribú Cines.

Camacho, M. (Producer and Director) (2015). *Illa* [Motion picture]. Bolivia: M. Camacho.

Campos, E. (Producer) and Delgado, A. (Director) (2017). *Retablo* [Motion picture]. Peru: Sexto Sentido.

Campos, E. (Producer) and Pérez, E. (Director) (2014). *Climas* [Motion picture]. Peru: Siri Producciones.

Canchari, Q. A. (Producer and Director) (2015). *Varayuqkuna* (Ancestral Authority) [Documentary]. Peru.

Canchari, Q. A. (Producer and Director) (2014). *Minkakuy* (Collective work) [Documentary]. Peru.

Carreras, L. and Ovando, L. (Producers) and Cruz, A. (Director) (2021). *Nudo mixteco* [Motion picture]. Mexico: Madrecine.

Casas, A. (Producer) and Pérez Solano, J. (Director) (2008). *Espiral* [Motion picture]. Mexico: CUEC-Foprocine-Imcine.

Castro, Á., Rodríguez, H. and Vargas, F. (Producer) and Vargas, F. (Director) (2005). *El Violín* [Motion picture]. Mexico: Camara Carnal-Fidecine.

Castro, H., Alvarez, C. (Producer) and Franco, S. (Director) (2012). *Tiempos menos modernos* [Motion picture]. Argentina-Chile: Cine-Ceneca-INCAA.

Catacora, T. (Producer) and Catacora, O. (Director) (2017). *Wiñaypacha* [Motion picture]. Peru: Cine Aymara Studios.

Chavarrías, A., Llosa, C. and Morales, J. M. (Producers) and Llosa, C. (Director) (2009). *La teta asustada* [Motion picture]. Peru-Spain: Oberón-TV3-TVE-Wanda Visión.

Chavarrías, A., Llosa, C. and Morales, J. M. (Producers) and Llosa, C. (Director) (2005). *Madeinusa* [Motion picture]. Peru-Spain: Oberón-Vela Producciones.

Cicerol, M. and Martínez Arredondo C. (1910). *El suplicio de Cuauhtémoc* [Short]. Mexico.

Cine Experimental Ayacucho (Producer and Director) (2008). *Frágil* [Motion picture]. Peru: Cine Experimental Ayacucho.

Cineminga collective (Producers and directors)(2010). *Jiisa weçe* [Short]. Colombia: Cineminga Collective.

Colectivo Cineminga (Producer and Director) (2010). *Jiisa Weçe (Roots of Knowledge* [Documentary]. Colombia: Cineminga.

Comenzana, I., Santana, A., Pace, J. and Agazzi, P. (Producers) and Gil, M. (Director) (2011). *Blackthorn* [Motion picture]. Spain-Bolivia-France-United Kingdom: Eter Pictures, Nix Films and Manto Films.

Connelly, C., Fischer, D., Fishwick, P. J. and Holland, M. (Producers) and Hyde, J. (Director) (2010). *Postcards* [Motion Picture]. United States-Peru: Lofu Productions.

Contreras Matias, J. (Producer and Director) (2007). *Sin sentimiento* [Motion picture]. Peru: Zankay Producciones.

Coppola, S. and Katz, R.(Producer) and Coppola, S. (2003). *Lost in Translation*. [Motion picture]. United States-Japan: Focus Features, Tohokushinsha Film Corporation and American Zoetrope.

Coria, J. F. and de Lara, M. C. (Producer) and Cecchetti, F. (Director) (2016). *El sueño del Mara'akame* [Motion picture]. Mexico: CUEC/IMCINE.

Cox, M. (Producer) and Gamboa Martínez, J. A. (Director) (2003). *Pishtaco* [Motion picture]. Peru: Magnum Producciones.

Crespo, M. and Lorenz I. (Producers) and Crespo, M. (Director) (2015). *Dauna: Lo que lleva el río* [Motion picture]. Venezuela: Asociación Civil Yakarí and Alfarería Cinematográfica.

Cruz, R., Solórzano, J. and Sánchez, J. (Producer) and Echevarría, N.(Director) (1991). *Cabeza de Vaca* [Motion Picture]. Mexico: Coproducción México-España, IMCINE and RTVE.

Cuarón, A., and Celis, N. (Producers) and Cuarón, A. (Director) (2018). *Roma* [Motion picture]. Mexico: Esperanto Filmoj.

Davey, B., Gibson, M. and Miranda, S. (Producers) and Gibson, M. (Director) (2006). *Apocalypto* [Motion picture]. United States: Icon Productions, Mayan Ruins and Touchstone Pictures.

De Morais, A. A. (Producer) and Andrade, S. and Baldo, F. (Directors) (2016). *Antes o Tempo Não Acabava* [Motion picture]. Brazil: Rio Tarumã Films.

Deckert, H. (Producer) and Brosens, P. and Woodworth, J. (Directors) (2009). *Altiplano* [Motion picture]. Belgium-Peru: Filmfreak.

Disse, I. (Producer and Director) (2010). *Siguiendo las estrellas* [Motion picture]. Panama-Ecuador: Pinima Films-La Mirona.

Domenech, B., Gallelli, S. and Catani, V. (Producers) and Martel, L. (Director) (2017). *Zama* [Motion picture]. Argentina: Rei Cine-Bananeira Filmes.

Domingo, P. (Producer) and Carrasco, S.(Director) (1998). *La otra conquista* [Motion Picture]. Mexico: Carrasco & Domingo Films and Conaculta.

Eguino, A. (Producer and Director) (2007). *Los Andes no creen en Dios* [Motion picture]. Bolivia: Cinema Ventura and Ibermedia.

Enginger, F. (Producer) and Dutilleux, J. P. (Director) (2004). *Amazon Forever* [Motion picture]. France: Gentleman Films, Skylight Produções and Gentleman Film.

Enriquez, B. (Producer) and Contreras, E. (Director) (2017). *Sueño en otro idioma* [Motion picture]. Mexico: Alebrije Cine y Video.

Epieyu, A. (Producer and Director) (2014). *Wachikua: Nuestra Historia* [Documentary]. Colombia.

Erbs, S. (Producer) and Said, M. (Director) (2013). *El verano de los peces voladores* [Motion picture]. Chile: Jirafa.

Escobar, M. (Producer) and Uriana L. (Director) (2012). *Jukua'ipamajatü wayuu (Asuntos Indigenas)* [Documentary]. Venezuela.

Escriba Palomino, N. (Producer and Director) (2011). *Jarjacha vs. Pishtaco: La batalla final* [Motion picture]. Peru.

Escuela de comunicación propia Putumayo (Producer and Director) (2012). *Ga´tëya sziaya co´ca, kudumani kat jainui huai, dachi druade embera bedea banduvada ñucata allpa yacuta micham, atun llagta putumayo alpa iakup ri*mai (Palabras de Agua) [Documentary]. Colombia.

Espinoza, M. (Producer and Director) (2011). *Mari Mari* [Short film]. Chile: Complot Estudio Creativo.

Estévez, M. (Producer and Director) (2013). *Hidrofractura: El agua, el aire, la tierra ... la muerte* [Documentary]. Argentina: TVC Neuquén SOTERMUN- Spain: Unión Sindical Obrera (USO).

Fernandez, P., Villarreal, J. and Montenegro, P. (Producers) and Estévez, M. (Director) (2012). *Hidrofractura: El agua, el aire, la tierra ... la muerte*. [Documentary] Argentina: Asociación Trabajadores del Estado.

Figueira, E. and Filho, R. (Producers) and Arraes, G. (Director) (2001). *Caramuru* [Motion picture]. Brazil: Sony Pictures.

Films colonial (Producer) and González, C. E., Ramos, J. M. and Sayago, F. (Directors) (1917). *El milagro de Tepeyac* [Motion picture]. Mexico: Films Colonial.

Fink, A. J. (Producer) and Fernández, E. (1943). *María Candelaria* [Motion picture]. Mexico: Films Mundiales.

Galiano, R., Guanes, C., Ramirez Jou, M. V. and Schémbori, T. (as Schembori T.) (Producers) and Maneglia, J. C. and Schémbori, T. (Directors) (2012). *7 Cajas*. [Motion picture]. Paraguay: Maneglia Schémbori Realizadores and Synchro Image.

Gallego, C. (Producer) and Gallego, C. and Guerra, C. (Directors) (2015). *El abrazo de la serpiente* [Motion picture]. Colombia-Venezuela-Argentina: Buffalo Films.

Gallego, C. (Producer), Guerra, C. (Director) and Gallego, C. (Co-director) (2018). *Pájaros de verano* [Motion picture]. Colombia-Denmark- Mexico: Blond Indian Films.

Gandara, S., Lopez, M. and Trafford, N. (Producers) and Scherson, A. (Director) (2005). *Play* [Motion picture]. Chile: Parox -Morocha Films-Paraiso Productions.

García, H. J. (Producer and Director) (2000). *Pewma jadkulu* (El conflicto en el sueño Mapuche) [Documentary].Chile.

García, J. J. (Producer) and Cabllero, S. J. (Director) (2012). *Por la tierra vivimos* (We live for the land) [Short film]. Mexico.

Gibson, M., and Davey, B. (Producers) and Gibson, M. (Director) (2006). *Apocalypto* [Motion picture]. United States: Touchstone Pictures.

Gil, N. S. (Producer and Director) (2012). *Zhamayama: Nuestra música* [Documentary]. Colombia.

Gómez, M. F. (Producer and Director) (2004). *Dulce convivencia* (Sweet gathering) [Documentary]. Mexico.

Gonzalez, E. (Producer) and Gonzáles, Ó. (Director) (2009). *Marcados por el destino* [Motion Picture]. Peru: Expresión 7 Cines Andes and Aborigen Producciones.

Gonzalez Rubio, P., and Romandia, J. (Producers) and Gonzalez-Rubio, P. (Director). (2009). *Alamar* [Motion picture]. Mexico: Lumiere.

Gordon, J. (Producer) and Bollaín, I. (Director) (2010). *También la Lluvia* [Motion picture]. Spain-France-Mexico: TVE-AXN-Canal+-Eurimages-Natixis Coficiné-ICAA.

Greene Flaten, P. and Tejos Martignoni, M. (Producers) and Huaiquimilla, C. (Director) (2021). *Mis hermanos sueñan despiertos* [Motion picture]. Chile: Lanza Verde and Inefable.

Grupo Ukamau (Producers) and Sanjinés, J. (Director) (1969). *El enemigo principal/ Jatun auka* [Motion picture]. Bolivia: Ukamau.

Grupo Ukamau (Producers) and Sanjinés, J. (Director) (1977). *Fuera de aquí/Llosky Kaymanta* [Motion picture]. Bolivia: Ukamau, Departamento de Cine de la Universidad de Los Andes and Universidad Central del Ecuador.

Gualinga, E. (Producer and Director) (2012). *Puma chirikuna (Los descendientes del Jaguar)* [Documentary]. Ecuador.

Guévara Torres, G. (Producer and Director) (2002). *Vicio maldito* [Motion picture]. Peru: Del Carmen Productions.

Gutiérrez, C., Pérez Solano, J. and Ramirez, T. (Producers) and Pérez Solano, J. (Director) (2014). *La Tirisia* [Motion picture]. Mexico: Tirisia Cine.

Gutiérrez Vega. P. (Director) (2013). *La flor que vive* [Short film]. Peru.

Gutiérrez Vega, P. and Chirapaq (Producers) and Gutiérrez Vega, P. (Director) (2015). *La flor que vive* [Short]. Peru: Chirapaq and Wapikoni Mobile.

Gutierrez, Z. F. (Producer and Director) (2014). *Cholitas con fútbol de altura* [Documentary]. Bolivia: CEFREC- Telesur D.R.

Hermida, T., Iglesias, G. and Palacios, M. (Producers) and Hermida, T, (Director) (2006). *Qué tan lejos* [Motion picture]. Ecuador: Corporación Ecuador para Largo.

Hermida, T. and Palacios, M. (Producer) and Hermida, T. (Director) (2011). *En el nombre de la hija* [Motion picture]. Ecuador: Corporación Ecuador para Largo.

Huamán Berrocal, J. (Producer and Director) (2011). *El destino de los pobres* [Motion picture]. Peru.

Huanca, H. O. (Producer and Director) (2013). *Ayni, un viaje al futuro* [Documentary]. Bolivia.

Hughan, I., Sabaté, S. and Slot, M. (Producers) and Encina, P. (Director) (2000). *Hamaca Paraguaya* [Motion picture]. Paraguay-Argentina-The Netherlands-France-Austria: Arte-Fortuna Films-Silencio Cine.

Inga Huamán, N. (Producer and Director) (2005). *Sangre y traición* [Motion picture]. Peru.

Jaguar, X. (Producer and Director) (2008). *El mito del tiempo* [Motion picture]. Guatemala-Mexico: Scorpion H.

Jonsson, A. (Producer and Director) (2016). *La carga* [Motion picture]. Mexico: Esfera Films.

Kamikia, K., Suya K., Suya W. and Suya K. (Producers and Directors) (2012). *Txejkho Kham Mby* (Warsome Women) [Documentary]. Brazil.

Komori, K. (Producer) and Matsushita, T. (Director) (2008). *The Gift of Pachamama* [Motion Picture]. Japan-Bolivia: Dolphin Productions.

Lanza, R., Moreno, A. and Ranvaus, D. (Producers) and Bellott, R. (Director) (2007). *¿Quién mató a la llamita blanca?* [Motion picture]. Bolivia: Buena Ona.

Larico F. (Producer and Director) (2004). *Triste realidad* [Motion picture]. Peru: Wary TV Producciones.

Larraín, J. d. D. (Producer) and Sepúlveda, S. (Director) (2013). *Las niñas Quispe* [Motion picture]. Chile: Fabula Productions.

Layers, T. (Producer) and Van den Berghe, G. (Director) (2014). *Lucifer* [Motion Picture]. Belgium-Mexico: Minds Meet and Mollywood.

Leon, E. (Producer) and Liza Alauie, O. (Director) (2013). *Trampas de tu lado oscuro* [Motion picture]. Peru: Audiofama Producciones.

Limberger, V., and Rovai, P. C. (Producer) and Svartman, R. (Director) (2000). *Tainá: A Origem* [Motion picture]. Brazil: Globo Filmes-Tietê Produções-Teleimage.

Loayza A. and Loayza D. (Producers and Directors) (2005). *El plan Papanoeal* [Motion picture]. Bolivia.

Lopez, B. (Producer and Director) (2005). *Taínos: La última tribu* [Motion picture]. Puerto Rico: Innova Entertainment.

López, T. W. (Producer and Director) (2013). *El día de las com*adres [Short film]. Argentina: Itín Productions.

Maire, G. (Producer) and Valdivia, J. C. (Director) (2009). *Zona Sur* [Motion picture]. Bolivia: Cinenómada.

Manzano, A. and Molina, C. (Producers) and Mondaca, D. (Director) (2020). *Chaco* [Motion picture]. Bolivia: Murillo Cine, Color Monster and Pasto.

Marcondes, M. A. and Rovai, P. (Producers) and Lamarca, T. and Bloch, S. (Directors) (2000). *Tainá – Uma Aventura na Amazônia*. Brazil: Tietê Produções.

Maire, G. (Producer) and Valdivia, J. C. (Director) (2009). *Zona Sur* [Motion picture]. Bolivia: Cinenómada.

Martínez Arredondo, C. (Producer and Director) (1914). *La voz de su raza* [Short]. Mexico.

Maxakali, I. (Producer and Director) (2012). *Kotkuphi* [Documentary]. Brazil: Pajé Films.

Méndez, J., and Campos, E. (Producers) and Méndez, J. (Director) (2008). *Dioses* [Motion picture]. Peru: Global Lens.

Mérida Coimbra, L. (Producer and Director) (2012). *Manuelas, heroínas de la Coronilla* [Motion picture]. Bolivia: Wallparrimachi Producciones.

Milchan, A., Smith, I. and Watson, E. (Producers) and Aronofsky, D. (Director) (2006). *The Fountain* [Motion picture]. United States: Regency Enterprises, Protozoa Pictures and Foy Inc.

Montahuano, Y., and Santi, R. (Producers) Montahuano, Y. and Castro, S. (Directors) (2019). *Vestimenta Sapara: Una tradición en peligro* [Documentary]. Ecuador: Tawna Films.

Morales, H. (Producer and Director) (2008). *Cuando te vuelva a ver* [Short Film]. Ecuador.

Morales, J. M. (Producer) and Puenzo, L. (Director) (2009). *El niño pez* [Motion picture]. Argentina-Paraguay: Wolfe Video.

Morales, J. M., Sikojev, A. and Tasioulis, S. (Producers) and Olivares G. (Director) (2006). *La Gran Final* [Motion Picture]. Spain-Germany: Wanda Films and Greenlight Media AG.

Moreira, J. P. (Producer and Director) (2014). *Saraguro* [Motion picture]. Ecuador: HandH.

Muenala, A. (Producer) and Cabascango D. (Director) (2011). *Apaylla* [Short film]. Ecuador.

Muenala, F. (Producer and Director) (2011). *Ella* [Short film]. Ecuador.

Muenala, W. (Producer) and Conejo N. (Director) (2008). *Malki* [Documentary]. Ecuador.

Muniz Wanderley, O. (Producer and Director) (2020). *Equilíbrio* [Short docufilm]. Brazil: Yawar.

Murat, L., and Aché, C. (Producers) and Murat, L. (Director) (2001). *Brava gente brasileira* [Motion picture]. Brazil: Europa.

Navas, W. (Producer) and Mora Catlett, J. (Director) (2006). *Erendira Ikikunari* [Motion picture]. Mexico: Eréndira Producciones.

Negrón, C. (Producer) and Tamayo, A. (Director) (2001). *Bien esquivo* [Motion picture]. Peru-Spain: Argos Producciones.

Nofuentes, I. (Producer) and Bustamante, J. (Director) (2015). *Ixcanul* [Motion picture]. Guatemala-France: La Casa de Producción-Tu Vas Voir Production.

Nozik, M., Tenenbaum, E. and Tenkhoff, K. (Producers) and Salles, W. (Director) (2004). *Diarios de Motocicleta* [Motion picture]. Argentina-Brazil-Chile-France-Germany-Peru-United Kingdom-United States: FilmFour.

Ocularis Films (Producer) and Ocularis, M. R. (Director) (2010). *El regreso de Lencho* [Motion picture]. Guatemala: Ocularis Films.

Ortega Matute, P. (Producer and Director) (2007). *El pecado* [Motion Picture]. Peru: Peru MOvie EIRL and Fox Perú Producciones.

Ortega, P. (Producer and Director) (2013). *El regreso* [Motion picture]. Venezuela: Mandrágora Films.

Pagani, A., Bechis, M., Gullane, F. and Gullane, C. (Producers) and Bechis, M. (Director) (2008). *A terra dos homens vermelhos* [Motion picture]. Brazil-Italy: Homescreen.

Parra, I. (Producer) and Arregui, V. (Director) (2013). *El facilitador* [Motion picture]. Ecuador: Otra Cosa Producciones.

Payá, I. (Produce) and Quemada Diez, D. (Director) (2013). *La Jaula de Oro* [Motion picture]. Mexico-Spain: September Film.

Peña, S. (Producer) and Zorraquin, L. (Director) (2015). *Guaraní* [Motion picture]. Paraguay-Argentina: Pelicano Cine.

Pereira, M. (Producer and Director) (2006). *El destino* [Motion picture]. Argentina: ABS Productions.

Piranha Films (Producer) and Larraín, E. (Director). (2008). *Alicia en el país* [Motion picture]. Chile: Piranha Films.

Polanski, R., Benmussa, R. and Sarde, A..(Producers) and Polanski, R. (Director) (2002). *The Pianist* [Motion Picture]. France-Germany-Poland-United Kingdom: R.P. Productions,Heritage Films,Studio Babelsberg, Runteam, Studio Canal +,Bac Films, Canal + Poland, Telewizja Polska S. A., Agencja Produkcji Filmowej, Filmboard Berlin-Brandenburg (FBB), FilmFernsehFonds Bayern and Filmförderungsanstalt (FFA).

Quispe, F. (Producer and Director) (2009). *El hijo del viento* [Motion Picture]. Peru. F. Quispe.

Rada, R. (Producer) and Sanjinés, J. (Director) (1969). *Yawar Mallku* [Motion Picture]. Bolivia: Ukamau.

Riandee, C., King, T., Dumas, S., Eckstein, P., Escolar and J.L., George, J.(Producers) and Baiz, A., Kubota Wladyka, J., Coimbra, F., Naranjo, G., Navarro, G., Padilha, J. and Ripstein, G. (Directors Producer) (2015). *Narcos* [Television Series]. United States: Dynamo, Gaumont International Television and Netflix.

Rimbach A., and Rimbach H. (Producers) and Kronthaler, T. (Director) (2009). *Escribeme postales a Copacabana* [Motion picture]. Bolivia: Coproducción Bolivia-Alemania and Avista Film.

Rivadeneira, G. (Producer) and Vivanco, J. (Director) (2008). *Sara la espantapájaros* [Motion picture]. Ecuador: Mirarte.

Rovai, P. C. (Producer) and Lima, M. (Director) (2004). *Tainá 2: A aventura Continua* [Motion picture]. Brazil: Globo Filmes-Lereby Productions-Tietê Produções.

Rovai, P. C. (Producer) and Bloch, S. and Lamarca, T. (Director) (2004). *Tainá 2: Uma Aventura na Amazônia* [Motion picture]. Brazil: Marcondes-Tietê Produções Cinematográficas.

Ruddy, A. S. (Producer) and Ford Coppola (Director) (1972). *The Godfather* [Motion picture] United States: Paramount Pictures.

Sabino, O., Menezes, F., Mor, R. and Migliano, M. (producers) and Whinti Suyá, Kambrinti Suya, Yaiku Suya, Kamikia P. T. Kisedje, Kokoyamaratxi Suya (Directors) (2011). *Txêjkhô khâm mby – Mulheres guerreiras* [Short]. Brazil: Aik Produções - Vídeo nas aldeias.

Sala, X. (Producer and Director) (2019). *El ombligo de Guie'dani* [Motion picture]. Mexico: Xavi Sala p.c.

Sanchez, J., and Ehrenberg, M. (Producers) and Valdivia, J. C. (Director) (2013). *Yvy Maraêy: Tierra sin mal* [Motion picture]. Bolivia-Norway: Cinenómada-Río Negro.

Sanchez, M. and Colectivo Igaryala (Producer) and Bollow, V. (Director) (2008). *Burwa dii ebo* [Motion picture]. Panama: Colectivo Igaryala.

Santiago, P. (Producer) and Ramírez, S. (Director) (2011). *Distancia* [Motion picture]. Guatemala: Producciones Concepción.

Sanz Palacios, C. (Producer) and de Oliveira Cézar, I. (Director) (2012). *Cassandra* [Motion picture]. Argentina: Costanza Sanz Palacios Films.

Schmit, D. and Sprimont, G. (Producers) and Diaz, C. (Director) (2019). *Nuestras madres* [Motion picture]. Guatemala: Need Productions, Perspective Films and Proximus.

Secué, H. (Producer and Director) (2012). *¡Y siguen llegando por el oro!* [Documentary]. Colombia: ACIN.

Skartveit, H. L. (Producer) and Araujo, D. (Directors) (2014). *Feriado* [Motion picture]. Ecuador-Argentina: Lunafilm.

Smucler, A. and Bicceci A. G. (Producers) and Bicecci, A. G. (Director) (2009). *Vaho* [Motion picture]. Mexico: Albricias Producción-Global Film Initiative.

Solares, A. (Producer) and Cortés, A. (Director) (2008). *Corazón del Tiempo* [Motion picture]. Mexico: Zalfra Video.

Stantic, L. (Producer) and Martel, L. (Director) (2001). *La Ciénaga* [Motion picture]. Argentina-France-Spain-Japan: 4K-Wanda Visión-Cuatro Cabezas-Ts Productions.

Stantic, L. (Producer) and Martel, L. (Director) (2004). *La niña santa* [Motion picture]. Argentina-Italy-Netherlands-Spain: El Deseo-RandC Produzioni-Hubert Bals.

Universidad del Cine – Centro de Investigación y Formación para la Modalidad Aborigen (Producers) and Lingiardi, S. (Director) (2010). *Las pistas – Lanhoyij – Nmitaxanaxac / The Clues* [Motion picture]. Argentina: Universidad del Cine – Centro de Investigación y Formación para la Modalidad Aborigen.

Urtizberea, A. (Producer) and Seggiaro, D. (Director) (2012). *Nosilatiaj. La belleza* [Motion picture]. Argentina: Vista Sur-Morocha Films-El Campo.

Valdez, M. (Producer) and Urrutia, Ó. (Director) (2000). *Rito Terminal* [Motion picture]. Mexico: UNAM-FOPROCINE-IMCINE.

Vallejo, J. (Producer) and Vallejo Torres, H. (Director) (2004). *El misterio del Kharisiri* [Motion picture]. Peru: Pioneros Producciones.

Verde, L. (Producer) and Huaiquimilla, C. (Director) (2016). *Mala Junta* [Motion picture]. Chile: Alpha Violet.

Yallico, P. and Gómez, R. (Producers and Directors) (2008). *Paktara* (Cuidado) [Short film]. Ecuador.

Zapana, B. (Producer and Director) (2013). *Q'uma chuyma* (Clean Heart) [Documentary]. Bolivia: CEFREC-CAIB.

Ziyasheva, D. (Producer and Director) (2015). *Defensores de la vida* [Motion picture]. Costa Rica: Popcorn and Friends.

Index

1492 (year) 17
1930s 71

A lenda de Ubirajara 82
A terra dos homens vermelhos 11, 110, 113, 167–9, 177, 180, 182, 198
aboriginal 17, 53, 135
academic interest 4, 56–8, 62, 88, 127, 194, 219
accent 24, 120, 124, 130–6, 140–3, 150, 152, 242
adolescence 92, 98, 104, 183, 149
advertisement 22, 151, 155, 248
Afro-descendants 20, 22, 28
agency 39, 67, 101, 111, 138, 159, 184, 221
Aguilar Gil, Yasnaya Elena 1, 17, 42, 227
Ajxup Pelicó, Virginia 231
Alamar 11, 160–2, 179, 208
Alicia en el país 11, 131, 139, 161–3, 177, 207, 258
alive Indian 23
Altiplano 107, 196–7
Altman, Rick 155
Amanecer en la selva 83
Amazon Basin 24, 67, 82, 110–12, 144–6, 160, 168, 195, 234
Amazon Forever 194–5
American Mutoscope 63
Amerindian languages 77, 82, 97, 112, 118, 120, 129–34, 143, 187, 206, 211, 243, 257, 259
Andean identity 99–109, 240–8
Antes o Tempo Não Acabava 11, 110, 112, 187
anthropology 6, 58, 65, 71, 77, 82, 83, 85, 88
Anzaldúa, Gloria 35, 250
Apaylla 235
Apocalypto 189, 194
Appiah, Kwame Anthony 202
archetypes 28, 176, 177, 206, 217, 220

Argentina 43, 60, 68, 76, 81, 113–18, 133, 140, 256, 258
Atempa sueños a orillas del río 236–7
audiences 4, 5, 8, 36, 38, 41, 49, 62, 66, 70, 73, 78, 80, 83, 93, 98, 100, 129, 132, 136, 139, 147, 150, 155, 165, 178, 182, 189, 190–4, 202, 205, 217, 220, 229, 238, 240, 243, 246–50
Australia 17, 194
authenticity 23, 37, 123, 125, 128, 143–51
auto-images 7, 10, 14, 35, 40, 44, 230, 265
Aymara 1, 5, 41, 69, 78, 81, 100, 131, 133, 154, 162, 173, 183, 196, 242
Ayoh'Omidire, Felix 136

Barbarian Meco Indians 55
Barrow, Sarah 100, 106–7, 138
Bataille, Gretchen 27, 175, 220
Baud, Michiel 61
beauty 75, 102, 117, 261
Bedoya, Ricardo 158, 241, 250
Belgium 196, 198
Berlin 4, 82, 146
Bien esquivo 11, 107, 277
Biograph Company 63
Birri, Fernando 77
Black Legend 54
Blacklivesmatter 6
blanqueamiento 28
blemmyes 51
blueprint 155, 210–20
Bolivia 41, 62, 69, 77–81, 87, 99–102, 127, 131–2, 173, 178–81, 195, 236, 257
Bourdieu, Pierre 129
Brava gente brasileira 11, 113, 137, 138, 258
Bravo, Sergio 84
Brazil 22, 43, 48, 53, 57, 62, 67, 71, 76, 81–2, 84–5, 110–13, 135–7, 160, 168, 176, 187, 218, 234, 236, 256, 258, 260
Brehme, Ernst Hugo 58

Burwa dii ebo 11, 207
Bussenius, Gabriela 70
Bustamante, Jayro 16, 38–9, 93
Butler, Judith 82

Cabeza de Vaca 86–7
camera obscura 57
Canada 62
Canessa, Andrew 21, 109, 133, 230, 250
Cannes Festival 145, 146, 193
cannibalism 50, 52–6, 81, 135
Caramuru 11, 53, 131, 135–6, 154, 203, 205, 258
Cariba 53
caricatured depictions 1, 6, 9, 22, 136, 150, 205
Carreño, Gastón 28, 57, 63, 124, 152, 156, 175, 258
casta paintings 54–5
Castillo, Debra 39, 93
Catacora, Óscar 249–50
Catholic values 106
CEFREC 87
Cenizas eternas 11, 108–9, 154, 182, 207, 260
censorship 69, 79, 80, 85, 150
Chambi, Martin 60
Che Guevara 191
Chicangana Bayona, Yobenj Aucardo 54, 56
Childhood 55, 92, 106, 139, 160–2, 183, 209, 210, 212, 219, 221, 244
Chile 24–25, 43, 70, 84, 113–15, 118–20, 129, 131–2, 142, 153, 161–2, 177, 231, 233, 235, 258
Chirapaq 24, 177
Chirix, Emma 18, 44
Cholitas con fútbol de altura 236
cholo 29, 154, 266
Cine de la Base 81
Cine regional 12, 15, 29, 40, 45, 227, 239–51
Cinema Nôvo 81
circulation 6, 48, 54, 58, 60–1, 72, 165, 191, 228–31
Cisneros, Vitelia 39, 40, 131
class 41, 60, 81, 98, 104, 115, 135, 183, 185, 192, 215, 219
Climas 11, 106, 142

cloned ethnotypes 216–20
Cochabamba 195–6
Cochochi 154, 161, 208–9
Cold War 20
collaborations 44, 83, 205, 229, 233, 250, 265
collotypes 57
Colombia 62, 71, 83, 87, 102–3, 121, 143–52, 163–4, 233, 236, 257
colonization 3, 20, 55, 86, 152, 166, 170–2
colours 50, 55–6, 149, 157, 173, 176, 207, 248, 260
Columbus, Christopher 48
Como era gostoso e meu frances 81
constructivism 6
Corazón Aymara 69
Corazón del Tiempo 97–8, 131, 179, 183, 208
Córdova, Amalia 3, 37, 78
core-periphery 2, 85, 105, 134, 193, 203, 230, 245–6, 262
corpus 9–14
Costa Rica 91, 260
Costumbrismo 56, 222
Crenshaw, Kimberlé 181, 187, 233
Crespi, Carlos 71
¿Cuando te vuelva a ver? 13
Cuarón, Alfonso 41, 44, 210–25
Cuba 90
Cuidado / Paktara, 232
cybernetics 228
  see also feedback, feedforward

D'Argenio, Maria Chiara 100, 109, 177, 249
daguerreotypes 57
Danse indienne 62
dark skin 23
Dauna: Lo que lleva el río 5, 108, 165, 177
De la Cadena, Marisol 19, 21, 243
De la Garza, Armida 27
De raza Azteca 66
De Sahagún, Bernardino 48
De Valck, Marijke 2
dead Indian 23
DeBry, Theodor 49–53
decolonized 80, 229, 273
Defensores de la vida 91, 183, 206, 260
Denmark 146–7

Desayuno de indios 62
Diarios de Motocicleta 190–1, 205
Dioses 131, 176, 186–7
discovery of Machu Picchu 60
discovery 48
discrimination 3, 18, 23, 24, 26, 37, 100–01, 115, 119, 152, 178, 181, 190, 207, 233
disease 75, 144, 171–2, 235
Distancia 93–4, 124, 199, 217
distribution 5–7, 36, 81, 90, 155, 164, 191, 194, 204, 206, 216, 231, 237, 241, 249, 254
domestic workers 185, 211
Dulce convivencia 12
dvd 100, 228

early acoustics 72
Ecuador 71, 80, 81, 84, 103–6, 127, 142, 232, 235, 257
Eden 57, 59
Edison Manufacturing Company 63
edition 39, 48, 54, 58, 189, 191, 246, 250, 264, 266
editorial strategies 39, 48, 54, 58
eighteenth century 17, 54–6, 126
Eisenstein, Sergei 59
El abrazo de la serpiente 40, 134, 144–6, 192, 230, 257
El bohío rebelde 83
El conflicto en el sueño mapuche / Pewma jadkulu 235
El destino de los pobres 243, 245–6
El destino 115, 124, 142, 180, 182, 207
El día de las comadres 236
El enemigo principal 79
El facilitador 11, 40, 103, 104–6, 131, 142, 177, 199, 205, 257
El hijo del viento, 244
El milagro de Tepeyac 65–6
El misterio del Kharisiri 246–7
El niño pez 115, 131, 133, 139–40, 185, 205, 258
El ombligo de Guie'dani / Xquipi' Guie'dani 95, 165, 169–70
El Pecado 243–5
El regreso de Lencho 93, 180, 207, 256
El regreso 108
El sueño del Mara'akame 95, 165

El suplicio de Cuahtémoc 64
El traspatio 94, 124, 142, 154, 207
El último malón 67–8
El verano de los peces voladores, 118, 142, 177, 180, 182, 205, 258
El Violín 5, 94–7, 177, 179, 208, 213
Eljaiek-Rodríguez, Gabriel 246
Ella 13
Encina, Paz 136–7
engravings 48–9, 52, 54
Enigma de las llanuras 76
environmental issues 80, 87, 156, 113, 197, 231, 233–5
epistemic systems 4, 9, 16, 48, 113, 135, 153, 163–4, 170–4, 203, 235, 265
epistemologies 15, 20, 92, 95, 108, 148, 153, 164, 166, 173, 227, 230, 234, 237, 247
Equilíbrio 234
Erase una vez en Bolivia 102, 208, 257
Erendira Ikikunari 30, 176, 179, 184–5, 208
Esperanto 214
Espiral 94, 142, 260
essentialism 58, 142, 242
ethnicity in Costa Rica 91
ethnotypes 2, 5, 6, 9, 25, 28, 29, 36, 39, 50, 61, 108, 167, 176, 188, 211, 216, 218–19, 253
Europe
  ancestry 19–21, 27–8, 114, 169
  art 4, 47–59
  influence 3, 18, 39, 61–8, 156, 160, 191–7, 249
  languages 131, 133, 237
  portrayals 135, 137, 161, 172, 184–5
Evo Pueblo 102, 176, 179
exoticism 35, 39, 50, 62, 110, 113, 146, 166, 194, 197, 204, 260
explorers 51–4

Falicov, Tamara 36, 120, 146, 204
feathers 53–5, 61, 135, 260
feedback 2, 4, 36, 191–2, 242
feedforward 2, 15, 192
Feriado 104–5, 142, 185, 205, 218, 257
Fernández, Emilio 74–5
fictional language 151, 187
Fiesta en el Volcán Higueras 77
Film Academy Awards 146, 193

film festivals 2, 5, 36, 37, 39, 106, 133, 146, 162, 167, 188, 191, 192, 204, 208, 216, 217, 228–9
Films-Geo Méliès 63
food 52, 141, 158, 169
Fourth Cinema 230
Frágil 244
France 18, 39, 48, 52, 57, 58, 62, 80, 82, 189, 190, 192–4, 260
French Revolution 18
funding 2, 3, 36, 41, 79, 81, 86, 95, 134, 146, 155, 167, 188–93, 205–6, 241, 260

Garðarsdóttir, Hólmfríður 90, 106, 182
Gauguin, Paul 59
gender
  adolescence 92, 149
  agency 39, 221
  archetypes 28
  childhood 55, 92, 245
  female protagonists 90
  femininities 106
  equality 106
  ethnicity 181, 217
  hegemony 44
  indigeneity 15, 109, 135, 187, 237
  masculinity 182
  mestizaje 70, 117
  paradigms 187
  patriarchy 5, 149, 185
  racism 169
  occupations 185, 211, 221
  portrayals 30, 38, 41, 70, 74, 101, 116, 149, 180, 184, 236
  self-representation 236–7
  sexuality 104, 185, 187–8, 218, 236–7
  social structures 97, 184
  stereotypes 184
  tradition 182, 185
  traits in films 30, 31, 255
  tropicalization 135
Genesis 53
genre 2, 8, 10, 44, 63–5, 72, 73, 100, 112, 148, 150, 153–6, 229, 241, 244, 246, 254, 262
Germany 50, 58, 59, 110, 144, 146
Getino, Octavio 63, 77, 80
Gleghorn, Charlotte 229

Global North-Global South 196
globalization 43, 95
good savage 52, 55, 108, 135, 167
Graham, Laura 20, 35
Great Voyages 50
Greca, Alcides 67
Greek 51, 157–8
van Groesen, Michiel 4, 52
Group Ukamau 78, 81
Guaraní language 113, 127, 133–4, 136–7, 173, 258
Guaraní 120
Guatemala 16, 38–9, 92–4, 176, 177, 192, 256
Gutiérrez Usillos, Andrés 53, 55
Gutiérrez Vega, Pelagia 234–5

Hamaca Paraguaya 120, 136–7, 258
Hans Staden 110–11
health 52, 172, 245
Hermógenes Cayo 77
Hernández Castillo, Rosalva Aída 18, 175
hetero-images 7–10, 16, 28, 42, 228
Hidrofractura: El agua, el aire, la tierra ... la muerte 232, 265
Hispaniola 49
histrionic indigeneity
  definition 35, 36
  emergence 2
  examples 40
  funding 206
  role of language 131
  transnationalism 137
  see also syntonic indigeneity
Holl, Ute 229
Hollywood 61, 63, 80, 88, 189, 247
Hubert Funds 146, 190

iconic citizen 109
iconography 49, 54, 101, 167
identity 117, 187, 237
imagined Other 5, 36–7, 42, 205, 267
imagology 6, 28
Inacayal 235
incest 186, 246
inclusion of language in cinema 72
inclusion 155, 194, 208
indianism 83, 98, 256

indigena (Latin) 16, 17
indigène, 17
indigeneity
   Indigenismo 73, 83
   Indigenous cinema 228–39
   indigenous heritage 60, 69, 73, 77, 82, 120, 126, 142, 207, 213
   indigenous knowledge 48, 75, 153, 170, 230
   indigenous (term) 17, 19–21
   LGBTQ+ 185, 187, 236, 237
Instituto Cinematográfico Boliviano 78
intersectionality 70, 107
   ethnicity and gender 15, 44, 109, 117, 135, 181, 182, 184, 185, 187, 217, 236, 237, 262
intertitles 72
introduction of sound 71
invention of cinema 61
Iracema, uma tramsa amazônica 82, 84–5
Italy 161, 168, 219, 223
Ixcanul 1, 38–40, 42, 93, 125, 134, 177, 182, 192

Janitzio 74
Japan 119, 198, 215, 234, 262
Jarjacha vs. Pishtaco: La batalla final 247
Jiisa weçe – Raíz del conocimiento 236
Justicia sin palabras 233

Kahlo, Frida 59
Kaiowá 168, 180
Katio people 83
Kazakhstan 5, 91
Kek'chí 93
knowledge transfer 162, 165, 202, 228, 230
Könun Wenu 124
Korean 120, 223
Kotkuphi 236
Kukuli 82–3

La carga 170–3
La Ciénaga 115–16, 186
La flor que vive 230, 234–6
La Jaula de Oro 98, 141–2
La leyenda del Ekeko 247–9
La limpia / Chiqui Pichay – Wayrachirina 236

La mujer sin cabeza 205
La niña santa 177
La noche de los Mayas 73
La otra Conquista 86
La Profecía del Lago 70
La Sirga 163–4
La teta asustada 106, 124, 140, 165–7, 185
La Tirisia 125
La voz de su raza 64
labour 30, 222
languages 123–52
Las Indias 17
Las niñas Quispe 165
Leerssen, Joep 7
León Gaumont et Compagnie 63
LGBTQ+ 104, 185, 187, 188, 218, 236–7, 245
Lie, Nadia 155
Lima 140, 240
linguistic ethnotypes 123, 131, 140, 146
Llosa, Claudia 39, 106, 139, 165
Los descendientes del jaguar / Puma chirikuna 232
Los ojos azules 206, 260
Los viajes del viento 146, 206
Los Warao 77
Lumiére company 62
Luna Victoria, Jaime 241, 250

Maclovia 76
Madagascar 186
Madeinusa 39, 157–9, 186
Madre, una ilusión convertida en pesadilla 244
Magallanes 138–40
magic 248
Main character 29–34
Mala Junta 231
Malik, Kenan 19
Man of the Secotan 49
Mapudungun 129, 132, 235
Marcados por el destino 244
Mari Mari 232
María Candelaria 15, 75, 76, 170
Martel, Lucrecia 115–16, 186
Martínez de Arredondo, Carlos 64
Mateus Mora, Angélica 71, 83, 175, 178
medicinal plants 171, 230, 234–5

medieval imagination 50–3
mental schemas 26–7
mestiço figure 110
mestizaje 18, 21, 88, 109, 135, 208
mestizo identity 182
Mexican civil war 73
Mexican Revolution 64
Mexico City 57, 169–70, 212–13, 219–24
Mexico 57–67, 72, 76, 94–9, 127, 169, 171, 211, 213, 220, 233
Middents, Jeffrey 83, 146, 180, 263
Middle East 20
migration 87, 103, 152, 161, 249
Minkakuy 236
Mocovís 67–68
modernity 23, 39, 44, 60, 68, 76, 83, 93, 108, 127, 157, 179, 180, 199, 246
Monette, Marie-Eve 159, 197
Monteforte, Guillermo 178, 231
Morelia 2
Moreno Figueroa, Mónica 208
Mother and the Child 49
Muerte y pueblo 76
music 119, 133, 139, 166, 212, 278
musical instruments 83, 97, 147, 166
mutilation 52

Nación Clandestina 87
Nagib, Lúcia 82
Nahmad Rodríguez, Ana Daniela 5, 178
Nakaq 247
National Geographic 60
Nepal 197
Netflix 148, 211, 215, 219, 223
New Latin American Cinema 86
New York 146
Ngöbe 91–2
NGOs 229
nineteenth century 17, 55–7, 63
nineteenth-century photography 56
Niños pobres 244
noble savage 36, 42, 56, 88, 255
Nobleza Araucana 70
Norway 216
Nosilataj. La belleza 116–17
nostalgia 37–9, 85, 95, 143, 146
nudity 48, 53, 57, 105, 110

Nuevo Cine Chileno 84
Nutuayin mapu 84

occupations 50, 55, 116, 214
oil 231–2
ontology 154, 156, 160–3, 168, 173, 227–40
Ortega Matute, Palito 245
Os Sertões do Mato Grosso 67
Ouweneel, Arij 7, 17–18, 26, 35, 250

Pagán-Teitelbaum, Iliana 158
Page, Joanna 16, 157
paintings 47–57
Pájaros de Verano 146–52
Palabras de agua / Gatë ya sziaya co'c 236
Paloma de papel 107
Panama 177, 180
panoramic vistas 58
Paraguay 120–1, 126, 129, 133–4, 136–7, 185
Parque Nacional do Xingu 111
Pathé Frères de Paris 63
Penny, Glenn 20, 35
Perception of the Image of the Indigenous Peoples of Mexico 23
perception 22–7
Peru 62, 70, 82, 106–7, 138–39, 234, 239–51
photography 39, 56–61, 203
pigmentocracy 182
Pinazza, Natália 115
piracy 228
Pishtaco 247
Play 118–20
Plascencia, Fabila 178, 231
Podalsky, Laura 91, 114, 191
Por la tierra vivimos 232
Portugal 48, 135
postcards 57
postcolonial 85, 90, 162
post-production 36, 228
Pratt, Mary Louise 18–21, 49, 52
Pre-Columbian 4, 19, 20, 36, 43, 64, 162, 176, 184, 191, 194, 228
preconception 27–8
Prelorán, Ricardo 76–7
primitivism 17, 54, 135, 137, 167
promiscuity 53, 135

psychoactive substances 165
Pueblo de indios 17
Pueblos dormidos 76
Puerto Rico 90

Q'uma chuyma 236
Qarquacha, el demonio del incesto 243
Quechua 1, 40, 79, 81, 105, 127, 130, 132, 140, 159, 186, 190, 242–6
¡Que Viva México! 59
¿Quién mató la llamita blanca? 12, 100–2, 131, 140, 154, 177, 199, 207
quinceañera 117, 237
Quispe-Agnoli, Rocío 203

racism 3, 6, 169, 182, 186
Ramírez Berg, Charles 65, 178
Rappaport, Joanne 18, 55
Razón de estado 233
Rebelión de los Colgados 76
religion 18, 48, 52, 65, 73, 77, 83, 106, 137, 196
Retablo 154, 187–8
Retorno a Aztlán 86
Ribeiro, Darcy 82
Richards, Keith John 78, 230
Río Escondido 76
rites of passage 92
Rito Terminal 94
Rituais e festas 67
Rivera Cusicanqui, Silvia 241
Rivera, Diego 59
road movies 155, 209, 190
Roma 210–24
Ross, Miriam 146, 190
Rubiés, Joan-Pau 48, 52, 54, 255
Ruiz, Jorge 78

Sánchez Cruz, Jorge 237
Sangre inocente 244
Sangre y traición 247
Sanjinés, Jorge 69, 78–81, 87, 101, 103
Schiwy, Freya 14, 229
School of Lake Titicaca 55
science 62, 63, 71, 167, 234
secondary character 29–34
Segato, Rita Laura 182
self-identification 19–22, 24, 228

Sendero Luminoso 106
seventeenth century 50, 54, 56, 137
sex 74, 116, 133, 158, 176, 184, 246
shaman 92, 144, 168, 242, 246–7, 260
Shaw, Deborah 37, 190, 208
Shohat, Ella 110, 143, 177
Siguiendo las estrellas 180, 199
silent cinema 62–71
Sin sentimiento 247
sixteenth century 17, 48, 50–2, 111, 170–1
slavery 19, 172
smallpox 172
social media 138, 145, 232, 238, 248
Société Lumière 63
soft power 203, 210, 219
sound 71–81, 130–9, 143–8
Solanas, Fernando 77, 80
Spivak, Gayatri Chakravorty 143, 193
Stam, Robert 110–11, 175, 177
Starn, Orin 19, 21
stereotypes 22–26
structuralism 22
subtitles 130, 132, 137–8, 206, 207, 215, 242, 259
Sueño en otro idioma 187–8, 206
surveys 23–26, 176–7
Sweden 216
syncretism 65, 77, 83, 159
syntonic indigeneity
    definition 35, 40, 264
    examples 41
    Roma 220–5
    see also histrionic indigeneity

Tabaré 66
Tacca de, Fernando 67
Tahiti 59
Tainá 160
Taínos: La última tribu 90
También la Lluvia 125, 180
Tarica, Estelle 101, 132, 256
technology 143, 153–56, 162, 189, 197, 202, 227–9
The Adoration of the Magi 48
The Netherlands 38, 48, 190, 223
Third cinema 80
Thornley, Davinia 230
Tiempos Mayas 64

Tiempos menos modernos 156–7, 208
Tompkins, Cynthia 5, 27, 114, 175
tourist books 58
touristic ruins 60
Trachtenbuch 48
traffic of children 38, 93
training 64, 191
Trampas de tu lado oscuro 244
transgression 185
translation 132, 136–9, 149
transsexual 187, 245
Triste realidad 244
tropicalization 110, 113, 134–6, 256
Tupi 112
Tupinambás 82
Txejkho Kham Mby 236
Tzotzil 2, 98, 141, 142

United Kingdom 49, 52
United States 64, 79, 90, 106, 144, 194, 211, 262
Uruguay 66, 114

Vaho 207, 218
Valdivia, Juan Carlos 41, 133, 173–4, 183
Varayuqkuna 236
Vargas, Francisco 96
Venezuela 83, 108–9, 150, 170, 177, 260
Venice Biennale 223
Vestimenta Sapara: Una tradición en peligro 163, 233
Veyre, Gabriel 62
Vicio maldito 22
viewers' reactions 238
Villas-Boas brothers 111–12

Villazana, Libia 190
violence 97, 107, 133, 136, 138, 163, 186, 194, 246
Vitagraph Company of America 63
vocative framing 124, 152
Vuelve Sebastiana 78

Wachikua: Nuestra Historia 236
Wade, Peter 21
Wara Wara 69, 70
Wernitznig, Dagmar 27, 54, 167
West Indies 54
western (genre) 63, 156
Western attitudes 92, 192–4
Western influence 28, 37, 83, 88, 103, 146
White, John 49
Wichí Lhamtes 117
Wiñaypacha 40, 249–51
wise *Indian* 109

Xingu 110–12, 218
Xinico Batz, Sandra 1, 18, 38–9

Yanomami 108–9
Yawar Mallku 79
¡Y siguen llegando por el oro! 12, 232
Yvy Maraêy: Tierra sin mal 173–4, 207

Zama 115–16, 258
Zamorano Villarreal, Gabriela 230
Zapatista resistance 97–8
Zhamayama: Nuestra música 236
Zona Sur 5, 41, 132, 176, 183
Zorrilla, Enrique 84

www.ingramcontent.com/pod-product-compliance
Lightning Source LLC
Chambersburg PA
CBHW052147300426
44115CB00011B/1560